RECREATION LEADERSHIP

H. DAN CORBIN
Purdue University

RECREATION

THIRD EDITION

Prentice-Hall, Inc.

Englewood Cliffs, N.J.

LEADERSHIP

13–767970–X

Library of Congress Catalog Card Number 70–76313

Printed in the United States of America

Current printing (last number):
10 9 8 7

Prentice-Hall International, Inc., *London*
Prentice-Hall of Australia, Pty. Ltd., *Sydney*
Prentice-Hall of Canada, Ltd., *Toronto*
Prentice-Hall of India Private Limited, *New Delhi*
Prentice-Hall of Japan, Inc., *Tokyo*

Title page illustration: **Games,** *by Breughel. Courtesy of Wilhelmstrasse Museum and Frank Lerner*

TO JEFFREY AND LESLIE

*whose world will be as promising as the vision,
forthrightness, and dedicated effort of sound
leadership can make it*

One of the occupational hazards in professional preparation
is despair. Whatever pitfalls we succumb to, we should remain
steadfast keepers of vision, hope, and determination: vision
that is based on principles, high standards, and research; hope
that springs from having witnessed the "impossible" take place
through concerted effort; and enlightened determination that is
the catalyst, the priceless ingredient, in our advancement
as a profession.

H.D.C.

PREFACE

The purpose of this book is to present in a single work the major aspects of recreation leadership. In this third edition, all chapters have been expanded and brought up to date. Due treatment has been given to the practical as well as to the theoretical, in an effort to provide students and leaders with a balanced treatment of the whole field. "How" and "where" are emphasized as much as "why" and "when" in the presentation of the principles and techniques essential to the adequate training of leaders.

Although the field is so broad, each subject has been treated as thoroughly as possible. Background and theoretical material are presented in Parts One and Two; they provide the setting for, and add significance to, the essentials of programming, covered in Parts Three, Four, and Five.

I am happy to acknowledge my debt to the pioneers in the field, without whose groundwork this book might not have been possible. Incentive for undertaking this work is also traceable to the many students I was privileged to teach while they were preparing themselves for this field.

Most particularly, I wish to express my gratitude to those who contributed chapters to this book: Edna Bottorf, Professor Emeritus and former Chairman of the Art Department, Pennsylvania State College, Lock Haven, for her chapter on arts and crafts; Dorothy W. Lynds, Assistant Professor of Speech and Dramatics, State University of New York, Geneseo, for the chapter on dramatics in recreation; and Spencer G. Shaw, Specialist in Story Telling, Nassau County, New York, libraries.

In addition, I should like to extend my thanks to my colleagues Gordon Starr, Ernest Schmidt, Don Neer, Gerald O'Morrow, James F. Jones, Jr., and Arden Johnson for their assistance in the preparation of this revision. Furthermore, I should like to thank Mrs. Judy Beck, Mrs. Wilma Talbott, Miss Linda Mellady, and Mrs. Donna Repp for their unstinting secretarial services.

H. Dan Corbin

Lafayette, Indiana
October 1969

CONTENTS

PART V: PROGRAM ESSENTIALS:
C. OUTDOOR RECREATION

Part I

BACKGROUND

Chapter 1

HISTORY OF THE RECREATION MOVEMENT

INFLUENTIAL FACTORS

Recreation leadership, one of the newcomers in the family of professions, has been preceded by many influences. The events that led to its recognition as a profession with a specialized body of knowledge, ethical standards, and a service to mankind will be highlighted. Therefore, this section proposes to trace historically the landmarks which line the road.

While organized recreation is a relative newcomer to the educational arena, its roots penetrate rather deep into the social, emotional, and mental fiber of our people. An understanding of the recreational pursuits of a people reflects and reveals the cultural and economic conditions that prevail at any period.

Eighteenth-century recreation in New England was a concomitance of the lives of the colonial settlers. To build homes in the wilderness and to supply themselves with the necessities of life were their major concerns; these were reflected in the eminently practical leisure-time pursuits of the New Englanders. Husking bees and apple bees not only brought people together, they helped provide food for the community. Quilting parties, famous in song, motivated the production of much-needed clothing. The avocations and vocations were related and much the same.

The southerners, in striking contrast, engaged in a great variety of enjoyable activities: card playing was general, and horseracing and popular games of skill and strength were frequent diversions. As one might suspect, these were the sports of the well-to-do, which meant that the ordinary settler played no part in them.

1

With the beginning of the nineteenth century and the onset of the industrial revolution came radical changes in our mode of living. When the major portion of a nation that has been principally agrarian is shifted to an urban life, definite problems are inevitable. The farm, with its rural life, is the antithesis of the city, wherein hurry, anxiety, and artificiality abound. A deeply ingrained manner of living cannot be cast off in a relatively short period of time without profound and serious consequences.

Despite the sore need for recreational expression and release, no real action was forthcoming. For the advent of the nineteenth century found the citizenry frowning upon the types of recreation indulged in by the upper classes. While many sporting clubs thrived among the wealthy, the attitude of governmental agencies was decidedly cool toward innovations and toward assuming its leisure-time obligations; recreation remained at first a matter of individual concern. The disfavor of American leaders for games of chance so colored public opinion that little was accomplished during the first half of the century to overcome the inertia.[1]

During the two decades from 1820 to 1840 a few American universities, influenced by the German physical training movement, provided outdoor gymnasia, at which students participated in formal gymnastics. Later, the English experimentation with games and athletics resulted in American imitation and a reduced emphasis on gymnastic activities.

EARLY DEVELOPMENTS

The first step in "a democratic attempt to fill a proven need,"[2] was taken in 1853, when it was decided to purchase land at the public's expense for use by the public. In that year, New York City's most famous green, Central Park, was bought. It served as an example that was quickly followed by other communities. These parks, however, were not intended for recreation as we know it today, but rather for landscaping and scenic beauty.

It is, however, the city of Boston that has left the chief imprint on the road to public recreation. There, in 1866, the first vacation school in America was opened as a church project. It was widely copied immediately. Twenty years later, Newark made its vacation schools an integral part of its school system and initiated singing groups, nature study, and handicraft activities. The first land purchase for purely playground purposes was in 1872 in Brookline, Massachusetts.

[1] J. F. Steiner, *Americans at Play* (New York: McGraw-Hill Book Company, 1933), p. 4.
[2] F. J. Olmstead and T. Kimball, *Central Park* (New York: G. P. Putnam's Sons, 1928), p. 30.

Modern recreation in America may be said to have been born in 1886.[3] In the city of Boston, palely imitating the example of Berlin, the first truly recreational achievement in the United States was made. A sand garden was opened by the Massachusetts Emergency and Hygiene Association. Here under the supervision of a woman living in the neighborhood, about a dozen children whose homes were in the immediate vicinity were permitted to play in the sand. The garden was used three days a week and was open throughout the summer months. It served the purpose of taking children off the hazardous streets and remedying their maladjustments to city life.[4]

Within the next two years the success of this unique undertaking had led to the inception of ten centers; and as the uncertainties of using volunteer workers became apparent, arrangements were made to pay the matrons who supervised them. Gradually, these centers were replaced by school yards, and the public recreational aspect of this new activity was clearly indicated. Other cities soon adopted the sand garden concept, thereby initiating what later became the playground movement.[5]

OTHER INNOVATIONS

Since the expansion of facilities in Boston so closely parallels that of the entire country, it may be well to continue, at this point, the story of Boston's pattern. By 1890 additional innovations had occurred: Trained kindergarten teachers had replaced the first unskilled ones; a small amount of play apparatus had made its appearance.

At the same time (1889) Boston opened its first outdoor gymnasium, a development that was to have a great influence all over America. The direction of social consciousness is evident in that the tract of land utilized was in a highly congested area. It was fenced in and well equipped with such modern paraphernalia as swings, seesaws, and a running track. In addition, there were facilities for wading and swimming under excellent supervision.

Insistent demand by social workers resulted in similar playground projects in congested areas, not the least of which was that begun at the end of the nineteenth century in Seward Park, New York City. A short time previously the first recreation pier as well as the first evening recreation centers were also instituted in that city.

[3]Steiner, *Americans at Play*, p. 14.
[4]C. E. Rainwater, *The Play Movement in the United States* (Chicago: University of Chicago Press, 1921), p. 46.
[5]National Education Association and American Association of School Administrators, *Educational Policies For Community Recreation* (Washington, D.C.: The Commission, 1940), p. 7.

Second only to Boston in its influence on the public recreation movement was Chicago, where a "model" playground was started at Hull House as early as 1892. Although by that year over a hundred American cities had made provision for municipal parks, very few of this number actually had afforded facilities for recreation. In 1903 Chicago voted $5,000,000 for "small parks" and two years later opened ten of them to the dwellers of slum districts. These spaces were to be devoted to enthusiasts of all ages and were organized to serve both indoor and outdoor events. Among the innovations were field houses containing showers, lockers, and even libraries, with trained personnel in charge of activities. In 1934 the various park districts were consolidated into the Chicago Park District under a board appointed by the mayor.[6]

While Chicago was intent on the operation of its parks, Los Angeles was laying out its first tax-supported playgrounds. In 1904 Los Angeles organized the first separate department of municipal recreation.[7] This step was a forerunner of the 1911 legislation passed by the state of Wisconsin which permitted a 0.2 mill tax to be levied for recreational purposes. This praiseworthy legislation has enabled Milwaukee to expand its community playground program with marked success.

In 1906 the Playground Association of America was formed[8] with the aim of assisting communities in developing recreational activities. Theodore Roosevelt, pioneer in conservation, justly became its first honorary president. Because of its constantly increasing scope, its name was changed in 1911 to The Playground and Recreation Association of America and in 1930 to The National Recreation Association. It has provided national leadership, skilled field counseling, and a monthly publication, *Recreation*. The National Recreation Association's emphasis has been on civic responsibility for recreation, and it has helped call public attention to the need for city-wide play projects. Indicative of its success was the commission it received during World War I to organize the War Camp Community Service for members of the armed forces.

There were three other landmarks in the twentieth century's first decade: the organization of Rochester's "social and civic" centers, the calling of the first Play Congress in Chicago, and the publication of the first course of study in play.

The new importance of recreation was underscored by the National

[6]Elizabeth Halsey, *Development of Public Recreation in Metropolitan Chicago* (Chicago: Chicago Recreation Commission, 1940), p. 57.
[7]*Recreation: A Post-War Plan for the City of Los Angeles* (Los Angeles: Playground and Recreation Commission, 1946), p. 1.
[8]Steiner, *Americans at Play*, p. 144.

Education Association, which in 1918 listed as one of the cardinal objectives of American education "the worthy use of leisure." During the ensuing period, this stress showed itself in increased recreational budgets, in a professional literature that compared favorably with other well-established writings, and in a comprehensive and varied range of activities: golf courses, swimming pools, bathing beaches, picnic areas, baseball and other game fields—expanding programs for all, rich and poor, babies, children, youths, older girls and women, whites, and Negroes. Of more recent date, the Educational Policies Commission considered "the recreation development of the individual to be a part of the flowering of individual personality—the foremost objective of education."[9]

PROFESSIONAL PREPARATION

Development of the professional preparation of recreation leaders pursued a path similar to the growth of the recreation movement. The usual informal approach, used by perhaps all professions in the early stages of their development, was followed by training institutes and then college and university specialization.

Professionalization was spurred on by such more formal efforts as the People's Institute of New York in 1916 and the Playground and Recreation Association's training institutes. This was first undertaken in 1918 when the forerunner of the NRA was commissioned by the U.S. Department of War to conduct training institutes in localities adjacent to military cantonments. The P.R.A.A. also operated Community Recreation Schools, where basic essentials were covered in six-week training institutes, and the National Recreation Graduate School, established in 1926.

Purdue University in 1937 was first to embark on an undergraduate curriculum in recreation; the University of Minnesota, New York University, and the University of North Carolina followed.

Park acreage was multiplied many times, with a new appreciation of the need for play spaces in housing developments. Whereas in 1900 there had been some ten thousand paid recreation workers, by 1930 this number had almost trebled; their salaries had risen in that period from seven to thirty-three millions.

GOVERNMENTAL EFFORT

With the depression, community resources for leisure-time programs had perforce shrunk, while the need had increased. Unemployed people

[9]National Education Association and American Association of School Administrators, *Educational Policies For Community Recreation*, p. 11.

required just the morale building that the neighborhood center could provide. At first makeshift volunteer workers attempted to fill the void, but Federal funds had to be earmarked for relief of the situation.

The governmental agencies that were organized to meet this situation were (in the order of their creation) the Federal Emergency Relief Administration, the Works Progress Administration, the Civilian Conservation Corps, the National Youth Administration, and the Public Works Administration. Despite some of the shortcomings attributed to these agencies, they made an indelible and worthwhile contribution toward the furthering of the recreation movement.

With the advent of World War II, recreation adapted itself to this change in our "way of life." The U.S.O., the Army's Special Service Division, the Navy's Welfare and Recreation Section, not to mention the yeoman work performed by the Office of Community War Services, the American Red Cross, and the Federal Works Agency, were of immeasurable worth. These are but a sampling of the agencies that served and supplemented community agencies.

With the return to a peacetime footing, effective steps were taken to set up living war memorials in the form of playground and recreation centers. This was aptly aimed to direct the patriotic fervor toward social betterment through added recreational facilities rather than, as was done after World War I, the erection of monuments and statues.

Recreation is now on the threshold of attaining its full stature in our democracy. The unmistakable trend is toward a shorter working day, with the five-day week a rule rather than the exception.

Increased life expectancy is coupled with "more life to the years," thereby yielding greater participation at all ages. Increased mechanization and automation yield a worker with residual energy sorely in need of recreational opportunities through which to express himself. Moreover, our prospering economy finds the worker with somewhere between five and eight per cent of his income expended on recreational pursuits. In addition, the gradual dissolution of the Puritan ethic which associates goodness with hard work adds its contribution toward a forthcoming Golden Era of recreation. The fact that we are becoming more and more a population of adults plus retirement at an earlier age and social security augur well for our expanded leisure.

SUGGESTED READINGS

Butler, George D. *Introduction to Community Recreation*. New York: McGraw-Hill Book Company, 1959.

DeGrazia, Sebastian. *Of Time, Work and Leisure.* New York: The Twentieth Century Fund, 1962.

Dulles, Foster Rhea. *A History of Recreation: America Learns to Play.* New York: Appleton-Century-Crofts, 1965.

Jacks, L. P. *Education Through Recreation.* New York: Harper and Brothers, 1932.

Kaplan, Max. *Leisure in America: A Social Inquiry.* New York: John Wiley & Sons, Inc., 1960.

Meyer, Harold D., and Brightbill, Charles K. *Community Recreation.* Boston: D.C. Heath & Company, 1964.

Miller, Norman, and Robinson, Duane. *The Leisure Age.* Belmont, Calif.: Wadsworth Publishing Co. Inc., 1963.

Outdoor Recreation for America. Washington, D.C.: Outdoor Recreation Resources Review Commission, 1962.

Steiner, Jesse F. *Americans at Play.* New York: McGraw-Hill Book Company, 1933.

Vannier, Maryhelen. *Methods and Materials in Recreation Leadership.* Belmont, Calif.: Wadsworth Publishing Co. Inc., 1966.

Chapter 2

LEADERSHIP PRINCIPLES
AND PROCEDURES

WHAT IS RECREATION?

What ingredients of recreation are bound to include a leisurely mood if not a slice of time to do with as the spirit moves one, an itch from within that motivates a response, and socially acceptable activities concerned with outcomes to the participant rather than coming out on top.

The range of activities may extend from "doing nothing slowly" to that which is purposeful and creative; it is essential that satisfactions accrue as the individual expresses himself. It is a way of life that can pervade and influence one's approach toward any activity, even gainful employment. It is less concerned with what is done to the ball than what the ball does to the player.

"Recreation" means to refresh, restore, recreate, rejuvenate, to invest with vigor and strength, and to build anew physically, mentally, spiritually. It is often called on to provide challenges and satisfactions which work is offering less and less. The mere fact that an activity is volitional and based on a choice does not assure that it has recreational value. All

SELF FULFILLMENT
ADVENTURESOME
SELECTIVE
SATISFACTIONS
EXPRESSES SELF
CREATIVE
VOLUNTARY PARTICIPATION
CONSTRUCTIVE
DIVERSITY OF INTERESTS
SOCIAL

◁ ◁ ◁   "Well-Rounded Individual"

RECREATION LADDER

too often, the activities are repetitive rather than creative, superficial rather than meaningful, and enervating rather than restorative. Obviously, all that goes under the guise of recreation does not genuinely qualify. Riesman alerts us to the possible consequence wherein leisure "may become what workers recover from at work (as children recover from vacations at school)."

Recreation can be compared to a ladder with its rungs consisting of worthwhile and lifelong activities and hobby pursuits that embody adventure, satisfactions, choice making, self-expression, creativity, voluntary participation, and socializing among other factors.

THE NEED FOR LEADERS

There are over 40,000 full-time recreation directors and leaders employed throughout the United States in public and private agencies. Starting salaries compare favorably with many professions. With a shortage of trained personnel, the well-qualified advance rapidly. The need exceeds the supply by far.

Men and women with professional training in recreation are finding employment in governmental, private, and voluntary agencies. Positions are available in communities, the Y.M.C.A., Y.W.C.A., Boy Scouts, Girl Scouts, Boys' Clubs, Girls' Clubs, settlements, 4-H Clubs, churches and synagogues, industry, hospitals, camps, American Red Cross, and the armed forces.

WHAT ARE WE SEEKING?

The question may be rephrased to read, "What kind of person are we trying to develop?" This obviously delves into the philosophical realm. Certainly, we are seeking a social being with diversified appreciations and skills. William Lyon Phelps, the famous Yale English professor, informed us that the happiest people are the ones who harbor the most interesting thoughts.

Hence, we are desirous of developing individuals who are equally at ease in the drawing room as in the sports arena, are familiar and embody basic understandings and skills in individual and team sports, when alone and when in groups, and have active as well as passive pursuits. Arts and crafts, camping, music, dramatics, social recreation, canoeing, boating, sailing, athletics, sports and games, aquatic activities, nature lore, and hobbies are prominent in the appreciation and skill makeup of outstanding leaders in this field.

Therefore, we are seeking a well-rounded individual. One can achieve this state only through well-rounded experiences. As Alfred North Whitehead so ably stated: "There is only one subject matter for education and that is life in all its manifestations."

RECREATION AS A PROFESSION

As we peer into the future, the one thing that is certain is that of change. It is noteworthy that change and progress are not synonymous; we can easily confuse motion with progress. For one, progress is marked by advancement beyond the status quo. It is fundamental for the survival. A profession either advances or regresses. It cannot survive in a time of rapid change without doing one or the other.

RECREATION INCLUDES:
Arts and Crafts
Boating, Canoeing and Sailing
Club Organizations
Dance
Dramatics
Hobbies
Individual and Dual Sports
Leadership Principles
Leadership Techniques
Low and High Organized Games
Music
Outdoor Education and Camping
Social Recreation
Special Events

The significance of a profession is dependent on the values, objectives, outcomes, principles, standards, and services it renders to society. Consequently, it is vital that the leaders that graduate from our institutions of higher education be steeped in the humanities and appreciate fully the factors that contribute toward a well-rounded individual.

The pace of change is so rapid as to be virtually alarming. Professionally, we often devote too much time "putting out fires" instead of concerning ourselves with "fire prevention." Little League is an example wherein recreation and physical education could have headed off many of the practices we now condemn. By not filling the void, nonprofessionals have.

We are confronted with a number of explosions: the explosions of leisure (time), knowledge, and population (see p. 31). How successfully we cope with these explosions will determine the degree to which we prosper as a people, not to mention as a profession. With an increasingly adult population, greater recognition in programming is vitally needed for this significant percentage of our populace. Moreover, our leisure-oriented society is making increased demands on our established facilities and leadership. The indistinguishable gap between adult education and adult recreation (and frequent overlapping) points up the need for greater effort in this area. This is particularly applicable in the leisure time arts, hobby pursuits, great books, linguistics, and the like.

The recreation major that we prepare in our institutions of higher education must be a versatile, enterprising, and flexible individual. He needs to be prepared to cope with situations that we cannot as yet envision as well as with the conventional requirements of the profession. Hence, there is wisdom in emphasizing general education or the liberal arts for fifty per cent of the total curriculum.

Recreation is one of the newest and most rapid growing professions. Our expanding leisure coupled with our "double quick and triple action" mode of living magnify the need for recreation. Restorative and recreative experiences are an increasingly vital need of our times. It must not be left to chance. We must "educate for leisure."

RECRUITMENT AND SELECTION

Fundamental to the success of any profession is the quality of the individuals that are attracted to its preparatory institutions. The essential feature of furthering the recreation profession requires a multipronged effort on the part of interested leaders in this profession.

A field as varied and exacting as recreation requires that the recruitment of students be carefully planned. The selection of students should be compatible with the personality requirements and the character traits which are of prime importance. An interview should certainly be an essential part of selection. References and recommendations should also be factors in arriving at a decision as to whether the candidate has the wherewithal for this work. There should be an examination of his leisure-time interests, activities, and experiences at leading.

The use of mass media, brochures, prospectuses, films, slides, recordings, and word of mouth ought to be developed so as to better inform the guidance personnel. It is here where the effort may bring bountiful rewards. In addition, the image of the recreation leader needs to be sharpened and glamorized so as to make the field more appealing to the prospective candidate.

In a field as relatively new as recreation, there are bound to be practitioners with varying degrees of educational preparation and background. With recreation rapidly growing in stature and importance throughout the nation, the need for adequately trained and qualified leaders is greater than ever.

RECREATION AND SPECIALIZATION

The specialized training of recreation leaders has been recognized only recently. It was long felt that anyone with talent in recreational activities was thereby capable of setting up a recreational program.

Due to the myriad leisure-time activities, principles, standards, methods, and objectives that comprise recreation, it is essential that the recreation leader be specially prepared for this field; the scope of recreation is governed only by human imagination. The field is so extensive that it is utterly impracticable to prepare students for all specialties. Just as medicine has had to face the problem of where the "practitioner" ends and the "specialist" begins, so must recreation. At best the training for "general" practice plus specialization in one or two phases can be achieved. Although the duties of recreational positions may vary, they do contain identical elements.

A recently held conference[1] advocated five years of professional preparation for the field of recreation. The fifth year was felt to be vital due to the expansion of knowledge. The fifth year could be taken before service or after a period of experience.[2] Undergraduate preparation should contribute a "background for future growth and the minimum competencies for beginning professional service." Attention was directed at recognizing that professional education is a continuing and lifelong commitment.

It was agreed that responsibility for deciding the nature of professional education should rest with the recreation profession. The establishment of standards is the profession's responsibility. In professional education, "the profession, the institution and the agencies employing professional personnel should share responsibility."[3]

After giving due consideration to "general education" and "related areas of professional recreation education," the Professional Preparation Conference enumerated competencies essential to the recreation profession. They are:

1. Understanding the concepts of leisure, the philosophies of recreation, and the development of a personal and professional philosophy of recreation.

[1]*Report of a National Conference: Professional Preparation in Health Education, Physical Education and Recreation Education* (Washington, D.C.: American Assn. for Health, Physical Education & Recreation, January 8–13, 1962).

[2]*Ibid.*, p. 23.

[3]*Ibid.*, p. 22.

2. Knowledge of the nature, history, and development of the recreation movement, including factors influencing the origin and the continuing progress of the movement.

3. Knowledge of the place, scope, and importance of recreation in the community setting.

4. Knowledge and understanding of the interrelationships and relationships to the recreation profession of social institutions such as government (local, state, federal), hospitals, business and industry, schools, religious organizations, home and family, armed services, youth-serving organizations—public and private, institutions—penal, correctional, etc.

5. Appreciation of the roles of the leader and his function in the guidance and counseling of the individual in social, personal, and leisure concerns.

6. Personal experiences, practical application, and skill in the following program areas: aquatics, arts and crafts, camping and outdoor recreation, dance, dramatics, mental and linguistic activities, music, service activities, social recreation, sports and games, hobbies, special interests, and special events, with respect to:

Scope (breadth of program)
Possible rewards and values
Methods of organization
Resources
Safety procedures and practices
Acquisition, use, and care of equipment
Leadership needs and techniques
Program planning and promotion
Practical experiences

It is understood that one individual will not be proficient in all program areas, but it is desirable that he be adept in at least two and that he have knowledge concerning the scope, values, and program opportunities in all.

7. Knowledge of these principles which guide recreation program development and execution in a variety of settings, including hospitals, playgrounds, parks, churches, community centers, and camps, under the auspices of governmental, private, and voluntary agencies or organizations and schools.

8. Knowledge of the planning and operations of park and recreation facilities.

9. Ability to train, supervise, and utilize both volunteers and professionals.

10. Ability to interpret the role of the recreation profession to colleagues, community groups, and participants in recreation programs.

11. Knowledge of professional, service, and related recreation organizations—their development, structure, aims, objectives, services, values, and problems of interrelationships.[4]

THE UNDERGRADUATE PROFESSIONAL CURRICULUM

The trend in institutions that train majors in recreation is toward a greater emphasis on general education with fifty per cent usually devoted to this area; the remaining fifty per cent is thereupon allocated to professional recreation education and its related areas. At the latest major professional preparation conference,[5] the second fifty per cent incorporated thirty-three per cent to special professional recreation education and seventeen per cent to related areas. It recommended the inclusion of numerous and diversified laboratory experiences to achieve greater skill learning and a greater familiarity with the professional recreation field starting with the first two years.

Stress was placed on the undergraduate curriculum as a professional recreation core with elective courses allowing for some specialization; the inclusion of a desirable number of elective hours was pointed out as necessary. Consultations with the major advisor are needed to assure integration of courses in allied disciplines as well as the interrelationships between laboratory and theoretical experiences. To help assure desirable outcomes, basic professional courses should precede laboratory experiences.

THE GRADUATE PROFESSIONAL PROGRAM

In building on the undergraduate curriculum, the graduate professional program must take even greater cognizance of the importance of screening its candidates. As they are called on to assume positions of leadership, the degree to which these standards measure up to the realistic demands the various leadership positions require will determine the effectiveness of the curriculum.

Therefore, the level of competence acquired during the undergraduate program must be closely scrutinized. The effectiveness with which the candidate handled his laboratory experiences is to be examined as

[4]*Ibid.*, pp. 88, 89.
[5]*Report of a National Conference: Professional Preparation in Health Education, Physical Education and Recreation Education*, pp. 89, 90.

are the depth and diversity of these opportunities. The need to acquire additional seasoning in the appreciations, understandings, and skills in sample areas of so broad a discipline must be met satisfactorily.

Also, graduate preparation should capitalize on the candidate's previous experiences. Opportunities to plan, organize, deputize, and supervise programs of worth are to be afforded the students. A familiarity with basic evaluative and research techniques as well as acceptable ability to make oral and written presentations are to be assured.

The conference[6] specifies depth of understanding in the following areas: (1) philosophy and principles of recreation, (2) administration of recreation, (3) research and evaluation, (4) personnel management, (5) public relations. Opportunity for additional specialization in such areas as park and recreation administration, therapeutic recreation, camping, and outdoor education should be offered. Individual preference calling for other specializations are to be worked out in consultation with the major advisor.

IN-SERVICE EDUCATION

In addition to the skills essential for the recreation leader stated earlier in this chapter, there is the need for appropriate training methods. Whether to employ one or several methods depends on the subject matter to be imparted and the trainee in question.

Needless to say, the professional advancement of the leader should never end. While there is much learning which results from experience gathered on the job, it is advisable to consolidate these gains by a well-organized in-service education program. In all likelihood a more effective program will result.

The techniques that follow are often used: institutes, conferences, staff meetings, seminars, symposia, workshops, individual or committee projects, and home study or correspondence courses. In addition, radio and television, films and slides, and periodicals and bulletins are other supportive measures.

INSTITUTES

The setting up of a training institute is a common practice of many Recreation Departments. The institute is often held periodically, with a higher rate of incidence for the summer recreation program. One will therefore find that the institute for summer playground leaders is possibly the more common example of this type of training procedure. In

[6]*Ibid.*, p. 91.

camp management the precamp session, in which the camp director meets with his counselors and instructs them in the camp program to be conducted, is another example of recreation institutes.

The topics to be covered at an institute should be adapted to the needs and the leadership concerned. The program may include a discussion of the problems usually confronted, program planning, and workshops in arts and crafts, dramatics, and music. Briefing in the special events to be held during the season, supplementary instruction in accident prevention and first aid, game leadership, tournament organization, rules interpretation, and assignments are other likely topics to be covered.

In some cities alertness credit is given for attending recreation classes at colleges in the area. This is deemed a sign of professional advancement and is one of the factors given recognition when considering the worker for possible promotion.

FIELD WORK

Clinical experiences. The medical and dental professions have for years employed clinical experience as a vital part of the training program. These exposures have provided concentrated experiences and have assisted in rounding out the practitioner's knowledge and skill. In a similar vein, field work offers the leader laboratory situations in which lifelike situations are confronted. As an aftermath, added significance is given to classroom study, since the discussions that follow become more meaningful. Field work also serves as a stimulus to further investigation, the formulation of desirable attitudes, and the learning of essential skills.

Graded laboratory experiences. A graded plan for laboratory experiences is highly desirable in the training of recreation leaders. Needless to say, these experiences should be adapted to the knowledge and the abilities of those who are to be exposed to these experiences. The recreational climate on the campus should be such as to symbolize a well-rounded recreational program.

Participation in these activities should be encouraged and perhaps be required from the freshman year through graduation. In this manner, the leader will develop certain skills and will absorb the essentials of a recreation program, the organizational steps employed, the provisions made for executing the program, and the problems, if any, that may arise. He will thereby have been in a position to learn by concept and through experiences in the cocurricular program. During the sophomore year, clinical observation can be made and related to his class experiences. In the junior year, experience at leading groups should be afforded under close guidance. As a culmination of these graded experiences, the senior should be placed in full charge of an activity group. While the supervision need not be as frequent as during the junior year, it should be considerably more exacting and complete in its constructive and analytical approach.

Field work. According to the Conference Report, Professional Preparation of Recreation Personnel,[7] directed field experiences can be divided into two types: (a) *observation* and *participation*, which encompasses "Introductory," "Laboratory," "Concurrent," and "Summer" experience; (b) *internship*, which is a "culminating" experience toward the end of undergraduate preparation.

The principles of field work. The provision of field work experiences can be readily justified on the following grounds: (1) They help to make the classroom subject matter and observation more meaningful. (2) They serve to impress upon the student the importance of the social agencies (settlement houses, boys' groups, community centers, the "Y," and the like) in modern day living. (3) They augment lectures and assignments in an appraisal of community institutions, groups, and individuals. (4) They provide real situations wherein the strengths and weaknesses of the students may be readily observed under "firing-line" conditions; the supervisor can thereupon gauge the program to the students' needs.

TYPES OF POSITIONS

There are innumerable types of recreational positions to complicate one's quest due to the lack of agreement on the part of our city recreation heads to standardize their listings. It is therefore desirable to be guided by the recommendations of the National Recreation Association:[8]

EXECUTIVE
1. Superintendent of Recreation. Chief executive officer in charge of a recreation department or division and its personnel, responsible for planning, promoting, and administering a comprehensive recreation service for all the community.
2. Superintendent of Recreation and Parks. Chief executive officer in charge

[7]*Conference Report, Professional Preparation of Recreation Personnel* (1957), pp. 24, 25.
[8]*Recreation Leadership Standards* (New York: National Recreation Association, 1965), pp. 8–57.

of a recreation and parks department and its personnel, responsible for the administration of a comprehensive recreation program for the entire community and for the administrative management of the public parks, playgrounds, and other recreation facilities. (In communities utilizing a combined recreation and park department the superintendent of recreation heads the recreation division within this department.)

3. Assistant Superintendent of Recreation. Executive officer responsible for administrative planning, organization, and supervision of the recreation program as general assistant to the superintendent of recreation; acts for the superintendent in his absence.

SUPERVISOR

1. Recreation Supervisor (General). Responsible either for all recreation services for a district or a large subordinate geographic area of the community, or for all services or facilities of a similar type.
2. Recreation Supervisor (Special Activity). Responsible for the planning, promotion, development, and supervision of a specialized activity phase of recreation at a community-wide program, such as music, athletics and sports, arts and crafts, and outdoor recreation for all, including the ill and handicapped.

CENTER DIRECTOR

1. Recreation Center Director. Responsible for the direction of a comprehensive program for a single recreation center, which may include a recreation building or indoor center, playground, playfield, camp or day camp, or combination of any of these.
2. Assistant Recreation Center Director. Responsible for personal direction of assigned portions of the recreation program for a large or complex recreation center; serves for the recreation director in his absence.

LEADER

1. Recreation Leader (General). Under close supervision, responsible for the promotion, organization, and personal leadership of a variety of recreation activities at an indoor and/or outdoor recreation center and for related work in the community.
2. Recreation Leader (Special Activity). Under close supervision, responsible for the organization, development, and personal leadership of one recreation activity or several closely related activities at one or more recreation centers.

TRAINEE

(The trainee positions are for preparing young people for professional recreation leadership; they should not be considered as substitutes for professional positions.)

1. Recreation Intern. Responsible for various administrative, supervisory, and leadership functions in a rotated work program under supervision of the

superintendent. This is a professional internship for graduates of recreation curricula.

2. Student Recreation Leader. Under close supervision of full-time staff member, responsible for the promotion, organization, and personal leadership of a variety of recreation activities in a field work program supervised by agency and college.

3. Junior Recreation Assistant. Under continuous supervision, assists recreation leaders to conduct games, special events, and other activities. Oversees free play activities and does routine tasks in both leadership and nonleadership work.

CERTIFICATION

One of the areas where the number of opportunities exceeds those reaching out for them is recreation. This anomaly can be explained in several ways. For one, some cling to the antiquated concept that a college education is not needed for this area, or they fail to see the worthiness of expending four years or more of the time, expense, and energy required to develop the competencies for this specialty. Certainly, the fact that the work entails odd-hour assignments as well as weekend employment is a hastily conceived deterrent for some.

The lack of certification in most states is a major deterrent to the field of recreation. As a consequence, standards are kept at a low or almost nonexistent ebb in many communities. Political appointments are often an aftermath. Salaries are bound to suffer because of the lowered requirements and the increased numbers who can qualify.

New York and California are leaders in that they have certification requirements. In *Certificates for Teaching Service*; the State Education Department at Albany, New York, refers to California's certification practices:

"The validity of a permanent certificate for teaching physical education, health and recreation, issued upon five years of approved preparation, shall be extended by the Commissioner of Education to include service as a director of physical education, health, and recreation on evidence that the holder thereof has completed eight semester hours in approved courses and has completed five years of approved and appropriate experience." Certification is limited to employees of Boards of Education and consists of two levels: 1. Certification of recreation teachers, and 2. Certification of the Director of Health, Physical Education and Recreation.

In California, a voluntary registration plan has been in effect since January 1, 1956. To qualify for the examination leading to registration, the applicant must have graduated from an accredited university or college with a recreation major and a B.A. or B.S. degree. If not a major in recreation, the college graduate is required "to have had satisfactory recreation leadership experience, which is to be evaluated by the Board of Recreation personnel."[9]

EVALUATIVE MEASURES

Efforts at accreditation necessarily include appraisal based upon accepted standards. Since October 10, 1956, the National Council on Accreditation in Teacher Education has been restructured and officially designated by the National Commission on Accreditation as the accrediting agency for teacher education.

Evaluation Schedules in Recreation is being replaced by the newly effected *Standards and Guide for Evaluation of Professional Preparation in Health Education, Physical Education and Recreation Education.*[10] To a great extent, these standards and guides are included in those of the National Council for Accreditation of Teacher Education. Essentially, they afford a device by which colleges can appraise themselves and use the findings to improve their health, physical education, and recreation programs.

TYPICAL AGENCIES

The report of the National Conference at Jackson Mill[11] emphasizes the problem confronting our undergraduate training institutions in their preparation of leaders for the varied job assignments. To illustrate the point, it categorizes the typical agencies with recreation functions, as follows:

Municipal Recreation	Settlement Houses
County Recreation	Boy Scouts and Girl Scouts
Rural Recreation	College Campus Recreation
State Recreation	(Including Student Unions)
Federal Recreation	Churches
Industrial Recreation	Labor Unions
Hospital Recreation	Camps
School Recreation	Commercial Recreation Agencies
Boys' Clubs and Girls' Clubs	Institutions
Y.M. & Y.W.C.A.'s	Play Schools

[9]*California Board of Recreation Personnel Annual Report*, 1955 (Sacramento: California Recreation Commission).

[10]*Standards and Guide for Evaluation of Professional Preparation in Health Education, Physical Education and Recreation Education* (Washington, D.C.: American Assn. for Health, Physical Education & Recreation, 1958).

[11]*Report of The National Conference on Undergraduate Professional Preparation in Physical Education, Health Education, and Recreation*, 1948, p. 32.

EDUCATIONAL BACKGROUND

In view of the course requirements, laboratory experience, and overall educational requirements, a four-year course in the field of recreation or its equivalent would appear to be a minimum requirement; the five-year program is in evidence in a few institutions. As these major curricula increase in number, recreation departments will train more qualified workers. Until that time, equivalent training in such fields as physical education, sociology, and the like may be studied for part of the background that is required. For those students who are enrolled in other departments, such as dramatics, speech, music, sociology, and physical education, the election of a minor in recreation may provide a strong allied field of study. In a similar vein, those who have completed undergraduate study in these related fields might do well to consider graduate work in recreation.

EXPERIENCE BACKGROUND

The requirement of experience as a recreational leader is often instituted by recreation executives. Some specify that the experience shall be gathered while in a salaried capacity while others make no such distinction.

In a study conducted by the author, a group of experts were requested to recommend the amount of experience required for recreational leadership. They were also requested to specify whether the experience should be paid or whether that specification ought not be a factor in deciding upon the worthwhileness of the experience. All agreed that one year of experience should be required, and seventy-five per cent of those questioned agreed that the experience be that of the "paid" type.

PART-TIME RECREATION PERSONNEL

The common practice of employing large numbers of part-time and temporary recreational personnel is a grave problem facing many cities. The employment of a high percentage of part-time and temporary workers should be considered a weak link in the recreation chain. While no issue is taken over the use of added personnel during the months when attendance is highest, it invariably contributes toward lowered efficiency. Careful selection can do much to mitigate this effect. Furthermore, the proportion of part-time to permanent employees should be kept at a low level, and their assignments should be so regulated that they may work with more experienced and capable permanent leaders.

The use of training institutes and workshops before the season gets under way is another device that has proved worthwhile.

SHORT-TERM RECREATION PROGRAMS

In most communities the recreation program is predominantly a warm-weather one. However one should consider the fact that during the warm-weather months there are numerous leisure-time opportunities for individual and family picnicking, camping, swimming, hiking, and the like.

It is not intended to minimize the importance of organized recreation programs at any time of the year; it is a year-round need. If anything, though, the need for recreation is greater during the fall and winter months, when the days are short and idle hours are more apt to weigh heavily on the hands of our youth. A generous portion of the recreation budget should be allocated for this usually slighted, although highly important, period of the year.

LEADERSHIP

A leader has been variously defined from one who has a follower to one who possesses the ability to guide and direct others in activities which are desirable and wanted by his group. To this might be added that the leader should possess qualities that are sought by his followers. Among these one may find the ability to initiate, an understanding of his group's needs, and the determination to carry the activity through to completion.

Personal qualifications. It is a known fact that the nature of recreational work has to place the leader in close contact with the members of his group. His ability to adjust himself to the varied situations that may develop is extremely important. While the ability to execute certain skills is of importance, it is even more essential that he be well versed in techniques of leading groups, of discerning interests, and of securing the cooperation of those in his charge.

In an application of the Q-Sort technique in Oakland, California, thirteen personality traits most descriptive of an "ideal" recreation director were designated as follows:

1. Is a genuinely dependable and responsible person
2. Is productive; gets things done
3. Has a wide range of interests (N.B. Superficiality or depth of interest is irrelevant here.)
4. Has warmth; has the capacity of close relationships; compassionate

5. Tends to arouse liking and acceptance of people
6. Is skilled in social techniques of imaginative play; pretending and humor
7. Is calm and relaxed in manner
8. Is socially perceptive of wide range of interpersonal cues
9. *Behaves* in an ethically consistent manner; is consistent with own personal standards
10. Appears straightforward, forthright, candid in dealing with others
11. Emphasizes being with others; gregarious
12. Able to see to the heart of important problems
13. Has social poise and presence; appears socially at ease.[12]

In a study conducted by Jackson M. Anderson,[13] there were ten personal qualifications selected by a jury of experts that would be important for leadership work. They are as follows: (1) considerateness, (2) courage, (3) health, (4) intelligence, (5) leadership, (6) professional knowledge, (7) efficiency, (8) sociability, (9) judgment, and (10) dependability. He adds that a greater-than-average abundance of all ten personal qualifications is vital for the performance of all leadership responsibilities in public recreation.

Desirable personality traits of a leader. While it is not intended to overemphasize the part that the leader's personality plays in the success of his program, it is nevertheless well to keep in mind that it is a determining factor, if but in part. There have been various attempts at rating leaders, but these have not been without flaws. Among the desirable personality characteristics of a successful leader one will find the following: A leader (1) is fair and impartial, (2) plays no favorites, (3) has a good sense of humor, (4) plays and mingles with the group, (5) is interested in each child, (6) possesses a cheerful disposition, (7) is patient, (8) does not "fly off the handle," (9) praises good work, (10) encourages the slower ones, (11) dresses appropriately, (12) is always willing to help, (13) is punctual, (14) is courteous, (15) has varied interests.

What leadership can do. It is well to acknowledge that an activity may be either good or bad, with effective leadership often the determining factor. A varied program will be more apt to attract a youngster to the leader's fold. Among the activities are sports, games of low and high organization, social recreation, dramatics, dancing (folk, tap, and so-

---

[12]Fred Darrell Weaver, *The Research Letter* (New York: National Institute of Recreation Research of the National Recreation Association, 1966).

[13]Jackson M. Anderson, *The Development of Personal Standards for Leadership Duties in Public Recreation* (unpublished doctoral thesis, New York University, 1948).

cial), handicrafts, music, hobby groups, and club organization. These activities afford the participant opportunities for expressing the self, playing with and sharing experiences with others, finding oneself in successful undertakings coupled with the recognition of one's mates, and developing the integrated personality that is a likely aftermath.

Duties of the recreation leader. The duties of the recreation leader will vary with the amount of responsibility afforded him by his recreational supervisor. As a rule the recreation leader is responsible for the organization, direction, and supervision of recreational activities. In some areas he is in full charge of the program, even to the extent of being responsible for handling the publicity, securing the cooperation of reliable community agencies, and choosing volunteer leaders. On the whole, the recreation leader will be responsible to a supervisor who may delegate to him most or all of the aforementioned responsibilities, with the provision that the supervisor must always be informed of the contemplated steps to be taken.

In addition, the duties of the recreation leader are to: (1) Encourage greater use of the recreation facilities as much as possible. (2) Conduct a well-balanced recreational program geared to the needs of those who frequent the play area. (3) Place due emphasis on such varied activities as dramatics, music, club organization, story telling, low and high organized games, tournaments and sports leagues, crafts, dancing, and nature lore. (4) Be responsible for the safe maintenance and cleanliness of the recreation area. (With careful planning and supervision, mishaps can be reduced to a minimum. See the chapter on Safety and First Aid for details on this subject.) (5) Keep records of attendance, supplies, accidents, special events, so that they are available to his superiors. (6) Periodically hold special events in addition to the usual recreational activities to stimulate further interest in the program. (This subject is discussed at length in the chapter on Special Events.) (7) Administer first aid efficiently to the injured. (A report of each accident with a statement from at least two witnesses should be presented to the supervisor within twenty-four hours.) (8) Inspect daily the recreational area and the equipment as a safeguard against accidents attributable to defective equipment and facilities. (9) Familiarize himself with the neighborhood surrounding his area. (His interest in the neighborhood will often result in an added response and support from the parents.) (10) Be interested in each person who visits the playground. (Each individual should be made to feel that he is important and wanted on the area.) (11) Be attired in clothing appropriate to his work. (Some departments require a special uniform to be worn.) (12) Exemplify considerateness, politeness, and courtesy. (These and other signs of good manners can often best be taught by concept and have a direct bearing on the children's behavior.)

VOLUNTEER LEADERSHIP

The volunteer in recreation can be described as one who offers his services and time without any financial reward, as distinct from the part-time or professional leader. His contribution may extend from one period per week up to a day or more.

The field of recreation is so broad that there is a real place for volunteer leaders. By the very nature of recreation with its countless interests and activities, it is too much to expect that any leader be capable of directing all interest groups. In directing special activities the volunteer leader can be used to good advantage. Aside from extending the scope of the program, the volunteer provides a link between the community and the professional. By so doing, the scope of the program can be extended, thereby narrowing the gap between the varied interests of the community and the recreational activities offered its members. Tasks should be assigned to the volunteer leader in keeping with his background and ability. Failure to heed this may deprive him of the challenge that may conceivably be responsible for his presence.

Sources of volunteer leadership. With the multitude of activities that comprise recreation it is conceivable that almost anyone can qualify for some type of volunteer leadership. The better-than-average athletic performer, the person with a better-than-average skill in a hobby, the former teacher, the college student who is seeking field work experience, people who were formerly in the recreation field, and parents or relatives of those taking part in the activities who have sufficient skill are among those who might be recruited.

How to attract the volunteer leader. It is well to remark that the volunteer will usually have to be ferreted out from the community. He will not offer his service as a rule, because he may not feel that what he has to offer will be exactly what is sought. The task of interesting potential leaders in assisting on a volunteer basis calls for definite measures. For one, the community should be appraised of the job to be done along with the number of volunteers required to supplement the existing leadership. The qualities desired in a group leader should also be emphasized as the qualifications for each position are outlined; newspapers, radios, announcements before fraternal organizations, service clubs, and auxiliaries are among the devices that can be employed.

No attempt should be made to impress the potential volunteer that it is a simple undertaking. Able people want to be challenged and are apt to shun trivial assignments. On the other hand, the volunteer is to be accepted as a member of the staff whose suggestions are respected and whose contribution is appreciated. In such a group the volunteer is more apt to enjoy his experience and, by the same token, recruits are more likely to be attracted.

THE PLACE OF LEADERSHIP

The place recreational leadership has earned in the public's esteem has been arrived at only after hard and arduous effort. It is noteworthy that leadership is still making progress. Following are accomplishments in this sphere:[14]

1. A continuing and accelerating of the change to a leisure orientation of the American way of life.
2. An emphasis on creative and constructive recreation as the worthwhile use of leisure time; and public responsibility for the provision of an ever-widening basic program of recreation opportunities for adult citizens as well as youth.
3. A continuing increase in the number of communities employing full-time recreation leadership.
4. A rising level of basic minimum qualifications required for professional employment, combined with a more definite understanding of the skills, abilities, and knowledges required of recreation leadership personnel.
5. An increase in the number and quality of undergraduate recreation major curricula.
6. A broadening and improvement of opportunities for graduate education in recreation leadership and administration.
7. A new emphasis on in-service training and education for both executive and staff leadership and for volunteers.
8. An improvement in the economic and social status of recreation leaders.
9. A continuation of the trend toward more standardized recreation leadership positions and functions.
10. A broader interpretation of the community recreation leadership function on the part of both citizens and professional leaders.

PLAY OBJECTIVES AND ACTIVITIES
FOR VARIOUS AGE GROUPS

Ages four to six. The four- to six-year-old is characterized as a highly individual child insofar as playing interest is concerned. There is a thirst

[14]*Personnel Standards in Recreation Leadership* (New York: National Recreation Association, 1957) p. 2.

for physical activity involving the fundamental muscle groups. Infantile characteristics are still in evidence. While the span of attention is rather short, a highly curious and imaginative mind is evident. On the social relations side, he displays a lack of ability to cooperate.

Among the suggested activities likely to meet the needs of the four-to six-year-old are dramatic activities such as story plays, animal dramatizations, and imaginative imitations of adult activities in store play and kitchen play.

Rhythmic activities such as marching, running, skipping, galloping, and hopping to musical accompaniment are popular. In addition, the use of simple body rhythms such as clapping and rhythm-band play is recommended.

Solo activities play a dominant role in their lives, a form of play often retained while playing alongside others. Socialization can be enhanced by low organized games. Stunt activities are popular. Block building, clay modeling, painting, and sewing are among the suitable arts and crafts activities.

The *seven to ten age group.* On the average, boys are slightly taller and heavier than girls in this age group. Here again, we find a thirst for active play with definite signs of progress in coordination. There is an appreciable improvement in the use of the accessory muscles of the hands and fingers. Interest in cooperative play is marked as domineering individualism becomes less noticeable. A thirst for adventuresome activities becomes apparent at this stage. While an interest in low organized games will still be apparent, one will notice a definite drift toward high organized games and team games.

Children of this age group are partial to imaginative play as is exemplified by dressing up for Hallowe'en or playing cowboys and indians. This is also true of rhythmic activities, such as folk dancing. High organized games will prove very entertaining as well as stimulating. Singing games are also popular. Handicraft activities involving modeling of planes and boats, clay modeling, soap carving, chip carving, the making of kites and snowmen, and miscellaneous construction projects are eagerly accepted.

The *eleven to fifteen age group.* In this age group the average girl is taller and heavier in weight. While it is often suggested that boys be separated from the girls during vigorous competitive play, they should be encouraged to play together whenever feasible. This is the period during which growth is so rapid that the "anatomy runs away with the physiology." Awkwardness is a natural outgrowth of this stage of rapid growth. There are strong indications of gregariousness and interest in group activities, clubs, and team games. An interest in adventuresome activities is apparent with a desire to assert oneself before others. Also, the period is one of hero worship and craving of independence from the family while pretending to "know it all."

The desire to participate in team games and other group activities is felt by both sexes; organized activities are vitally desired to meet this need. As an adjunct to the growing social awareness, folk and social dancing as well as social recreation are advised. Highly organized games and sports activities are also indicated for growth in the ability to cooperate and carry out an assignment. Social recreation and varied arts and crafts activities are also worthwhile, as are dramatics, musical activities, camping, nature lore, and hobby activities.

SEX DIFFERENCES IN PLAY

Special play provisions for the sexes are not needed for the period prior to adolescence. With the advent of adolescence, the separation of boys and girls is often the rule. This change has been urged, particularly for competitive activities, due to physiological differences. Nevertheless, it is this observer's conviction that recreation objectives can be served best by permitting play between the sexes so long as the activity is not too vigorous and body contact is not involved. It is particularly advisable that boys and girls be represented on each side of play rather than to have boys compete against girls. Very successful tournaments have been conducted in mixed volley ball, softball, deck tennis, as well as the usual mixed-double activities such as tennis and badminton. This listing is not complete but merely suggestive of the possibilities.

It is well to recognize that there are significant differences in both structure and function of both sexes. Among these one will find that the structure of the pelvis in the female is such as to affect the running speed. In addition, the female has fewer red corpuscles per cubic centimeter, which has a bearing on the ability to endure prolonged periods of physical exertion. The boy has greater strength and often possesses advanced motor ability.

As a rule, although there are many exceptions in evidence, the boy prefers more vigorous activities than does the girl. It has been contended that girls are less interested in competitive play; this belief is rapidly losing ground with increased opportunities for competition. It is noteworthy that well-organized programs for girls under the leadership of capable women place less emphasis on competition than do the leaders of boys. The relegation of competition to a less prominent role on the part of our women leaders is deserving of recognition and acclaim. Certainly they come closer toward achieving the over-all objective of play for "play's sake."

ROLE OF SUPERVISION

That effective supervision can do much toward improving the program is indeed a truism. This can be achieved only if there exists a cooperative spirit and a meeting of minds between the supervisor and leaders. This concept is a far cry from the "don't" stage of "snoopervision."

The rapport which should exist between leader and supervisor calls for a two-way road with a free exchange of ideas. The supervisor is afforded an opportunity to observe the leader as he conducts his groups. On the other hand, the leader may encounter difficulty in the handling of certain phases of the program. The resulting exchange of thought between these two should help to achieve a more satisfactory program.

It is highly important that the relationship between the supervisor and the leader be on an amicable basis and that the problems that arise be on a factual rather than an emotional plane. Professional equality should be emphasized with the fact that both have distinct assignments with a common objective: a more effective and satisfactory program for the individuals that frequent the play area.

In addition to the discussion which is often a part of the supervisor's visit, there are other worthwhile measures to be taken: The following are suggested for consideration and possible use: (1) organization of the program; (2) conferences with individual leaders; (3) round-table discussions between the supervisor and the leaders in his charge; (4) demonstration of that which is desired, preferably at a leaders' conference; (5) a change of assignment should the leader encounter repeated difficulties; (6) encouragement of professional development by suggestion and example; (7) recommendations of guided reading and study; (8) evaluation of the leaders' work and progress; (9) organization of an in-service training program for the leaders.

ESSENTIALS OF PROFESSIONALIZATION

A profession is distinguished from a trade in that it includes ethical procedures which serve as guideposts for its members. The recreation profession is in need of greater cohesiveness and higher standards. Professional organizations can help raise their standards to achieve true professionalization. In addition to state associations, the National Recreation and Parks Association and its branches: the American Association of Zoological Parks and Aquariums, the American Park and Recreation Society, the National Conference on State Parks, the National Therapeutic Recreation Society, and the Society of Park and Recreation Educators; the National Industrial Recreation Association; the American Association of Group Workers; International Recreation Association; and the American Association for Health, Physical Education, and Recreation, among others, serve a vital need. Adequately trained leaders are the building blocks with which the recreation profession can be constructed. Training and certification should go hand in hand, with the power of certification a function of the state.

RECREATION AND THE CONSUMER

According to Riesman[15] people will look (there is mounting evidence that they are) "to their employers for financial security in old age . . . consumption will increasingly move toward making life now comfortable and 'well-rounded.' " This has greatly influenced installment buying of boats, golf and other sports equipment, and skiing holidays to Sun Valley, even Innsbruck.

There has been a cross-fertilization of recreational pursuits in American society. Golf clubs are a common sight in the industrial worker's automobile trunk or station wagon; he also pursues such former aristocratic sports as sailing, pedigreed dog breeding, and horseback riding.

Americans are looked upon as frenetics with a built-in restlessness whether at work or during their leisure-time pursuits. Mumford[16] in his *The Transformations of Man* covers man's reactions from Old World to the New World. He is portrayed as possessing a dynamism and buoyancy from the start that explains our emergence as a nation of dabblers, hobbyists, and fun lovers. A hedonistic philosophy pervades. This is borne out by the fact that approximately ten per cent of the G.N.P., or seventy billion dollars, is expended in this direction.

The overwhelming influx of leisure leaves many confused; they are unprepared and often waste or dissipate it. A significant number solve this dilemma by moonlighting. This lack of preparedness poses a question that our schools need to handle with greater effectiveness. Education for leisure is one of the great needs of our times.[17] This need is bound

---

[15]David Riesman, *Abundance for What?* (New York: Doubleday & Company, Inc., 1964), p. 119.

[16]Lewis Mumford, *The Transformations of Man* (New York: Harper and Brothers, 1956).

[17]Riesman in *Abundance for What?* states: "For many people today, the sudden onrush of leisure is a version of technological unemployment: their education has not prepared them for it and the creation of new wants at their expense moves faster than their ability to order and assimilate these wants."

to increase as we are called on to devote less energy and time toward each day's endeavors.

Currently, the nearest we come to the "leisure class" is the "group of artists and intellectuals who regard their work as play and their play as work"; work is the center of their lives without walling it off from "the rest of life either by its drudgery and severity or by its precariousness."[18] At the other end of the spectrum, the unemployed are devoid of leisure since they have not "earned" it. For the vast majority, it is to their leisure and consumership that they must go to fill this void in their lives.

"EXPLOSIONS" INFLUENCE RECREATION

A number of "explosions" have occurred which exert a tremendous influence on the profession. This is bound to continue and multiply as a force.

The *population explosion* entails more than a mere increase in numbers. There has been a phenomenal increase in those sixty-five years of age and over with its attendant influence toward Senior Citizen Clubs and activities. We are told that one half of the population in the United States will be under twenty-five.

Knowledge has increased to an extent that the estimates appear to be incredible. Whether one accepts that knowledge has doubled in the last three, or even ten years, the fact still remains a staggering one. The implications this holds for recreation are almost overwhelming. Not only do we encounter a vast increase in the number and depth of hobby pursuits, but there is also a greater alliance with adult or continuing education.

In addition, there is the explosion of gadgetry. Labor-saving devices are constantly on the increase. In the last fifteen to twenty years, we have seen a tremendous influx of electronic products, electric knives and toothbrushes, detergents, and powered labor-easing products.

Consequently, there is the expansion of leisure which is the trend of our era. That this is a natural outgrowth of the advanced mechanization, automation, and cybernetics few will question. There is also the fact that whether it is a blessing or a curse rests in the hands of each one of us. Hence, the need for education and guidance becomes all the greater as the strains and stresses become magnified. Moreover, the gap between work and recreation widens as the industrial worker is confronted with more specialized tasks and consequently more tedious work.

[18]*Ibid.*, pp. 168, 169.

What the future holds forth staggers the imagination. The increased leisure and residual energy for the worker—including the housewife—augur well for all family participation. The prospect of overloading existing facilities is already evident. Adequate provisions need to be made to meet increasing pressure from present and future needs.

PHILOSOPHICAL REFLECTIONS

A philosophical treatment should take into account phenomena supported by justification causes, and their application. To a considerable extent there are philosophical implications in many sectors of this book. A philosophy should be practical in its systematic organization of concepts.

Work in the traditional image was a more complete and satisfying experience. It involved seeing a task through to the completion phase with considerable opportunity for socializing experiences attendant to the work. Furthermore, the less pressured life and slower pace, though still warranting recreational outlets, called for restorative and satisfying avocational pursuits to a reduced degree. The gap between work and recreation has been widening steadily as industry progresses via specialization of labor, automation, and cybernetics.

Recreation is an indispensable ingredient of the Good Life. We never outgrow our need for recreation. Like the other aspects of education, the appreciations, understandings, and skills of recreation cannot be left to chance. Rather, there is an increasing need to educate for leisure so that the broad spectrum of its offerings can be appreciated.

The average person has close to 120 days of leisure each year.[19] Additionally, the average worker has at his disposal five hours of free time daily with more energy available at the end of his working day, due to use of the machine, automation, coffee breaks, and other improved working conditions. In the words of the outstanding pragmatist, John Dewey: "Education has no more serious responsibility than making adequate provision for enjoyment of recreation leisure . . . for immediate health . . . for lasting habits upon the mind."

True leisure must be earned. As Margaret Mead so aptly expresses it: "Unearned leisure is something which will have to be paid for later. It comes under the heading of vice—where the pleasure comes first and

[19]H. Dan Corbin, *Education for Leisure, 1962 Yearbook, The Growing Years: Adolescence* (Washington, D.C.: American Assn. for Health, Physical Education & Recreation), pp. 223–235.

the pain afterwards—instead of virtue, where the pain or work precedes the reward."[20]

The trend toward placing excessive stress on the material things of life at the expense of those which nurture the spirit is increasingly evident. This is apparent in the industrial sphere as well as in the manner in which we regulate our lives away from work. Our very civilization is at stake. Mumford grasps this danger by saying: "Civilization begins by a magnificent materialization of human purpose; it ends in a purposeless materialism. An empty triumph, which revolts even the self that created it. The sudden evaporation of meaning and value in a civilization, often at the moment when it seems at its height, has long been one of the enigmas of history. We face it again in our time."[21]

And Riesman states: "Just as we are lowering our water table by ever deeper artesian wells and in general digging even deeper for other treasures of the earth, so we are sinking deeper wells into people in the hopes of coming up with 'motives' which can power the economy or some particular sector of it. I am suggesting that such digging, such forcing emotions to externalize themselves, cannot continue longer without man running dry."[22]

The shorter work day has not been an unmixed blessing. Reduced working time, though a fringe benefit of employment and used by union and management as a financial equivalent, has been misused by many; they have resorted to second jobs, a practice displeasing to the unions since it is counter to the intent of reduced hours of employment. Secondly, it reduces the number of jobs to be spread among its constituency. It is prophesied that the thirteen-week sabbatical of the Steel Union will be handled by having four so involved undertake a moonlighting assignment.

A recent issue of the Labor Department's monthly review disclosed that one out of every twenty workers is holding more than one job. Government workers, especially those in the postal service, were moonlighting in greatest numbers.

SUGGESTED READINGS

Brightbill, Charles K. *Education for Leisure-Centered Living.* Harrisburg, Pa.: The Stackpole Company, 1966.

[20]Margaret Mead, "The Pattern of Leisure in Contemporary American Culture," *Annals of the American Academy of Political and Social Science*, 11; (September, 1957), 313.

[21]Lewis Mumford, *The Transformations of Man*, p. 69.

[22]David Riesman, *Abundance for What?* p. 180.

Butler, George D. *Introduction to Community Recreation*. New York: McGraw-Hill Book Company, 1959.

Carlson, Reynold, Theodore Deppe, and Janet MacLean. *Recreation in American Life*. Belmont, Calif.: Wadsworth Publishing Co. Inc., 1963.

Conference on Education for Leisure. Washington, D.C.: American Assn. for Health, Physical Education & Recreation, 1957.

Conference on Professional Preparation of Recreation Personnel. Washington, D.C.: American Assn. for Health, Physical Education & Recreation, 1957.

Conference on Recreation for the Mentally Ill. Washington, D.C.: American Assn. for Health, Physical Education & Recreation, 1958.

Danford, Howard G. *Creative Leadership in Recreation*. Boston: Allyn & Bacon, Inc., 1964.

Fitzgerald, Gerald B. *Leadership in Recreation*. New York: A.S. Barnes & Co., Inc., 1951.

Goals for American Recreation: A Report. Washington, D.C.: American Assn. for Health, Physical Education & Recreation, 1964.

Jacks, L. P. *Education Through Recreation*. New York: Harper and Brothers, 1932.

Kaplan, Max. *Leisure in America: A Social Inquiry*. New York: John Wiley & Sons, Inc., 1960.

Kraus, Richard. *Recreation Today, Program Planning and Leadership*. New York: Appleton-Century-Crofts, 1966.

Personnel Standards in Community Recreation Leadership. New York: National Recreation Association, 1965.

Professional Preparation in Health Education, Physical Education and Recreation Education, Report of a National Conference. Washington, D.C.: American Assn. for Health, Physical Education & Recreation, 1962.

Shivers, Jay S. *Principles and Practices of Recreational Service*. New York: Crowell Collier and Macmillan, Inc., 1967.

Standards and Guide for Evaluation of Professional Preparation in Health Education, Physical Education and Recreation Education. Washington, D.C.: American Assn. for Health, Physical Education & Recreation, 1958.

Ziegler, Earle F., *Philosophical Foundations for Physical, Health and Recreation Education*. Englewood Cliffs, N.J.: Prentice-Hall, Inc., 1964.

Part II

ORGANIZATION AND ADMINISTRATION

Chapter 3

CONDUCTING A RECREATION SURVEY

There are many types of recreation surveys that may be conducted in connection with recreational fact gathering. Aside from the appraisal type of survey, there are also the limited and comprehensive. The "appraisal survey determines the community's resources—facilities, areas, finance, personnel, etc.; the "limited" is more restricted in scope, embracing a population breakdown, financial resources, and administrative breakdown among others; the "comprehensive" is the broadest and involves population, economic forces, social factors, physical resources, recreational practices, interests, and related data.

The successful administration of a recreation system and, in a similar vein, efficient play direction call for advancing from the known to the unknown. The recreation survey is an effective device for accurately gauging the known and much of the unknown. It provides a means of measuring that which is at hand in the line of available recreational resources, the number and sex in each group to be served, the varied interests and needs to be met, the adequacy of the program being conducted, and recommendations for improvement.

Ideally, the survey should precede the inauguration of a recreation program. However, there is ample evidence to substantiate the opinion that it can be of inestimable value to recreation departments already in existence. An appraisal of the department periodically will serve to alert its members and may lead to a program which comes closer toward meeting the needs of the vast majority in the community. If properly conducted and implemented, it can be a powerful influence in strengthening the department.

NEED FOR A SURVEY

John Dewey's emphasis on a felt need holds equally true for a survey. The community should feel the need for a survey or much of the public support that will be necessary for its success will be reluctantly extended. Informing the public of its advent through the newspapers, radio, and by talks at service clubs, P.T.A. meetings, and business and professional groups, will do much toward encouraging public support. After all, the venture is directed at improved recreational offerings for the citizens, families and themselves.

Whenever possible, the survey should be sponsored by a responsible community agency or group. As in the case of the Lock Haven Survey, the Recreation Commission sponsored this undertaking in conjunction with the State Teachers College of that city. If the Community cannot afford to pay, the services of graduate students may be secured from a nearby college. The students will volunteer their services so that they may gather material. In addition to recreation departments, sponsorship may come from boards of education, business and professional groups, park boards, and social agencies (community chests and councils, merchants' bureaus and chambers of commerce, and service clubs).

SCOPE

The survey can encompass any or all of the following four sources of recreational activities:

1. *Public recreation* refers to governmental bodies that derive their financial support exclusively from tax funds: parks, playgrounds, and community centers.
2. *Voluntary agencies* derive their financial support from endowments, gifts, grants, and moneys other than from tax sources: boys' clubs, "Y's," and settlement houses.
3. *Quasi-public recreation* secures its funds partially from private sources and the remainder from tax moneys: many libraries and museums.
4. *Commercial recreation*, such as bowling alleys, theaters, and dance halls, is conducted by business enterprises for the profit to be secured.

Most studies appraise facilities and areas as to age group and population needs. Still others attempt to single out specific phases such as delinquency and recreation, and the influence recreation may have on the automobile accident rate among those age groups reached by the program. Studies are undertaken to compare the administrative setups or financial management of cities of comparable size.

ORGANIZATIONAL STEPS

At the outset, a survey committee should be organized consisting of representatives who have a genuine interest in recreation and are will-

ing to devote their energies to this venture. This may have been preceded by a steering committee, although it is not absolutely necessary.
A survey director may be chosen to take direct charge and to supervise
the survey.

By all means, a series of conferences should take place preliminary
to and concurrent with the survey so as to arrive at a clear-cut concept
of the objectives, scope, procedures, conclusions, and recommendations
of the study. The present author, who served as the Lock Haven survey
director, was instrumental in arranging a meeting of the members in
the community who had displayed an active interest in recreation as
leaders of activities, members of recreation and athletic boards, sponsors
and coaches of tournament play, directors of youth organizations such
as the "Y," Little League, scouts, and the like. The current trends as they
apply to a city the size of Lock Haven were outlined. The scope of
the study included an interest questionnaire and a door-to-door survey to ascertain the ages of those in each household and the concentration of population in order to determine whether the existing play
areas were easily accessible from the densely populated districts. This
brief overview was presented to enlist the support of these community
leaders and secure any suggestions they might contribute.

SUPPLEMENTAL PROCEDURES

In surveying interests, the children at the public and parochial schools
as well as the members of the service clubs and women's groups were
asked to fill out the questionnaire which is reproduced on pages 198–199
for the hobby portion and hereafter for the music, sports, and adult interest parts. The findings were tabulated on big rolls of white wrapping
paper to accommodate the many responses.

MUSIC
1. What instrument do you play? ....
2. What instrument do you own? ....
3. Do you belong to an orchestra or a band? ....
4. Do you go to music concerts? ....
5. Would you be interested in organizing a community
   a. Orchestra .... b. Choral group ....

SPORTS

	Sports you take part in	Seasonal favorites	Have never taken part but would like to
1. Air Rifle Shooting			
2. Apparatus Stunts			

	Sports you take part in	Seasonal favorites	Have never taken part but would like to
3. Archery			
4. Badminton			
5. Bag Punching			
6. Bait or Fly Casting			
7. Baseball			
8. Baseball Fly Catching			
9. Basketball			
10. Shooting Baskets			
11. Beagling			
12. Beach Bathing			
13. Bicycling			
14. Billiards			
15. Pocket Billiards (pool)			
16. Bowling			
17. Box Hockey			
18. Boxing			
19. Calisthenics			
20. Camping			
21. Picnicking			
22. Canoeing			
23. Rowing			
24. Sailing			
25. Aquaplaning			
26. Croquet			
27. Darts			
28. Deck Tennis			
29. Fencing			
30. Field Hockey			
31. Fishing (still)			
32. Fishing (casting)			
33. Fishing (fly)			
34. Football			
35. Football (passing)			
36. Football (touch)			
37. Golf			
38. Practicing Golf			
39. Handball			
40. Hiking			
41. Walking			
42. Horseshoes			

	Sports *you take* *part in*	*Seasonal* *favorites*	*Have never* *taken part* *but would* *like to*
43. Hunting (animals)			
44. Hunting (birds)			
45. Ice Hockey			
46. Ice Skating			
47. Jacks			
48. Juggling			
49. Kite Flying			
50. Marbles			
51. Mass Games (tag and so forth)			
52. Mountain Climbing			
53. Mechanical Exercises			
54. Object Balancing			
55. Ping Pong			
56. Riding			
57. Roller Skating			
58. Rope Spinning			
59. Rope Skipping			
60. Speedball			
61. Sledding			
62. Shinney			
63. Skiing			
64. Shuffleboard			
65. Sidewalk Tennis			
66. Social Dancing			
67. Tap and Clog Dancing			
68. Folk Dancing			
69. Square Dancing			
70. Soccer			
71. Softball			
72. Squash			
73. Swimming			
74. Diving			
75. Rifle Shooting			
76. Pistol Shooting			
77. Skeet Shooting			
78. Trap Shooting			
79. Track and Field			
80. Tumbling			
81. Tennis			
82. Tobogganing			

	Sports you take part in	Seasonal favorites	Have never taken part but would like to

83. Semiorganized Games
84. Relays
85. Volleyball
86. Weight Lifting
87. Water Polo
88. Wrestling
89. Walking on Stilts
90. If there are any other sports not listed above that you would like to take part in, please state here.

ADULT INTEREST (SUPPLEMENT)

1. Are you interested in forming a city softball league for all ages? _____
2. If you take part in recreational activities, state the name of the area used
   _____
3. What is your idea of a good activity for your age group? _____
4. What is your hobby(s)? _____
5. Are you sufficiently skilled to lead a hobby group? _____

The map of Lock Haven was reduced photographically into twenty-four sectors. A sectional map was given to each member of the class who was assisting with this project as a partial fulfillment of the laboratory requirement of thirty-six hours per student. The door-to-door portion of the survey wherein each family in Lock Haven was visited elicited the following information:

1. The number in each family and age grouping.
2. The relative density of population in each sector.
3. The places where the children go to play.
4. Where the adults go for their recreation.

A very large map of the city was secured and was used to record the findings of this part of the survey. A system was devised wherein multi-colored pins were used to denote the various age groups. To keep from overcrowding the map, each pin represented five of that age group. Through this means, the density of population and their age groupings could be readily observed. The assortment of colors and their age group designations were as follows:

Pin Color	Age
Red	3–5
Orange	6–8

Yellow	9–11
Green	12–15
Blue	16–18
Purple	19–21
Tan	22–25
Brown	26–35
Black	36–45
Plain	46–over

Following is the home-visit survey blank designed to elicit recreational information:

Address .... *Name* ....

No. in Family ..... *Age Group*

Male: 3–5 ( )   6–8 ( )   9–11 ( )
        12–15 ( )   16–18 ( )   19–21 ( )
        22–25 ( )   26–35 ( )   36–45 ( )
        46–over ( ).

Female: 3–5 ( )   6–8 ( )   9–11 ( )
        12–15 ( )   16–18 ( )   19–21 ( )
        22–25 ( )   26–35 ( )   36–45 ( )
        46–over ( ).

Where do children play? ....
Where do adults go for recreation? ....
....

RECOMMENDATIONS

It is noteworthy that the existing recreational areas were marked so as to be clearly visible on the map. After an analysis of the findings concerning the density of population and the number in each age group, the recreational needs of the city became more evident. A comparison of the findings with accepted standards revealed the need for a minimum of six recreational areas.

In determining the location of the play areas, two related factors were taken into consideration: the density of population and the distance to be covered to reach a play area. It was decided that children should not be required to walk more than half a mile to a play area; older youths and adults might avail themselves of other means of transportation and could be expected to cover a greater distance. Six play areas were recommended: three play lots for children, one playfield for adolescents and adults, and two neighborhood playgrounds for all age groups.

The revelations of the interest questionnaire were also made available to the Recreation Commission. It was apprised of the hobby, music, sports, and adult interest findings. In view of the fact that over half of Lock Haven's population is twenty-six years of age and over, it was recommended that adequate provisions be made for this large segment as well as for the younger groups. Other recommendations included an outdoor swimming pool in connection with a neighborhood playground, a bicycle and walking path along the river, and additional picnicking facilities which could be constructed adjacent to this path.

INFORMING THE PUBLIC

After the fact gathering and analysis is completed, there is still work to be done. Agreement as to the findings and recommendations should be secured before any facts are released. The sponsoring group should receive copies of the original report. Afterwards, the facts should be synthesized into a form for public consumption. Copies should be issued to the press and radio so that the public may be made cognizant of the results. In addition, copies should be distributed to cooperating agencies and individuals. Leaders of the various public and private recreational agencies and members of the board of education should also receive copies.

The power of the public to influence action should never be underestimated. Every effort toward informing the public is usually considered to be effort and time well spent. The sponsoring group will, therefore, be very desirous of publicizing the findings. In the case of the Lock Haven Survey, the *Lock Haven Express* devoted practically an entire issue toward the survey findings, accompanied by profuse illustrations.

NOTABLE SURVEYS

Quite a few worthwhile surveys have been conducted in recent years. While all have not been equally effective, there is little room to doubt that all have served to develop an awareness of the recreational needs in their localities.

The *Teen Age Recreation Survey in Long Beach* embodies an interest survey of junior and senior high-school pupils; a questionnaire was circulated with the assistance of the physical education instructors in those schools. Adult interests have been surveyed by a number of studies. The National Recreation Association has compiled the findings of a survey of the interests and activities of adults. This study benefited from the cooperation of participating recreation departments. The *Schedule For the Appraisal of Community Recreation*, also issued by the National

Recreation Association, has proved helpful to many communities. Also, *Planning for Recreation Areas and Facilities in Small Towns and Cities*, issued by the Federal Security Agency, is another helpful aid in this regard.

A thorough-going survey was conducted for Los Angeles by Community Surveys Associated. It encompassed a community plan for Metropolitan Los Angeles and was appropriately titled *Recreation for Everybody*. On the county setup, the *Hamilton County Recreation Survey* which is issued by the Bureau of Governmental Research, Cincinnati, Ohio, is recommended.

SUGGESTED READINGS

A Study of Recreation and Parks for the City of Tulsa and Its Metropolitan Area. Tulsa, Okla.: The City of Tulsa, 1957.

A Teen Age Recreation Survey in Long Beach. New York: National Recreation Association.

Brown, J. Lee. *Planning for Recreation Areas and Facilities in Small Towns and Cities*. Washington, D.C.: Federal Security Agency, Government Printing Office.

Clawson, Marian. *How Much Leisure, Now and in the Future*. Washington, D.C.: Resources for the Future, Inc., 1961.

Meyer, Harold D., and Charles K. Brightbill. *Community Recreation: A Guide to Its Practices*. Englewood Cliffs, N.J.: Prentice-Hall, Inc., 1964.

Outdoor Recreation for America. Washington, D.C.: Outdoor Recreation Resources Review Commission, 1962.

Outdoor Recreation Trends. Washington, D.C.: Bureau of Outdoor Recreation, Department of the Interior, April 1967.

Planning Areas and Facilities for Health, Physical Education and Recreation. Chicago: The Athletic Institute, 1965.

Recreation—A Post-war Plan for Los Angeles. Los Angeles, Calif.: City of Los Angeles, 1946.

Recreation Research, Collected Papers from National Conference on Recreation Research. Washington, D.C.: American Assn. for Health, Physical Education & Recreation, 1966.

Recreation Surveys of the Cities of Buffalo, Rochester, Baltimore, Los Angeles, Toledo, Tulsa.

Schedule for the Appraisal of Community Recreation. New York: National Recreation Association.

Sitte, C., *City Planning*. New York: Random House, Inc., 1965.

Wingo, Lowdon, *Cities and Space*. Baltimore, Md.: Johns Hopkins University Press, 1963.

Chapter 4

ADMINISTRATIVE SETUPS

The administration of recreation, as hereinafter considered, will incorporate federal, state, county, and regional recreation. Each branch of government has an agreed-upon function to perform. With the evolvement of recreation has gone, in some instances, a shifting of responsibilities. For example, the more direct and comprehensive involvement of the federal government in recreation has been accompanied by greater financial support to the states; consequently, the states have found themselves in a position to provide services that are broader in scope and more detailed in nature. The emphasis is predominantly on public or tax-supported recreation in this chapter except for the brief reference to church recreation.

MUNICIPAL RECREATION

Just as efficient leadership is the *sine qua non* of the recreation program, so proper organization and judicious administration is the *sine qua non* of the recreation department. Suffice it to say, there are varied types of administrative setups throughout the country. It is therefore essential to scrutinize the cities under consideration so as to ascertain how recreation is administered in representative cities. While the population of the cities to be dealt with in this chapter are 300,000 and over,[1] the revelations are symbolic and applicable to smaller municipalities.

Recreation Commission. A vast majority of the recreation departments throughout the land operate under a board or commission setup. The commission is usually comprised of five members, although there are quite a few with seven. Cincinnati, Ohio, is typical of many cities wherein the Board of Park Commissioners and the Board of Education were responsible for the management, administration, and financing of the city's recreational activities. Its Public Recreation Commission was

[1]H. Dan Corbin, *A Comparative Study of Public Recreation in Cities of 300,000 Population and Over with Special Emphasis on New York City* (unpublished doctoral dissertation, New York University, 1946).

44

formed by the adoption of a new provision to the Cincinnati City Charter in 1926. The law stated:

There shall be a Public Recreation Commission consisting of one member of the Board of Education appointed by said Board, one member of the Board of Park Commissioners appointed by said Board, and three citizens appointed by the Mayor, to serve without compensation. The term of office of said members and the powers and duties of said commission shall be fixed by ordinance of the Council, but all funds obtained from levies for recreational purposes, appropriated by other public bodies, or donated for such purposes to the City of Cincinnati or the Public Recreation Commission shall be expended by said Commission.[2]

The Director of Public Recreation is in charge of administering Cincinnati's recreational programs in the play areas of the schools, parks, and playgrounds. The school system cooperates with the Public Recreation Commission by interchanging the use of playgrounds. The Board of Education accepts a joint responsibility for the maintenance of these playgrounds.[3]

The Recreation Commission of San Francisco is administered by the City and County of San Francisco. Seven members comprise the Commission, five appointed by the mayor of the City, for a period of four years, one term expiring each year; and two exofficio members, one the Superintendent of Parks, and the other the Superintendent of Schools. The activities of the Recreation Department are coordinated with other public and private agencies through practical cooperation. Two of the members of the Recreation Commission, which serves without compensation, must be women.

Among the smaller communities with a recreation commission setup are Evansville, Indiana; Lawrence, Kansas; Lake Charles, Louisiana; and Frederick, Maryland.

In 1942, by act of Congress, a Recreation Board was created for the District of Columbia. Pertinent provisions follow:

ARTICLE I: MEMBERSHIP OF THE RECREATION BOARD

Section 1. The Board shall consist of seven members as follows: A representative of the Board of Commissioners selected by that Board; a representative of the Board of Education selected by that Board; the Superintendent of the National Capital Parks ex-officio; and four members, who shall have been for

---

[2]Article VII, Section 14.
[3]Letter of Wendell H. Pierce, Acting Director of Research, September 19, 1945.

five years immediately preceding their selection bona fide residents of the District of Columbia, appointed by the Commissioners of the District of Columbia for a term of four years, each, except of the original appointments, which shall be for terms of one, two, three, and four years, respectively.

The appointment of the four citizens shall be without regard to race, sex, or creed, and shall take judicious account of the various parent, civic, and other organizations through which residents of the District voice their civic wishes and advance the common welfare. The two members of the Board representing the Board of Commissioners and the Board of Education shall be designated annually by their respective agencies.

Section 2. The members of the Board shall serve without compensation for such service.

Section 3. The Board shall select from among its citizen membership its Chairman and its secretary and is hereby authorized and empowered to adopt all necessary rules and regulations for the conduct of its business.

The Board was also authorized to appoint a Superintendent of Recreation.[4]

The District law authorizes the Board to enter into agreements with other agencies that have jurisdiction over property. Through representation from the District Commissioners, the Board of Education, and the National Capital Parks office, cooperative use of the facilities belonging to each group is fostered.

Separate recreation authority. The trend as indicated by national studies conducted by the author and others[5] is toward administration by combined park and recreation authorities. This form of administering public recreation is especially suited for large communities. Through the authorization of a separate bureau or department of recreation to make use of all public facilities, an efficient setup is in the offing. Cooperation with the private as well as the public agencies is simplified under a single authority so that a comprehensive recreation program can be achieved for the entire city. Moreover, overlapping or duplicated programming and wasted effort and funds are precluded. Efficiency is thereby heightened so that more valuable services can be rendered at minimal cost.

The 1966 *Recreation and Park Yearbook* reports that the number of

[4] Article II, Sec. a, Public Law 534, 77th Congress.

[5] Cf. George D. Butler, *Introduction to Community Recreation* (New York: McGraw-Hill Book Company, 1959), Chapter 30; G. Hjelte, *The Administration of Public Recreation* (New York: The Macmillan Company, 1947), Chapter IV; J. F. Williams and C. L. Brownell, *Administration of Health and Physical Education* (Philadelphia: W. B. Saunders Co., 1947), pp. 58–59.

combined park and recreation agencies increased from 466 in 1960 to 1,304 in 1965. During that period, the number of separate recreation departments decreased from 949 to 818, and separate park agencies from 543 to 428.[6] More than fifty per cent of all public agencies solely responsible for park and/or recreation services are combined park and recreation departments.

At the city level, separate recreation authorities outnumbered separate park authorities. The opposite was true at the county level. The *Yearbook* states that the trend toward combined park and recreation authorities is expected to continue.

Divided responsibility. Under this administrative plan, the public recreational services are handled by more than one municipal agency. For example, New York City has divided control between the Board of Education and the Department of Parks. The Division of Community Education of the Board of Education conducts programs in the schools and on athletic fields. The Bureau of Recreation of the New York City Department of Parks is responsible for the programming of recreational activities in more than 600 playgrounds and gymnasia. In addition, the Bureau operates designated recreation areas in conjunction with the Board of Education. There are more than 20 sites that have been arranged so that the school playgrounds are made available for community-wide use during the after-school hours. These play areas are operated under Park Department supervision. This cooperative policy is to be followed in future school construction.

Board of Park Commissioners. As early as 1905, the City Council of the City of St. Paul passed an ordinance providing for the establishment of a playground system under the supervision of a park board; the mayor was empowered to appoint a committee of three as the Advisory Playground Board, and the Board of Park Commissioners was to appoint a supervisor for playgrounds and public recreation. This plan has continued in operation.

Other cities where the Board of Park Commissioners administers recreation are Wilmington, Delaware; Fort Wayne, Indiana; Wichita, Kansas; Spokane, Washington; and Cambridge, Massachusetts.

Board of Education Rule. Boards of education have been gaining in taking charge of the "preparation for the worthy use of leisure time," pronounced by the National Education Association in 1918, as one of its seven Cardinal Principles of Secondary Education. The matter of finan-

[6]*Recreation and Park Yearbook*, 42nd ed. (New York: National Recreation Association, 1967), pp. 44, 45.

cial support has been one of the deterrents, with education supported to a considerable extent by state funds whereas recreation is on the whole a municipal function.

This argument has been obviated in the Commonwealth of Pennsylvania by Act 141 which became effective May 27, 1947. Recreation is administered through the Extension Education Division of the Department of Public Instruction. The state aid is apportioned on the basis of the salary permitted, multiplied by the "reimbursement fraction" for that district for recreation teachers and supervisors holding a standard provisional or college certificate; state aid varies from twenty-three per cent in the wealthiest districts to more than ninety-five per cent in the poorest ones. The median fraction for all of the Commonwealth's school districts is more than seventy-five per cent.

Community Schools. It is indeed true that there is increasing evidence of community recreation under board of education rule. That the highest percentage of a community's capital investment rests in school properties is also a fact in practically all communities and especially in smaller ones. Each school is replete with facilities that can be utilized for recreational purposes.

The American Association of School Administrators and the Educational Policies Commission have long advocated that public school properties be kept open for public use during the after-school hours.

However, the ever-increasing demands for expanded services upon boards of education have accounted for the willingness of some to yield the handling of community-wide recreation to another agency. In many cases where this has taken place, effective cooperation between the recreation agency and the school has occurred. The auditorium (entertainments, town hall meetings, speakers' forums, concerts), gymnasium (games, sports, dances), shop (carpentry, machine tooling, handicrafts, hobby groups), pool (swimming, diving, life saving), music rooms (instrument practice, band rehearsals, community chorus, community sing), home economics rooms (cooking, baking, sewing, interior decorating), and classrooms (club meetings, adult education) are highly suited to meet a community's needs until specially constructed facilities are available. Modern school construction plans often call for the placement of most of these facilities in a wing of the school plant so that the problem of winter heating, of lighting, and of policing are simplified.

Evidence of board of education administration of recreation is to be found in such municipalities as New Bedford, Massachusetts; Albany, New York; Newark, New Jersey; Kansas City, Missouri; and Milwaukee,

Wisconsin. In Milwaukee, the Department of Municipal Recreation and Adult Education operates under the direction of the Milwaukee Board of School Directors. The state law empowers the Board of School Directors to request a special tax not to exceed eight-tenths mill on the city's valuation with the moneys to be used expressly for leisure-time activities for both children and adults.

The law also stipulates that the Milwaukee School Board may cooperate with any other municipal board or commission that has facilities usable for recreation. Under this arrangement, the School Board is to provide the instruction and supervision with the outside board furnishing the facilities. Pursuant to this provision, the public parks are used for athletics and playground activities, and the pools under the jurisdiction of the Board of Public Works are used for swimming instruction and aquatic meets.

Another example of a city that is making around-the-clock use of its schools through its adult education and recreation program is Flint, Michigan. Funds are realized through state support for adult education, board of education appropriations, the public-spirited Mott Foundation, and other cooperating agencies.

By making fuller use of its schools for recreational purposes, Flint is readily afforded the use of such "municipal luxury items" as community centers and recreation halls. Duplication of facilities is avoided through the less expensive substitutes utilizing areas that would otherwise go unused.

CHURCH RECREATION

A significant contributor on the recreational front is the church. Certainly, churches have utilized the sylvan setting for religious instruction with the church camp. That they have emphasized recreational activities in conjunction with their ecclesiastical objectives is also recognized.

In addition, churches have employed recreation as an adjunct to their religious activities. The Riverside Church in New York City has for years operated a successful recreational program. Many churches throughout the land have put to sound use recreational pursuits as a means of impressing on the minds of their congregants that the church is interested in the welfare of each member as an integrated individual. As a consequence, the physical, emotional, mental, and social well-being were most compatible with the spiritual. The efforts of the Catholic Youth Organization (C.Y.O.) are deserving of special commendation for their measures on a faithwide basis.

STATE RECREATION

It is becoming increasingly apparent that recreation is largely a state function. Recreation, as an accepted member of the education family, is deserving of the same treatment accorded its other "children." For decades states have operated parks, forests, camp sites, winter sports, and picknicking, hunting, and fishing facilities, so that recreation is not a new phenomenon to them.

Moreover, the taxing power of the average municipality is very slight at best. In many instances, the taxing powers of municipalities are barely adequate where they do exist. The municipal government is left with the "pickings" after the federal and state governments have exercised their prior taxing rights. That, plus the necessity for enabling legislation before the municipality can exercise these powers, leaves recreation in a highly dependent position. The state possesses existing services which can, with little added effort, assume the added responsibility of serving the local recreation departments.

Control by State Boards of Education. In *Recreation—A New Function of State Government*, Charles K. Brightbill[7] provides these arguments in favor of the state board of education control of recreation:

1. State Boards of Education have Physical Education Bureaus and there are those who see a very close relationship between physical education and recreation.
2. It has been held that inasmuch as recreation has educational values, it makes sense to turn over the administration of recreation to the educators.
3. Because of the fact that local school boards many times control the grounds and buildings required for a community recreation program, it is wise to place control in Boards of Education. Moreover, it is held that this argument is strengthened by virtue of the fact that not only are new school facilities being designed to provide recreation space, but State Boards of Education are consulted on such problems.
4. Education has access to large groups of teachers with knowledge of education principles and practices and with experience in handling children.
5. Education has respect and prestige in both local and State government and, consequently, the public may be more willing to accept recreation as a cofunction with education.
6. State Boards of Education have access to machinery for training instructors and leaders and have had a wealth of experience in this field.
7. The recreational interests of education have gone beyond mere physical

[7]Charles K. Brightbill, *Recreation—A New Function of State Government* (Washington, D.C.: Recreation Division, Federal Security Agency 1944).

activities, as evidenced in the expansion of extracurricular activities such as orchestras, choruses, drama groups, hobby clubs, and the like.

Outside of the state services mentioned above, the states assist the municipalities in the technical planning of play areas, in programming, and through financial support. Technical services are made available by some states for the planning and layouts of play areas. In-service training programs are conducted by such states as Pennsylvania (through its State Planning Board in cooperation with the Public Service Institute of the Department of Public Instruction) and Alabama (through its State Department of Education). Municipal recreation departments receive financial assistance through the education departments of the states of Washington, Florida, and Pennsylvania. To help integrate their services, many states have inaugurated interdepartmental or interagency committees.

State colleges and universities have contributed splendidly toward furthering effective community recreation. This work has been conducted largely through their extension divisions by field recreation consultants. Outstanding examples of this service are in evidence at Purdue University, the University of Minnesota, and the University of New Hampshire. In addition, there are the Agricultural Extension Service (which is administered by the state agricultural colleges), the United States Department of Agriculture, county governments, and farm organizations. Recreation is being accorded added stress in its efforts at improving rural living. The 4-H clubs are a popular outgrowth of agricultural extension service with about two million enrolled in 81,000 4-H clubs.

State recreation commissions. Up to the present, there are three states with recreation commissions: North Carolina, Vermont, and California, in the order of their inauguration. The North Carolina Recreation Commission came into being on March 19, 1945, with a board of seven appointed members and four ex officio members. Vermont's State Recreation Board started to function by April 1, 1947, with three members comprising the board. On July 8, 1947, the California State Recreation Commission of seven members was organized. Its staff consists of a director, assistant director, and four recreation specialists who are assigned to designated sectors of the state.

The commissions provide advisory and consultant services to the municipalities. Among their services are conferences, in-service training, surveys, and technical assistance. In the relatively short time since their advent, the recreation commission plan has more than justified its existence.

State recreation services. A national plan of coordinated action can result best from cooperative planning and coordinated efforts of all state and municipal agencies in concert with their federal counterparts. Through the interagency committee, the synchronization of these efforts is more readily assured; interagency recreation committees function in the states of Indiana, Michigan, Minnesota, Missouri, North Carolina, Ohio, and Virginia.

FEDERAL RECREATION

Significant changes have taken place in the area of federal recreation starting with the January 1962 issuance date of the Outdoor Recreation Resources Review Commission report. This was followed by the establishment of the Bureau of Outdoor Recreation by the Secretary of the Interior of April 2, 1962. Shortly thereafter the Recreation Advisory Council was formed by executive order on April 27, 1962. The following year, the Bureau of Outdoor Recreation Organic Act provided the Secretary of the Interior with broad recreation planning authority. Of relatively recent date are the Land and Water Conservation Fund Act and the Federal Water Projects Recreation act passed in 1965.

The Open Space Program of grants-in-aid to urban areas was widened to incorporate urban beautification by the Housing and Urban Development of 1965. The Federal Interagency Committee was replaced by a "new look" involving intergovernmental relationships, resulting in the newly formed Recreation Advisory Council. The planning and research functions of the new Bureau of Outdoor Recreation was a prime mover in this change.

LAND AND WATER CONSERVATION FUND

The Federal Interagency practices and federal–state relations were modified upon passage of the Land and Water Fund. In order to take advantage of the $75–100 million fund available annually, the states have revamped in many instances their plans of operation. A state official has been designated to deal with the Bureau of Outdoor Recreation throughout the nation. This person serves as the coordinator of state recreation plans and programs and provides a liaison between the Federal Outdoor Recreation Assistance Program and the local recreation agencies.

The Fund Act requires a comprehensive outdoor recreation plan on a statewide basis in order to secure the fifty per cent matching funds for land acquisition and development of facilities. This has spurred on concerted efforts on the part of the many states which, prior to that point, did not have plans of action. The plan of action calls for federal funds to be meted out to the municipalities by way of the state. This "chain of command" holds true for the submission of proposals to the Bureau of Ourdoor Recreation as well as for the granting of funds.

COOPERATIVE FEDERAL EFFORTS

The newly formed Department of Housing and Urban Development and the Bureau of Outdoor Recreation has cooperated to expedite a speeding up of plan formation and their implementation. Wherever state outdoor recreation plans apply to urbanized areas, the Department of Housing and Urban Development takes over. In the matter of Open Space Projects outside urbanized areas, the Bureau of Outdoor Recreation reviews proposals to see that they are consistent with statewide recreation plans. On the whole, the Open Space Program is centered in highly urbanized areas providing facilities of neighborhood utility. Moreover, Land and Water Funds for the acquisition of recreation areas of statewide, metropolitan, or regionwide significance are stimulated. The federal agencies that benefit from the Land and Water Conservation Fund are the National Park Service, the Forest Service, and the Bureau of Sport Fisheries and Wildlife. Generally, the federal share of Land and Water Conservation Funds is directed at the acquisition of land for many authorized areas.

The Recreation Advisory Council is concerned mainly with major policy matters to help assure that a unified approach will be employed by all federal agencies. To expedite this, the Council has formulated criteria to determine whether an area warrants being selected as a National Recreation Area. Consequently, the application of these criteria by the Bureau of Outdoor Recreation has helped to assure high standards. Policy guidelines are also in the process of being formulated by staff study groups.

PLANNING AND RESEARCH

By 1968, it is believed that the National Outdoor Recreation Plan will be completed. It will guide the apportionment of public resources to meet the nation's outdoor recreation needs. This plan will bring up to date and extend the coverage of the 1962 report of the Outdoor Recreation Resources Review Commission. Parallel questions to the ORRRC survey will be employed to help establish trends in public preferences. As an outgrowth, it will reveal the changes which five years of concerted effort have accomplished.

Study teams have proposed a national system of wild rivers, the nationwide system of trails, a series of national recreation areas, and the
conservation use of excess military lands. Furthermore, interagency efforts are directed at developing new types of outdoor recreation resources.

HISTORICAL HIGHLIGHTS

The federal government's interest in recreation was first evidenced in
1864 when, by congressional act, Yosemite Valley and the Mariposa
Big Tree Grove were given to California for recreation purposes. In 1872,
President Grant affixed his signature to the bill that created Yellowstone
National Park. As early as 1868, the Commissioner of the *Office of Education* recognized in its first report that a relationship existed between
education and recreation.

The *Bureau of Fisheries* was set up by 1871 and later became the
Fish and Wildlife Service. Congress authorized the use of national forest
areas for recreation in 1897 thereby providing for picnic areas, camp
sites, and the like, for outdoor recreation, including fishing, hunting,
camping, and picnicking. The federal government's interest in recreation gained real impetus at the turn of the twentieth century. Increased
efforts were exerted for the use of federal land and water areas for recreational purposes. By 1906 authorization was given the President to establish national monuments.

In 1914 the *Extension Service of the Department of Agriculture* came
into being under the Smith–Lever Act whereby impetus was given to
recreation in rural areas. The *Forest Service* was given added authority
in 1915 to permit "the construction of summer homes, hotels, and other
structures, under permits not to exceed thirty years of duration in national forest areas."

The *Children's Bureau* came into existence, in 1912 and soon became
cognizant of the recreation problems and needs of our children and
youths. By 1915 it had made a study of the play facilities for children
in the District of Columbia. In addition to other important studies the
Bureau was prominent in Children's Year activities in 1918, and in the
1919, 1930, 1940, and 1950 White House Conferences on children, with
the recreational needs of children and youth highlighted. The child welfare programs administered under the Social Security Act have been
concerned with the recreational needs of children coming within the
Act's provisions.

In order to provide recreational services for the military personnel at
the start of World War I, the Commission on Training Camp Activities

was organized. As a result, programs were instituted under private auspices in and around camps and in war industrial centers. To administer the national monuments, parks, and reservations, the *National Park Service* was organized in 1916. Not until 1933 did those national monuments, parks, and military parks shift over to the *National Park Service*. The depression recreation services of the federal government are considered under "Brief History of the Recreation Movement," pages 1–7.

The *Federal Housing Division* activities of the *Public Works Administration* were inaugurated in 1933. Recognition of the role recreation can play in planning housing projects was rendered from its inception. Indoor and outdoor recreation facilities have been included in housing projects. Recreation programs have been developed in conjunction with the neighboring community. It is noteworthy that the *Federal Housing Administration*, which is a loan insurance agency, insists on outdoor recreation space allocations wherever present facilities are inadequate. It is now known as the *Public Housing Administration*.

A *Technical Committee on Recreation* was instituted by an *Inter-Department Committee* in 1936 to coordinate health and welfare activities pursuant to the recognition of recreation as a vital federal function. In fact, several federal agencies organized recreation programs for their employees. The *Travel Division* was set up to promote travel throughout the United States. In 1944 Congress designated that the *Department of the Army* provide through its *Corps of Engineers* for the recreational use of its reservoirs.

During World War II, the *Army* and *Navy* instituted extensive recreational programs. Along with the *American Red Cross*, which handled recreational services in on-the-post hospitals and in communities of combat areas, the temporary *Division of Recreation of the Federal Security Agency* encouraged and offered counsel in communities to provide recreation for servicemen and war workers. It also maintained affiliations with the United Service Organizations and recommended projects to the *Federal Works Agency* for recreation buildings and services. The Commissioner of Education, through his reorganization plan of 1944, recommended that a special section on school–community recreation with a staff of specialists be organized. This was advocated to expedite meeting the needs of education in the development of programs of training in recreation skills, extracurricular activities, after-school and vacation play, the use of school facilities, and community recreation resources.

The *Federal Inter-Agency Committee on Recreation* was created in 1946 to make possible coordination and planning to cope with the growing demands for recreation facilities and services. By acting as a clearing house for the exchange of policies, plans, methods, experiences, and procedures among the agencies, it contributes toward more efficient federal service. It also undertakes to ease the dissemination of information dealing with the federal recreation services, while aiming to round out governmental contributions to the states and their peoples with special emphasis on small communities and rural areas, minority groups, young people, older adults, and women and girls. This committee function has been largely preempted by the Bureau of Outdoor Recreation.

Among the federal agencies with recreation functions are the following:

Corps of Engineers	Department of the Army
National Park Service	Department of the Interior
Fish and Wildlife Service	Department of the Interior
Bureau of Reclamation	Department of the Interior
Bureau of Land Management	Department of the Interior
Federal Extension Service	Department of Agriculture
Forest Service	Department of Agriculture
Office of Education	Department of Health, Education and Welfare
Public Health Service	Department of Health, Education and Welfare
Public Housing Administration	Housing and Home Finance Agency

To augment that which was presented, other governmental agencies which contribute to the nation's recreational life are added:

The Bureau of Indian Affairs provides limited recreational opportunities for the public on Indian lands as well as facilities and programs for the Indians themselves.

The National Capital Park and Planning Commission was created to plan and acquire an adequate system of parks, parkways, and playgrounds, to preserve the forest and natural scenery in and about the national capital, and to prepare a coordinated city and regional plan for the District of Columbia and environs.

Under the *Department of Health, Education, and Welfare* the Public Health Service furnishes information on sanitary problems relating to construction and operation of park recreation developments, such as swimming pools, camps, and beaches.

The *Federal Works Agency's* Public Roads Administration cooperates with the National Park Service and the Forest Service in constructing roads in areas under the jurisdiction of these services. As a considerable part of the national use of all public roads is estimated to be for recreation purposes, the total program of this agency has an important bearing on the recreation of the people. The Bureau of Community Facilities administers federal grants and aids made in connection with the defense and war program for recreational facilities and services to local communities. It also disposes of recreation properties to local and federal governmental agencies.

The *Department of Agriculture's* Soil Conservation Service has set aside the developed recreation areas in connection with its land utilization projects.

The *Tennessee Valley Authority* assists state and local governments within its area of operation to plan and organize their recreation services. It has also developed a number of demonstration parks, most of which have been transferred to state or local agencies for administration.[8]

SUGGESTED READINGS

Butler, George D. *Introduction to Community Recreation.* New York: McGraw-Hill Book Company, 1959.

Colbern, Fern M. *Buildings of Tomorrow: Guide for Planning Settlements and Community Buildings.* New York: William Morrow Co., Inc., 1955.

Commission on Architecture. Architecture for Adult Education Association, 1957.

Conference on Professional Preparation of Recreation Personnel. Washington, D.C.: American Assn. for Health, Physical Education & Recreation, 1957.

Hall, J. Tillman. *School Recreation: Its Organization, Supervision and Administration.* Dubuque, Iowa: William C. Brown Company, Publishers, 1966.

Hjelte, George, and Jay S. Shivers. *Public Administration of Park and Recreational Services.* New York: The Macmillan Company, 1963.

Kraus, Richard G. *Recreation and the Schools.* New York: The Macmillan Company, 1964.

Meyer, Harold D., and Charles K. Brightbill. *Community Recreation: A Guide to Its Organization.* Englewood Cliffs, N.J.: Prentice-Hall, Inc., 1964.

——. *Recreation Administration: A Guide to Its Practices.* Englewood Cliffs, N.J.: Prentice-Hall, Inc., 1956.

Recreation and Park Yearbook, 42nd ed. New York: National Recreation Association, 1967.

Rodney, Lynn S. *Administration of Public Recreation.* New York: The Ronald Press Company, 1964.

[8]*The Role of the Federal Government in the Field of Public Recreation* (Washington, D.C.: Federal Inter-Agency Committee on Recreation, June 1949), pp. 4, 5.

Chapter 5

PROBLEMS CONFRONTING
THE PROFESSION

Professions, like individuals, are often confronted with matters or questions requiring solution. These problems are of various degrees of difficulty. An examination of the problems listed will reveal this fact on quick examination.

It therefore follows that the recreation profession would have its share of questions to be resolved. As a profession that is undergoing rapid growth, it is challenged by significant problems which are but a natural feature of development. In fact, the more strongly entrenched educational subjects have been confronted with similar vital problems and, though much older, are still not without them. In view of the fact that recreation is in somewhat of a probationary state, it must be especially conscious of its weaknesses.

Recreation can be compared with the adolescent who suddenly finds himself growing so rapidly that he becomes gawky—his physiological development can't keep up with his anatomical growth. That many of the gains made have been consolidated is indeed true. That there are numerous other gains to be made and much consolidation to be achieved is also true.

PROFESSIONAL OUTLOOK

Still, despite all this the prospects are far from gloomy. In fact, the outlook is a bright one, considering the fact that the number of cities which are inaugurating recreation departments is rapidly growing. The inevitable trend toward an increasing leisure will continue to be a selling point for the field. With a steadily more mechanized industry and greater specialization of effort, the need for recreational outlets and creative play mounts. As was mentioned previously, the gap between work and play is constantly widening due to the increased monotony of industrial work, with the individual laborer's contribution toward the finished product diminishing in importance and discernibility.

Improved roads and faster modes of transportation have eased the task of reaching heretofore inaccessible recreation areas; state and federal parks and play areas are being used more extensively annually. Advances in medical science have contributed toward an increased span of life, a more rapid population growth, as well as a more adult population; herein, we find one of the great challenges to recreational leadership.

TRENDS

The trend toward grants-in-aid from the state governments augurs well for the profession. As an acknowledged branch of education, it is deserving of generous state support. State departments of education as well as institutions of higher education are becoming increasingly aware that recreation is a specialty calling for distinctive training. A growing number of institutions are inaugurating major programs. Through the realization that this form of education warrants special training in specific skills there has grown a curriculum which is gaining in stature. Although the training given physical education teachers parallels that required of recreation majors in part, this exacting field calls for added specialized courses of instruction.

In this connection, we see evidence of a trend toward a minor in recreation. When associated with a major in physical education, music education, dramatics, or fine arts, a minor in recreation can provide the profession with well-trained specialists in these program areas.[1]

The Recreation Commission Plan has risen in popularity as an organizational setup for community recreation. With representation from the board of education on it, it offers an opportunity for the use of the school system's facilities and equipment. It forestalls duplication of effort on the part of separate governmental agencies, such as the park department and the board of education.

Outdoor recreational areas are being given greater utility through floodlights whereby their use can be extended until ten or eleven o'clock at night. This advance stands to benefit all ages, particularly adults, since they are generally deprived of public recreation opportunities during their after-work hours because of the early closing time of outdoor areas. This is especially true during the winter months.

Efforts are being expended at the careful selection of prospective leaders. Since leadership in recreation makes greater demands on the

[1]Henry O. Dresser, "The Need of a Recreation Minor," *Recreation Magazine* (January 1958).

personality, considerable effort is being exerted at securing suitable criteria for the selection of candidates. Before long the measures that are being employed will be refined and probably adopted by more colleges and universities.

PROBLEMS AND PROJECT LISTINGS

This selection will concern itself with a listing of timely questions and problems. It is noteworthy that discussions of problems confronting the profession can be related to subjects under consideration by classes of recreation trainees. This technique is to be encouraged since it provides situations wherein original thinking on the part of the students is encouraged. Furthermore, the exchange of ideas that results, if kept within bounds by the instructor and augmented by his contributions, can yield effective learning. In addition, many of the problems can be utilized as project subjects to be used for termpapers. Also, quite a few are usable as examination questions.

For the convenience of the instructor and student as well, the problems and project suggestions are categorized into four general topics: Finance, administration, recreational leadership training, and miscellaneous.

FINANCING RECREATION

1. What are the accepted ways of raising revenue for the operation of a parks and recreation department?
2. The problem of financing local public recreation is omnipresent. State and explain the various means of financing this service.
3. What should be the recommended per capita expenditure needed to provide a well-balanced community recreation service? Would the city's size affect the amount?
4. What are the advantages and disadvantages of the special mill tax for financing local recreation?
5. State the principles that underlie sound budget procedures. How are these principles to be put into effect?
6. What shall be the basic policies that underlie the levying of fees for recreational services and facilities?
7. Has the levying of fees and charges had much effect on participation?
8. What financial records should be kept by the recreation department in addition to those required by the city? Is there evidence that unit cost records have helped secure increased appropriations?
9. How will the tendency of cities to establish a pay-as-you-go policy for capital improvements affect the acquisition of needed recreation areas and facilities?

10. What procedures are recommended in handling recreation funds as, for example:
    a. Income from concessions?
    b. Collections on golf courses, swimming pools, and so forth?
    c. Funds taken in by activity groups?
11. In a nationwide survey, clear and thorough financial reports were virtually nonexistent. How can a city formulate a financial report devoid of these shortcomings?
12. Is a time–cost accounting system an indispensable aid in computing the maintenance costs of a recreation program? Explain.
13. What are the pros and cons of charging fees for tax-supported recreational activities?
14. To what extent should the recreation department set aside added funds so as to stockpile equipment suitable for use in the event of a sneak attack or national emergency?
15. Should state funds be made available to support a study of camping needs and facilities in each community? If so, how shall it be administered?
16. How can the following administrative procedures of school camping be solved?
    a. How shall school camping be financed?
    b. What ages or grades should go camping?
    c. Who are to be the leaders?
    d. What should be the ratio of teachers to campers?
    e. Should the camp be coeducational?
17. How should day camps be financed?
18. In order to extract additional value out of each tax dollar, the multiple use of space and facilities are to be encouraged. Outline acceptable measures to help assure this fund-saving procedure.

ADMINISTRATION

1. State the principles of sound practice in the development of a staff organization chart.
2. Present an administrative analysis of a large city's recreation department. State the various positions and justify their existence.
3. Describe the supervisor's role in a recreation system. Present arguments for and against.
4. Give instances of effective use and abuse of supervision.
5. How have activity interests changed in the past twenty-five years? What are the trends evident in these changes?
6. How can more effective recreational use be made of county, state, and national parks?
7. Are the standards for municipal recreation areas and facilities as set up by the National Recreation Association adequate?
8. Have the principles of the National Facilities Conference been accepted:

    a. In the planning of community-wide interrelated facilities?

    b. In determining the kinds of facilities needed?

    c. In developing standards for functionally designed facilities?

9. Is standardization of municipal recreation department reports feasible? If so, how can it be arranged?

10. Is it possible to bring about unified planning, joint financing, and integrated use of recreation facilities.

    a. In urban areas?

    b. In rural areas?

    c. In the region?

11. Organize a joint plan for a community of 35,000 which would provide adequate facilities for an all-age recreation program making use of:

    a. City parks and recreation areas.

    b. County parks and recreation areas.

    c. State parks and recreation areas.

    d. Public beaches, streams, and so forth.

12. How can we sell communities on the idea that recreation should be community-wide rather than restricted to a select few, of year-round duration instead of limited to the summer months, and for all ages instead of for the younger elements only?

13. What can a recreation department do to assure properly executed publicity?

14. Widespread duplication of the recreation function by various community agencies has been a great deterrent to its progress. What measures ought recreation take to reduce or eliminate these overlappings?

15. Should the school be the hub of a community's recreational activities? If so, justify this policy. If not, explain why not.

16. How would you proceed to sell a community on the importance of extending the use of its facilities through floodlights and indoor play areas for after-dark use?

17. Present the steps you would follow in securing the acceptance of a community-wide recreation program.

18. How can a recreation department evaluate the effectiveness of a recreation program?

19. Justify cooperative planning among municipal, county, and state park officials in providing recreation facilities outside the city.

20. Suggest ways local recreation departments can more effectively use the facilities of county and state parks.

21. What procedure should be followed by the director of recreation in formulating a long-range plan for the development of areas and facilities?

22. How can we effect greater participation of adults in such activities as mothers' and fathers' clubs and the like?

23. Should federal grants-in-aid become an actuality? How should they be administered?

24. How can municipal and school authorities work together for a long-range plan to acquire and develop recreational properties and facilities?
25. What consultant services shall the states make available to recreation directors and agencies who may require advice and counsel as to:
    a. Layout and design of recreation facilities?
    b. Program?
    c. In-service training and institutes?
26. How would you go about justifying recreation as a twelve-month need and not just for warm weather?
27. An effective community recreation program calls for cooperative relationships among the various community agencies, such as the "Y," boys' clubs, settlement houses, service clubs, boards of education, PTAs, health, parks, and police departments, near-by educational institutions, industries, and commercial recreation establishments. How should an administrator proceed to secure this cooperative action?
28. Present accepted planning concepts for the construction of park–schools that meet the "education–recreation" needs of pupils and serve as effective community centers.
29. Examine the recreation commission or board plan for its merits, legal status, and suitability for areas that already have organized recreation and for those inaugurating it.
30. What is the place of day, short-term or weekend, and family camping in the municipal recreation program?
31. What should desirable standards for day camps be with relation to:

a. Objectives?	d. Finance?
b. Organization?	e. Leadership?
c. Program?	f. Facilities?

32. What are the characteristics of an effective administration?

RECREATIONAL LEADERSHIP TRAINING

1. What can teacher-preparation institutions do to assist in the development of proper professional attitudes?
2. Training for citizenship is very vital in a democracy. How can recreation contribute toward this end?
3. What are the skills that a teacher-preparation institution for recreation leaders ought to stress?
4. Should there be a differentiation of objectives for different ages and sexes? If so, what should these objectives be?
5. Should there be a differentiation of objectives for the various socio-economic groups? If so, state what they should be.
6. Plan a model recreation area and justify each piece of equipment in the light of existing needs.
7. What can teacher-preparation institutions do to emphasize physical recreation safety?

8. State the personal qualities essential to recreation leaders.
9. What are the objectives in the professional preparation of recreation leaders?
10. Give a description of a well-trained and effective leader with emphasis on educational qualifications, experience background, and leadership traits.
11. The recreation leader's role is not merely to meet the interests of people; he should be equally concerned with creating new interests which will meet the needs of the group. How can he proceed to achieve this end?
12. Analyze activity interests with emphasis on locality, socio-economic factors, age, and sex.
13. How can colleges recruit recreation leaders?
14. What should the professional preparation of the part-time recreation leader be?
15. What should the in-service training program of recreation leaders include?
16. State the types of laboratory or field work experiences most desirable for the recreation major student. How can they be administered?
17. What standards should the college or university preparing recreation leaders meet with reference to the following:

    a. Staff?
    b. Facilities?
    c. Campus recreation program?
    d. Recreation consultant service?
    e. Placement?
    f. Follow-up?

18. How much emphasis should be placed on recreation therapy in the preparation of recreation leaders?
19. Far-reaching advances in preventive medicine and the new specialty of geriatrics among others have contributed toward a more and more adult population, What significance does that have as to:
    a. Teacher-training institutions?
    b. Types of recreational activities?
    c. Time scheduling of activities?
    d. Facility needs?
20. Should the certification of recreation personnel be agreed upon, what shall the qualifications be for:
    a. The recreation director
    b. The supervisor?
    c. The leader?
21. How can the institutions that train recreation leaders cooperate with agencies and leaders in the field to improve the quality of recreation personnel?
22. Analyze the legislation in your state as to:
    a. Strong points
    b. Loopholes
    c. Measures to be taken to correct the weaknesses detected.
23. Justify the contention that an understanding of individual and societal

problems as they relate to leisure time marks the professional delineation of the recreation leader.

24. How much skill attainment should be required of the recreation trainee.
25. Should there be a relationship between campus recreation opportunities and the offering of professional courses in this field? If so, how would you implement it?
26. Should sociology or physical education be charged with the responsibility of preparing recreational leaders?

MISCELLANEOUS

1. What are the similarities and differences between public and voluntary agencies?
2. Urbanization, automation, cybernetics, and the multiplication of conveniences have not added necessarily to the quality of our lives. Explain this point of view.
3. We often hear of the re-creative and restorative effects of recreation. What are they?
4. What are the character-training opportunities to be found in recreation?
5. List the various positions in the field and their duties.
6. The need for creative opportunities is great in our highly mechanized and specialized labor era. What can recreation do to help overcome this void?
7. What is the effect of recreation on health?
8. Can recreation serve as a corrective force in regard to the cardiovascular-renal diseases and the increase in mental disorders?
9. What can recreation contribute toward the reduction of crime and delinquency?
10. What are the recreational needs of the residents in your locality?
11. What would constitute a well-rounded recreation program for a community? Justify each activity.
12. How can public recreation meet the threat of commercial recreation?
13. How does recreation contribute toward the "worthy use of leisure" in the home, school, and community agencies?
14. How can we effect wider use of the schools as centers of community life and recreational activities?
15. What is the responsibility of the recreation department for co-recreation?
16. Should the participants in recreational activities be classified? If this is deemed advisable, state how it can be achieved.
17. Should the teaching of fundamental skills be included in the recreation activity program? If so, to what extent?
18. What are the pros and cons of the volunteer in recreation?
19. What are the steps to be considered in the initial development of the school camp?
20. State and explain the standards needed for the certification of recreation leaders by an agency of the state.

21. What are the functions to be relegated to the federal and state governments?
22. How far shall the participants' interests influence the recreational program?
23. Justify the inclusion of co-recreational activities in the program as to social values. What percentage of the recreational program should be devoted to this phase of recreation?
24. How can the profession influence needed research studies?
25. How can available research findings be implemented through professional action?
26. What phases of recreation need to be studied and evaluated?
27. How far shall the recreation profession go toward establishing standards for the training of new leaders?
28. Explain how teacher-preparation institutions can foster the professionalization of its trainees.
29. How far shall leadership training go in organizing and conducting testing programs?
30. What emphases are to be placed on the cultural aspects of recreation in our training institutions?
31. Shall leadership-training courses be organized according to job assignment duties and functions?
32. Shall colleges and universities be in sole charge of recruiting leaders, formulating courses of study, placement of leaders, and follow-up on their job assignments?
33. Leadership is the key to an effective recreation program. Imagine you have just finished observing an agency executive at work. *List* the observable characteristics of this person which would characterize him as an effective executive.

Chapter 6

CLUB ORGANIZATION

One can say with reasonable assurance that there are more influences rampant in the average community to mislead our youth than there are of a positive nature. There is need for creative leadership which can uncover interests and develop them under group situations such as is embodied in a soundly conducted club. The good that can emanate from a properly led club is enough of a justification in itself. Added benefits can be extracted in drawing individual and group recreations before they escalate into flare-ups, rumbles, and the like. As will be noted, the group provides admirable learning situations and a preparation for citizenship.

Group work delves into the group setting without losing sight of the individuals in its midst. The interplay of personalities is guided toward social growth. Democracy in action and its attendant procedures call for a recognition of the role of the individual precisely as he relates himself to the others in the group. The leader's role in this phase of recreational leadership calls for a recognition of these and related factors. In addition, it calls for a working understanding of both individual and group behavior problems. The vast majority of recreational activities lend themselves admirably to the group work approach.

Group work concerns itself with all recreational activities with the group providing the nucleus for recreational expression. These lifelike experiences offer admirable opportunities for learning to associate with others, for social recognition, self-expression, and finding oneself through successful participation. Through an acceptance of the responsibilities that go with group endeavors, dependability, cooperativeness, initiative, leadership, and the acquisition of new skills often develop. The club offers a splendid means for the organization of a group wherein common interests can find expression and be strengthened, with the individual's welfare a prime concern.

67

THE LEADER'S ROLE

The role of the leader can be compared to the helmsman of a ship. His job is to stick to the course and to steer clear of shoals, reefs, debris, and rocks. The decision as to which course to follow, the speed at which to travel, and the destination that is sought are decided by the members of the club. Their needs and interests are paramount and are to be translated into activities which are stimulating and joyful.

Unless the participants find the activities pleasant and captivating there is a good likelihood that the size of the group will dwindle. The fact that the participant in any phase of the recreational program attends of his own volition accentuates the challenge to the leader's tact and ingenuity. Once the club member finds the proceedings not to his liking, the leader is not fulfilling his obligations to the group. Furthermore, his job is to lead, not to control. He should be sensitive to the wishes and desires of his group. On the other hand, the leader can make suggestions to the group. He can couch his suggestion "as though he said it not." For after all, the leader is responsible to see to it that the activities and outcomes are socially compatible and conducive to the development of well-rounded boys and girls, men and women.

CLUBS DEFINED

Clubs are a grouping of individuals possessing a common interest. Opportunities are afforded for fellowship and the expression of one's gregariousness. They are refined versions of gangs in socially acceptable settings. Since interests play so prominent a part in the organization of a club, the leader must consider it a part of his strategy to unearth these interests and to capitalize on this discovery by channeling them into appropriate clubs. Whether we will it or not, individuals from six to sixty crave the acceptance and recognition of belonging to a group. Isn't a club preferable to a gang?

Types of clubs. The varieties of clubs possible are only limited by the imagination. Any attempt at categorizing clubs must start with the gang or the natural grouping of individuals. A mutual-interest group is also a common starting point for a club with its activities centered around music, dramatics, athletics, hobbies, or any other interest. A dynamic leader creates the focal point for a club with his personality as the guiding spirit: The members' admiration for him creates a cohesive force which can be transformed into a very effective and active group.

There are unlimited horizons in scanning the different clubs which are possible. The following are but a few that have been tried successfully:

Archery	Radio	Dramatics
Square dancing	Ornithology	Book review
Spelunking	Model train	Painting
Newspaper	Art	Tap dancing
Folk dancing	Knitting	Winter sports
Choral	Sewing	Photography
Hiking	Naturalist	Cooking
Camping	Boating	Stamp collecting
Crafts	Social dancing	Cycling

How to organize. At the start, an informal meeting might be held with those who are interested. This informal approach may take place in the outdoors, on the playground, under a tree, or in the confines of the recreation center. While the possession of a common interest bond is usually in evidence, it need not be. The leader may find that the group is predominantly concerned with playing together without any specific activity interest. In that event, the leader should help the group in its "gang urge" to find itself through a wide range of activities.

The spark for a club based on a more specific interest may come in time. At any rate, the urge is a real one and should be given recognition. With the leader serving as an adviser, the group may decide on a meeting time, place, officers, constitution, and by-laws. Or if it is not ready to do so, it may decide to remain on an informal basis for the time being. The wishes of the group should be respected. Other symbols in a club's growth are the decision by the group on an appropriate name to give it identity, or the possible use of a uniform or jacket for an athletic club to bolster the members' sense of belonging.

Objectives of clubs. Basically, the club should be concerned with pleasurable activities and outcomes. That there is nothing inconsistent in coupling fun with desirable objectives has been repeatedly demonstrated by successful leaders. The following objectives can serve to guide the leader in his quest for a purposeful club:

1. To explore and develop interests
2. To create and nurture social values
3. To strengthen the ability to initiate and lead
4. To develop the ability to follow intelligently with appreciation and agreement as to the ends sought
5. To foster desirable character traits
6. To employ the gregariousness in youths as an opening for socializing influences.

International aspects. The concept of one world and the advent of the United Nations as a vital force for peace need not be lost sight of in group work. A growing awareness of the worth of other cultures' is becoming increasingly apparent. An exploration of the cultures of other countries can be undertaken by groups as they relate to the club's program. For example, a music club can discover that the music of other lands can easily unfold an understanding of the composers' background and the cultural factors which influenced their compositions.

In a similar vein, the folk dancing club can acquaint itself with the background which accounts for the pageantry and gyrations of the dances of different lands. An art club can explore the customs, mores, and cultural life of the artists whose paintings are under consideration. The aforementioned exemplify but a few of the possibilities that are available to the astute leader who is interested in widening the scope of his club's achievements. Is not better international understanding one of the vital needs of our day? Will not prejudicial thinking yield to better understanding?

THE COMMITTEE

Definitively, the committee is a group charged with the responsibility of fulfilling a task, preparing recommendations, or arriving at a solution to a problem. After an appraisal of the committee's function, the president should select prospective members who are interested and suited for the job to be handled. Since the committee chairman is the one who should set the pace for his committee, it is highly essential that he be capable of inspiring the group to operate as a unit.

This aim can be furthered by the chairman's friendly though determined striving for accomplishment. He should elicit responses from all members and should not superimpose his ideas to the exclusion of the others on his committee. Appreciation of the wishes and contributions of each member should be expressed by the chairman. His receptiveness to the ideas expressed by others on the committee can do much toward making it a functioning unit. Through efficient committees the president can extend the scope of the club's activities and further the accomplishments of his regime. Involvement is one of the keys to successful club direction; assignment to committees is a valuable means toward this end.

PREPARING THE CONSTITUTION

The preparation of the constitution is to be delegated to a group committee by the president or the temporary chairman of the group; this committee should consist of a minimum of three members. The constitution committee will need the advice of the leader in this task. As soon as the constitution is completed, it should be presented to the group at its next regularly scheduled meeting. At that time, the constitution should be read before the group, section by section. Each section should be read, discussed, and approved or disapproved before passing on to the next.

Not until each section is accepted should the constitution be considered for approval. The constitution can then be adopted in toto. This measure comprises a very important part of a club's life and deserves careful and thorough consideration. The leader should be alert to the fact that the democratic process is to be respected with regard to new membership as well as in adopting each section of the constitution.

Sample Constitution and By-Laws
for an Athletic Club

CONSTITUTION AND BY-LAWS

of the _____ A.C.
of the _____ Community Center

Articles

ARTICLE 1—*Name*

This organization shall be known as the _____
Athletic Club of the _____ Community
Center.

ARTICLE 2—*Purpose*

To awaken and promote a thorough and sane interest in healthful physical activities, fellowship, wholesome living, and to live up to the ideals of the _____ Community Center.

ARTICLE 3—*Membership*

All members in good standing in the Community Center shall be eligible for membership. (Election at a regular meeting by a two-thirds vote may be included if desired.) (A stipulation as to age may also be stated at this point.)

ARTICLE 4—*Officers*

There shall be a President, Vice-President, Secretary, and Treasurer, to be elected as hereinafter provided. The club adviser shall be _____
of the _____ staff.
(play area)

ARTICLE 5—*Amendments*

This Constitution may be amended by a two-thirds vote of the membership. All amendments are to be submitted in writing and signed by three members and to be read at a regular meeting.

Bylaws

ARTICLE 1—*Officers*

Section 1. All officers shall be elected annually (or semiannually) by a majority of the members on a ballot.

Section 2. Election of officers are to be held in the month(s) of _____

_____

ARTICLE 2—*Executive Committee*

Section 1. The officers of the club and the club adviser shall comprise the Executive Committee.

Section 2. The Executive Committee shall meet whenever circumstances warrant or on the advice of any Executive Committee member, including the adviser.

Section 3. The adviser shall serve as chairman of the Executive Committee.

Section 4. The club Secretary shall also be secretary of the Executive Committee.

ARTICLE 3—*Meetings*

Regularly scheduled meetings shall be held every _____ at
                                                              (day)
_____ in the club room of the _____
   (time)   (play area)

ARTICLE 4—*Dues* (if deemed necessary)

Section 1. Membership dues shall be _____ for each _____
                                              (amount)   (period)
(A majority of the membership may change the dues.)

Section 2. Failure to pay the dues for _____ periods shall cause the
                                           (number)
matter to be brought before the Executive Committee. After due consideration of hardship factors, the Executive Committee may recommend suspension. (Note: For hardship cases, some clubs provide added duties so that these members may work for their dues.)

Section 3. The Secretary shall inform the suspended member of the Executive Committee's action. Voting privileges shall be denied the suspended member until the account is paid.

ARTICLE 5—*Expulsion of Members*

The repeated failure of a member to support the club's objectives and activities may call for Executive Committee action. The member shall be permitted to defend himself before the membership. Only after a warning to mend his ways has failed shall expulsion be considered. A four-fifths vote of the membership shall be required to expel a member.

ARTICLE 6—*Amendments and Quorum*

Section 1. An amendment to the Constitution shall be possible when a two-thirds vote of the membership favors it.

Section 2. A quorum of _____ members shall be necessary
(number)
before a meeting is held. (A quorum usually is considered a majority of those on the club's rolls.)

Order of Business

The President is charged with the duty of following the accepted order of business:

1. Call the meeting to order
2. Secretary reads the minutes
3. Reading of letters and other communications
4. Committee reports
5. Unfinished business
6. New business
7. Adjournment

DUTIES OF OFFICERS

There should be a clear-cut understanding of the duties of each officer. This can prevent confusion and lead toward a better and smoother functioning club. The duties of each officer are as follows:

President. The President (1) presides as chairman of the meeting; (2) calls the meeting to order; (3) follows the order of business and enforces the bylaws; (4) repeats clearly all motions under consideration after a member has seconded them; (5) preserves order; (6) appoints the necessary committees; (7) does not express personal opinions while presiding (hands over the gavel when he desires to speak on a question); and (8) calls special meetings.

Vice-President. The Vice-President (1) serves in place of the President during his absence; (2) assists the President in executing various tasks; (3) helps to administer and serve on committees; (4) acts as presiding officer when the President decides to speak on a motion; and (5) assumes the Presidency when the office of President becomes vacant until it is filled by an election.

Secretary. The Secretary (1) keeps the minutes of each meeting; (2) records a statement of every motion made; (3) notifies the members of each meeting (this may not be necessary where the group meets more often than once per month); (4) keeps a record of all committee members; and (5) records the resolutions passed, along with the number for and against them.

Treasurer. The Treasurer (1) collects dues; (2) pays all bills (checks should be countersigned by one other officer); (3) presents a periodic financial report; and (4) keeps the group informed as to money taken in, money expended and for what, and the balance as of a given date.

DEFINITION OF TERMS

The following extracts from parliamentary law and terminology are intended to assist in club management:

The Chair.   The President or one serving momentarily in his stead.

Addressing the Chair.   Making a statement directed at the President.

Obtaining the Floor.   Securing the right to speak from the President.

The Motion.   In presenting a motion, the member is to stand. After receiving recognition from the Chair, he is to state his motion. It is to be a single proposal. Upon being seconded by another member, the President then presents it for group action. Discussion for or against the proposal may ensue or an amendment to it may be proposed. The member who presents the motion is permitted to speak first and last on that motion.

Amendments.   The modifying or changing of a *motion's* wording while adhering to the form and intent of the original motion. No more than two amendments to a motion may pend at any time. Should there be an amendment under consideration, then the amendment to the amendment is taken up first. Once it is rejected, the President restates the motion as originally stated; if the amendment is accepted, the motion should be restated in the amended form. A vote on the motion in its final wording follows.

Question.   Matter or business under consideration. After adequate discussion, the President may ask, "Are you ready for the Question?" Should no one ask for the floor, then the President takes a vote on the motion (puts the motion). Those who are for it are requested to say "Aye" and the opposed to say "Nay." The outcome is then announced.

Calling for the previous question.   A request that the motion pending be voted on after due consideration.

Tabling the motion.   Postponing action on a motion to a later meeting so that added consideration may take place.

Question of privilege.   Securing attention from the Chair immediately for the purpose of asking a question, and making a point of order (a question growing out of a previous question or motion). It does not call for a second and is not debatable. Takes priority over a member on the floor.

Two-thirds vote.   A two-thirds vote is required for: (1) suspension of rules; (2) amendment to bylaws; (3) discharging a committee; (4)

considering business out of order; (5) stopping or restricting debate (calling for the previous question); (6) unwillingness to consider a business matter; and (7) special order of business.

Suspension of rules. Rules may be suspended: (1) when there is no question on the floor; (2) while a question is on the floor, providing the purpose of the suspension is related to the question. Privileged motions take priority when a motion to suspend the rules is presented; a motion for suspension is not to be amended and cannot be debated.

Special orders. A question under consideration may be put off for a future meeting. It can be debated, amended, and passed by a two-thirds vote.

Viva voce vote. This is a voice vote with "Ayes" designating those for and "Nays" indicating those against the business under consideration.

Ballot vote. Voting for election of officers and on controversial issues usually are by a closed ballot.

Pro and con. A "pro" vote is a vote for a position; a "con" vote is one against a position.

Unfinished business. The inability to complete business at one meeting calls for its transference to the next session for consideration. Unfinished business also may be referred to as old business.

Agenda. An agenda is a list of matters to be considered at the meeting.

Time limit. A time limit is a limit placed on the amount of time and the number of pros and cons which can be imposed on a motion.

Refer to committee. The President may refer a question to a committee for further study.

Recommitted. A question may be referred to the committee for a second time after it has been reported to the group.

MONEY-RAISING VENTURES

Clubs are confronted quite often with the problem of raising money to help support their activities. In other instances, money may be needed to pay for uniforms, jackets, going to camp, refurnishing the club rooms, and to pay for dues. The leader can suggest projects that are most suitable for the particular problem at hand.

Some money-raising ventures for club or member purposes are:

Grocery delivery concession	Doughnut sale
Scrap paper, magazines, junk	Candy sale
Magazine subscription sale	Lemonade sale
Metal coat hanger collection	Comic book sale
Snow removal	Plays, movies, shows

Errands   Kennel
Porch washing   Board animals
Baby sitting   Carnival
Mowing lawns   Dance
Cleaning basements   Concert
Ash removal   Rummage sale
Christmas card sale   Car wash and wax

Here again, projects of this nature feature involvement of the membership. The more each member is called on to do for his club, the more he is apt to support its efforts. As a consequence, his appreciation level will rise, thereby serving to strengthen its hold on the membership. The entire venture will have greater significance for all.

Chapter 7

WHAT'S YOUR LEISURE QUOTIENT?

Recreation is becoming increasingly a necessity in modern life. In fact, we never outgrow our need for recreation. While our expanding leisure has brought to the fore the need for recreation, it has existed since primeval man. However, as our responsibilities and lives grow more complex, the need for recreation becomes more pronounced. It is then that the splintering effects of our "double-quick and triple-action" lives cry out for the restoration that recreation can so effectively provide. In essence, it helps to integrate the individual to his former semblance of wholeness. It can serve to "re-create" each and every one of us as can no other force in our lives. Balanced living is not possible without it.

Leisure, uncommitted, or spare time are often used synonymously. Unfortunately, those least prepared for it are getting it first, namely those with low levels of education. Hopefully, this will spread throughout all strata of society. There is already mounting evidence of this fact.

TAKING STOCK

In arriving at a leisure quotient, no attempt is being made at following hard and fast rules. Just as taking inventory provides the businessman with a spot check, one's leisure quotient can serve as a stock-taking measure. If it stimulates "dusting off the shelves" and refurbishing with some new stock, it will contribute toward more effective living. It is also intended as a device to encourage the development of recreational resources from which the individual can draw during his waking hours. Also, it can serve as a reservoir that can be tapped throughout life. While the checklist rating chart is there to facilitate your "stock taking," it may be used simply to peer into your uncommitted pursuits for a quick appraisal.

Our concern should be for activities that one can partake of alone as well as with others. It is also of extreme importance to pursue interests that will sustain us into our later years. Some lend themselves toward both indoor and outdoor participation. Whenever feasible, the out-of-doors is to be preferred because of the additional lift we usually experience in the open. In this regard, southern and western residents are afforded a bonus because of the balmier weather for longer periods throughout the year. In a study confined to outdoor summertime recreation experiences by the Bureau of Outdoor Recreation, a highly significant fifty-one per cent increase was noted between 1960 and 1965.

Those who find themselves in colder regions are extending their outdoor seasons by insulated garments, sleeping bags, etc., which enable extended camping, picnicking, and canoeing. This is aside from the usual winter sports of sailing (frostbiting), ice fishing, deep sea fishing, mountaineering, ice boating, tobogganing, skiing, and ice skating. We are simply becoming more and more active.

It is well do establish that we need a "bag" of interests or pursuits from which to achieve a more meaningful life. By drawing on these from time to time, we tend to enrich our lives. The richer and more varied our recreational resources, the more interesting and productive our lives are apt to be. Nowhere does the aphorism "Whatsoever ye soweth so shall ye reap" apply more appropriately. Ideally, an exposure to varied activities during our early, formative years is the more desirable way to assure a bountiful adulthood and later life.

OUR AGING POPULATION

In recent years, there have been many forces at work to contribute toward an increased life expectancy. Advances in immunology, public health services, the antibiotics, and geriatrics plus vacations with pay, labor-saving devices, and recreation outlets have contributed toward this encouraging state of affairs. Since 1900 our total population has roughly doubled while those sixty-five years of age and over have quadrupled.

The elderly of today have more vigor than their counterparts a generation ago. Moreover they are more financially solvent due to retirement plans and the various benefits of social legislation. Consequently, they are in a better position to participate and benefit from organized programming in Senior Citizen Centers or on their own.

Activity nourishes the mind and spirit while helping to keep us physically young. "We don't stop playing because we are old; we get old because we stop playing." In this connection, a study conducted in New York City revealed that programs for the senior citizen made him less introspective and reduced the need for medical assistance.

The eminent psychologist Thorndike dispelled the previously held concept of being too old to learn some time ago; hence, the need for greater emphasis on adult education and acquiring new recreational skills throughout life. Recreation is vitally concerned with the present, reflects and draws on the past, and recognizes that the future can be enriched by leading a bountiful present. By cultivating a variety of recreational resources, they can serve as a reservoir which can be tapped throughout our lives.

OUR LEISURE POTENTIAL

UNCOMMITTED TIME

The growth of uncommitted time brings to mind the contributions made by the mechanization of industry, specialization of labor, automation, and cybernation which have emancipated man, at least in much of this civilization, as the beast of burden. Hence, the worker finds himself with more energy and time for leisure-time pursuits. In the home, we observe countless mechanical aids for the housewife. Processed foods, mixes, frozen foods and dinners, plus the myriad household gadgets have eased the burden of operating a home. Consequently, the mother can join her family in recreational pursuits.

The Puritan ethic with its glorification of work is a vanishing factor in our lives. This is most notable since the advent of our leisure-centered society. We have imparted to leisure-time pursuits a badge of dignity that seemed incredible a mere generation ago. Improved productivity and greater income have contributed toward increased sums for discretionary buying; close to $50 billion are expended annually on goods and equipment for recreational purposes.

DISTORTED VALUES

The need for developing sound judgment and good taste is vital. Edgar Dale alerts us: "to have good taste is to enjoy with understanding. . . . We learn good judgment by exercising judgment. We learn taste by tasting good things."

Simply being exposed to what life has to offer without selectivity is one of the great dangers of our times. For the cheap and tawdry outnumber by far the desirable and edifying. The opportunities to view violence and the sexually suggestive in our mass media are many times more plentiful than those that stress the better examples of music, dramatic arts, interpretive dancing, and the like. There is proof everywhere to support this belief as we face the droves of cheap magazines, paperbacks, TV shows, and movies. Moreover, their mounting reliance on sex and violence as attention-getters call for more positive action on the part of educators, parents, and psychiatrists. We cannot afford to leave this to chance.

The reaching out among our youth for thrills and unusual sensations via glue sniffing, barbiturates, marijuana, and LSD is alarmingly on the increase. Not only are these individuals turning their backs on parental and institutional authority, they are also contributing disproportionately to delinquency, thefts (automobile, shoplifting, etc.), aggravated assault, homicide, and forcible rape. Recognition must be given to adequate support for coordinated efforts by education, health, welfare, employment, law enforcement, correctional, and recreational agencies concerned with youth.

DESIRABLE INFLUENCES

A greater percentage of effort is to be exerted toward positive (preventive) influences which these agencies can cooperativly undertake. Our youth need more opportunities to secure challenge and adventure through organized community-wide physical and social activities. These satisfying and rewarding experiences can serve as wholesome outlets for the seemingly limitless energies and drives of our youth. Furthermore, they can serve to channel our youth toward lifelong interests; this is a concern that we need for all youth and not merely for a relative few who get caught in harm's way.

How can we establish sound interests? (1) They should be meaningful and acceptable to one's peers. (2) They should be stimulating and satisfying. (3) They should be put into use at every opportunity. (4) Attempt to sharpen skill levels, for satisfaction usually rises with proficiency. (5) Encouragement and approval are stimulants and are to be used effectively. If used sparingly and appropriately, competition or special events can spur on added enthusiasm.

ENTERTAINMENT AND/OR RECREATION

In this vein, two avenues for filling the gap of uncommitted time are left open to us: entertainment and/or recreation. Entertainment is essentially a passive, though usually satisfying, experience; therein, the participant absorbs the outpourings of others. In the realization that we have more than doubled the number of community orchestras and bands in a recent ten-year period and that we have more symphony orchestras than the rest of the world combined, our level of entertainment is still deplorably lowbrow. Our TV fare and movies, with occasional exceptions, leave many flustered and frustrated.

On the other hand, recreation (play) has a "give and take" element which allows for expressing one's self in a stimulating and satisfying manner. It can be enjoyed for its own sake. We never outgrow our need for these essential experiences in our lives. It has restorative qualities to help offset the splintering effects of our mechanized and pressured lives. The need here is for the broad spectrum of experiences ranging from the physical (running, jumping, climbing, throwing, and dodging) to the cultural and the fine arts (dramatics, music, and dance). Within these extremes are nature lore, winter sports, camping, picknicking, social, and aquatic activities with boating and skiing among the most rapid in growth of popularity.

The tendency toward specialization is ever on the increase. Here we encounter a clash; for the more we specialize, the greater becomes our need for general education and the fine arts to add balance to our lives. In fact, one threatens the other. The time extracted from our schooling for specialization reduces the amount available for general education and the leisure-time arts in our curricula. Our post-Sputnik era of emphasizing mathematics, science, and the language arts has made a sacrificial lamb of the liberal arts; the "why" has been forsaken for the "how."

Check List or Rating Chart

RATING SCALE

3	Applies always
2	Applies regularly
1	Applies seldom
0	Applies never

I. Home
1. Is a room or a portion set aside?
2. Is there a climate of freedom in the household?
3. Are friends free to come and go?
4. Is noise tolerated?
5. Are there games, books, play materials in generous supply?
6. Are there outdoor play materials for all age groups?
7. Is an outdoor area available for play? (Badminton, croquet, quoits, shuffleboard, swings, sandbox)
8. Is musical play encouraged? (Piano or other instrument, record player, dancing)
9. Is the family able to entertain itself on a rainy day?
10. Are vacations considered "essential" in the family budget?

Always (3) *Regularly (2)* *Seldom (1)* *Never (0)*

II. *Individual*

1. Are pursuits varied?
2. Are creative activities included?
3. Are outdoor activities stressed?
4. Can you enjoy a game whether or not you win?
5. Do you share interests with others?
6. Do you have 3 indoor pursuits? (Score 3 for 3 pursuits, 2 for 2, etc.)
7. Do you have 3 outdoor pursuits? (Score as in 6)
8. Will most (over fifty per cent) of your interests be useful in later years?
9. Do you have community-wide interests? (Scouting, "Y," PTA, church groups)
10. Do you like to meet new people?
11. Do you visit new places with keen anticipation?
12. Do you enjoy doing something new?
13. Do you go out of your way to assist or share experiences with others?
14. Do you like to sing?
15. Is dancing (social, square, folk) of interest to you?
16. Is time allocated for reflection?

III. *Family*

1. Is play with others encouraged?
2. Does the family spend an "evening in?"
3. Are all-family pursuits stressed?
4. Is emphasis on doing instead of viewing?
5. Are family members afforded a choice?
6. Does your family share evenings with other families?
7. Are interests of all age groups considered?
8. Are cultural pursuits (going to museums, art galleries, and attending concerts) regularly shared by the family?
9. Are discussions (current events, sports, travel, foreign cultures) a regular part of the family's shared experiences?
10. Is some form of physical recreation (tennis, bowling, walking, swimming, bicycling) shared by the family?
11. Are storytelling and reading (other than newspapers) enjoyed by all members?
12. Are space and time allotted for hobby pursuits?

IV. *The Elderly:*[1] *Those approaching or having reached retirement*

1. Do you relish or seek out new experiences?
2. Do you have a special recreation interest for indoors?
3. Do you have a special recreation interest for outdoors?
4. Do you have a hobby in which you participate alone?
5. Do you have a hobby which you enjoy with others?
6. Do you and your spouse[2] have a hobby in which you take part together?
7. Are you contemplating or planning a new recreational pursuit which you can continue for a prolonged period of time or even for years?
8. Do you have active interests that you can pursue year around?

Always (3) Regularly (2) Seldom (1) Never (0)

SCORING

Excellent	101 or more
Very good	81—100
Good	61—80
Fair	41—60
Poor	21—40
Inferior	20 or less

CHARACTERIZING OUR ERA

The changes in our lives occur often at overpowering rates. The stress, emotional conflicts, frustrations, suppressions, and repressions prove overwhelming to many. Hurry, anxiety, worry, insecurity, and the myriad pressures of day-to-day living are part of our way of life. As a consequence the adjustments called for prove insurmountable to a significant portion of our population. Is it any wonder that more beds are occupied by the mentally ill than for all other infirmities combined? It is a supportive fact that fifty-two percent of all confining illnesses are mental.

Whether we perform complex or simple tasks during our work day, our bodies crave diversion, change of setting, or rhythmical expression.

[1]These are relatively reduced in number for they are in addition to those listed under II.

[2]Of course, this question does not apply to those who are single or no longer have a spouse.

The need to do what one wants to do when it suits one most has a highly sanative influence on our minds and spirits. It can serve as a neutralizing force for the disintegrating forces of our pressured and highly competitive lives. It calls for planning. Certainly, it should not be left to chance.

The range of activities and hobbies is as vast as human interest. Hence, the lists on page 198 hold no pretense at being complete. Rather, they are suggestive of the activities that may be employed to add sparkle and verve to life. Carry-over activities are those that can be continued into later years. An examination of those listed under hobby, cultural, and miscellaneous will reveal that they are suited for all ages and all-family participation with few exceptions. They also support the fact that groups of diverse age can share these experiences or take part separately.

SUGGESTED READINGS

Brightbill, Charles K. *Education for Leisure-Centered Living*. Harrisburg, Pa.: The Stackpole Company, 1966.
——. *Men and Leisure*. Englewood Cliffs, N.J.: Prentice-Hall, Inc., 1961.
Kaplan, Max. *Leisure in America*. New York: John Wiley & Sons, Inc., 1960.
Mead, Margaret. *Cultural Patterns and Technical Change*. New York: Mentor Books, 1955.
Russell, Bertrand. *The Conquest of Happiness*. New York: Liveright Publishing Corporation, 1958.
Shivers, Jay. *Leadership in Recreational Service*. New York: Crowell Collier and Macmillan, Inc., 1963.
Williams, Arthur. *Recreation for the Senior Years*. New York: Association Press, 1962.

Part III

PROGRAM ESSENTIALS:
A. PLANNING AIDS

Chapter 8

AUDIOVISUAL AIDS

Much recreational literacy and skill is acquired through the sense of sight as well as the kinesthetic sense. With the realization that the more senses appealed to during the learning process the more effective the teaching, the growth of visual aids as an adjunct to the teaching process has been tremendous. If properly produced, visual aids can serve as a very efficient teaching device. Certainly, the armed forces in the last war showed convincingly how the learning process could be shortened through the use of visual aids. The importance of careful selection as to their suitability cannot be overemphasized. Obviously, the mere use of visual aids offers no assurance of the desired outcome.

Many think of motion pictures as the sole visual aid. This is perhaps traceable to the fact that it is possibly the most popular one in the minds of most people in the field. In addition to motion pictures, however, there are opaque projection slides, filmstrips, posters, blackboards, charts, maps, graphs, models, specimens, and television. Each one of these will be discussed briefly as they relate to recreation. (Movies and recordings in the field of music are listed under *Music and Recreation.*)

MOTION PICTURES

The motion picture is a very valuable and interesting visual aid. In the recreation field, the motion picture reproduces skills with continuity that resembles real-life situations. For example, the stroke in badminton can be conveyed through the motion picture better than perhaps any other medium.

Suggested sources for films and examples for various recreational activities will be presented later in this chapter. To enjoy fully the benefits of the motion picture, the group should be prepared for the showing so that continuity may exist between the group's objectives and the film. Furthermore, a thorough discussion should follow the showing in order to answer any questions that may arise. A demonstration of the disputed point before the group will do much to clarify it as well as to reinforce the learning process through repetition. Some projectors make it possible to stop the action at any frame desired and to slow down the action to simplify the viewer's observations. These two modifications of regular motion should be considered whenever showing a film. The use of noninstructional films for entertainment value can be advantageous if carefully chosen. One of the less costly developments is 8-mm sound.

OPAQUE PROJECTION

One of the most versatile and simple to use projection devices is the opaque projector. For one, it does not require a completely dark room, though, of course, the darker the room, the sharper the image. It can project pictures, charts, or any content from a book, magazine, or any object that will fit within the opaque projector's base, which is usually 6 by 8 inches. Some opaque projectors come with accessories that permit, in addition, the projection of slides 2 by 2 inches and 3¼ by 4 inches as well as 35-mm filmstrips.

The projection of a still picture or similar device is considered one of the most effective means of instruction, since time for analysis and discussion is more apt to be taken and used fully.

SLIDES

As mentioned previously, slides can be an effective teaching device. Moreover, they lend themselves to ample discussion and can be readily made by most any age group as a project; or the leader can make his own slides. Photographic slides are two inches square, while silhouette and etched-glass slides are 3¼ by 4 inches in size. The easiest to construct is the etched-glass slide. The object desired is simply drawn on the slide's rough side. A mere erasure makes the slide useful for another drawing. The silhouette slide can be made by placing a cutout of the drawing between two clear glasses of slide size. While a variety of things may be done with the glass or plastic slide which is 3¼ by 4 inches, India ink slides and cellophane slides may be made on the etched glass. In addition, transparencies made of 35-mm black and colored negatives can make effective slides. A projector that is adaptable to the side of each slide is necessary.

FILMSTRIPS

Filmstrips offer a relatively inexpensive and desirable instructional aid. They possess the same advantages as do slides and are much less expensive to purchase than films. Less technical skill is needed to make one's own filmstrips than motion pictures. Projectors are available that can be used both for slide and filmstrip projection.

The Athletic Institute has available filmstrips in archery, badminton, campcraft, cycling, fencing, fishing, games, golf, ice skating, skiing, skin and scuba diving, softball, table tennis, and tennis to name but those that are more closely related to recreation; there are thirty-six popular sports subjects in all. They are available with or without 33⅓ rpm narrative records and available through direct purchase or rental. Rental can be arranged through Ideal Pictures, 1840 Alcatraz Ave., Berkeley, California, 94703; Ideal Pictures, 1558 Main Street, Buffalo, New York, 14209; and Ideal Pictures, 417 N. State Street, Chicago, Illinois, 60610.

POSTERS

Through proper planning and care in preparation, posters can serve as a graphic visual aid. They are one of the oldest devices for visual instruction. By leaving a poster up for prolonged periods of time at one site, it loses much of its effectiveness, for the viewer ceases to pay any attention to it. Periodic changing of posters as well as their shifting from one spot to another can add to their effectiveness as a device. In addition, the use of vivid colors, third-dimensional figures and lettering, and pictures or drawings denoting action can add to their attention-getting power and message-bearing quality.

BLACKBOARDS

The use of the blackboard is so common as to be virtually overlooked as an easily available and very valuable medium. Its utility is enhanced by the ease with which it can be erased in part or in its entirety. The use of colored chalk can make the illustrations more vivid. Blackboard illustrations can find many uses, in dramatics (stage layouts, planning of props, and so forth), recreational sports (plays, strokes, angle of bounce with topspin, etc.), music (lyrics, list of song selections, etc.), and handicrafts (designs, knot tying, construction plans, etc.). Whenever feasible the material to be placed on the board should be written or drawn before the group's arrival.

MISCELLANEOUS AIDS

The overhead projector is a device similar to the opaque projector. It differs in that it will project on a screen placed above the blackboard that which is written on a plastic slab or transparency. The leader can draw or write at his desk while his group views it instantaneously. Erasures can be made with a cloth and the board used again.

There are numerous other visual aids at the leader's disposal. Charts find uses in handicrafts (use of tools, types of wood, and so forth) and in recreational sports (charting plays in basketball, stroke illustrations in badminton, and the like). Maps can be used in hosteling (planning an itinerary) and for art work (studying influence of terrain on a nation's culture). Graphs are useful for indicating scoring in sports while models and specimens are exceedingly useful in nature lore (bird study, insect collections, leaf study, and so forth). Hikes and field trips are allied activities which take the viewer to an on-the-spot visual aid. Collections of specimens are to be encouraged during these excursions.

A medium that has unlimited possibilities is that of television, which combines hearing and viewing with motion. Opportunities are afforded for group musical instruments, arts and crafts, dramatics, sports, and hobby instruction, to mention a few. If the medium realizes its potentialities, it can constitute an unprecedented force in pleasant leisure-time use as well as instruction. Up to the present, it has aped many of the mistakes that have plagued radio. Perhaps the answer rests in the allocation and availability of community-owned television stations throughout the country to assure the needed number of educationally sound telecasts.

ON-THE-SPOT PHOTOGRAPHY

The use of slides that can be made on the spot are limitless. The Polaroid Land Camera loaded with transparency film yields a slide to be projected right away. Recreation Departments can use regular film that takes but ten seconds for a print, useful in reporting without delay activities, contest winners, arts and crafts exhibits, and countless other graphic portrayals. Thus, the pictures are shown readily when their newsworthiness is at its peak.

In addition, this rapid form of photography lends itself admirably to making social functions memorable. A humorous prop with a cutout for one or two heads can be a highlight at a daylight picnic or at an indoor social with flashlight or floodlight photography. In fact, it can be used as a fund raiser with a charge of approximately a dollar a pose. Photographs snapped as the guests arrive can also be used as place cards.

PREPARATORY STEPS

Before projecting a motion picture, filmstrips, slides, or transparencies, it is good practice to make the needed preparations to assure a successful showing. For one, it is advisable to preview that which is to be shown. This is particularly advisable before projecting a motion picture. The projector and screen should be so situated as to clear all heads and be as easily visible as conditions will permit. The seating arrangement should be checked with this in mind. No one should sit closer to the screen than twice the picture's width nor more than 30° off to the side. The speaker should be near the screen at about the level of the audience's ears.

A preview of the film will help iron out these possible wrinkles as well as whether the film is inside out and ready to go, whether the film needs splicing, and whether the take-up reel is large enough. After the preview test, rewind the film. Rethread it and run the film up to the title, whereupon you are ready for the audience.

Before ordering a film, ask the source of supply for literature describing the film. Look up the descriptions incorporated in sources such as *Educational Film Guide*. Ascertain whether the film size available (16 mm, 35 mm, or 8 mm) fits your projector and whether it is a sound or silent film.

Other considerations are of almost equal importance. Be sure to have the instructional material that comes with the machine at hand; it generally includes troubleshooting information use should the machine get out of kilter. Spare fuses and bulbs should be part of a repair kit. A flashlight will prove helpful for checking things while the machine is in operation. It will be invaluable for the projectionist to know how to splice film and to have the equipment accessible. The projector should not be left while it is working. Assign someone to handle the room lights so that they can go off as the showing starts and on at its completion without any delay. Have the sound system warmed up before the lights go off so as not to interfere with the film's continuity. As a last consideration, try to assure adequate ventilation, for the discomfort associated with viewing a film in an overheated room detracts vastly from the message to be gotten across.

AUDIOVISUAL AIDS FOR RECREATION[1]

ARCHERY

Set of four filmstrip units involving history of archery, shooting, aiming, and archery rules (Athl., sound or silent, color). The film *Archery for Beginners* demonstrates the techniques found useful in stance, nocking, aiming, the draw-through, and the follow-through. Extensive use of the close-up shot is made to show fingers and arm action (U.W.F., 12 min., 16 mm, silent, black and white.)

In the film *Archery for Girls*, the basic steps essential for skillful archery are broken down and illustrated. (Coronet, 10 min., 16 mm, sound, black and white.)

Expert shooting form via slow motion is demonstrated in the film *Archery with Larry Hughes*. Techniques of stringing, nocking, drawing, and shooting with a heavy bow, are clearly shown with close-ups. (B.F.S., 7 min., 16 mm, silent, black and white.)

BADMINTON

Set of six filmstrip units involving the game of badminton, service, overhead strokes, forehand strokes, backhand strokes, and badminton rules simplified (Athl., sound or silent, color). In the film *Flying Feathers*, High Forgie and Ken Davidson show how to make the various shots in badminton. The basic techniques involved in playing this fast-growing sport are presented. (Pictorial, 10 min., 16 mm, sound, black and white.)

Let's Play Badminton is a film in which Ken Davidson demonstrates fundamental steps in playing the sport. Slow-motion shots clearly show the properly executed techniques. (G.S.C., 16 min., 16 mm, sound, color.)

The film *Tips on Better Badminton* is concerned with singles and doubles play by Canadian and American champions. Position play, footwork, and wrist action are clearly demonstrated. (S.T.T.A., 20 min., 16 mm, sound, black and white.)

BASKETBALL

Basketball, with Branch McCracken of the University of Indiana, points out basketball fundamentals. Ball handling, passing, dribbling, guarding, and shooting are demonstrated. (Coronet, 15 min., 16 mm, sound, black and white.)

[1]Full names and addresses for the films are listed alphabetically at the end of the chapter.

The film *Basketball for Girls—Fundamental Techniques* demonstrates ball handling, passing, and shooting fundamentals. The importance of practice and skill are stressed along with team play. Slow and regular motion are used in portraying skillful action. (Coronet, 1 reel, 16 mm, sound, black and white.)

The film *Fundamentals of Basketball* consists of a five-reel series of successful practices of leading coaches including Clair Bee, Long Island University; Dr. H. C. Carlson, University of Pittsburgh; George Keogan, Notre Dame; John Bunn, Stanford; Dr. Forrest Allen, Kansas; with Chuck Taylor also featured. (B.F.S., 76 min., 16 mm, sound, black and white.)

BOATING

Floating Fun: Simple wording is used by a teacher to point out how to sail. A sailing dinghy race is used as a laboratory situation wherein the learners put into practice what was taught them. It is a Grantland Rice Sportlight. (U.W.F., 10 min., 16 mm, sound, black and white.)

Learning to Sail: How-to-sail skills are demonstrated by competent sail trimmers. Enthusiasts of all levels of competency will be fascinated by this film. (H.L., 1 reel, 16 mm, sound, color.)

Oars and Paddles: The prevention of accidents in boats and canoes is emphasized. How to launch a boat and canoe, fundamentals of rowing and canoeing, rescuing others and oneself when a boat overturns, and surf rescue work are dealt with capably. (Castle, 24 min., 16 mm, sound, black and white.)

BOWLING

Bowling Skill: In this film the sport's history is explained. Basic shots are demonstrated by experts. Ted Husing is the narrator of this Grantland Rice Sportlight which is recommended for school use exclusively. (T.F.C., 10 min., sound, black and white.)

Fundamentals of Bowling: This film stresses six common faults along with instructions on how to overcome them; proper ball selection, proper stance, approach, delivery, follow-through, and spot bowling are clarified. (T.F.C., 20 min., 16 mm, sound, black and white.)

Another worthwhile film, *Set 'Em Up,* features fundamental techniques of bowling exemplified by bowling stars. It is produced by Metro-Goldwyn-Mayer and is available exclusively for school use. (T.F.C., 10 min., 16 mm, sound, black and white.)

The *Beginning Bowling Series* consists of a unit containing an instructor's guide and student pocket books. Fundamentals of bowling are explained by Ned Day and Milton Raymer. The slidefilms are three in number: *The Sport, Delivery,* and *Aiming and Scoring.* (Athl., 3 slide-films, 35-mm filmstrips, silent and sound, black and white, and color.)

CAMPING

Camping Education, a "March of Time" film, portrays the training program at the National Camp for Professional Leadership, which is sponsored by Life Camps, Inc. A graphic presentation of the impressive program at Life Camps for Boys and Girls is given. (Assoc., 2 reels, 16 mm, sound, black and white.)

Therapeutic Camping. The role of camping as related to adjustment needs and learning problems in the Maine woods. An example of camping for special groups. (Severeux Schools, Devon, Pa., 28 min., 16 mm, color, free.)

A Key to Conservation. Conservation is stressed as an adjunct to camping. The rewarding experience earned through camping are emphasized. (Ind. U., 23 min., 16 mm, color, rental.)

Another interesting film, *Camping for Girl Scouts,* displays varied activities of a Girl Scout camping program. (Girl Scouts, 15 min., 16 mm, sound, color.)

The film *Winter Camping* demonstrates hiking and camping in the deep snow, selecting a camp site, putting up a tent, fire building, cooking, and making a bed. Personal hygiene problems are also dealt with. (Assoc., 2 reels, 16 mm, sound, black and white.)

COMMUNITY RECREATION

A greater insight into how recreation can be organized and the values to be derived from a well-organized program can be furthered through the films that follow. A brief description accompanies each film to facilitate a more effective choice.

Town and County Recreation displays the reasons for the steps to follow in analyzing a community's recreation facilities and services. How to plan for the future is stressed. (Athl., 20 min., 16 mm, sound, color.)

Pastimes in Young America emphasizes the various types of recreation evolving out of the three basic early American philosophies that amusement is akin to sin, games must have a purpose to them, and fun for fun's sake. (Assn. Films, 30 min., sound, black and white.)

Planning Recreational Facilities is an aid toward more effective organization of a community's facilities. The complexities of planning the development and construction of recreation areas are pointed out. (Assn. Films, 15 min., sound, color.)

The film *All-American Way* points out the contribution recreation and sports make toward the sportsmanlike behavior of young men and women. Emphasis is also placed on the development of healthy and sound citizens. (Chic. Trib., 26 min., 16 mm, sound, black and white.)

Another film in the recreation series, *Fitness Is a Family Affair*, illustrates how group action can help to meet recreational needs. In this situation, neighbors unite to effect community recreational opportunities. (N.F.B., 19 min., 16 mm and 35 mm, sound, black and white.)

As a school project, children convert a barn into a recreation center in the film *Lessons in Living*. The children perform the cleaning up, carpentry, and painting, among other jobs. (N.F.B., 22 min., 16 mm, sound, black and white.)

The vivid film *$1,000 for Recreation* shows the importance of recreation as a community need. Tax-supported recreation is given preference to private support. It thereupon shows how service clubs and other agencies can contribute toward a well-rounded community recreation program. (Athl., 12 min., 16 mm, sound, color.)

"*Aging in America*" is a two-part 1967 film shown on the *Look Up and Live* television series. It is an excellent overview of the reactions of experts and the aged as to the problems associated with aging and retirement. (C.B.S. News—Special Projects, 524 W. 57th St., New York, N.Y., 50 min., 16 mm, sound, black and white, free.)

Of time, Work and Leisure, based on Sebastian de Grazia's monumental book, highlights such modern societal problems as pressured living and faulty values. (Ind., U., 20 min., 16 mm, sound, black and white, rental.)

In *As Tall as a Mountain*, the motivating and adventuresome experiences of the Outward Bound camping experiences will stay with the viewer. Rugged and challenging adventure are made available to youth from all strata. (Adolph Coors Company, Golden, Col., 35 min., 16 mm, sound, color, free.)

A beautiful and poignant film, *The Land Between the Lakes*, reveals what is available for family camping under the Tennessee Valley Authority. The potentials of the Barkley Dam are featured. (T.V.A., Golden Pond, Kentucky, 30 min., 16 mm, sound, color, free.)

Careers in Recreation analyzes the varied duties of a recreation professional and also points up the need for qualified leaders in this rapidly expanding profession. (Athl., 27 min., 16 mm, color, rental.)

Leaders for Leisure portrays the complexities of recreation leadership in order to justify the need for professional education. Success in community-wide recreation can thereby be more readily assured. (Athl., 21 min., 16 mm, color, rental.)

A tragedy stimulates a town to inaugurate a youth program in the film *Make Way for Youth*. Frictions are forgotten, as are racial and religious differences, as the program gets underway. (Pa., St., 22 min., 16 mm, sound, black and white.)

In the film *Play Is Our Business* the need for leisure-time pursuits for children is pointed out. Assorted activities suitable for various age groups are presented. Materials used by play schools are shown. (Pa. St., 22 min., 16 mm, sound, black and white.)

A Chance to Play, portraying the need for playgrounds and recreation centers for our youth, stresses a growing need for meeting the needs of the aged. The film also indicates means by which these facilities can be secured. (G.E., 20 min., 16 mm, sound, black and white, free.)

When All the People Play shows how a community recreation program revitalizes a rural district. The locale of the film is Annapolis Royal, Nova Scotia. (N.F.B., 16 mm, sound, black and white.)

The film *Playtown U.S.A.* shows how a community can organize to form a year-round, all-age recreation program. This film is especially suited for showings to school boards, park boards, service clubs, and fraternal organizations. At the start, community indifference spurs to action an individual who starts the ball rolling. (Pa. St., 25 min., 16 mm, sound, color.)

The final film we have chosen for this series, *Re-creation*, portrays how a family is re-created by vacationing in some of our national forests. It is produced by the United States Department of Agriculture. (Assoc., 3 reels, 16 mm, sound, black and white.)

FIRST AID AND SAFETY[2]

The film *Athletic Injuries—Their Prevention and Care* studies the prevention and care of injuries incurred during play. Strapping is demonstrated. This film is particularly useful for trainers and coaches. (Bike, 35 min., 16 mm, sound, color.)

Produced by the United States Navy and depicting the medical facilities and techniques used in reserve work, the film *Essentials of First Aid* features examination of the injured and the treatments employed. (Castle, 32 min., 16 mm, sound, black and white.)

The film *Help Wanted* discusses fundamentals of first aid and their

[2]Other safety films are mentioned under *Riflery* and *Swimming*.

utilization on the injured. The film offers a dramatic portrayal of the extensiveness of injuries and the assistance that is so vitally needed in such cases. (Johnson, 31 min., 16 mm, sound, black and white.)

Prevention of athletic injuries and how to care for athletic injuries are emphasized in the film *Prevention and Immediate Treatment of Athletic Types of Injuries.* Detailed handling of tendon, muscle, groin, hip bone, shoulder, and rib injuries are among those portrayed. (B.D., 45 min., 16 mm, silent, color.)

Approved methods of play and playground care are demonstrated in the film *Safety at Play.* It offers instruction in safe-play practices geared to the elementary level. First aid measures for minor involvements are illustrated graphically. (A.B., 7 min., 16 mm, silent, black and white.)

A film which should prove helpful to coaches, trainers, and teachers of first aid is *Taping Techniques.* The role of taping as a preventive measure in activities is extolled and how to tape is shown clearly. This film is advised for male groups of high-school age or older. (Bike, 45 min., 16 mm, silent, black and white.)

Realizing that the sought-after vacation period may be crammed with hazards, the film *Vacation Safety* considers swimming and boat safety, fire safety, poison ivy, and other hazards in a camp setting. (E.B.F., 14 min., 16 mm, silent, black and white.)

GOLF

Duffer's Swing is the first of the Johnny Farrel Gold Instruction Films. Fundamental strokes and form for male and female duffers are portrayed. Driving and putting are emphasized as well as other game essentials. (U.W.F., 10 min., 16 mm, sound, black and white.)

Lawson Little, Jimmy Thompson, Harry Cooper, and Horton Smith show the viewer the correct way to play the game in the film *Golf Mistakes.* The wrong way is also exemplified to point out the pitfalls. This film is produced by Metro-Goldwyn-Mayer and is available exclusively for school use. (T.F.C., 10 min., 16 mm, sound, black and white.)

In the film *Good Golf*, Ralph Guldahl, Johnny Revolta, Gene Sarazen, and Sammy Sneed are the male golfers, while Opal Hill, Helen Dettweiler, and Helen Hicks are the women in this display of good golf practices. Shots of varying difficulty are made with ease. (U.W.F., 35 mm., 16 mm, sound, black and white.)

HORSEMANSHIP

Basic steps of saddling, bridling, mounting, and preparations prior to riding a horse are shown in the film *Ground Technique.* The correct techniques are given greater emphasis through the intermittent use of slow motion. (Minn., 2 reels, 16 mm, silent, black and white.)

In the film *Riding Technique* the three elemental gaits of the English style of riding are demonstrated. Close-ups and slow motion are employed to emphasize correct form. (Minn., 25 min., 16 mm, silent, black and white.)

The third film we have chosen to list here is titled *Saddle Sense*. Fundamental steps of horsemanship are shown. The walk, trot, and canter are analyzed, portrayed, and related to the use of the weight, hands, and legs. (V.V., 25 min., 16 mm, silent, color.)

JUVENILE DELINQUENCY

Three case histories of boys stemming from unsatisfactory homes are presented in the film *A Criminal Is Born*. This film aids in the development of an appreciation of the causative factors in crime. (Assoc., 21 min., 16 mm, sound, black and white.)

The film *Dead End* emphasizes the influence slum conditions bring to bear on juvenile delinquency. With slums adjoining fashionable homes, a series of events take place after a wealthy boy's watch is stolen by boys from the slum area. (Assoc., 1 reel, 16 mm, sound, black and white.)

Another interesting film, *That Boy Joe*, approaches juvenile delinquency from the causative and preventive angles. That it is a problem calling for prolonged and relentless effort is stressed. (Assoc., 2 reels, 16 mm, sound, black and white.)

RIFLERY

The details involved in the wise use of the rifle are graphically shown in the film *How to Shoot the Rifle*. Considerable detail is given in the fundamentals of sighting, triangulation, pulse and breathing, and prone, sitting, kneeling, and standing positions. (N.R.A., 35 min., 16 mm, sound, black and white.)

A most important film, *The Making of a Shooter*, shows how a lad is trained to handle firearms safely. He is taken to the National Rifle and Pistol Matches where he observes champions in action. (N.S.C., 24 min., 16 mm, sound, black and white; 40 min., 16 mm, silent, black and white.)

Equally important is the film *Safety On!* which shows safe and unsafe ways of handling firearms. Accident records accompany each dangerous scene. Out-of-state borrowers are confined to the months of June, July, and August. (M.C., 13 min., 16 mm, sound, color.)

SKIING AND SNOW PLAY

Skiing is growing rapidly as a winter sport. In the film *Basic Princi-*

ples of Skiing, emphasis is placed on caring for and adjusting skiing paraphernalia. Slow motion is used effectively to point out the more essential positions of ascending, descending, walking, turning, and running. (N.Y.U., 4 reels, 16 mm, sound, black and white.)

Skiing trips to Sun Valley, Mt. Hood, Mt. Lassen, and Yosemite are featured in the film *Ski Safari.* Methods used in cross-country skiing, slalom racing, and straight-down skiing are illustrated. (Pa., St., 10 min., 16 mm, sound, color.)

In the film *Play in the Snow,* three children and their friends build a snow man, play fox and geese, coast, and ski. Stress is placed on health habits, dress, and safe snow play. (Pa. St., 11 min., 16 mm, sound, black and white.)

TABLE TENNIS

In the film *Ping Pong,* the game is described and taught by champions. Footwork and stroking are demonstrated fully by very capable performers. It is produced by Metro-Goldwyn-Mayer and is available for schools exclusively. (T.F.C., 1 reel, 16 mm, sound, black and white.)

Offering a more advanced portrayal of table tennis techniques, *Table Tennis,* with Ann Sigman, Stanley Fields, and Sol Shiff, features strategic play and advanced stroking as well as the more elemental phases of the game. (Assoc., 10 min., 16 mm, sound, black and white.)

In *Table Tennis Techniques* a young boy and girl are taught the fundamentals of the game by experts Coleman Clark and Hamilton Canning. Close-ups and slow motion add to the effectiveness of the film. Toward the end, the experts go at it to exemplify the other end of the achievement scale. (Dav., 11 min., 16 mm, sound, color.)

TENNIS

Featuring Don Budge, *Fundamentals of Tennis* stresses the fundamental steps that result in better tennis. Simple strokes are demonstrated in addition to the more advanced ones. (B.F.S., 20 min., 16 mm, sound, black and white.)

The film *Technique of Tennis* illustrates how to grip the racket correctly for forehand, backhand, service, and general stroking. It is handled by Lloyd Budge, Don's brother, and is produced by Columbia Pictures for schools and recreation areas only. (T.F.C., 9 min., 16 mm, sound, black and white.)

For the more advanced player and to inspire the less capable one, Fred Perry, in the film *Tennis Tactics,* puts on a display of the brilliant tennis that made him prominent internationally. It is produced by Metro-

Goldwyn-Mayer and is available to schools and recreation areas exclusively. (Assco., 10 min., 16 mm, sound, black and white.)

Mention should also be made here of the *Beginning Tennis Series*, which comes with an instructor's guide and student pocket books. It's titles are: *The Game, The Forehand Drive, The Backhand Drive, The Service,* and *The Rules Simplified.* (Athl., 5 slidefilms, 35 mm, silent, color; 35-mm filmstrip.)

VOLLEYBALL

In the film *Play Volleyball*, Bill Slater clarifies the "how" and "what" of this very popular sport. Among the fundamentals that are considered are serving, receiving, setting up, and blocking. Through the medium of slow motion, close-ups, and stopping the motion, skills are graphically described. (Assoc., 20 min., 16 mm, sound, black and white.)

Again, volleyball is a sport appealing to both sexes. *Techniques in Volleyball for Girls* emphasizes volleyball play geared to girls' rules. Individual skills are stressed and applied in team-play situations; slow motion is generously employed. (Schol., 16 min., 16 mm, silent, black and white.)

In *Volleyball for Boys*, the rules are interpreted in play situations. Allowance is made for circumstances that warrant modifications of the rules. Slow motion is used to emphasize important points of the game. Fundamentals are emphasized throughout. (Coronet, 11 min., 16 mm, sound, black and white.)

SOFTBALL

The film *Play Softball* demonstrates through slidefilm the fundamental skills of batting, fielding, and pitching. The need for team play is also conveyed. A printed commentary is supplied. (Assoc., 35-mm slidefilm, black and white.)

Skills involved in position play are analyzed through slow motion in the film *Softball for Boys*. The skills involved in pitching are stressed as is also the need for team play. Fundamentals of base running, catching, pitching, batting, fielding, and sliding are stressed. (Coronet, 1 reel, 16 mm, sound, black and white.)

Since softball is growing in popularity as a sport for both sexes, the film *Softball for Girls* should be considered here. The skills involved in throwing, catching, fielding, and batting are shown. Emphasis is placed on position play for each player without overlooking the importance of team play. (Coronet, 1 reel, 16 mm, sound, color.)

SWIMMING

Fred Cady of U.S.C., noted for his success as a teacher of swimming, instructs a child of ten in the film *Beginning Swimming*. The essential techniques involved in learning to swim are shown. (B.F.S., 10 min., 16 mm, black and white, and color.)

Another film featuring Fred Cady is titled *Advanced Swimming*. Here Cady reveals how to help average swimmers to overcome their common faults. Ken Carpenter is the film's narrator. (Assoc., 20 min., 16 mm, black and white.)

A valuable film, *Boy Scout Methods of Waterfront Safety*, demonstrates how not to rescue a victim and portrays the use of buoy, rope, stick, log, and boat. Canoe and rowboat safety are also considered. (B.S.A., 12 min., 16 mm, silent, black and white.)

MISCELLANEOUS AUDIOVISUAL AIDS (RECORDINGS INCLUDED)

In the film *The Chesapeake Bay Retriever*, the raising of this only home-bred hunting dog is presented. Training procedures are also presented in an interesting fashion. (Assoc., 1 reel, 16 mm, sound, black and white.)

Ted Allen, a world's champion, demonstrates fundamentals and expert techniques in the film *Horseshoes*. (T.F.C., 10 min., 16 mm, sound, black and white.)

The film *Speedball for Girls* describes and demonstrates the essential skills of this splendid game for both sexes. Individual skills and team play are shown by girl performers. (Coronet, 1 reel, 16 mm, sound, color.)

In the film *The Years Between*, the general role of scouting between boyhood and manhood is portrayed. (Boy Scouts, 17 min., 16 mm, sound, black and white.)

A slidefilm, *Beginning Camping*, is a two-unit slide kit covering the fundamentals of camping. Unit I, "Building and Using a Campfire," and Unit II, "Camping Safety," are suited for outdoor education classes, scout troops, camp classes, etc. (Athl., 2 units, slidefilm, sound, color.)

The recording *Nothing's Free But Time* is one of the series *Youth Tells Its Story*. The need for adequate recreational facilities for our youth highlights a significant problem. (A.Y.C., 16-inch record, 33⅓ rpm recording.)

Vacation Hazards presents the ten prominent summer vacation dangers along with suggestions on how to steer clear of them. This recording is one of the *Help Yourself to Health* series produced jointly by the United

States Public Health Service and the United States Office of Education. (O. of E., 16-inch record, 15 min., 33⅓ rpm recording.)

Another recording, *Contributions to Athletics*, is one of the *Freedom's People* series. The contributions of the Negro to American life is dramatized. Negro celebrities volunteer their services in this effort at promoting national solidarity and improved race relations. (O. of E., 30 min., 33⅓ rpm recording.)

Books and publications such as those listed in the reading list for this chapter can offer other suggestions and ideas to the instructor who wishes to take full advantage of these most effective tools for learning, the audiovisual aids.

SOURCES OF FILMS

A.Y.C.—American Youth Commission, Washington, D.C.

Assoc.—Associated Films, 35 W. 45th St., New York 19, N.Y.; 206 S. Michigan Ave., Chicago 3, Ill.; 351 Turk St., San Francisco 2, Calif.; 3012 Maple Ave., Dallas 4, Texas.

Athl.—Athletic Institute, 805 Merchandise Mart, Chicago, 54, Ill.

B.F.S.—Bailey Film Service, 2044 N. Berendo, Hollywood 24, Calif.

Bike Web—Bike-Web Manufacturing Co., 41 W. 25th St., Chicago 16, Ill.

Boy Scouts—Boy Scouts of America, 2 Park Ave., New York, N.Y.

Castle—Castle Films, 1445 Park Ave., New York 22, N.Y.; 542 S. Dearborn, Chicago 5, Ill.; Russ Bldg., San Francisco 4, Calif.

Chic. Trib.—Public Service Office, Chicago Tribune, Tribune Tower, Chicago 11, Ill.

Coronet—Coronet Instructional Films, Coronet Bldg., Chicago 1, Ill.

Dav.—Kenneth R. Davidson, General Sportcraft Co., 215 Fourth Ave., New York 3, N.Y.

E.B.F.—Encyclopaedia Britannica Films, Inc., 207 S. Green St., Chicago 7, Ill.

G.E.—General Electric, River Road, Schenectady 5, N.Y.

G.S.C.—General Sportcraft Co., Ltd., 215 Fourth Ave., New York 3, N.Y.

H.L.—Hawley-Lord, Inc., 61 W. 56th St., New York 19, N.Y.

Ind. U.—Indiana University (Audio-Visual Center), Bloomington, Ind.

M.C.—Michigan Department of Conservation, Room 328, State Office Bldg., Lansing 13, Mich.

Minn.—Bureau of Visual Instruction, University of Minnesota, Minneapolis 14, Minn.

N.F.B.—National Film Board of Canada, 620 Fifth Ave., New York 20, N.Y.; 84 E. Randolph St., Chicago 1, Ill.

N.R.A.—National Rifle Association, 1600 Rhode Island Ave., Washington, D.C.

N.S.C.—National Safety Council, Film Service Bureau, 20 N. Wacker Drive, Chicago 6, Ill.

N.Y.U.—New York University Film Library, Washington Square, New York 12, N.Y.

O. of E.—U.S. Office of Education, Washington, D.C.

Pa. St.—The Pennsylvania State University, Audio-Visual Aids Library, University Park, Pa.

Pictorial—Pictorial Films, Inc., R.K.O. Bldg., Radio City, New York 20, N.Y.

Schol.—Scholastic Coach, 220 E. 42d St., New York, N.Y.

S.T.T.A.—Sport Tips and Teaching Aids, 16801 Park Side Drive, Detroit, Mich.

T.F.C.—Teaching Film Custodians, Inc., 25 W. 43rd St., New York 18, N.Y.

U.W.F.—United World Films, Inc., 1445 Park Ave., New York 22, N.Y.

V.V.—Phyllis Van Vleet, 1803 Highland Place, Berkeley 8, Calif.

SUGGESTED READINGS

Brown, James W,. Richard B. Lewis, and Ford F. Harcleroad. *A-V Instruction Materials and Methods.* New York: McGraw-Hill Book Company, 1959.

Cross, A. J., and Irene F. Cypher. *Audio-Visual Instruction.* New York: Thomas Y. Crowell Company, 1961.

Dale, Edgar. *Audio-Visual Methods in Teaching.* New York: The Dryden Press, 1954.

De Kieffer, Robert, and Lee Cochran. *The Manual of Audio-Visual Techniques.* Englewood Cliffs, N.J.: Prentice-Hall, Inc., 1962.

Kinder, James S. *Audio-Visual Materials and Techniques.* New York: American Book Company, 1959.

Minor, E. *Simplified Techniques for Preparing Visual Instructional Materials.* New York: McGraw-Hill Book Company, 1962.

Visual Sports Instruction Aids. Chicago: The Athletic Institute, 1966.

Wittick, W. A., and C. F. Schuller. *Audio Visual Materials: Their Nature and Use.* New York: Harper & Row, Publishers, 1962.

White, Jane F., and Thadys Dewar, Jr. *200 Ideas for Visual Teaching.* J. Weston Walch, 1962.

Chapter 9

SAFETY AND FIRST AID

Adventure is a vital ingredient in a wide variety of recreational pursuits. Its presence in these activities sparks the satisfactions that are among the outcomes. Hence, the presence of the risk factor is one that needs to be recognized as an integral part and allowances made. This should be highlighted in the instruction of the assorted skills involved in the activity. In addition, proper attire, conditioning, lens guards, and the like are to be employed whenever appropriate. By its very nature, recreation attracts large numbers of participants. These large groups are often accommodated in relatively small areas. The intensive activities coupled with the great number participating tend to increase the possibilities of accidents. These facts bring to light the need for careful planning and for skillful leaders so that the number of accidents can be kept to a bare minimum. The recreational situation is further complicated by the fact that the child comes and goes as he pleases. This freedom, which is an integral part of recreational philosophy, creates a need for adroit organization and leadership. In addition, the recreation area finds itself confronted with the problem of handling various age groups with scant opportunity for classifying the players as to their physiological needs.

The use of age or height factors for classification is indeed inadequate, although better than helter-skelter classifying. Wherever feasible, simple motor ability and skill tests are to be used, especially when body contact is involved. Of equal value is the matter of having each youngster examined by a medical doctor prior to participating in competitive athletics. That the play leaders should be well versed in training procedures and accepted first aid practices goes without saying. It is popularly regarded that American Red Cross First Aid certification is a good indication that the individual has completed the minimum training required for first aid work. A knowledge of anatomy, physiology, hygiene, and body mechanics will also prove helpful.

SAFETY EDUCATION

We are all aware that conserving human life is one of the fundamental justifications for safety work. It is of equal importance for recreation-loving people to be free from injuries so that they may continue their quest for interesting activities and adventures. The leader should inform his charges that the taking of needless risks is a sign of foolhardiness and should not be mistaken for heroism. On the other hand, such games as bronco buck and chicken fight wherein body contact takes place may result in minor injuries. However, ought we not to balance them against the benefits and joys that accompany these activities? To restrict one's life to a highly safe and sheltered existence at the expense of invigorating and adventuresome activities would indeed be more damaging to an individual than the occasional bruise.

Safety for what? Safety for bigger and better adventures. Safety for more-rounded living and for the many and varied recreational activities which can help to make life interesting and worthwhile.

ACCIDENTS ANALYZED

A highly regarded study[1] ranks injuries as to type in the following order:

1. Sprains	4. Bone injuries
2. Strains	5. Internal injuries
3. Wounds	

The parts of the body that are most frequently subject to injury are also listed in this study:

1. Leg and foot	5. Pelvis
2. Arm and hand	6. Back
3. Head and neck	7. Thorax and abdomen
4. Shoulder	

Accidents do not just happen; they are caused. A high incidence of accidents in any recreational area warrants an analysis to help discover the causes. A spot map of the recreational area with pins to designate the exact place where each accident took place would be in order. The leader will deduce from a cluster of pins which area is most dangerous

[1] F. Lloyd, G. Deaver, and F. Eastwood, *Safety in Athletics* (Philadelphia: W. B. Saunders Co., 1936), p. 27.

and can devote extra effort at supervising that sector. The permanent marking of lines to designate boundaries of activities can help immensely. The selection of assistant leaders from among the youngsters can do much toward making the play area safer. In addition, the use of assembly programs wherein a state trooper or the local policeman may address the group can prove helpful. Safety information and suggestions may be printed in the play area newspaper and in the local paper.

It is alarming to note that accidents injure and kill a very large percentage of our population; in fact, someone is injured through an accidental cause every three seconds. Close to one hundred thousand people die annually from accidents. This last fact doesn't take into account the many who are seriously injured or permanently disabled. Only a small percentage of the accidents are what one might call unavoidable. The vast majority are therefore preventable with thorough organization, effective leadership, and compliance on the part of the participants.

LEADERSHIP AND ACCIDENT PREVENTION

The importance of effective leadership in a soundly conceived program borders on the obvious. This is particularly true of accident prevention. A competent leader is alert to the common dangers that lurk in a play area in which many participate in active games. Not only is he conscious of the possible hazards but he is conscientiously impelled also to take the necessary steps to forestall avoidable injuries. Acknowledging that accidents do not just happen but are caused, the alert leader is in a strategic position to prevent the vast majority from taking place.

The relationship between competence in an activity and reduced accidental injuries is attested by experts. Recreation should therefore concern itself with instruction in skills without infringing on the fun element. While recreation does not care to emulate the exactitude of varsity sports instruction, it should concern itself with minimal skills especially where the activity is somewhat on the hazardous side.

PLANNING THE PLAY AREA

The play area should be large enough to accommodate the equipment and the number of participants who will partake of its activities. There should be enough space to avoid the dangerous overlapping of play areas. Whenever feasible, apparatus should be located off to the sides of the playground so as to reduce interference with general play and activities. The rules dealing with the safe use of the apparatus should be made known to the children and posted for all to see. Walks should be so situated as to provide safe entry and exit from the play area.

Outdoor play areas should be fenced in to control their use when supervision is available. If this is not possible, the movable pieces of equipment should be removed or chained fast before the play leader departs. Picket fences are no longer approved since they provide hazards unless the pickets are curved. Chain-link fencing has proved itself to be most popular and desirable; wire-mesh fencing is also widely used.

Planning should include the assurance of a safe approach to the play area. Signs warning motorists that they are approaching a play area should be erected. Lines should be plainly marked at the intersections, with signal lights highly desirable. As a project, each child can be asked to plan and write out the safest route from his home to the playground. This project may be worked out at home prior to its presentation to the play leader. In this manner, the child will be apprised of the safest approach to the play area while fully sensing that the responsibility is his. A map of the community or the city may be placed before the group so that each youngster may show the rest how he reaches the play area.

PLAYGROUND SAFETY

The safe conduct of a playground depends in the last analysis on the quality of leadership. No matter how well planned the array of play apparatus and their placement on the playground may be, it is up to the play leader to create a relatively safe place for children to play. Otherwise, it may well be an attractive nuisance with danger lurking everywhere. The following suggestions for play directors and rules for children are borrowed from an article written on this very subject when the author directed play activities for the Recreation Bureau, New York City Department of Parks.[2]

Safe swinging. Swings should be surrounded by a guard or fence. The use of baby swings should be limited to children up to the age of six; large swings are for those over six. Chains are safer than ropes and even these should be tested and oiled regularly.

Instructions for children: Sit alone in the swing—never kneel or stand —and swing back and forth facing the same direction as all the other children. When you decide to stop swinging, bring the swing to a gradual stop before getting off. Don't push or twist the empty swing. Take off your roller skates before starting to swing.

[2]H. D. Corbin, "Ensuring Safety in the Use of Playground Facilities," *Recreation Magazine* (April 1941), pp. 29–31.

Safe sliding. The slide, which must be kept free of stones, slivers, and similar objects, should lead into a soft landing of mats, loosened earth, or shavings. The small slides are for children up to five years old; the taller ones are for the older children. All slides should be checked regularly for any weakening of the structures.

Instructions for children: Climb to the top of the slide using the ladder and slide down sitting erect with your feet stretched out in front of you, after having made sure there is no one on the slide before you start. Be on the alert as you reach the bottom, dig your toes into the landing pit, and leave the slide as soon as you hit.

Safe seesawing. Inspect the seesaw bolts and the handles, tightening any that may be loose. Check all wood parts for cracking and oil all moving parts.

Instructions for children: Remember that only two children can use the seesaw at one time. When lowering the seesaw, touch the ground with both feet, keeping the seat from bumping. Balance the seesaw by facing the child opposite you as you sit on it. When you are through, notify your partner, hold on to the board, and lower it gradually so that he can get off safely.

Safe skating. No more than two children should hold hands; trains and snake skating should be discouraged. Examine the skating surface for cracks and make sure that all poles and supporting structures are well padded. Bicycles and pushmobiles ought not to be allowed on the rink. At least four inches of ice is needed for skating by all ages.

Instructions for children: Wait until you reach the rink to put on your skates. Do not speed and remember to be even more careful when there is someone in front of you. Trick skating is dangerous for you and bumping and pushing is dangerous for the others. Skate around a group rather than through it and keep your mind open and alert all the time.

Safety on jungle gym. Give the children instruction in the safe use of the jungle gym and do not allow more than a safe load—approximately twenty children. Test the apparatus for rigidity and make sure that all bolts are tight.

Instructions for children: Be certain that your hands are dry and hang on tightly with both hands. Do not try any risky stunts. Shaking the jungle gym may cause someone to fall off. Remember that pushing and shoving are more dangerous when you are off the ground.

Safety in using the bars (high bar and parallel bars). An attendant should be present when this apparatus is in use and he should restrict its use to those within age groups designated according to the apparatus in use. The landing underneath the bars should be softened by loosened earth, skidproof mats, or shavings. All faulty equipment should be removed.

Instructions for children: Keep a firm grip with dry hands at all times. French chalk or powder will help. Don't take unnecessary chances and never try a difficult stunt unless a leader is nearby. Stay away from the apparatus when you are not using it.

Safe wading. Keep the pool free from debris and allow no glass objects near it. Test the water periodically; use chlorinated lime or a similar purifying agent to keep the water pure. Require every child to pass through a one-per-cent solution of hypochlorite of lime before entering the pool and admit none with a skin lesion.

Instructions for children: Do not enter the pool when you are overheated and leave the pool when you begin to feel cold. Take no toys or breakable objects with you to the pool. Do not jump or dive in and don't splash or push the other children.

Sandbox safety. Strain the sand periodically and clean the sandbox at least once a day and at other times if warranted. Make sure the sand is thoroughly dry before allowing the children to enter and never permit bottles or sharp objects to be brought in.

Instructions for children: The sandbox is used by others as well as by you, so be considerate. Do not take pointed or breakable toys with you to the sandbox and never eat or drink there. Do not jump in the sandbox and don't throw sand; it may get in someone's eyes.

Safe toy play. The acceptance of toy play as a necessary part of a child's development goes without saying. A selection of toys should be made with the full realization that toys improperly chosen may create needless hazards to mar the child's fun. The use of fireworks as part of holiday celebrations has caused innumerable injuries and many fatal accidents. For example, during the Fourth of July celebration in 1941 there were over two thousand nonfatal injuries not to mention the countless injuries which were not reported.

Adequate instruction should be given in the use of such playthings as skates, bicycles, skis, sleds, and similar devices. Further information relative to this discussion is included in the chapter, *Toys and Child Play.*

Safe gymnasium play. Safe conduct in the gymnasium is also highly essential to forestall injuries. The apparatus normally found in a gym (the high bar, parallel bars, horse, spring board, etc.) should be used only after adequate instruction has been imparted. A spotter should be required for the more hazardous stunts. Certainly, mats should be placed underneath the pieces of equipment so that falls may be cushioned.

It is noteworthy that nineteen per cent of all the accidents in and about the school during 1947 occurred in the gymnasium. The wearing of rubber-soled shoes and the removal of breakable personal articles such as rings, eyeglasses, watches, pins, pencils, and bracelets may do much toward reducing the number of accidents.

Safe swimming. Skill in swimming is one of the most essential abilities one can acquire. Safe behavior in and about the water is of equal importance in that it regulates the "when" and "where" to employ the skill. In the selection of a place, it is important that the water be sufficiently pure and that the area be patrolled by a skilled lifeguard. The use of the "buddy" system while swimming is not to be overlooked when bathing in the surf or in very crowded swimming areas. Furthermore, instruction in life-saving techniques can do much toward making the individual a safer swimmer as well as a dependable companion when at the beach or pool. The importance of skill in swimming is highlighted by the fact that thousands drown each year. There is a vital need for responsible and well trained leaders.

Softball safety. The growing popularity of softball appears to have no bounds; it is indeed an interesting and pleasurable activity. However, there are many possible dangers inherent in this sport. One of the most notable is that of throwing the bat. The player should be informed at the start that as soon as he has completed the swing, the bat should be dropped and not thrown. This seemingly simple advice may have to be repeated for certain players. Also, the players other than those who are at bat and "on deck" should be kept behind a restraining line to prevent possible mishaps.

Bicycle safety. It is a common practice for youngsters to travel to the recreation area by bicycle. This practice creates the need in many areas for bicycle safety projects. The examining of bicycles to determine whether they are free from mechanical defects should be very definitely included. The brakes should be tested for their gripping power. The height of the handlebar and seat are to be adjusted in keeping with the size of the rider. Ability of the rider to control his bicycle can be determined through accepted skill tests.[3]

The Bicycle Institute of America has been a prominent organization in fostering safety practices for the bicycle rider. It has pioneered in the establishment of bicycle paths to help assure safe places for this highly satisfying activity for all age groups; it will even assist in the planning and architectural layout. Furthermore, it will provide literature for distribution to bicycle safety groups on request.

[3]*Bicycle Safety Tests* (New York: Bicycle Institute of America).

Boat safety. The rapid growth in popularity of boating and sailing has exceeded the prophecies of most enthusiasts. There is little doubt that if handled in a sane manner, boating and sailing can be safely conducted. On the debit side we note that in 1947 nine hundred lives were lost in water transport accidents. It is a fact that a great proportion of these deaths occurred in the handling of small craft.

The ability to swim is highly desirable for anyone who handles a boat and particularly so in handling canoes or sailboats. An awareness of the number it can safely hold and the ability to handle it under all conditions should be assured. The boat should be checked for defects and leaks and an approved boat cushion which doubles as a life preserver or a vest-type life preserver should be on board for every passenger. Should it have a motor, added precautions are necessary; it should be checked thoroughly before starting out. Maritime regulations require a fire extinguisher on boats that are motor-driven.

The Bureau of Marine Inspection and Navigation[4] of the United States Department of Commerce suggests the following "don'ts" to prevent boat accidents:

1. Don't overload the boat. No boat is safe when overloaded.
2. Don't rock the boat (that's like saying, "I didn't know it was loaded").
3. Don't try to show off in a boat.
4. Don't fool in a boat.
5. Don't change seats in a small boat.
6. Don't venture too far in a small boat.
7. Don't brave a thunder squall. Seek shelter in time.
8. Don't take chances when nonswimmers are along.
9. Don't forget spare oars and anchor.
10. Don't fail to provide life belts for children.
11. Don't expose others while you are learning.
12. Don't be afraid of a boat—respect it.

Small sail boats must be cautiously handled.

1. Don't make fast the main sheet.
2. Don't jibe in a heavy wind.
3. Don't be afraid to shorten sail.
4. Don't attempt to carry sail through a thunder squall.

Motor boats have particular hazards.

1. Don't take chances with fire and explosives.
2. Don't tolerate an installation which lacks modern safeguards.

[4]*Safe Operation of Motor Boats*, Vol. II, No. 12 (June 1938).

3. Don't allow gas or oil in the bilge.
4. Don't forget your wake can damage others.
5. Don't operate near swimmers in the water.

Winter sports safety. The need for interesting recreational activities does not respect the seasons. Therefore, the recreation leader should take full advantage of the activities that are most suitable for the winter season. Sledding is an ever-popular activity and is also one of the most hazardous ones. Some recreation departments close off streets so that safe sledding on a hill can be assured. Roped-off areas in parks are also often used.

Ice skating is another highly popular winter activity. Here again, precautions are to be taken if a river, lake, or pond is to be used. It should be assured that the ice is sufficiently deep for skating. Members of the fire department or police department often assist in the checking of the depth of the freeze and in patrolling the area. Perhaps the fastest growing winter sport is that of skiing. While it is not without its share of hazards, skiing can still be a relatively safe activity providing a special area is designated without the danger of having interference from sled riders. Properly fitting shoes and skis plus adequate instruction in their use is highly important.

FIRST AID

Now that the prevention of accidents has been dealt with, the "first" handling and treatment of injuries likely to occur on the recreation center, playground, or athletic field is to be considered. When parents entrust their children to a leader's supervision, they have a right to expect competence in the meeting of emergency situations.

The presence of large numbers on the play area taking part in running jumping, climbing, throwing, and kicking increases the exposure to possible injuries. It follows, therefore, that the play leader should be well versed as to how to cope with the injuries that might take place. The initial treatment that is administered can prove to be of inestimable worth in preventing complications and further harm. Responsibility for the handling of emergency situations and injuries falls within the recreation area's province. It would be foolhardy to entrust the welfare of hundreds of participants to an inadequately trained leader.

The first aider's role. Upon arriving at the scene where there is an injured or ill person, the first aider should be observant and inquisitive to determine all of the facts in the case. He can serve best by preventing further damage and pain. In addition, he may employ accepted measures which may help the victim on the way toward recovery. His role is not to displace that of the physician but rather to institute basic first aid measures which will gibe with the physician's efforts to follow.

The following steps are presented in the order of importance:

1. The victim should be made to lie down if he is not already in that position. Should chest injuries or a heart involvement cause his breathing to become difficult, then prop up the head and shoulders no more than absolutely necessary. Shock and strain on the mechanism are accentuated in the upright position.
2. Inspect thoroughly for all possible involvements and then cover him up to keep him warm and to control the amount of shock. Varying amounts of shock are evident in all serious injuries. Reassure the patient so as to reduce his fears.
3. Preferential and instantaneous care are to be given to serious bleeding, stoppage of breathing, and poisoning.
4. Send for a physician and inform him of the extent of the victim's injuries, the first aid measures being applied, and the place where the patient may be found.
5. Liquids are not to be given if there are internal injuries or if the victim is unconscious.
6. The victim is not to be moved unless it is absolutely necessary. Suitable transportation should then be procured.
7. Crowds are to be kept clear of the patient.

Wounds. Any break in the skin creates the possibility of infection. Wash with tincture of green soap (if not available, then any soap). Remove grease with naphtha, ether, turpentine, kerosene, or benzine. If bleeding persists, apply direct pressure over a gauze pad. When required, apply tourniquet a fist's length from the armpit for bleeding in the arm or a fist's length from groin for bleeding in the leg. Then apply antiseptic (physician will recommend whether to use two per cent iodine, tincture of merthiolate, or metaphen), allow it to dry, and apply sterile dressing.

Extensive cuts or puncture wounds should be referred to a physician for possible suturing, dressing, and the administering of antitetanus serum.

Shock and fainting. While fainting need not follow the pallor, lusterless look, weak and rapid pulse, mental sluggishness, nausea and uneven breathing of shock, it does at times; the symptoms are similar for both shock and fainting except that unconsciousness or semiconsciousness always accompanies fainting.

Keep the patient warm and reclining with the head slightly lower then the rest of the body (elevate the foot of the cot or bed by placing books under the posts). The exceptions include possible fractured skull, stroke, or brain injury. Send for a physician if the victim does not come to in a matter of seconds. When consciousness is restored, a mild stimulant such as coffee, tea, or aromatic spirits of ammonia (one half teaspoon in a half glass of water) may be given.

Sunstroke and heatstroke. At the outset, dizziness, headache, stoppage of sweating, and vomiting may take place. Later, hot and dry skin, rapid and strong pulse, high temperature up to 110°, and possible unconsciousness and delirious behavior may be evident. It is a serious condition as attested by its approximately twenty-five per cent fatality rate.

Shift the victim to a cool and shady place. Remove unnecessary parts of the clothing and place him in a reclining position while elevating his head. Cold compresses are to be applied to the head. The body can be cooled by saturating the undergarments or by wrapping in a sheet which is moistened. Send for a physician immediately.

Heat exhaustion. At the outset, there are signs of dizziness with nausea and vomiting also possible. A cold sweat, weak pulse, shallow breathing, pallor, great weakness, and a temperature as low as 96° may be observed.

Take the victim to a cool place and put him in a reclining position. Heat may be restored by blankets, hot-water bottles, hot tea, coffee, or aromatic spirits of ammonia. Up to a tablespoonful of salt can be administered with water. A physician's services should be secured if exhaustion persists.

Heat cramps. There are severe cramps in the extremities and abdominal muscles. Signs of heat exhaustion may be evident, although this is not always the case.

Handle as for heat exhaustion with salt to be included in the treatment. Hot applications are to be applied to the abdomen. Massage the limbs with firm hand pressure.

Animal bites. A dog or cat bite is usually accompanied by punctured wounds which are highly infectious. Moreover, there is the added danger of rabies or hydrophobia that is spread through the rabid animal's saliva; scratches licked by a rabid animal have been known to cause rabies. It cannot be cured after it develops.

The wound is to be washed to remove the saliva by holding it under a faucet of running water. Next, dry the wound with gauze, apply antiseptic, permit it to dry, and dress the wound. Secure the services of a physician.

One should be careful to seize the animal without exposing oneself to its bite. The animal should be isolated for ten days to ascertain whether or not it will develop rabies. If the animal does, there is still time to institute treatment. Should the animal be shot to prevent others from being bitten, the head of the animal is to be examined to determine whether or not it is rabid.

Insect bites. There is swelling and inflammation at the site of the bite. Baking-soda paste or an ammonia-water compress should be applied. If a sting is seen, remove it by scraping.

Poisoning. Immediate steps should be taken before the poison is absorbed by the stomach. Look about the victim for evidence of the container and examine the mouth for signs of the type of poison. Nausea, stomach ache, and vomiting often are present.

Do not spend time searching for the antidote. Rather, dilute the poison with large quantities of liquid. Continue to encourage vomiting by giving an emetic (use salt water, baking-soda solution, dish water, milk, etc.) until clear liquid is regurgitated. After the stomach is washed out, the known antidote may be given. Epsom salts in generous amounts may also be given at this time. Food poisonings are treated in the same manner. An emetic is not to be used in poisoning cases caused by acids or alkalies.

Burns. The majority of burns are caused by dry or moist heat with electricity and acids a frequent offender. There are three degrees of burns:

First degree—red skin
Second degree—blistered skin
Third degree—charring of flesh marked by deep tissue destruction

In proceeding to treat burns, remove clothing about the burn while cutting around the parts that stick to the skin. Extensive burns warrant immediate medical attention since shock is great with the added danger of infection. A baking-soda solution on sterile gauze is highly recommended. For minor burns, a baking-soda paste or a salve of half baking-soda and half petroleum jelly is satisfactory. Apply a dressing to help prevent infection.

Foreign body in the eye. Caution the victim not to rub the eye. Do not persist in removing an object from the eye after initial attempts are unsuccessful. A drop of sterile olive oil or mineral oil in the eye accompanied by a cold compress will reduce further irritation while the patient is being taken to a physician (preferably an ophthalmologist or oculist).

Gently force the upper lid over the lower one to encourage watering of the eye. This procedure if followed in the early stages will remove a vast majority of specks from the eye. If this is unsuccessful, ask the victim to shut his eyes while directing his eyeballs to look straight ahead. Question him as to where he feels the speck. Otherwise, look first at the lower lid, then at the eyeball, and finally at the upper lid by rolling it back over a wooden match or applicator. When the object is detected, remove it with an applicator or sterile gauze.

Suggestions for a first aid cabinet. The following items are recommended for inclusion in a first aid cabinet for use in a playground, play field, community center, and the average play area. It should be readily accessible and kept well stocked at all times. In addition to a collapsible-type stretcher and splints, the items to be stocked are:

Triangular bandages	Naphtha
1-inch compress on adhesive	Adhesive tape
1- and 2-inch roller bandages	Aromatic spirits of ammonia
3-inch gauze squares	Glass or paper cups
Scissors	Calamine lotion (2% phenol added)
Antiseptic (2% iodine, merthiolate,	Splinter forceps
or metaphen)	Absorbent cotton
Petroleum jelly	Applicators

SUGGESTED READINGS

American Red Cross. *Swimming and Diving. Life Saving and Water Safety. Safety in Athletics. First Aid Textbook.* Washington, D.C.: American Red Cross National Headquarters.

Morehouse, Laurence E., and Philip J. Rasch. *The Scientific Bases of Athletic Training.* Philadelphia: W. B. Saunders Co., 1963.

National Safety Council. *Safety in Physical Education and Recreation.* Chicago: The Council, 1941.

Planning Areas and Facilities for Health, Physical Education and Recreation. Chicago: The Athletic Institute, 1965.

Seaton, Don Cash. *Safety in Sports.* Englewood Cliffs, N.J.: Prentice-Hall, Inc., 1948.

Springfield Safety Council. *Recreational Leadership and Safety.* Springfield, Ill., 1944.

Stack, H. J., and J. D. Elkow. *Education for Safe Living.* Englewood Cliffs, N.J.: Prentice-Hall, Inc., 1966.

Chapter 10

BEHAVIOR PROBLEMS
AND DELINQUENCY

Behavior problems can range from minor situations to those that warrant inclusion in the Federal Bureau of Investigation's Crime Index offences; during the first six months of 1966, the Index recorded a nation-wide increase of eight per cent over the same period in 1965 entailing aggravated assault, robbery, forcible rape, murder, and property crimes. Suburban areas continued to record the sharpest overall percentage rise. Suffice it to say, crime is predominantly a social problem and warrants community-wide concern.

A youth is neither good nor bad. He merely behaves in a manner that we associate as being either acceptable or not. The question to be asked then is what makes him behave as he does. Certainly, more of the leader's energies should be expended at finding and treating the cause rather than concerning himself with the symptoms exclusively. Symptomatic treatment of behavior difficulties simply results in new symptoms when the old ones are removed.

A delinquent child is defined as one who breaks a law, is repeatedly truant, wayward, or is disobedient. His behavior is such that it threatens his own morals and those of others. The approach called for is sympathetic appraisal and assistance so as to ameliorate or correct the difficulty.

According to school law, the truant is a delinquent and responsible for an offense which would be a misdemeanor were he an adult. Truancy is one of the most common early signs of delinquency or maladjustment. Obviously, behavior problems signify an inability to adjust satisfactorily to societal requirements, whether they be of the home, school, or community.

There are numerous factors that contribute toward behavior short-comings and delinquency. In modern American society we observe an unmistakable weakening of the home life, each member so preoccupied with his own needs that there is no real family life. We are witnessing an alarming increase in illegitimate births. It is equally astounding to note that thirteen per cent of the children under eighteen are living with but one parent. Among Negroes about forty per cent of the households are without a husband.

On the whole, we find that there are inadequate provisions for recreation throughout the country with but a few exceptions. This inadequacy is even more pronounced for those in their late teens and older age groups. Although we observe signs of added expenditures for recreational facilities, equipment, and leadership, they are not commensurate with the mounting needs traceable to normal population growth and the boom in births which started with the first peacetime draft, continued during World War II, and is still perplexing our population experts. Nor do they take into account the longer life span with a constantly older average age.

CITY LIVING

With the highest rate of juvenile delinquency anywhere, the city has much with which to concern itself. Crowded living conditions cause the individual to lose his identity. As a result, some misbehave under the guise of a reduced likelihood of being detected. The high rate of industrialization has opened up more job opportunities, not only for the head of the family but for the mother as well. This has done much toward weakening the structure of the home.

Moreover, city living is devoid of the many challenging situations normally present in rural areas. The lack of opportunity for such racially old activities as hunting, fishing, hiking, and camping has created a real void. By eliminating the chores that were commonplace in rural living, the city leaves our youth with enforced leisure and a paucity of opportunities to take their place. To quote Hollingshead:[1]

"The adolescent's ambiguous position in the society may be a product of the loss of function for this age group in our culture. The increasing expectancy of life coupled with the harnessing of physical energy and the development of mechanical techniques on the farm and in industry have turned society from the direct dependence on the adolescent in the productive process."

According to Daniel P. Moynihan,[2] director of the Joint Center of Urban Affairs of Harvard University and the Massachusetts Institute of Tech-

[1] A. B. Hollingshead, *Elmtown's Youth* (New York: John Wiley & Sons, Inc., 1949), pp. 149–150.
[2] *New York Times*, July 25, 1967, p. 18.

nology in Boston, the rash of riots throughout the United States finds class, rather than race, at the root of things. In his view, the present violence was caused by "a large, desperately unhappy and disorganized lower-class community in American cities that happened to be prevalently nonwhite." His 1965 government report titled "The Negro Family: The Case for National Action" argued that the explanation for the American Negro's predicament was less the matter of segregation than an unstable family structure nearing "complete breakdown." This he traced to centuries of discrimination and economic deprival.

City life is notoriously deficient in adventuresome outlets for our youth. With the value of land at a premium, the availability of adequate space for adventure is conspicuous by its absence. Space allocated for recreational use is inadequate by any standard. It is therefore all the more urgent that the existing areas be used intensively and under capable leadership.

We are reminded that it is just as natural for a youth to steal second base as to steal fruit from a stand. All too often, the stealing is attributable to a craving for the challenge that goes with attempting to take something without being apprehended rather than a genuine desire for the object pilfered. In order to abort a misdirection of energy, it is highly essential that adequate facilities, equipment, and programming be made available; above all, the deep need of leadership must not be overlooked.

THE HOME

Many authorities contend that behavior problems and delinquency get their start in and near the home; apparently they do not begin at the play area or school, although symptoms may crop up there. It therefore follows that anything done to strengthen a youth's home life and his immediate environment can prove of inestimable worth. It is commonly agreed that the first six years of life are the most impressionable in determining attitudes, moods, emotional stability, and the like. The home should be a pleasant place to come to and at which to stay. The need for a nook to call one's own where one can work, study, or just be alone is recognized as an essential of homelife. Further, the feeling of belonging and being wanted in a secure setting cannot be ignored.

The home should also be a place where there is respectful and cheerful treatment of all. It is desirable that it be a place to which our youth can feel free to invite their friends and where they can entertain them without being subjected to any embarrassment. Experts inform us that there is a direct relationship between substandard housing and juvenile delinquency; it constitutes a contributing environmental factor toward delinquency with an influence on youth much greater than on grown-ups.

Professor Sheldon Glueck and Dr. Eleanor Glueck of Harvard Law School conducted a study[3] of 500 delinquent boys from the slum areas of Boston and a control group of 500 boys from the same area who did not get into difficulty with the police. They discovered that if the child's family life was desirable, the chances were but three in one hundred that he would become a delinquent; on the other hand, if his family situation was inadequate, the chances were ninety-eight out of one hundred that he would end up a delinquent. The factors that were most prominent were: "A father whose discipline was lax or overstrict or erratic (not firm and kindly); a mother who left the boy to his own devices without provision for a healthy use of his leisure time; a family whose home was 'just a place to hang your hat.'" They warned that "little progress can be expected in the prevention of delinquency until family life is strengthened by a large-scale, continuous, pervasive program designed to bring to bear all the resources of mental hygiene, social work, education, and religious and ethical instruction, upon the central issue."

In this regard, one should note that the maximum age of a juvenile is seventeen; therefore he is considered a delinquent rather than a criminal and subject to handling by juvenile courts. This marks the delineation between juvenile delinquency and crime.

BEHAVIOR OBJECTIVES

Society has set up standards of behavior to maintain law and order and thus protect the rights of each individual. Any attempt at usurping the rights of others is incompatible with the legal statutes. In a like manner, the recreation leader instills standards of behavior for those in his charge. He aims to set a climate that is conducive to desirable behavior. He also attempts to prevent unsatisfactory behavior through an increasing and challenging program of activities.

By the same token, he is alert to aberrant behavior so as to nip it in the bud before it gets out of hand. He is concerned with determining the underlying causes for these misdeeds rather than merely with the symptoms. As an overall objective, the leader strives to develop a code

[3]Sheldon Glueck and Eleanor Glueck, *Deliquents in the Making* (New York: Harper and Brothers, 1952).

of behavior that is fair, courteous, and considerate of others. The development of well-balanced personalities through purposeful activities based on individual needs can be termed an overall objective.

ADULT STANDARDS

The imposition of adult standards on our youth is wrought with danger. Rebellious behavior is a possibility which ought not to be viewed with alarm since it is typical of many adolescents. The contention by each generation of adults that youth is "going to the dogs" is traceable to forgetfulness on the part of elders of their own youth. Overstrict homes may contribute to delinquency. The leader and parent should earnestly try to understand the problems of our youth. A genuine impression of a desire to help them is to be conveyed. Every effort to assist them should be willingly extended. Opportunities for varied recreation activities, and the development of new interests and outlets should be encouraged at every turn; emphasis on physical activities are advised as outlets for youthful zest and vigor. For the less amenable children, reference to psychological or behavior clinics is advised so that their delinquent tendencies can be studied as a problem to be solved rather than a crime to be punished.

THEORIES OF DELINQUENCY

We are often reminded of certain factors that contribute to delinquency. Many of these do not stand up under analysis, e.g., being born with a predisposition toward delinquency and being of the biologically criminal type. Environmental factors loom large in influencing the delinquent with broken homes, vicious and demoralizing homes, defective discipline, bad companions, and unsatisfactory school experiences prominently mentioned.

Caution drawing hasty conclusions is to be heeded for fear of oversimplifying the problem. It is one that calls for close observation and analysis of the individual. Delinquency is caused predominantly by social factors evolving around the home and the youth's immediate environment. According to Carroll,[4] delinquency is attributable to poor family ties and is not to be blamed on comic books or motion pictures.

This is not intended to preclude other factors which are brought to light as one studies this problem more closely. Further research is warranted to unearth the effects of the following: (1) The influence of the

[4]Herbert A. Carroll, *The Dynamics of Adjustment* (Englewood Cliffs, N.J.: Prentice-Hall, Inc., 1956), pp. 279–281.

annual one-billion-copy and 100-million-dollar comic book sales, (2) the influence of TV on our youth (during one week over Los Angeles TV stations crime pictures featured 161 murders, twenty-four conspiracies to commit murder, seven attempted lynchings, sixty justifiable homicides, and two suicides); (3) the effects of reading retardation as a contributing factor or concomitant to the upheaval; and (4) the role of the community school center and neighborhood houses as a positive force in community life.

SCIENTIFIC APPROACHES

There are few fields that call for closer scrutiny and concern for the individual than behavior problems and delinquency. Finding the cause is fundamental to a solution of the problem. A better comprehension of the individual can be secured by the following approaches:

Medical. A thorough medical examination may reveal whether there are any clinical shortcomings, such as faulty vision, hearing, or strains on his vitality. For example, the youth who cannot hear what is said to him may be accused of being disobedient or may try to compensate for not being challenged by resorting to antisocial behavior.

Behavioristic. Behavior problems are due to improper conditioning, according to Watson. Unconditioning and reconditioning are recommended.

Psychometric. An appraisal via suitable tests may reveal whether the problem is accountable, if but in part, to an inability to learn and adapt.

Psychiatric. The service of a psychiatrist is used to unearth whether mental disease is a contributant.

Sociological. Environmental and societal influences are studied in relationship to behavior difficulties.

Other supportive measures are to be found in sincere adult interest as to the whereabouts of their children and in the support of community efforts at providing challenging and wholesome experiences for our youths in properly equipped play areas under capable leadership. Child guidance clinics can be utilized both as a preventive and corrective force. The referral of delinquents to juvenile courts that are manned by qualified legal minds and probation officers is another factor. It is alarming to note that many delinquents are held in jails throughout the country and are exposed to rubbing elbows with hardened criminals and prostitutes. As an example of enlightened treatment, we find the Brooklyn Plan wherein first offenders are placed on probation for two years without trial. The records are torn up if the parolee lives up to his probation pledges. Of almost one thousand cases, only five were reopened. In another survey, Grünhut showed the sanative effects of probation. He discovered that juvenile delinquency rose to a peak in areas where probation was not employed.[5]

THE PROBLEM CHILD

This term has been used perhaps too loosely. Indiscriminate use of a term is often resorted to by people who consider it smart to speak the language of the expert without any regard for its appropriate applications. Child psychologists tell us that all children are individuals and therefore differ. As soon as a child differs somewhat more than the rest, he is stamped as a problem without any consideration for the scarring that may result.

Basically, all children are the possessors of similar wants. The desire for attention and love is perhaps uppermost. They want to be accepted by their mates as well as to do, handle, putter, build, and, yes, even destroy. These wants, at times, get youngsters into difficulty with their elders because they do not "conform with the wishes of the group." Aren't the group's wishes apt to be adult-conceived? Might not the activity be so removed from the individual's wants as to fail to challenge him completely?

These individual sparks can be kindled by an alert leader. The shy and retiring youngster is often the one who fails to draw attention although he may be more of a real "problem" than the boisterous and bullying type. Encouragement and praise may be needed whereas the aggressive youngster may benefit from the chances to blow off steam during vigorous play. The intelligent leader is constantly on the search for the cause of behavior difficulties.

DELINQUENCY, A COMMUNITY PROBLEM

Delinquency is certainly not restricted to the United States. It is worldwide in scope and attributable, in part, to the chaotic state brought about by wars, shifting allegiances among nations, and cheapened values among their peoples. Instability in the adult world is prominent. A *New York Times* worldwide survey concluded in 1957 revealed that although notable progress has been achieved abroad, the situation in the

[5]Max Grünhut, *Juvenile Offenders Before the Courts* (London: Oxford University Press, 1956), p. 27.

United States is becoming worse, aside from London, all cities abroad indicate they are "gaining the upper hand."

In the United States, by and large, apathy appears to be the keynote. We mislead ourselves into believing that housing projects are the answer but find they often become newly created slums; failure to prepare the new occupants in their flats and their adopted neighborhoods to receive them properly have brought on "chaos, conflict, and confusion." By restricting admission to those of low income levels, new-style ghettos have been created—this time perforce of "the sharp knife of income" rather than by religion or color. A community organization to help tenants bridge this veritable abyss is very much needed.

Community needs are dynamic and therefore are subject to change. It therefore follows that each community agency would do well to reappraise its services. An organization pooling all community agencies dealing with children and youth is advised so that overlapping can be avoided, duplications removed, and overlooked needs assigned. The services call for a concerted attack by all agencies. The coordination of these community agencies is a "must" in tackling this vital community need. State Youth Agencies have come into being in Indiana, Massachusetts, Minnesota, New York, and Wisconsin to assist community agencies in their efforts.

THE ROLE OF RECREATION

While recreation does not pretend to have the answer to all that ails our youth, it does have a significant role to play. Needless to say, it recognizes the indispensability of the home and the community agencies in this triangular attack at the problem. In contributing toward a positive environmental influence, recreation is in a strategic position. When boys and girls do what they want to do, they are then in their most impressionable and malleable state. What community force finds itself in a more enviable position?

Recreation, as probably no other means, can contribute toward the prevention of antisocial behavior. During his play experiences, a youth reveals much of his inner self. A competent leader can detect faulty behavior tendencies in their incipient stages; he can constitute a vital preventive force. Lastly, recreation can contribute toward the corrective phase of this social problem. Here again, it can reach our youth through activities that they like most. It can offer wholesome energy and interest outlets in its overall aim at well-rounded living. The importance of cooperative action on the part of the home and the other community agencies is mentioned again to emphasize the magnitude of the problem and the need for total action.

DISCIPLINARY SUGGESTIONS

The role of the leader has been extolled and not without justification. For one, his task is not a simple one. He is expected to symbolize the desirable traits he is to encourage. His most effective teaching in this regard is through concept rather than precept. When he imposes discipline, he should impress the reason (the "why") without losing his composure so that it approaches the personal level.

If the leader should lose control of his temper, the issue at stake is lost sight of and the personality clash becomes the dominant factor. As in Gilbert and Sullivan's *The Mikado*, the punishment should suit the crime. Consistency is another trait that is helpful in leading youths. An unwavering sense of fairness topped by a pleasing though objective manner will forestall possible accusations of playing favorites. An abiding faith in youth and interest in the welfare of each individual are also considered essential.

Furthermore, emphasize that which the child does well rather than harping on his shortcomings. Look for his strengths rather than his weaknesses and by so doing you are making him more aware of his strong points. You are also bolstering his self-regard and confidence in his abilities. He will be more willing to initiate and try things, for a stultifying fear will not be his. He will have acquired an exploring mind unhampered by the impatient "don't." Recognition, unfiltered opportunities, and sympathetic appraisal mark the astute leader. Criticism may be necessary on occasion. When it is, it should be constructive and stem from appreciation, with encouraging comments.

SUGGESTED READINGS

Brightbill, Charles K. *The Challenge of Leisure.* Englewood Cliffs, N.J.: Prentice-Hall, Inc., 1964.

Carroll, Herbert A. *Mental Hygiene: The Dynamics of Adjustment.* Englewood Cliffs, N.J.: Prentice-Hall, Inc., 1964.

Danford, Howard. *Creative Leadership in Recreation.* Boston: Allyn & Bacon, Inc., 1964.

Glueck, Sheldon, and Eleanor Glueck. *Delinquents in the Making.* New York: Harper and Brothers, 1952.

Hollingshead, A. B. *Elmtown's Youth.* New York: John Wiley & Sons, Inc., 1949.

Moore, Wilbert E. *Social Change*. Englewood Cliffs, N.J.: Prentice-Hall, Inc., 1963.

Slavson, S. R. *Re-educating the Delinquent*. New York: Harper and Brothers, 1954.

Shivers, Jay S. *Principles and Practices of Recreational Service*. New York: The Macmillan Company, 1967.

Sullivan, Katherine. *Girls on Parole*. Boston: Houghton Mifflin Company, 1956.

Task Force Report. *Juvenile Delinquency and Youth Crime*. Washington, D.C.: U.S. Government Printing Office, 1967.

Chapter 11

SPECIAL EVENTS

The special event is an accepted highlight or culminating activity in recreational programming. It can provide added impetus and meaning if properly thought out and sensibly handled. For one, the special event should be related to the program being conducted. It should also be compatible with the objectives of the program so that it does not dominate or interfere with the other important phases of the program. If properly planned and executed, it can add meaning and give substance to the program.

By the same token, misguided enthusiasm can so distort one's sense of judgment as to cause everything to become secondary to the event. By giving the special event the emphasis it warrants and no more, it can be relegated to its rightful place in the program. As a laboratory situation for the knowledge and skills that were mastered, it can assume a legitimate role in the instructional process. The leader should assume direction that is well thought out and balanced in perspective to assure this outcome.

The special event can be given added impetus if it can be built around a special occasion, celebration, or holiday. Such occasions as St. Valentine's Day, Memorial Day, Parents' Night, Boys' and Girls' Week, Easter, Christmas, Independence Day, and Labor Day provide splendid themes around which to build a special event. It will serve as an added spur to interest, which the activity itself cannot muster.

HOW TO ORGANIZE

The organization of a special event can be started by contacting the recreation leader's immediate superior for discussion and advice. If the project is deemed acceptable, an organization meeting should be held which all interested parties can attend and where they can be told the plan and details. The next step is the formation of committees so that various duties can be delegated.

While all special events may not require the committees mentioned, the following have proved of value in the planning of numerous special events:

Program.   The program Committee sets up the plan and arranges the program.

Publicity.   The Publicity Committee handles the preparation of the publicity and its distribution to the newspapers, magazines, and radio and television stations. The sending of invitations and the posting of notices also fall within this committee's duties.

Music.   If the occasion calls for it, arrangements for musical accompaniment are to be handled by this committee either in the form of recorded music, a pianist or accordionist, band or orchestra or whatever the event may warrant.

Safety.   Should there be the need for parading or the handling of large numbers, this committee can notify the police department for permission and escort service; the police may also be requested to rope off the area. If the activity is indoors, there may be the need to notify the fire department as well.

Finance.   When admission charges are to be made or whenever funds are to be handled it is advisable to delegate the responsibilities to the Finance Committee.

Equipment.   The handling of equipment and properties falls within the province of the Equipment Committee.

Reception.   Greeting the invited guests and ushering them to their seats can be handled by the Reception Committee.

It is noteworthy that smaller occasions may not warrant this many committees or that the occasion may be such as to require other committees. This is but a general plan and can readily be modified. Larger ventures, on the other hand, may call for Steering and Executive Committees.

SPECIAL EVENTS 'ROUND THE YEAR

The following special events lend themselves for inclusion during the designated months. Many of these can be used equally well during other months of the year; the leader's knowledge of his situation will often guide him effectively.

January
Snow and Ice Activities
   Ice Hockey Tournament
   Ice Skating Carnival
   Ice Show

Snow Sculpture
Skiing Demonstration
Checker Tournament
Chess Tournament
One-Act Play Contest
New Year's Party

February
Holiday Celebrations:
Lincoln's Birthday—patriotic observance, play, project, readings
St. Valentine's Day—dance or party
Washington's Birthday—patriotic observance, storytelling, films, party, play
Roller Hockey Tournament
Indoor Paddle Tennis Tournament
Musical Instrument Contest
Father and Son Night
Mother and Daughter Night

March
St. Patrick's Day—entertainments, dance, party, dramatic presentation, contests
Whistling Contest—bird calls, novelty whistling
Stunt Contest—judged according to difficulty, perfection, originality
Outdoor Basketball Tournament
Pet Show
Brother and Sister Party—a cousin may be substituted where there is no brother
    or sister
Hobby Exhibit

April
Doll Exhibit
April Fool's Day—dance, prank contest for cleverness, party
Kite Flying Contest
Easter Activities—egg decorating contest, party, dance, egg hunts
Bicycle Decorating Contest—in conjunction with a bicycle safety campaign,
    with skills tests and bike inspections included
Track and Field Meet
Play Day
Boys and Girls Week

May
Marble Shooting Contest—boys and girls 12 to 14 years of age
Handball Tournaments
    Boys under 17
    Boys 17 to 21
    Men 21 and over

Girls 16 and over—singles only
Mixed doubles
Model Sailboat Races
Memorial Day Celebration—patriotic exercises, dramatics, group singing
Mother's Day Celebration—party, play
May Pole Activities

June
Flag Day Celebration—flag ceremonies, oratory, dramatic presentation, contest
Horseshoe Pitching Contest
Field Hockey
Folk Dance Exhibition
Softball Tournament
Hopscotch Contest for Girls
Father's Day Celebration

July
Independence Day—July 4 Celebration—patriotic observance, oratory, dramatic
    presentation, appropriate music, parade
Field Day—track, field, and novelty events
Amateur Photo Contest
Boys' Softball Throw for Distance
Baseball Tournament
Jacks Tournament for Girls
Model Airplane Flying Contest
    Gasoline Engine (Conventional)
    Jet Propulsion

August
Swimming Events
    Exhibitions—diving, synchronized swimming, and rescue work
    Events—dashes and relays
    Novelties—Viennese night, clown acts, Buccaneer Party, Bathing Beauty
        Contest
    Learn-to-Swim Campaign
Golf Tournament
Paddle Tennis Tournament
Tennis Tournament
Quoits Tournament

September
Handicrafts Exhibit
Amateur Singing Contest
Labor Day—holiday observance, oratory, picnic, athletic contests
Nature Exhibit
Barber Shop Quartet Contest

Volleyball Tournament:
  Boys
  Girls
  Mixed
Shuffleboard Tournament

October
Holiday Celebrations:
  Columbus Day—dramatics, oratory, party, dance
  Halloween—party, dance, original costume contest
Table Tennis Tournament
Badminton Tournament
Harvest Festival and Dance
Amateur Photo Exhibit
Art Exhibit
Roller Skate Carnival

November
Holiday Celebrations:
  Veterans' Day—patriotic services, oratory
  Thanksgiving Day—party, dance, pageantry
Arts and Crafts Projects—for Christmas gift presentation
Storytelling Contest
Harmonica Contest
Glee Club Concert
Band Concert

December
Christmas Observance:
  Christmas Tree—decorating and lighting
  Carol Singing
  Plays and Parties
  Glee Club and Band Concerts
  Dramatic Presentations
Toy Repair Project—repair of used toys for presentation to the needy
Decoration of Recreation Area
Christmas Party
Christmas Dance
Gift Exchange

Halloween. Halloween is singled out for more detailed consideration because many communities are harassed annually by costly and disconcerting pranks and vandalism. Unfortunately, most communities expect to deter the pranksters by emphasizing the punishment in store for the culprits. The more enlightened communities resort to a positive approach. In the realization that our youth require outlets for their energies, they arrange occasions wherein the holiday spirit can be given vent to without incurring costly damage to property. It will usually be found that Chambers of Commerce will gladly cooperate and even offer prizes to add encouragement to this approach to a perplexing problem. A contest for the best drawing of the Halloween motif on the store windows can prove a highly popular event; jack-o'-lanterns, witches, goblins, bats, owls, and cats are often included. The community-wide parade is an annual feature in many areas. Prizes are often awarded to the best attired and to outstanding floats. Halloween parties are sponsored by the Recreation Departments in many communities. These and numerous other events geared to the interests in each community can remove the dread many people have of this holiday.

THE EXHIBIT

An exhibit, just as any other special event, may add incentive to the activities that lead up to the exhibit stage. The photography group may work with greater thoroughness and enthusiasm when it is directing its picture taking, developing, printing, enlarging, and coloring at the impending exhibit. In a like manner, the handicrafts group will be more apt to exert special effort in planning and constructing models, jewel boxes, wallets, book ends, stools, etc., when they are to be placed on exhibit for all to view.

So long as the exhibit does not become so grandiose an undertaking that the participants are carried away by it, there is much to be said in its favor. The exhibit can be displayed in the local library, school, store window, or at the play area itself. It should be publicized over such available media as the local newspaper, radio and television stations, mimeographed notices to parents, and posters scattered throughout the community. Exhibits offer a splendid means of informing the public.

THE DEMONSTRATION

A panoramic view of recreational activities can be displayed with effectiveness by the demonstration technique. It is considered possibly the finest means of publicizing recreational activities. The demonstration can take the form of an aquatic show, stunt and pyramid program, dancing, circus, carnival, or field day.

Whenever possible, the program should be knit together by a central theme such as a May Day or Boys' and Girls' Week program. The activities that are portrayed should illustrate a cross section of the play area's recreational program as much as possible. The use of invitations to the occasion adds an aura of importance. Added significance can be given to the event by employing civic officials as judges or merely as representatives of their departments. Sponsors in the form of beauty-contest winners chosen by judges drawn from the high-school art department and local photographers, among others, may add interest to the demonstration.

SPORTS DAYS

Sports days offer a form of competition for the rank and file of the recreation center or school. They provide a splendid opportunity for co-recreation although they can be restricted to a single sex grouping. At the start, all participants are segregated into teams, with each team or group retaining its identity. The activities program can include the gamut of team games (volleyball, softball, track and field, basketball, etc.), dual games (doubles in tennis, badminton, and paddle tennis—mixed or plain), and water activities. Each grouping may have more than one team representing it.

Opportunities for the building of group spirit and fellowship are afforded by the sports day. A half or a whole day devoted to this occasion will turn out to be time well spent for its recreative value, giving the participants a feeling of comradery and pride in being members of the play area. The day can be made even more pleasant by topping it off with a picnic.

PLAY DAYS

Under the play day plan, the recreation spirit is at a high pitch with joyful activity the prime objective. As in the sports day, all participants, regardless of ability, are encouraged to participate with the outcome of minor significance. Groups from different recreation areas are invited to take part in the play day and are mixed up with the others so that the identity of the individual or his group is lost. Each group, containing members from the different areas, takes part in assorted activities such as volleyball, softball, tennis, badminton, basketball, and the like. Only a relatively short period is devoted to each activity. While the play day concept is used most commonly for female groups, it can be used with equal, if not greater, success as a co-recreational activity.

SAMPLE SPECIAL EVENTS

Football skills contest. It is conducted between-the-halves of a college game annually and attracts athletes from a radius of about eighty miles. The four events are run off in the fifteen minutes permitted by the rules. It affords the athletes representing schools of different sizes an opportunity to compete on a par with each other. In addition to individual cups presented to the winners of each event, there is a team trophy which is retained for the year. Outright possession is not earned until the team championship is won three times. A letter to the coaches, a reply form, and information for the coaches are included to help guide the holding of a special event of this type.

INFORMATION FOR COACHES

Football Skills Contest

A. Place Kicking for Accuracy:
   1. The college will furnish men to hold the ball.
   2. One kick will be made from the 12-yard line, directly in front of goal posts.
      Two kicks will be made from the 15-yard line, one from each side of field, 18 yards in from sideline.
      One kick will be made from the 25-yard line, directly in front of goal posts.
   3. There will be four kicks attempted.
   4. Scoring is one point if good from the 12-yard line, two points for each kick from the 15-yard line spots, three points if good from the 25-yard line.

B. Punting for Distance:
   1. Each punter will get three tries.
   2. The longest punt will count as his score.
   3. The punter will punt from the goal line toward midfield.
   4. The punter cannot step in or over the goal line.
   5. If punt goes out of bounds, the spot where it went out will be the official mark.
   6. Scoring the longest punt will receive first place; second place will go to the next longest punt; and so forth.

C. Pass for Accuracy:
   1. Each contestant will be given six tries.
   2. Tires will be mounted six feet off the ground.
   3. Three tries will be given each contestant from a distance of ten yards away from the target (a tire).
   4. Three tries will be given each entry from a distance of 15 yards away from the target.
   5. Scoring: 3 points will be given each time a ball goes through the tire; one point for a ball hitting the tire. The passer amassing the greatest number of points will be the winner.

D. Centering for Accuracy:
    1. Each contestant will be given six tries at the target (a tire).
    2. The tires will be suspended 3½ feet from the ground.
    3. Each contestant will be given three tries from a distance of five yards from the target.
    4. Each contestant will be given three tries from a distance of ten yards from the target.
    5. The scoring in this event will be the same as the scoring in the passing for accuracy event.

Note: Each player may contribute to the team score as follows: By placing first in an event, he earns ten points, second (seven), third (five), fourth (three), and fifth (one).

Conducting a parade. The occasion to conduct a parade in conjunction with a special event arises in recreation centers and schools from time to time. Exact timing and delegation of responsibilities to committees by the leader will help to assure the success of the parade and its associated event. In this case, we shall picture a bonfire as the event to accompany the parade.

The committees should include the following:

1) *Organization Committee* to set up the general plan in consultation with the other committees. Time of departure, broadcast, fire, wood collection, and incidentals fall within its province.
2) *Safety Committee* to secure permission from the police department, police escort, route to follow, roping off of the area (bonfire), and arrangement for the fire-fighting equipment at the fire. A round-the-clock watch of the bonfire may help to prevent a prankster from jumping the gun.
3) *Publicity Committee* to spread word of the affair via the newspapers, radio, posters, and announcements at assemblies and on bulletin boards; mimeographed notices containing a schedule of events and instructions will prove invaluable. A broadcast of a portion of the program may be arranged with the local radio station to add interest.
4) *Program Committee* to decide on events such as speeches, entertainment, music, and singing. In the event there is to be a dance and refreshments to follow the parade, then subcommittees in these two added phases are to be appointed.

Sample parade. A pep rally and parade is an annual affair at Lock Haven. Each of the four classes vie for the privilege of having its name inscribed on the plaque. This designation is awarded to the class that displays the most originality, initiative, and effort in dress, floats, and the number of participants. A committee of judges consisting of eminent people in the community is chosen to arrive at an indisputable decision.

The instructions to the students follow:

PRELIMINARY   NOTICE

Pep Rally   Pep Rally   Pep Rally   Pep Rally   Pep Rally

ATTENTION—CAMPUS QUARTERBACKS

Now is the time for all good students to come to the aid of our bench-warming orange-eaters. They need support!!! Let's give it to them by making our HOME-COMING DAY PEP RALLY on Friday, November 10, 1950, a really inspiring success. Surely the events of the evening are packed with all the fun you can handle, so BE THERE!

Look:

Parade in costumes	Radio broadcast
Prize for best class participation	Kingsized bonfire
Cheers	Eats
Songs	Topped off by dancing
Clowning	

Watch for further information as to time, place of meeting, and complete program in the SCOOP.

Time Schedule for the Pep Parade
(Issued on Day of Parade)
Friday, November 10, 1950

5:30   Assemble in dining hall
6:05   Assemble in front of administration building
6:20   Assemble in street near clock tower
6:25   Start the parade down Main Street
6:55   At the judges' stand in front of express office for judging of classes
7:15   At the radio broadcasting station
7:35   Start back by way of same route to the college
8:00   All classes at the bonfire
8:05   Start of bonfire
8:30   All classes to the girls' gym for dancing and refreshments

In order to avoid confusion, all classes will assemble Friday evening before dinner in class formation outside the dining hall. Class presidents will be informed where to assemble classes.

The classes will sit in respective indicated places in the dining hall. They will leave the dining hall in class formation to assemble in front of the Administration Building immediately following dinner.

Important! When the program is completed at the radio station it will be necessary for all classes to remain in their respective groups for the return to the bonfire. The police have been kind enough to give us an escort and to block off traffic for us. Let's cooperate with them by keeping our class formations and by coming back in a whole unit just as we went down.—Remember—stay in your class formation when returning.

Remember, immediately following the bonfire there will be dancing and refreshments in the girls' gym for all. We know you will be tired but drag yourself over and have a glass of cold cider and plenty of good eats.

Let's all pitch in and have a good time. Come on Freshies; let your hair down.

Formation of Parade
    Order of march
    College band
    Cheer leaders
    Senior class
    Junior class
    Sophomore class
    Freshman class
Radio Program and Schedule
    Band number
    Introduction
    Cheer
    Band number
    Now it can be told!!!???
    Men's group—sing Alma Mater
    All join in on Alma Mater
    Fade out
Program for the Bonfire
    Band number
    Lighting of fire
    Cheer
    Speeches: President of college
            and football coach
    Awarding of plaque by judges
    Comedy number
    Band number
    Cheer

Chapter 12

TOURNAMENTS

In our quest at making recreational activities more satisfactory and challenging, the dash provided by suitable tournament play deserves serious consideration. One of the prime responsibilities of the recreation leader is to organize competitive play so as to stimulate interest in the activities. Tournaments can serve this purpose admirably. It is noteworthy that special care is required in selecting the type of tournament and in organizing and managing it. Furthermore, uncontrolled competition during tournament play can create disastrous situations with tempers flaring and discretion cast to the wind.

The capable leader will arrange and administer his tournament in such a way that the possibility of conflicting situations will be reduced to a minimum. This can be achieved only after detailed thought, planning, and competent leadership are brought into play. Notifying the prospective contestants, eligibility regulations, registering for play, officiating, and scheduling, as well as the conduction and selection of the right type of tournament, are among the essentials to be considered.

PUBLICIZING THE TOURNAMENT

In order to publicize a tournament effectively, it is advisable to use as many approaches as possible. If the recreation area publishes a newspaper, that organ should be used. Posting an attractive announcement on the bulletin board is another indispensable device. The local radio station can prove a valuable medium through its sports announcer's sports résumé program. Certainly, the local newspaper(s) should be used to good advantage.

The personal approach should not be overlooked, since it has been proved to be a very effective device on its own and a splendid follow-up technique. Colorfully illustrated posters can be used at various vantage points on the play area or at prominent places. Through these means, not only will greater numbers be attracted to the tournament but, what may be of greater importance, the shy and reluctant individual is more apt to be reached.

CLASSIFYING ENTRANTS

The worth of an activity can be lessened by admitting entrants who are hampered by strains and drains on their mechanisms. This brings up the need for a medical examination prior to participation in a vigorous activity. The need is more pronounced when the competitive spirit is whetted by tournament fever; dysfunctions and aberrations are apt to be overlooked when that all-important contest is to be played.

It has been this observer's experience that it isn't too difficult to find a physician who will gladly examine the entrants without charge. This chore will be even easier if one of the participant's parents chances to be a physician. Of course, the physician's task can be eased by seeing to it that all entrants are present at an appointed time and place.

Classifications according to age, weight, and height are most commonly used in recreational areas. Certainly, classifying according to age is the easiest method to employ and is therefore most popular. Nevertheless, a more foolproof classification results as added factors are brought into play. It may be possible, in some communities, to avail oneself of the findings of more exacting tests, such as the Rogers, McCloy, and Brace tests, from the physical education teacher at the school. In smaller communities, the participants in the recreation program are the same as those who attend the local school. Quite often, the recreation leader is a member of the school's physical education department; under these conditions, a use of the school's classification findings can be assured.

ELIGIBILITY REGULATIONS

A major objective in setting up a tournament is to stimulate interest and to increase the number of participants in the recreation area's activities. Therefore, the eligibility rules should be few in number and as simply worded as possible. A rule should not be listed unless it will be enforced faithfully. The aim of attracting entrants of comparable ability and satisfactory mental, moral, and physical attributes should be borne in mind.

For the average situation, a vigilant leader rather than wordy regulations can assure a satisfactorily conducted tournament. Adherence to standards of good sportsmanship which embody a code of honest play, modest winners, good losers, nonabusive language, comradery, polite treatment of referees and umpires, and a desire to play the game according to the rules should be required implicitly.

SELECTION OF DATES

The recreation leader can decide on a registration period sufficiently long to permit a maximum enrollment in the tournament; it should be about two weeks before the start of play. Every effort is to be made to adhere to the closing date selected for all entries. By the same token, the date set for the start of the tournament should be followed faithfully. The uncertainty created by changing dates does much to mar the effectiveness of a tournament. Whenever feasible, conflicts and holidays should be anticipated in selecting tournament dates for registration, closing entries, and scheduling playing dates.

OFFICIATING

Whenever feasible, the leader should try to delegate the officiating to capable youths who are dependable and have earned the respect of the participants. This practice is recommended since it may be necessary to schedule more than one game at a time. Furthermore, the leader should be available for supervision of the entire program and to add zest to other activities that do not carry with them the popular appeal of tournament play. This is not to be interpreted as a rigid rule but rather as a general guide. There are usually older boys or girls who have proved ability in sports who will gladly volunteer to serve. In a similar manner, timekeepers and scorekeepers can be secured. Mimeographed or printed scorecards can be handed to the officials so that a record can be easily kept. An appeals committee consisting of elected members of the recreation area with the leader serving ex officio in a nonvoting capacity will prove helpful in ruling on disputes and appealed decisions arising from tournament play.

POSTPONEMENTS AND FORFEITS

Postponements should be discouraged whenever possible. When outdoor activities are involved postponements are unavoidable. Provision can be made by setting aside a period during the week for playing off postponed contests. Otherwise, postponed contests should be tacked onto the end of the tournament. In other words, proceed with the contest as scheduled with the understanding that the contests which could not be played are to be held after the regularly scheduled ones are played. Postponement of a game may be permitted by a leader providing it is mutually agreed upon and duly arranged in advance.

The regulation requiring that the teams be ready for play at the time it is scheduled should be strictly enforced. Failure to appear at the scheduled hour should result in a loss of the game by forfeiture to the team that did appear. In the event both teams are late, the leader can consider the playing of a shorter game should another contest be scheduled so as not to conflict with the playing of a regulation game.

TYPES OF TOURNAMENTS

The more popularly used tournaments—round robin, elimination, double elimination, ladder, and pyramid—are to be considered. Attention will be given to the strong points and weaknesses of each. Deciding factors in selecting the type of tournament are the amount of time available, the leadership on hand, number of courts or fields, number of entrants, availability of officials, and equipment. The type of tournament should be appropriate also for the sport to be played.

Round robin. One of the fairest and most highly recommended tournament systems is the round robin. It should be used at every possible opportunity so long as time and facilities permit. In the event the round robin tournament has so many entries as to warrant a division into leagues, the winner of each league can play off via an elimination tournament. Percentage is secured by dividing the number of games won by the number of games played.

$$\text{Percentage} = \frac{\text{Number of Games Won}}{\text{Number of Games Played}}$$

The number of games to be played is arrived at as follows: Number of games to be played $= \frac{N(N-1)}{2}$ (N=umber of teams entered).

The advantages of the round robin tournament are: (1) Each team or individual has a chance to compete against every other. (2) It assures a maximum amount of play for all entrants. (3) If time permits, it can be run through more than once while sustaining interest. (4) Whether a team is strong or weak, it is given the opportunity of playing through to the end of the tournament. This is especially valuable for the weak ones who need the play even more than the others. (5) Interest in the tournament is upheld until its end. It is perhaps the most satisfactory of all tournaments.

The disadvantages are: (1) Its effect is restricted to a minimum of four and a maximum of ten entrants. For a greater number of entrants, dividing the team into leagues is recommended. (2) A greater amount of time and space is required for the larger schedule of this tournament as compared to the elimination tournament, for example.

Round robin tournaments may be conducted by the use of either the numerical or the square technique. In the numerical technique, as is demonstrated below with an even number of entrants, each team or individual is given a number. The numbers follow each other as shown under #1 of the first diagram. In arranging #2, the numeral opposite 1 under #1 (in this case 6) is inserted in the vertical listing after which the numerical sequence is followed. The same procedure is followed under #3, #4, and #5. Each team plays the team opposite it in the listing.

#1	#2	#3	#4	#5
1₋6	1₋5	1₋4	1₋3	1₋2
2–5	6–4	5–3	4–2	3–6
3–4	2–3	6–2	5–6	4–5

To further exemplify this technique, an odd number of entrants is used. Herein, the letter B designates a bye. Otherwise, the procedure is the same as that demonstrated for six teams or, for that matter, for any number of entrants.

#1	#2	#3	#4	#5	#6	#7	#8	#9	#10	#11
1₋B	1₋11	1₋10	1₋9	1₋8	1₋7	1₋6	1₋5	1₋4	1₋3	1₋2
2–11	B–10	11–9	10–8	9–7	8–6	7–5	6–4	5–3	4–2	3–B
3–10	2–9	B–8	11–7	10–6	9–5	8–4	7–3	6–2	5–B	4–11
4–9	3–8	2–7	B–6	11–5	10–4	9–3	8–2	7–B	6–11	5–10
5–8	4–7	3–6	2–5	B–4	11–3	10–2	9–B	8–11	7–10	6–9
6–7	5–6	4–5	3–4	2–3	B–2	11–B	10–11	9–10	8–9	7–8

In the square technique (Figure 1) the letters denote the dates and each number signifies a different player or team. An X is placed where the horizontal and vertical boxes of a team or entrant meet. Starting with the second box of the horizontal row number 1, place the letter B and follow with the consecutive alphabet letters. The omitted letter A is placed under 12 since the letter X occupies its place. The last vertical row must be considered as the next consecutive regardless of the letter that appears in the space. Horizontal rows 1 and 2 illustrate the point as do the others.

Letter B is placed at the start of horizontal row 2. Since an X intercedes, the letter C which is displaced by the X is placed at the end of the row while D follows the X and so on. This procedure is retained

	1	2	3	4	5	6	7	8	9	10	11	12
1	X	B	C	D	E	F	G	H	I	J	K	A
2	B	X	D	E	F	G	H	I	J	K	A	C
3	C	D	X	F	G	H	I	J	K	A	B	E
4	D	E	F	X	H	I	J	K	A	B	C	G
5	E	F	G	H	X	J	K	A	B	C	D	I
6	F	G	H	I	J	X	A	B	C	D	E	K
7	G	H	I	J	K	A	X	C	D	E	F	B
8	H	I	˙J	K	A	B	C	X	E	F	G	D
9	I	J	K	A	B	C	D	E	X	G	H	F
10	J	K	A	B	C	D	E	F	G	X	I	H
11	K	A	B	C	D	E	F	G	H	I	X	J
12	A	C	E	G	I	K	A	B	F	H	J	X

Figure 1

right through horizontal row 11. The letters of vertical row 12 are placed on horizontal row 12. The completed square contains the complete schedule in codified form and ready for a double round robin. Let's imagine that letter A stands for July 1, B for July 3, and C for July 5. The sample listing in Figure 2 exemplifies how it can be worked out and listed.

The leader can graphically illustrate the standing of each team by placing a green color in the entrant's (horizontal) row when he wins and a red color in the same row when he loses. The second phase of the round robin can be illustrated by coloring the boxes below the X's similarly.

Use the same number of squares as there are teams entered. For an odd number of entries, add one vertical row. Follow the aforementioned procedure out to the last box. The last row indicates the dates during which a bye takes place.

Elimination. This tournament is not as popular as the round robin. Its disadvantages are that the weak player who needs the play most is usually eliminated by the end of the first round; that one half of the players are eliminated after the first contest; and that it fails to sustain interest, especially among those who are dropped. Nevertheless, this form of tournament does have advantages: It is the fastest type of tourna-

Sample Listing

Date	Teams	Scores	Teams	Scores
	1 vs. 12		4 vs. 9	
July 1	2 vs. 11		5 vs. 8	
	3 vs. 10		6 vs. 7	
	1 vs. 2		3 vs. 5	
July 3	3 vs. 11		6 vs. 8	
	4 vs. 10		7 vs. 12	
	1 vs. 3		5 vs. 10	
July 5	2 vs. 12		3 vs. 6	
	4 vs. 11		7 vs. 8	

Teams & Numbers

1. Browns
2. Cardinals
3. White Sox
4. Dodgers
5. Pirates
6. Cubs

7. Yankees
8. Red Sox
9. Giants
10. Indians
11. Phillies
12. Braves

Figure 2

ment to conduct and lends itself to play of short duration; less demand is made on the facilities so that fewer courts or fields will suffice; and it is relatively simple to administer.

Four types of the elimination tournament will be considered here: the single elimination, the standard consolation, the Bagwell-Wild version, and the double elimination.

In the single elimination (Figure 3) the number of games played is one less than the number of entries—$N-1$. A power of two is necessary in drawing this form of tournament. Assuming that 11 teams are entered in the tournament, the difference between the next higher power of two (2, 4, 8, 16) which is 16 and 11 yields five byes (do not play in first round). When there is an odd number of byes, in this case five, three are placed in the bottom half and two in the top half. Figure 2 illustrates how a single elimination with 11 entries is bracketed. As shown, all byes are taken care of in the first round with byes inserted at both ends. In this manner, a power of two is achieved going into the second round. When there is no seeding of players, the entries are placed in a hat and drawn to decide objectively where each entrant is

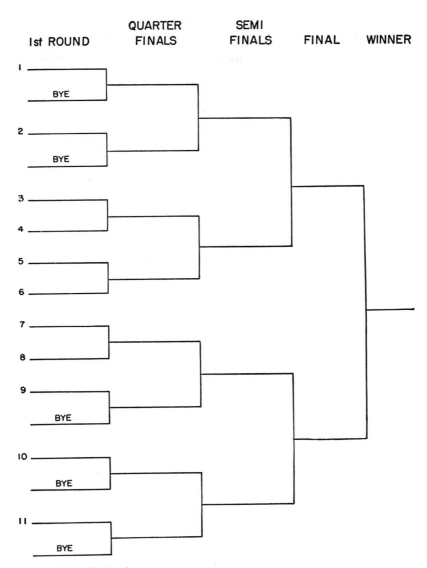

Figure 3. Single Elimination

to be placed. Should there be seeded players, the remaining entrants are to be placed on the basis of a drawing.

In the standard consolation (Figure 4) those who have lost out in the first round play-off the consolation phase. They are thus assured at least two contests. The defeated finalist is the winner of second place while the consolation winner takes third place.

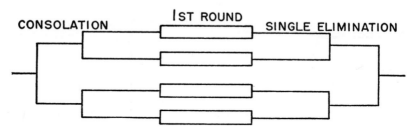

Figure 4. Standard Consolation

Basically, the consolation tournament is a weak tournament. Dynamic leadership is required to sustain interest in the consolation portion. The single elimination or the double elimination which follows are preferred; nevertheless, the consolation tournament is included in order to present all the popularly used tournaments.

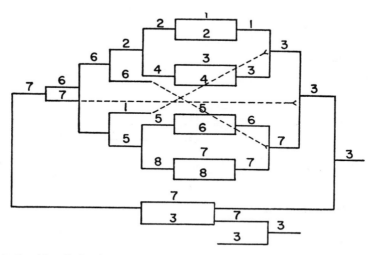

Figure 5. Double elimination

The double elimination (Figure 5) represents an attempt to keep from eliminating an entrant after one defeat; it takes two defeats to eliminate in this tournament. It is rarely used unless there are eight or fewer entries in the tournament.

The lowest bracketing can be explained best with the reminder that an entry is defeated as soon as two contests are lost. Since 3 has lost but one contest (to 7), he is eligible for another game. In this one, 3 is victorious and thereby wins the championship.

The Bagnell–Wild version (Figure 6) facilitates the selection of second and third places. However, it possesses the weakness of not permitting the start of play for the second and third places until the first-place winner is cleared. The illustration of the 11-entry elimination tournament (diagrammed in Figure 4) is used again to show this adaptation.

As you will note in Figure 5 the single elimination is completed to arrive at the first-place winner. To decide the second-place winner, all defeated by the winner prior to the final round play each other in an elimination play-off. The loser in the finals (10) plays the winner of this elimination play-off to decide the second-place winner. The third place can be decided as follows:

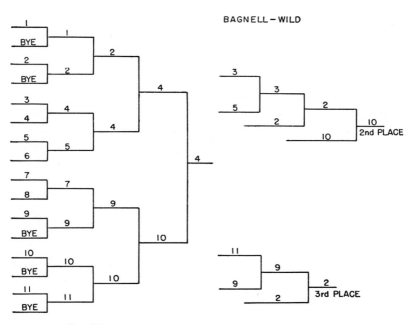

Figure 6. Bagnell-Wild

1.) When the entry that lost in the finals (10) of the single elimination is defeated in the second-place play-off, he becomes the third-place winner.

2.) Should he win second place, all who lost to him during the single elimination play-off. The winner of this phase plays the loser of the second-place finals to become the third-place winner.

Since Figure 6 shows no. 10 to have won second place, then all those he defeated in the single elimination (11 and 9) play one another, with the winner (9) opposing for third place the defeated finalist for second place (2).

Seeding. In seeding, the best teams or players are bracketed so that they will not eliminate each other early in the tournament. The judgment for seeding is based on the proved ability as revealed during previous play. An objective technique such as the results of a tournament that was held previously is preferred to the judgment of the leader. The risk of being accused of playing favorites is too high a price to pay.

A minimum of two contestants are advised for seeding in a tournament of about eight entrants, three for about 12, and four for 16. For recreational purposes, a maximum of four seeded entries is recommended. Caution should be exercised to place them well apart. For example, if there are but two seeded entries, place one at the top and the other at the bottom of the first round bracketing; third and fourth seeded entries are to be inserted in the second and third quarters of the first round and so on depending on the number of entries to be seeded. On the basis of the 11-entry tournament shown in Figure 4, entrants 1, 6, and 11 would be the seeded entrants.

Perpetual tournaments. The starting position in the ladder and pyramid tournaments (Figure 7) is decided by a draw. Starting and closing dates should be announced in advance. In the ladder tournament, the player is permitted to challenge either of the two directly above him. If it is a play area where the participants are there so seldom as to delay the tournament's progress, the leader may extend the challenge rights to any three above the challenger. Under the pyramid tournament, the contestant can challenge any one on the line above him. In both types, the challenger who wins exchanges places with the loser above him. The pyramid lends itself to more entries and more extensive challenging. Since fatigue may be a factor in one's defeat, the leader should limit the number of challenges that may be directed against anyone during a twenty-four-hour period; restricting the number of challenges will be needed especially as the closing date approaches.

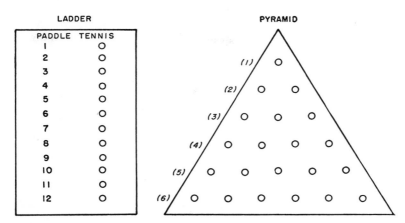

Figure 7. Perpetual tournaments

SUGGESTED READINGS

Forsythe, Charles E. *The Administration of High School Athletics.* Englewood Cliffs, N.J.: Prentice-Hall, Inc., 1962.

Leavitt, Norma M., and Hartley D. Price. *Intramural and Recreational Sports for High School and College.* New York: The Ronald Press Company, 1958.

Means, Louis E. *Intramurals, Their Organization and Administration.* Englewood Cliffs, N.J.: Prentice-Hall, Inc., 1963.

Voltmer, Edward F., and Arthur A. Esslinger. *The Organization and Administration of Physical Education.* New York: F. S. Crofts & Co., 1958.

Part IV

PROGRAM ESSENTIALS:
B. INDOOR RECREATION

Chapter 13

RECREATION FOR ADULTS
AND THE AGED

The aphorism "You cannot return from where you haven't been" applies even more so to the adult in general and the aged in particular. Full living at each stage of development is the best means of preparing for the succeeding periods. This is a challenge that we should stand ready to accept unremittingly if we are to acquire the flexibility and adaptability that contributes toward that perennially youthful outlook. "We don't stop playing because we get old but rather we get old because we stop playing" helps to prove this point.

Adult recreation is not to be thought of as a new form of recreation. On the whole, its activities are no different from those generally planned for the younger element. The distinction is often drawn so that recreation refers to adult avocational pursuits, whereas play connotes activities for children. Considerable overlapping exists in the activities themselves. There is a difference though in the approach to be employed in trying to reach members of adult age. Among the mistaken thoughts has been the one that the adult can take care of his own recreational needs. It is noteworthy that most adults have not had the benefit of instruction in leisure-time use.

With the steady growth of labor-saving devices and the commensurate increase of leisure, we find that the adult is coping with a problem for which he is ill-prepared. He is not well-versed in the basic skills nor is he extended the opportunity of making a rational choice as to type of activity. We are, therefore, confronted with too high a percentage who display that blank look while "watching the Fords go by." Herein rests one of the great challenges of our day at a time when cities are becoming more crowded and suburban parcels of land more costly; fifty-nine per cent of the total population resides in urban areas.

Furthermore, the community is the hub of the recreation wheel. It is charged with the responsibility of meeting the leisure-time needs of all, regardless of age or economic status. This need becomes more pronounced as the gap between work and play widens with the advancement of specialization and monotony of labor. These enervating experiences call for restoration which can best be achieved through recreational outlets.

Adult recreation is accepted as a governmental function in a democracy. It is also a truism that the aged are often ignored or slighted in recreational planning. This oversight assumes greater importance as we examine the trends of our population. A nation with all our opulence and human resources owes something to the aged who have contributed much toward society. At a time when their productivity is ebbing, are we to relegate them to the proverbial scrap heap? Or are we to impart to them the sensation of being wanted, of extending their usefulness through recreational outlets, new interests, and lay leadership opportunities?

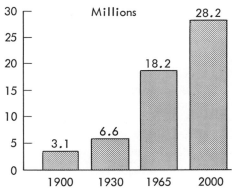

Source: Bureau of the Census

Figure 8. Older population growth

AN AGING POPULATION

That we are faced with the prospects of a constantly older population is becoming increasingly apparent. This state of affairs has been foreseen for some time. In 1900–1902 the average life span was 49.5 years; it is now 70 years. The percentage of older people has been steadily on the increase. Since 1900 the total population of the United States has doubled; the number of those 65 years old and over has quadrupled.

In that period those 65 and over increased from 3 million to more than 14 million. When projected to 1975, it is estimated (according to the Bureau of the Census) there will be 20 million.

One out of every eleven in the United States is 65 years of age and over (a total of 19 million men and women). In this age group, women outnumber men 129 per 100. Female life expectancy at birth is 73.7 as compared to 66.9 for males.

THE ELDERLY: THEIR PLIGHT AND FEDERAL ASSISTANCE

Many of our aged are not self-sufficient; some 2.6 million older couples have incomes under $3000. Almost 2.7 million older persons who live alone or with nonrelatives have incomes under $1500. Still another disturbing fact is that one sixth have anywhere from no assets of any kind to assets of less than $1000. It follows that the availability of The Older Americans Act was a needed development in that it "established needed services, opportunities, and facilities for older persons" as follows:

Establishing an Administration on Aging within the U.S. Department of Health, Education, and Welfare, to serve as Federal focal point and clearing-house of information on all matters of concern to older Americans.

Providing grants to the States to develop services for older people in their home communities.

Providing grants to public and nonprofit private agencies, organizations, institutions, and individuals for demonstrations and research of national and regional value.

Providing grants for training persons for work in the field of aging.

Through the Nelson Amendment to the Economic Opportunity Act, the Director of the Office of Economic Opportunity is authorized to make grants for special projects. It is aimed at the chronically unemployed poor who "are unable, because of age or otherwise, to secure appropriate employment or training assistance under other programs. . . ."

In addition, the Office of Economic Opportunity is cooperating with the National Council on Aging through Project Find. Surveying what the needs of the elderly are and appropriate programming are among the objectives sought. In all, the efforts are directed at the indigent, of which the elderly constitute a disproportionate percentage.

Although much of the progress in life expectancy is attributable to the remarkable reduction in infant mortality, advances in medical science, shorter working week, vacations, labor-saving devices, and recreational immunology, geriatrics, public health service, the antibiotics, plus the outlets have contributed toward this improved status.

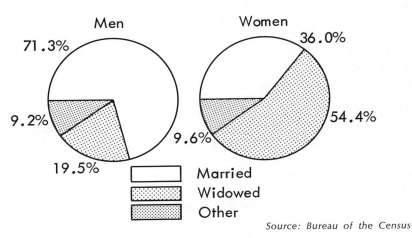

DISTRIBUTION OF OLDER PERSONS BY MARITAL STATUS, 1965

Men

Women

71.3%

36.0%

9.2%

54.4%

9.6%

19.5%

Married
Widowed
Other

Source: Bureau of the Census

Figure 9. Distribution of older persons by marital status

Adult recreational opportunities should keep pace with this rapid aging of our population. That they have failed to do so borders on the obvious. In this regard, nationwide renown has been earned by St. Petersburg, Florida, for its program geared for the aged. It has set aside a two-acre playground under the control of an organization to which each member pays four dollars in dues per year. In return, the members are afforded a wide variety of activities suited to their age grouping. The most popular of these activities is shuffleboard, with the 125 courts usually filled to capacity during much of the day and evening. Also, the "Happy Hours Club" of Lancaster, Pennsylvania; the "Golden Age Society" of Jamestown, New York; the "Middle Age Social Club" of Tacoma, Washington; the "Senior Citizens Calendar" of Rochester, New York; the "Friendship Club" of Edmonton, Canada; and the campsite for the aged (Camp Cleveland) in Cleveland, Ohio, are examples of programs geared to the needs of this growing and vital segment of our population.

RETIREMENT

While retirement ages do vary, we see evidence about us that Social Security considers sixty-five as the starting age for its benefits. Civil-service groups have set retirement plans at age fifty-five and labor unions are seeking retirement rights at sixty. No one will question that the trend is toward an earlier retirement age. Should technological advancement continue, the possibility of an earlier retirement becomes real. Furthermore, if a depression should set in, the further lowering of the retirement age may find many new supporters.

The retired person of today is in a more virile and healthful state than his predecessors and can therefore take fuller advantage of recreational opportunities. Besides, recreational pursuits can be of assistance in his aging gracefully while retaining mental alertness. A recreational interest that absorbs an oldster can restore that gleam in the eye. The elderly individual who becomes interested in a hobby, for example, becomes thereby a vivacious personality. An uninspired oldster finds time weighing heavily, with only his aches and pains as a basis for conversation.

In New York City the Department of Welfare operates numerous centers for older persons. Their programs are considered as "preventive medicine." Significant reductions in the number of health complaints and psychosomatic ailments are reported as the aged are exposed to varied recreational opportunities. According to Dr. Howard W. Rusk, the East Harlem Day Center membership had fewer visits to local welfare and family service agencies and medical clinics after joining in the Center's program. Recognition is given to the fact that the members have problems that are similar to children from broken homes. Their circle of relatives, dear ones, and friends is an ever-shrinking one. In addition, dwindling resources and energies often prompt tensions and frustrations. The need for satisfactory experiences with their peers becomes all the more vital.

The new medical specialty, geriatrics, reveals that a good deal of the physical and mental deterioration of our old folk is hastened by inactivity and the weariness of a dull existence. Shall we permit our oldsters to approach senility that much sooner simply because we have failed to stimulate them into active participation? This challenge plus that of the trend toward earlier retirement ages should give the recreation profession added concern to effect concerted action. As a nation, we must marshal our resources to cope with an inevitably increasing leisure in order to demonstrate that we are the masters and not the victims of the machine.

PRINCIPLES OF ADULT LEADERSHIP

Making arrangements for adult recreation is somewhat more difficult than making them for children. For one, adult interests are more diverse and therefore call for greater investigation. Many adults are illiterate, recreationally speaking, because they were not exposed to those opportunities the younger elements of the present generation have had. Since their more educable years were overlooked, the instruction planned for adults should be more fundamental and interestingly presented with others on a similar level of ability. Whenever the activity lends itself, co-recreational play should be encouraged.

When the older person finds active games to his liking, the leader should be alert to the fact that his level of endurance is lower and that he is to be deterred from overtaxing himself; this should be handled subtly without subjecting the player to needless embarrassment. He may react more slowly to new ideas and will require a longer warm-up period than younger folk. Active games can be modified to mitigate the strain on the older members. Mixing up these games with less-vigorous activities can serve as a general guide in program planning. Certainly, the teacher-training institution should include adult recreation as part of its recreation curriculum.

Industrial recreation also offers a desirable means of exposing adults to recreational skills and play. When the plant or industry fails to provide it, the public recreation authorities should consider stepping in to fulfill this need. A widely known example of this is the Oakland Industrial Recreation Association. Industrial recreation is but a supplement to and not a substitute for adult recreation; for it does not encompass the unemployed, the retired, or many of the adult females of the community.

ADULT NEEDS

The adult has need for activities that will satisfy his interests whether they include vigorous activities or those that call for sedentary outlets, such as hobbies, table games, and arts and crafts. Depending on their learnings, some may prefer one or the other while others may prefer a combination of the two. Since many have not mastered even fundamental skills, an instructional period, which includes those of similar attainments or lack of them, would provide a desirable setting for learning.

For many, the creation of new interests may be of great importance. They should be extended an opportunity to dabble in a variety of activities so that they might discover what they would like most. An honest-to-goodness choice of varied activities will aid them in selecting activities that suit their needs best. Instruction in the elements of these new activity-interests may develop into more lasting ones.

By exposing the adult to a variety of possible activity interests, he is more apt to be stimulated into action. What is of even greater importance, his interest is bound to be sustained since the selection is based on a varied rather than a restricted choice.

ADULT EDUCATION AND RECREATION

It is difficult to separate education from recreation, especially when one recognizes that recreation is a form of education. This thought is brought out very succinctly and emphatically by Jacks when he states, "The education which is not also recreation is a maimed, incomplete, half-done thing. The recreation which is not also education has no recreative value."[1]

Some states make different distinctions in this regard; we will cite two instances. The state of Michigan has decreed that its general adult education appropriation be earmarked for expenditure through the schools for "education recreation." Regular instructional classes are required to qualify for state aid. A class in swimming instruction that meets regularly and covers the fundamental strokes can qualify for state aid, while a period devoted to recreational swimming or water games would not. Pennsylvania is somewhat more liberal; its Extension Education Act provides that state aid be given for the leadership of out-of-school youth through the boards of education for any activity desired by fifteen or more individuals. A community band, a summer playground program, or even recreational swimming can justify state aid.

The adult is quite often a more difficult individual to reach than the youth. He is more standoffish, for one. Too many steer clear of participating for fear of displaying their crude ability. Rather than subject themselves to possible embarrassment, they forego the risk of participation. The astute leader is in a position to recognize these fears and can allay them by placing the novice in play situations with others of similar ability.

PROGRAM SUGGESTIONS

While active participation is to be encouraged whenever feasible, it can be supplemented by spectator or listening interests, which are called into play while attending athletic contests and musical renditions, to give but two examples. Instruction in rules, systems of play, strategy of sports, and music appreciation should be emphasized. To concentrate on spectating at the expense of participating would ignore a vital need. Moreover, attention should be given to activities that can carry over into later years, that do not lose their appeal as the advancing years result in less vigorous play. Swimming, fishing, hunting, walking, golf,

[1] L. P. Jacks, *Education Through Recreation* (New York: Harper and Brothers, 1932), p. 2.

tennis, badminton, skating, and the like are to be encouraged in recreational programs for our youths as carry-over activities into adulthood. By all means, they should be taught in adult recreation programs to those who have not been extended this opportunity in childhood.

Instruction in the rules, systems of play, and strategy of sports will help the viewer enjoy the athletic contest. The development of an appreciation of music through the symphonic, operatic, and instrumental forms among others can prove of lasting value. Added appreciations of art, literature, and hobby specialties provide other means of adding zest to the art of living well-rounded lives.

PROGRAM ACTIVITIES

Carry-over Activities	Hobby Activities	Cultural Activities	Miscellaneous
Badminton	Boat building	Music	Riflery
Tennis	Model building	Band	Shuffleboard
Golf	Airplanes	Orchestra	Card games
Croquet	Trains	Chorus	Bridge
Camping	Boats	Community sings	Pinochle
Hiking	Fly-tying	Concerts	Canasta
Sailing	Knitting	Appreciation of	Nature lore
Horseback riding	Sewing	Dramatics	Socials
Squash	Pottery	Lectures	Clubs
Bowling	Leather tooling	Discussion groups	Horseshoes
Fencing	Soap sculpture	Debating	Theater parties
Boccie	Clay sculpture	Town hall	Charitable activities
Paddle tennis	Block printing	Meetings	Constructing toys
Calisthenics	Collecting	Speakers' forums	Rebuilding toys
Weight lifting	Coins	Art	Collections
Swimming	Stamps	Sculpture	Bazaars
Dancing	Butterflies	Painting	Carnivals
Social	Insects	Designing	Pocket billiards
Square	Photography	Sketching	Darts
Folk	Picture taking	Drawing	Fly casting
Handball	Developing	Book reviews	Scrapbooks
Archery	Printing	Poetry	Chess
Table tennis	Enlarging	Storytelling	Checkers
Softball	Retouching	Library services	Outings
Fishing	Ornithology	Trips and excursions	Picnics
Hunting	Geology	Museums	Barbecues
Curling	Interior decorating	Planetaria	Patriotic celebrations
Bicycling	Magic	Historical shrines	Documentary films
Volleyball	Chemistry	Botanical gardens	Social recreation
Deck tennis		Libraries	Clubs
		Industrial plants	Festivals
		Travel	Weight-reducing clubs
			Leadership of youth groups

SUITABLE ACTIVITIES

Since the adult's interests parallel those of our more youthful citizens, the activities to be listed here will be chosen predominantly with the older person in mind. The "why" and the "how" have been treated which leads us to the "what." Emphasis is to be placed on the less-active interests and those activities that carry over even into the waning years.

A sharp line or distinction cannot be accurately drawn for the various states of adulthood. Nor is it desirable. Interests, skills, and levels of mastery do not follow standardized paths. The astute leader will not only select those activities that suit the interests and needs of the participants but will also concern himself with the educability and the degree of skill.

The activities are divided into four categories so as to facilitate the task of program planning. "Carry-over" activities are those that are somewhat more active in nature while retaining usefulness into and somewhat past middle age through regular participation and a slight letup in the style of play; a shift from singles to doubles play in the case of badminton and tennis or playing nine instead of eighteen holes in golf are examples. Hobby, cultural, and many of the miscellaneous activities possess vast carry-over value and are also to be encouraged; they can sustain interest, thereby giving incentive to further exploration and enjoyment.

SUGGESTED READINGS

Corson, John J., and John W. McConnel. *Economic Needs of Older People.* New York: Twentieth-Century Fund, 1956.

Counseling of the Older Person: Proceedings of the Governor's Sesquicentennial Conference on Aging. Indianapolis: The Indiana State Commission on the Aging and Aged, 1966.

Donahue, Wilma, and Clark Tibbitts (eds.). *Planning the Older Years.* Ann Arbor: University of Michigan Press, 1950.

Gernant, Leonard. *You're Older Than You Think.* Kalamazoo, Michigan: Division of Field Services, Western Michigan University, 1960.

Guide Specifications for Positions in Aging. Washington, D.C.: Administration on Aging, October 1965.

Kraus, Richard. *Recreation Today.* New York: Appleton-Century-Crofts, 1966.

Meyer, Harold D., and Charles K. Brightbill. *Community Recreation.* Englewood Cliffs, N.J.: Prentice-Hall, Inc., 1964.

Moore, Wilbert E., *Social Change.* Englewood Cliffs, N.J.: Prentice-Hall, Inc., 1963.

Shivers, Jay S., *Principles and Practices of Recreational Service.* New York: The Macmillan Co., 1967.

Chapter 14

ARTS AND CRAFTS*

Work in arts and crafts programs has brought purposeful activity to leisure moments otherwise empty or wasted in worthless activities; it has developed hobbies that have brought satisfaction to the worker or additional money to his pocket; it has even provided him a means of making a living. The government, recognizing these many values during the last war, established craft programs in the camps and U.S.O. centers for the services in action and also for the convalescents and crippled in the hospitals.

The values to be derived from craft participation by an individual are many. Working with the hands has been found to bring healing to mental, emotional, and physical aberrations. It relieves tension. It soothes and restores. Creating an original design or producing a piece of work well done brings satisfaction in accomplishment, in personal endeavor and success. Planning a project and bringing it to satisfactory completion develops initiative, self-reliance, and orderly thinking. It brings one a feeling of individual personal worth and respect extremely valuable in personality development and satisfying living.

There is no one, no matter what age or condition, who cannot be helped to a more useful or enjoyable life through developing some handcraft. Some crafts, such as weaving and clay modeling, can be pursued by all ages. Programs can bring the young and old of varying racial or economic groups together on common projects, resulting in better understanding and respect. Social or other differences are forgotten in admiration or recognition of another's abilities or accomplishments. Such programs also develop and further community or group spirit and esteem.

A job well done not only brings pleasure to the worker but develops in him a critical attitude toward other objects and skills, and appreciation of good design and excellent craftsmanship wherever found. Appreciation of other cultures and other people is formed. Better taste is developed.

*This chapter was prepared by Edna A. Bottorf.

158

A desire and demand for better products made by hand or machine results. A respect for the worker is engendered.

THE CRAFT ROOM

For the best program a suitable room should be found where equipment and materials may be conveniently kept and supervised, where an adequate working space is provided and competent supervision or teaching offered. Such a room need not be large or elaborate. A simple arrangement permits more ease in working and in supervision. Tools and equipment should be sturdy to survive handling by the unskilled, the uneven usage by many, and constant wear. Several strong tables are necessary for a working surface. Only basic tools are to be provided so that less time of the supervisor need be given to their care; more ingenuity can be developed among the workers to create or improvise additional tools. Likewise, although common or locally available materials should be supplied or pointed out, workers should be encouraged to be on the lookout for other possible materials, especially among waste products. Thus, an inquiring and critical attitude as well as respect for materials will be developed. Workers will become more alert to possibilities and personal creative abilities. New sources of material will be discovered. Finding tools and materials through one's own inventiveness will increase satisfaction, self-reliance, and respect.

THE CRAFT PROGRAM

The program of activities will, to a certain extent, be limited by the materials and equipment available. Under all circumstances, it should be related to personal or home needs as well as community services and activities.

The activities or crafts provided should take into consideration the age and abilities of the workers so as not to be too difficult or advanced, yet not too easy. There should be enough difficulty to create a feeling of satisfaction in having attained achievement over difficulty but not so much so that defeat or poor results will give a feeling of failure or frustration. Every project should bring a feeling of satisfactory achievement. At least, there should be fun in the doing.

CRAFT INSTRUCTION

Since people entering a class in arts and crafts usually do so with the desire of actually making some particular object they have in mind and can use, they do not care to spend time on preliminary exercises or projects. It takes careful handling to persuade a beginner to attempt a simpler project, if he has originally chosen one beyond a beginner's possibilities, without destroying his interest and enthusiasm. The relation between this substituted project and the desired one should be clearly established and kept in mind at all times so that the worker feels he is actually working on his chosen problem.

Likewise time spent at the beginning of a problem on theory, history, or research related to this form of activity may also destroy interest and enthusiasm. As the worker progresses in his activity his curiosity about such information may be aroused and then satisfied. For instance, someone wishing to learn to weave has some definite object such as a rug that he wants or needs in the home. He wishes to begin weaving the rug immediately. While weaving he may become interested in how the yarns are made, dyed, etc., how rugs have been woven in the past and by other peoples. Research and activities in these lines might follow depending upon the interest and curiosity of the individual. To insist upon such material first, except perhaps in an extremely brief review by the instructor, may kill all enthusiasm and interest. Even a brief presentation might better be withheld until the activity is under way and then given rather casually or informally.

AIMS AND STANDARDS

From the very beginning, originality and experimentation with techniques, tools, materials, methods, and designs should be encouraged—but not to the extent that the worker becomes discouraged or confused. Initial problems should be mainly concerned with the mastery of the materials being used and essential skills. Standards should always be high though related to the age and progress of the worker. Careless or slipshod work should never be permitted. All problems should be so well executed that they will be useful and give satisfactory service as well as elicit the admiration of both worker and others.

Explanatory notes. There are many crafts that may be utilized. Some require more tools, others have a wider range of application, while still others may be carried on by practically all ages. The following are easily handled and taught, have a wider appeal, are less expensive, and are practical.

Under each craft are given the necessary tools and materials, possible objects to be made, and directions for carrying on the activity. Where necessary, illustrations are furnished to explain a procedure, problem, or equipment. A bibliography is furnished for those who desire more detailed instructions or further study. In all crafts the designs and procedures are determined by the qualities inherent in the material. The worker should always keep these in mind and not attempt to use a material in a manner inconsistent with its nature.

CLAY MODELING

The materials of clay modeling are clay, water, and plaster of Paris. The necessary equipment includes a knife, a sharp stick or modeling tools, plastic bags, cloths, newspapers, containers, a board or oilcloth to work on, a rolling pin or length of broom handle, sandpaper, a sponge, a kidney rubber, brushes, glazes, and a kiln. Pottery, dishes, boxes, tiles, jewelry, figurines, and beads may be modeled from clay.

Preparation of the material. Clay can be secured from local deposits or purchased from a supply house. The native clay must sometimes be refined if firing is desired. Purchased clay comes wet or dry (flour) and in a variety of colors. Add water to clay flour and knead well the resulting mass. If it is sticky add more flour or spread the mass out and knead it until it comes freely from the hands. If objects are to be fired or turned on the wheel, pound the clay well until all air bubbles are removed and the clay is consistent throughout. After preparing the clay allow it to "ripen" in an air-tight container for at least a day. Clay is soft and pliable when wet but hardens when dried and baked.

Thumb, coil, and slab methods. A ball of clay can be pushed into a desired shape by manipulation of the fingers (thumb method). It can be rolled into evenly shaped coils or cut into strips. Objects can be built up by placing such coils or strips on top of each other, the shape being determined by the placing of the coils (coil method). Objects may also be made by rolling the clay with a rolling pin into sheets, cutting sections from the sheets and fastening these together (slab method).

To fasten clay pieces together securely, score the parts that touch, moisten with clay slip, and firmly rub together. Clay slip is made by mixing water and clay powder to the consistency of cream.

Wheel method. In making objects on the wheel, center the clay mass first. Keep the hands wet while working so that the object will not stick to them and be pulled loose. Shape the object by pressure of one hand on the outside and of the other inside.

Figure modeling. Animals or figures can be built up with coils or fashioned with the fingers, orange sticks, knives, or bits of wire. Pull out parts from the original mass or fasten on with slip. Hollow solid objects to facilitate drying without cracking. Flowers and other forms make interesting costume jewelry if pins are glued to their backs.

Mold method.   Objects may also be made by casting in a plaster of Paris mold. One-piece molds can be made from clay or other objects that have no undercutting. Objects must be coated with glycerin, vaseline, or clay slip to keep from sticking to the plaster of Paris. Place the coated object open side down in a cardboard box that is at least two inches larger on all sides than the object. Slowly sift plaster of Paris over a quantity of water (large enough to fill the box) until dry powder rests on the top. Slowly stir mixture with the fingers until it is creamy throughout. Carefully pour this over the object to fill the box. Tap the box lightly on the side to dislodge air bubbles. When the plaster of Paris has heated and become firm, tear the box free and carefully remove the object.

After being dried thoroughly the mold is ready for use. Pour clay slip into it filling it completely. As the mold absorbs the water, note the thickness of the model and add more slip until the desired thickness is secured. Pour off the surplus slip. As it dries the clay form shrinks and separates from the mold. If it adheres at any point, gently loosen it with a knife to prevent warping or cracking. Reverse the mold to remove the form and dry thoroughly before using again.

Drying.   The clay shrinks when drying and, especially in the case of thick pieces, should be kept from draughts or heat until thoroughly dry. Quick drying and shrinking of the exterior may cause the object to crack. Dry forms are called "green" ware.

Finishing.   Surfaces of dried pieces can be smoothed with a wet sponge, finger, kidney rubber, knife, or fine sandpaper.

Decorating.   While still moist or after drying, objects can be decorated with colored underglaze paints or crayons or with colored clay slips (engobes). Designs may be scratched into the surface or through the dried colored slip (sgraffito decoration).

Firing.   Stack green ware in the kiln quite compactly for firing. Air should be able to circulate fairly well. Do not place heavy pieces on thin ones. Directions for firing are furnished with the kilns. Fired pieces are called "biscuit" ware.

Glazing.   To withstand water, biscuit pieces must be glazed. Glazes come in powder form and a variety of colors. The powder is mixed with water to the consistency of cream and applied to the object by dipping, pouring, spraying, or patting on with a brush.

Protect the surfaces of the kiln or shelves with a coating of kiln wash (a powder mixed with water to the consistency of cream and brushed on). Place the glazed objects on small stilts. Do not let them touch each other or the kiln. Follow the kiln directions for firing.

Experimentation in modeling objects, mixing glazes, or decorating should be encouraged.

Notes. In cold weather dryness can be checked by holding object against a window. If moisture gathers it is not dry.

When considered dry, the object may be placed on top of the kiln after it is heated to insure thorough drying.

Do not use the same brush, even if washed, in different colored glazes or engobes.

Protect working surfaces with paper or oilcloth. Roll out the clay in slab ware on the cloth side of oilcloth. Pull the cloth from the clay and not the clay from the cloth to prevent distortion of the shape.

If no kiln is available an "Indian kiln" might be tried. The objects are buried under stones and covered with wood which is then fired and kept hot for some hours. If this is not practical, objects can be painted with tempera paints and varnished or shellacked. Tempera paint and pencil marks will burn off in firing.

STENCILING

The materials used in stenciling are stencil paper, paint (tempera or textile), wax crayons, and cloth or paper. The equipment necessary includes a sharp knife, scissors or a razor blade, turpentine, and stencil brushes. For silk-screen painting one needs a wooden frame, silk or organdy, silk-screen stencil paper, adhering and block-out liquid, and a squeegee. Greeting cards, posters, bookplates, bookmarks, end papers, notebook covers, wrapping papers, wall hangings, articles of clothing, draperies, household linens, and colored prints (serigraphs and the like) may be made by the stencil process.

Stenciling is one method of repeating a design numerous times. The procedure involves brushing color onto the desired surface through openings cut into an (usually) oiled paper.

Planning the design. In making a design, avoid long narrow areas or much twisting or curving unless the space is broken at intervals, especially at turnings. Secure areas lying within other areas to an outer edge unless they are to be made in more than one color, in which case a separate stencil should be made for each color. Trace the design on

STENCILING

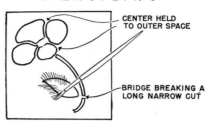

CENTER HELD
TO OUTER SPACE

BRIDGE BREAKING A
LONG NARROW CUT

Figure 10. Stenciling

the stencil paper. With a sharp tool, cut out the areas to be removed following on the outside of the line so that the opening will actually be larger than the desired shape.

Procedure. Place the cut stencil on the material to be stenciled. Load a brush with color but brush out thoroughly on a cardboard or dish so that the brush looks comparatively dry. Too much paint clogs the openings and gets under the stencil. Direct the brush briskly from the edge to the center of the opening (Fig. 10). If necessary repeat the stroke in order, especially with cloth, to insure that the paint will get into the material and not just on the nap. Remove the stencil. When the color is dry, apply the second color through the second stencil. Before using a stencil a second time check the back and wipe off any paint that may have run under the edges. In stenciling with textile paint on cloth, a second color may be added immediately after the first but allow twenty-four hours for complete drying. In stenciling on cloth with either textile paint or wax crayons, set the color by ironing over the reversed cloth using a pressing cloth, dampened with white vinegar, and a hot iron.

Stippling. Paint may be stippled on paper by dipping a toothbrush in tempera paint and brushing a stick or comb over the upturned bristles from the end toward the handle. A spray of fine drops is thus created and can be directed on the stencil. Be sure all surfaces not to be painted are well covered in this process.

If used in textile paint, brushes must be cleaned in turpentine and washed with soap and warm water.

Silk-screen printing. Silk-screen printing is a form of stenciling. It is used by artists in printing serigraphs or in industry for commercial work. It can be used for the same purposes as other stencils.

For amateur workers the following method is best. Stretch a fine and even-meshed silk or organdy tightly over a wooden frame. Cut a stencil from special silk-screen stencil paper and fasten it to the outside of the material according to the directions furnished with the stencil paper (there are several kinds). Seal the corners and edges on the inside of the frame with brown adhesive paper so that paint cannot get through. Put a quantity of thick paint in one end of the frame. Place the frame over the area to be stenciled. Insert a squeegee at the end where the paint has been placed and firmly draw it over the stencil to the opposite side pushing the paint ahead of it. Although one brushing is often sufficient, to insure a solid color, reverse the squeegee and put it back in the opposite direction. More than one color can be applied by preparing a separate frame for each color.

The stencil can be removed and the frame used again but the process is rather tedious. Directions for this come with the stencil paper used.

Notes. When using more than one stencil for a design, be sure the stencils match perfectly.

When using textile paints, prepare the paints and material according to the directions furnished with the paints.

Material must be tightly stretched during stenciling.

For a different and effective result, brush in from the edge without filling the opening completely; also brush a deeper tone or color in from the edge of an opening already filled with color.

Rough edges are the result of too much or too runny a paint on the brush.

BLOCK PRINTING

Block printing is another method of reproducing a design an indefinite number of times. Its basic materials are linoleum blocks (mounted or unmounted) or wood blocks, paper or cloth on which the design is printed, oil or tempera paint or printer's ink, a potato, inner tube, sticks of wood shaped with a knife or file, or a soap eraser. The necessary equipment is a slab of glass, rubber brayer, palette knife, hammer, spoon, or washing-machine wringer, and a knife, razor blade, or cutting tools. In addition to the articles which can be made by stenciling, illustrations for publications and calendars, notices, invitations, wall plaques, and book ends are often made by block printing.

Making the design. Scrap linoleum is much cheaper and more easily secured than mounted linoleum (mounted for use in a printing machine). Since linoleum is quite soft and chips fairly easily, designs should consist of large printed areas broken perhaps by small areas or lines of white rather than of thin printed lines.

Fine-grained wood blocks can also be used, the cuts usually being made on the end grain. Since wood is stronger than linoleum and finer lines can be cut and still be strong, the design usually puts less emphasis on mass than is the case with linoleum blocks.

Cutting the block. Paint the linoleum with a thin coat of a light-colored tempera paint so that the transferred design can be easily seen. Since the design will appear reversed when printed, reverse it before transferring it to the linoleum. Outline the areas to be printed with a sharp knife, gouge, or razor blade with the tool slanting away from these areas or lines. This leaves areas that widen toward the bottom and are therefore stronger. With the knife or wider gouge, remove the areas not to be printed. The larger the area, the deeper should be the cut; fine lines may be quite shallow (Fig. 11).

BLOCK PRINTING

SLANTING   DEEP CUT   SHALLOW CUT

Figure 11. Cutting the block   **Figure 12. Printing from sticks**

Printing the block. Put a drop of printer's ink on a slab of glass. Run a rubber brayer over this in different directions until the brayer is evenly coated with a fairly thin coat of ink. Run the brayer over the linoleum until all uncut surfaces are evenly covered. Place the material to be printed on a pad of paper or felt. Turn the linoleum over and place it on the spot to be printed. Hand pressure to the back of the block if unmounted linoleum is used, or several sharp blows with a hammer on the back of mounted blocks, will transfer the design to the material. Unmounted blocks placed on paper may be run through a wringer for printing. Ink the block again for each new printing. Clean the block, brayer, and glass slab with turpentine and wash the glass with soap and water.

Fasten a hook on the back of a cut linoleum block and hang it on the wall for a decoration. Parts may be colored if desired. A small piece of wood fastened on the front at the bottom of a block transforms it into one of a pair of book ends.

Printing with sticks and the like. Block printing can also be done by using sticks of varying shapes (match ends, pencils, wood scraps). Vary edges by chipping or filing. Press the ends on an inked pad or piece of felt on which paint has been spread thinly. Designs can be created by printing together sticks of varying sizes or shapes (Fig. 12). Designs can be cut into a raw potato or on a soap eraser and painted as in stick printing; color may be brushed on.

WEAVING

In weaving, certain threads (tightly spun so they will not stretch but remain firm) are arranged in a determined order as the "warp" threads. Other threads, or "woof," which may be soft and pliable are run through the warp threads. The simplest weaving consists of crossing over one thread and under the next. In pattern weaving on a loom this is called the "tabby." There are a variety of forms, or "looms," on which warp threads might be arranged. The mark of good weaving is a straight selvage. In weaving one needs a warp or cord, yarn, a loom, and a needle or stick to act as a shuttle. Table mats, rugs, caps, belts, dolls, hammocks, afghans, purses, pillow tops, chair seats, and scarves are among the many items which can be easily woven.

Card weaving. In *round mat* weaving cut an uneven number of points on the circumference of a cardboard circle. Starting from one of these with a cord or carpet warp, cross the circle to the opposite side; pass under a point; return, crossing the first thread, to the point next to the starting point and cross under this point (Fig. 13a). Continue back and forth until all points have been caught and tie the two ends of the cord on the back of the loom. Thread the needle with a long piece of yarn. Pierce through the circle at its center from the rear. Begin weaving by going under one thread and over the next. Continue until the outer edge of the loom is reached pushing the woof threads toward center while working. Be careful not to stretch the woof threads or the mat will curl when removed. Remove from the loom by bending up the points and pulling the loops over them. Run the end of the yarn down along one of the warp threads. If it is necessary to begin a new thread in weaving, run it alongside the end of the last thread for three or four warp threads. When the article is completed, the ends ·themselves may be cut off close to the surface.

A cap is made on a round loom. Instead of passing the warp ends under the points, they are caught onto the cardboard about halfway between the points and center on the back of the loom (Fig. 13b). After the weaving reaches the circumference on the front, the woof is continued on the back of the loom so that the warp there is also filled in. The cardboard is then pulled out.

In a *rectangular loom*, points are cut on two opposite sides of the loom. The warp is passed from side to side catching the points and returning. All warp threads are on the front of the loom. Fasten the ends together on the back until weaving is completed and then run them down along another warp thread.

A design may be worked on this loom by having a second color woven over the desired warp threads, both colors catching on the same warp where the design ends (Fig. 13c). Beat the woof closely together. Be careful not to stretch the woof, or else the sides will be pulled in.

A doll's hammock may be made on this loom by fastening two rings at the center of the back of the loom. Instead of passing the warp threads under the points they should be caught in the ring and then brought back between the next two points to the front, across it to the opposite side, then to the back to the other ring, and continue as on the other end (Fig. 13d). Weaving need be done only on the front of the loom.

WEAVING

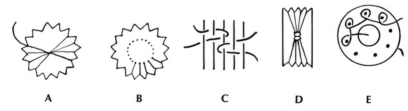

A   B   C   D   E

Figure 13. (a) **Winding the round loom** (b) **For a cap** (c) **For a design**
(d) **A hammock** (e) **Threading the spool**

Spool. An empty thread spool, a sharp tool such as a nail or heavy wire, thread, cord or yarn are needed. Several brads are spaced evenly around the top of the spool. Thread the end of the cord through the hole in the spool. Loop it over each nail (Fig. 13e). When the first nail is reached again, place the cord on the outside above the loop. With the nail, lift the loop over the cord and the nail without disturbing the cord (Fig. 14a). The end of the cord sticking through the spool is given a slight tug. Place the weaver cord on the outside of the second nail above the loop over the weaver and nail. Continue this as long as desired. A round braidlike loop appears at the opposite end of the spool at the end of this cord. Arrange this braid in any desired way (around a center to make a circular mat, or back and forth for a rectangular one) and sew the strands together.

A   B

Figure 14. Lifting the loop and threading the heddles

Loom weaving. *Looms* may be purchased or made. For pattern weaving it is best to buy a loom. Directions for stringing it up come with the loom. The warp threads are strung through the eyes in wire, metal, wooden, or string "heddles" (Fig. 14b), which when raised or lowered, raise or lower the warp. These heddles may be fastened to two or more rods so that different combinations of threads may be raised at a time creating a variety of "sheds" through which the woof thread is sent, relieving the worker of picking up these threads individually. Heddles are usually controlled by being fastened to treadles manipulated by the feet. In pattern weaving tabby threads alternate with the pattern threads.

Figure 15. Indian loom

Indian looms are made by running the warp threads between two sticks. Suspend this by a cord from a tree or other support. To keep the warp stretched tie a rock to the second stick (Fig. 15). Fasten a cord to the end of a third stick. Catch this thread under the second warp thread, wind it around the beam, pass it under the fourth warp, again around the beam, under the sixth warp, again around the beam, and continue across until the opposite side is reached. Fasten it to the end of the beam. Above this arrangement insert a flat piece of wood under the warps not caught and over the ones caught. When this flat stick is turned, half the warp threads are lifted, forming one shed. When this is flattened again and the beam lifted, the other warp threads are lifted and the second shed formed. Weaving begins at the bottom.

Popsicle weaving. A loom for belt weaving can be made from popsicle sticks. Drill a hole in the center of seven or eight of these sticks. Lay them side by side with an eighth of an inch between them (Fig. 16). Lay other sticks across the top and bottom of this row and fasten them together with a cord bound around them securely. Cut warp threads the length of the belt desired plus an added eighteen or so inches (warp threads are always cut longer because of waste at the ends). Thread these warp threads through the holes in the sticks and between the sticks. Gather the ends together and tie in a knot. Fasten one end to a doorknob or chair arm, the other end to a string tied around the weaver's waist. Pull the warp taut. By raising the popsicle loom, half the threads are raised forming the first shed; by lowering it, the other half are raised creating the second shed.

Egyptian card weaving. This makes beautiful belts. Unless drafts for patterns are secured from a reliable source the worker will not know what his design will be until after some weaving is done. Cut thin cardboard squares of four inches and round the corners slightly. Punch a one-quarter-inch hole in each corner three fourths of an inch in from the edges (Fig. 17). Letter these holes A, B, C, D. Number the cards for convenience. Cut colored threads the desired length allowing eighteen inches or more for waste. Taking the first card, pass the desired colors from the top to the bottom through the holes and lay the card face up

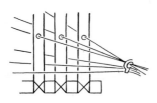

Figure 16. Popsickle loom

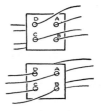

Figure 17. Stringing the cards

with the threads stretched in opposite directions. Thread the next card in the same way (changing the colors); lay it on top of the first with the letters corresponding. When half the cards are filled, pass the threads from the bottom to the top in the remaining cards with the colors in the two center cards being the same for correspondingly lettered holes; the next card being the same as the card on the other side of the center card, and so forth; and the final card with the same colors as the first card. This will insure a design that reverses itself.

When all cards are filled, tie the threads together at each end and stretch securely between two uprights. A shed appears at either side of the cards. Begin weaving at one side of the group of cards. Any color may be used as it does not show except at the edge. To change the shed move all the cards together a quarter turn in one direction. Repeat four or more times in this direction creating a new shed at each turn. Then reverse in the same manner until the cards are back at the original position. To repeat the design, turn the cards the same number of times as in the first pattern and proceed as before.

BRAIDING

Belts, rugs, mats, chair pads, bedroom slippers, bracelets, and lanyards may easily be made by braiding. No special equipment is needed for this, only the materials themselves: yarn, leather strips, old material or crepe paper (for flat braiding), gimp (for round or square braiding), and a hook for lanyards or a buckle for belts.

Flat braiding. Three or more strands can be braided together. The same principle of passing over and under strands as in weaving is employed in flat braiding (Fig. 18a). Variations can be secured by using two or more strands as one, keeping strands so used side by side (Fig. 18b).

Round braiding. Two strands of gimp are used in round braiding. Fold these at center to form four strands. (If this is to be a lanyard, place a hook at this fold.) There are two steps to follow (Fig. 18c).

1. Fold the left strand back of the two center strands, bring it forward, and place it between these center strands.

2. Fold the right strand back of the two center strands, bring it forward, and place it between the center strands. Continue with the first step, then the second until the desired length is secured. In making a lanyard, the braid is formed into a loop and finished with square braiding; the round braiding acts as a core around which the square braiding is worked (Fig. 18d).

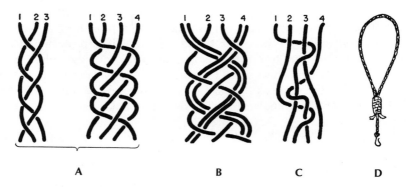

Figure 18. (a) **Flat braiding** (b) **Variation** (c) **Round braiding** (d) **Lanyard**

Square braiding.   Separate four strands to lie at right angles to each other (Fig. 19a).

1. Fold No. 1 back between Nos. 3 and 4. Fold No. 3 forward between Nos. 1 and 2. Fold No. 4 over No. 1 and under No. 3. Fold No. 2 over No. 3 and under No. 1. Pull ends together tight (Fig. 19b).

2. Fold No. 3 back. Fold No. 4 to the right over No. 3. Fold No. 1 forward over No. 4. Fold No. 2 to the left over No. 1 and under No. 3. Pull all strands tight (reverse of Fig. 19b).

3. Fold No. 1 back. Fold No. 4 to the left over No. 1. Fold No. 3 forward over No. 4. Fold No. 2 over No. 3 and under No. 1. Pull ends tight (Fig. 19b).

Alternate steps Nos. 2 and 3 until the desired length is secured.

Spiral braiding. Prepare for spiral braiding by performing the first step of square braiding. Then fold No. 2 back between Nos. 1 and 4 but do not pull tight. Fold No. 1 over Nos. 2 and 4. Fold No. 4 over Nos. 1 and 3. Fold No. 3 over No. 4 and through the loop left by No. 2. Pull all strands tight.

Repeat this step always folding each strand over the strand just laid over it as well as over the strand to its right until the desired length is secured.

To reverse the spiral, fold strands to their left instead of to their right.

Spiral and square braiding look alike when viewed from the top (the weaving surface).

Finish. With the strands lying as in Figure 19b, start with any strand. Slip it under the strand to its right and back under the strand crossing over it (Fig. 19c). Do not pull this first strand tight. Proceed

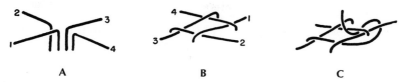

Figure 19. (a–b) **Square braiding** (c) **Finish**

with each strand, pulling these tight until the last strand. There the same procedure is followed except that this strand must pass through the loop left by the first strand in order to get back under the strand crossing over the first strand. Pull all strands tight and cut them off about one-half inch from the braid.

SQUARE KNOTTING

In square knotting, by which can be made belts, purses, doilies, and so forth, only a tightly spun, smooth cord is needed.

Procedure. To make a square knot use four strands of cord. If the knotting is to be fastened to some object such as a buckle for a belt, use two strands looped over the side of the buckle. The side strands are worked over the two middle strands which are held flat. Place the left strand over the center strands (Fig. 20a). Take the right strand and bring it over the free end of the left strand, pass it under the center strands, and bring it up through the loop formed between the left strand and center strands. This is the first step. The second step is the same except that "under" and "over" are reversed. Place the strand now at the left under the two center strands. Place the present right strand under the free end of the left strand, pass it over the two center strands, and take it down through the loop formed between the left strand and the center strands. Pull the cords tight (Fig. 20a).

KNOTTING

Figure 20. (a) **Square knot** (b) **Lazy Sqaw stitch** (c) **Figure 8 stitch**

To make objects. Objects are made by combinations of single knots. First row: Make as many as the object is to be wide. In the second row the first two threads (at the left) of the first knot are put aside. The two right strands of this knot and the two left strands of the next knot furnish the four strands from which the knot is now made. Proceed across the row using the right two strands of one knot with the left two strands of the next knot for each new knot. This leaves the right two threads of the last knot free. The third row begins by using the first two discarded strands and the next two strands to the right (the first two strands of the first knot in row 2). Proceed as in the second row. Alternate the second and third rows until the desired length is secured. Draw the ends back through thread on the back of the article and cut off.

To make a doily, make a small ring from the cord. Loop many cords over this ring spreading them out in all directions; the larger the doily, the more the number of strands. Proceed as above, going around the center ring. As the work proceeds, allow space enough between rows so that the work will lie flat.

Interesting variations can be secured by using groups of cords together instead of the single ones in some rows, by varying the space between the rows of knots, and by making strands using the same four cords for a specified space before combining cords from different knots. With a little experimentation, the worker can find many other variations for himself.

BASKETRY

Raffia. Baskets, bowls, mats, trays, coasters, and the like may be made of raffia. The only equipment needed—aside from the raffia itself and reed, old cloth, grasses, pine needles, and rush or corn leaves for core materials—is a large-eyed needle.

Take a group of raffia strands, a piece of reed, or a strip of cloth (twisted for compactness) for a core on which to work. Form a circle of about a half inch or less in diameter. Thread a needle with another strand of raffia. Wrap this strand over and over the circle until the original strands are completely covered and secured. Wrap the strand twice or for a quarter of an inch distance over the free ends of the core strands (or reed or cloth strip). Bring the weaving strand through the center of the ring (lazy squaw stitch, Fig. 20b). Again, wrap this strand around the core for the same distance as before. Again bring it through the center of the ring. Continue until the circle is completed after which pass the needle under the last row instead of through the center of the circle (Fig. 20b). Keep the work snug and tight.

The shape of the object is determined by the placing of each row against the previous row. It is easier to work from the outside of a bowl or basket than from the inside.

Add new strands of raffia to a raffia core to maintain an even thickness. When the weaving strand becomes too short, select a new long strand from the core or, in the case of a reed or cloth core, add one to the core an inch or so before it will be needed. Wrap the discarded strand around the core and continue with the new strand.

Variations are possible. (1) Instead of bringing the weaving strand from the back to the front when joining to a previous row, pass it from the front to the rear (a figure eight stitch, Fig. 20c); continue wrapping the core as before. (2) The number of times the core is wrapped between the stitches joining the rows can be varied from one to several; the fewer times wrapped, the tighter will be the weaving. (3) Make a lazy squaw stitch. Repeat the stitch through the same opening. Pass the strand around this stitch once or twice before wrapping the core again. This produces a more open weaving. (4) Designs can be produced by using different colors.

Reed. In working with reed or willow, for which a sharp knife is the only necessary equipment, one must remember to soak the reed for ten minutes before weaving. In making a basket, bowl, tray, or the like with a woven base, cut spokes long enough to form the sides, cross the bottom, and turn under at the top. Cross half the spokes over the other half at their center. Using a thinner reed, weave over the top spokes, and under the bottom ones for two or three times (Fig. 21). As an uneven number of spokes is necessary, cut off one at this point. Spread the remaining ones in pairs (there will be one single) so that they are spaced equally. Weave over and under alternate spokes. After a few rows of

Figure 21. Center weaving

B A S K E T R Y

A	B	C

Figure 22. Reed weaving

weaving, separate all spokes and continue weaving. Work from the outside of the object. Shape it by turning the spokes in the direction desired. Weave snugly.

A simple variation is to weave over two and under one spoke. Another is to weave with two strands instead of one. A third is to weave with two strands, one in front and one in back of each spoke, crossing the two strands between the spokes, always keeping either the back strand (Fig. 22a) or the front strand (Fig. 22b) on top throughout a row. Another variation is secured if the back strand is kept on top for one round and the front strand for the next round (Fig. 22c).

For a wooden base, cut a flat piece of wood to the desired shape. Drill an uneven number of holes around the edge; the holes should be large enough for the reed to pass through easily. The distance between holes is determined by the size of the reed and the closeness of spokes desired.

Cut the spokes twice the desired height plus the ends for turning under. Push the two ends through two adjoining holes and pull entirely through (Fig. 23). These form the spokes for weaving. Begin weaving at the base.

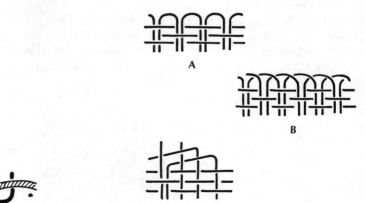

Figure 23. Spokes through wooden base

Figure 24. Finishes

A few of the most common finishes are the following:

1. Push each spoke down along the next spoke, forming a scalloped effect (Fig. 24a).

2. Push each spoke down the second spoke, forming overlapping loops. (Fig. 24b).

3. Pass the spoke to the left in front of the next spoke, behind the second spoke, and down along the third spoke (Fig. 24c).

Many other finishes can be found in the books listed in the bibliography.

Pine needles. Select long dry pine needles. Soak them ten minutes before using.

Take several needles to form a bunch about one-fourth inch in diameter. Wind a piece of raffia around one end for about an inch in length. Join to the end where wrapping started to form a small circle. Make joint secure by several wrappings. For the second row, wrap raffia around needles and take a stitch in the first circle (Fig. 25). Bring the needle through the same spot a second time. Wrap the needles again and take a stitch (twice in the same spot) in the circle. Repeat until the second row is completed. In succeeding rows, take the stitches in the top of the stitches of the preceding row. Stitches should be about half an inch apart. If stitches become too far apart add a stitch between. Add more needles when necessary to keep the bunch even.

The shape is determined by the placing of each row against the preceding row.

BEADWORK

Beads (wooden, tile, or seed) can be woven or strung to make belts, bags, tiles, bracelets, purses, headbands, and the like using only the beads themselves and an extremely thin, wirelike needle, thread, and a loom.

Seed bead weaving. Designs are worked on a cross-section paper, each block representing one bead. If planned with colored pencils or crayons the finished effect can be determined.

Figure 25. Pine needles

BEADWORK

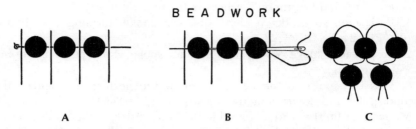

| A | B | C |

Figure 26. (a–b) **Seed beads** (c) **Tile or wood beads**

Warp threads are strung on a bead loom. The space between threads is the width of a bead. The number of threads used therefore determines the width of the finished object.

String a needle with strong thread and tie the thread to an outside warp thread. Following the pattern, string all of the beads of the first row on the thread, bring them up on the underside of the loom, each bead in its proper place (Fig. 26a-b). Pass the needle back through the beads but this time on the top of the warp threads ending at the starting place (Fig. 26b). Pull thread tight. Put the succeeding rows of beads on in the same manner.

Wooden and tile beads. Wooden and tile beads are used to make purses and tiles. Designs are made by using different colored beads. Beads on one row alternate between beads on the rows above and below it. This method of stringing the beads together is shown in Figure 26.

CHIP CARVING

Chip carving is a method of decorating flat wooden objects such as trays and boxes. Bass wood is the best material to use because it is easy to carve.

Designs are composed of triangular areas each representing a chip. They may vary in size and be arranged touching each other to form borders, spots, and so forth.

Each area can be cut out by a sharp knife or razor blade in one piece but until skill is acquired it is better to cut each as follows. Holding the knife in a vertical position, press the point into the center of the triangle and press the blade down toward a corner. Repeat in each corner (Fig. 27a). Holding the knife at an angle slanting toward the center of the triangle, begin at the upper corner. Press the knife point gradually down and deeper, following the cut previously made. Have the knife blade follow along the side of the triangle while pulling it down to the next corner of the triangle (Fig. 27b). This removes a small chip. Repeat on each side of the triangle.

If triangles touch in the design, remove alternate triangles first, then remove the ones skipped.

WOOD WORK

Among the innumerable objects which may be produced by wood working are pins, wall plaques, book ends, mail boxes, toys, coasters, wall brackets, bracelets, buckles, buttons, scrapbook covers, wastepaper baskets, lamp bases, and ornamental boxes. Saws, hammers, nails, and glue are the only equipment necessary.

The first thing to do in making an object is to plan a pattern on paper. Be original in your design; do not use or copy designs made by others.

Trace the design on the wood. Cut it out with a coping saw or power saw. For openings, drill a hole in which to insert the saw blade, fasten it to its holder, and saw out the area.

Objects can be decorated and finished in a great variety of ways: stained, painted, waxed, burned, carved, inlaid, crayonexed, filed, gessoed.

For buttons, designs can be created by filing triangular or round notches on the edges. To crayonex, rub a pressed crayon over the surface. After all surfaces are covered, an interesting effect can be secured by brushing India ink over the crayoned areas.

Gesso is made from whiting and glue. It can be made or purchased. It is a very thick liquid which can be applied with a brush to the surface to be decorated and creates a raised design. Allow the liquid to drop from the brush—do not smooth out. Higher modeling can be secured by repeated layers, allowing each to dry before applying the next coat. If liquid is put on too thick, it shrinks unevenly when drying. To secure

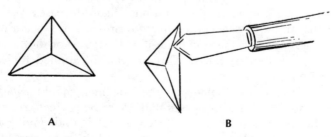

A   B

Figure 27. Chip carving

different colors, tempera paint can be added to the liquid or paint may be applied to the dry surface.

Leather, metal, or cutout cork designs can be glued or nailed to wooden objects.

CARVING

Sculptured objects can be carved out of wood, soap, plaster of Paris, sculpstone, or paraffin with a sharp knife or file.

Draw the top, sides, and end views of the desired figure to fit the block or material. Transfer these views to the block. Chip off the material down to the outline. Round off the corners and cut out desired detail.

It is better to cut off small chips to avoid splitting or breaking through the main figure. Plaster of Paris can be kept covered with a damp cloth to make cutting easier. It can be smoothed down with a file. If the paraffin is melted and green wax crayon added, the resulting material will look somewhat like jade.

Although wood and soap figures may be painted they look better if left in their natural condition.

PLASTICS

Plastic objects can be made from sheets or pieces of plastic or old toothbrush handles using a file, jeweler's saw, and plastic cement.

Procedure. Plastic materials can be shaped by heating and bending or by sawing and cementing. Designs can be applied by engraving with a sharp tool, filing, coloring, or drilling with a power drill. The object should be finished by rubbing with fine emery cloth, smoothed with 000 steel wool, and polished with a soft cloth and pumice or a buffing compound.

LEATHER WORK

Book covers, book ends, purses, billfolds, key cases, picture frames, bookmarks, belts, portfolios, pins, buttons, cigarette cases, pencil cases, knife sheaths, and desk sets can be made from leather. Generally, modeling tools or a nutpick, a sharp knife, a punch, stamps or dies, and a hammer are the only tools required. Designs can be applied to leather by tooling, stamping, or carving.

Tooling. Designs for tooling by the beginner should avoid narrow raised areas, straight lines, or curves that are to be perfect arcs or circles; these require more skill. It is easy to go out of bounds and not easy to correct such errors. Always allow a one-fourth-inch border for lacing. Cut the leather with a sharp knife to the size needed. Wet it with a sponge or under running water. If held under a spigot, let the water hit the under side. When it begins to show through on the right side, it is wet enough. If water appears when the leather is pressed, it is too wet and should be allowed to dry somewhat before using. Trace the design on the right side of the leather with a rather sharp metal tool, a knitting needle, or a nutpick. Be careful to keep the pattern flat (do not thumbtack it on the leather); do not cut through the paper. Remove the paper and go over the lines impressed on the leather. If desired, nothing further need be done.

To get a raised design, use a modeling tool or the back of the nutpick point. Work on a smooth firm surface so that no creases will show through on the leather. Although a hard wood slab or piece of glass is recommended, a pad of paper absorbs extra moisture and raises the design higher. Press with a rotary stroke over the area to be lowered. Outline the design again when finished.

A stippled effect is also interesting. Press the background area with a sharp pointed tool distributing the dots evenly but not mechanically.

If the design is not high enough, turn the leather over and use a rounded tool to press from the wrong side. Be sure to outline the design on the right side again. Be careful to keep the leather in shape. It stretches while wet and can get out of shape easily.

Stamping. Stamps can be made from a linoleum block. In this case cut out the part to be raised and cut to an even depth. Metal dies or stamps can be purchased or made from nails or firm wood blocks or sticks. File edges for variety.

Plan a design first on a blotter with the dies or stamps. Group them together to form larger patterns or to form borders.

Wet the leather and stamp the design where desired. Use hand pressure on the stamps.

Carving. Keep the design simple. Do not use narrow spaces. Use a carving leather such as cowhide. Cut the desired pieces. Soak for five minutes. Roll, grain side out, and place in an airtight container overnight.

Trace the design as for tooling leather. Using a sharp, straightedged knife, cut around the design with a vertical cut, piercing halfway through the leather. With a modeling tool, press the cut edges slightly to remove the sharp, raw-looking edge. Using a background stamp, press down the area around the design using sharp, strong blows on the stamp from a hammer so that the background will be pressed lower than the design. There are other stamps that can be used on the raised areas for variety and detail.

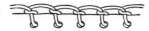

Figure 28. Lacing

Lacing. Holes for lacing are punched about one eighth of an inch in from the edge. A spacing tool may be used to space the holes evenly or they may be gauged by eye. If two edges are to be laced together, it is better to punch one side and mark the holes on the second from the first so that the holes will match perfectly.

The easiest lacing is to bring the lace through two matching holes from the back to the front. Do not let the lace twist or turn. Pull the lace through. Come through the next two matching holes. Pull the lace taut. Proceed around the piece. The ends can be drawn through to the inside and glued down or caught between the two pieces between the edge and the holes.

A more elaborate lacing can be secured by pushing the lace through the hole from the front to the back (Fig. 28). Repeat in the second hole. Do not pull tight. This leaves a loop on top. Bring the lace to the front but push it back through the loop. Now take up the loop by pulling it tight after which pull the end of the lace tight. Keep the lace flat; do not let it turn or twist.

Push the lace through the next hole. Again do not pull tight but leave a loop and proceed as before. Work always from the front of the object.

There are also other lacings possible.

Laces can be joined together by splicing the ends and cementing them together with rubber cement.

Finishing. Leather can be left in its natural color or colored with leather dyes, enamels, acids, or waterproof colored inks. Ink is somewhat easier to handle. Be careful to apply it evenly to avoid spots.

Leather can be cleaned with a lather from saddle soap. It can be darkened in several ways, one being by applying neat's-foot oil. Apply it evenly and not too heavily. Leather can also be finished by applying a liquid wax with a cloth. Rub well.

METAL WORK

Bowls, trays, bracelets, desk sets, bookends, paper knives, pins, wall plaques, pendants, coasters, buttons, screens, boxes, candle holders, masks, candle molds, wastebaskets, pierced lanterns (candle), and pen and pencil holders may be made from various metals.

Tooling. Metal foils, 32 to 36 gauge, are used for tooling. The foils are very soft and easily bent and manipulated; they must be applied to a firm surface after tooling. They can be nailed on wooden surfaces or bent around a cardboard form. Designs similar to those used in leather tooling are suitable.

With an old pair of ordinary scissors cut the metal to the desired size and shape. Lay the design on the metal (on a felt or paper pad) and go over the lines with a pencil, pressing firmly. Remove the paper and the lines can be seen pressed slightly into the metal. Turn the metal over. Use a smoothly rounded tool of metal or wood (a rounded end of a pen-holder, nail, or nutpick), and, using rotary movements, go over the areas that are to be raised while pressing more each time. If the metal is laid on a piece of felt or rubber pad, the work proceeds more easily. Occasionally, turn back to the front and go over the outline again as the background may become stretched too. Although designs may be raised quite high, do not stretch the metal too much or it may split. High areas should be filled with cotton or plaster of Paris to protect them from becoming crushed. Interesting textures can be secured by rubbing over a rough surface such as fine-meshed wire. Use a ruler to form straight lines. Use a linoleum-block design as for leather stamping. In this case, place the metal foil over the cut block and rub the foil into the cut areas.

Hammered. Metal of a harder guage (16 or 20) is used for forming bowls. Metal circles, from three to twelve inches in diameter, may be purchased, cut with tinner's shears, or sawn with a jeweler's saw from a piece of sheet metal.

Objects can be formed over an anvil (working on the outside of the object with the sides down) or on a hard wood slab, a sandbag, or a wooden mold (working on the inside and turning the sides up). A wooden mallet does not stiffen or mark the metal as easily as a metal hammer. A rubber mallet is better for pewter. A space in the center should not be pounded. Some people prefer beginning at this center line; others prefer starting at the edge. In either case, holding the metal at a slight angle, strike a series of overlapping blows following the center line or edge whichever is decided upon. The second row of blows should overlap the first as well as each other. Proceed to the edge, or to the center line depending upon the starting line.

Hold the metal at a sharper angle and repeat the rows again. Continue until the desired depth is attained. Be careful to raise all sides equally. If the form becomes uneven, reverse and gently strike the higher sections. When completed, reverse the form and give the center a few gentle strokes so that it will be raised slightly providing a more even resting place.

If the metal becomes too hard, hold it in a hot flame until it becomes red-hot. Then plunge it in cold water.

When finished the metal should be stiffened by pounding it as above with a metal planishing hammer over a metal plate. The hammer marks give an interesting texture to the surface. Pieces of metal can be fastened together by soldering or riveting. Edges should always be filed to remove any sharp points or edges. Scallops can be formed by bending with a pair of pliers. Ends can be turned in the same way.

Objects can be decorated by sawing, chasing, etching, or stamping.

Sawing. In sawing, background areas are cut out. It is therefore necessary to make sure that all design areas are joined to each other. Drill a hole in the area to be removed. Insert a saw blade and fasten it to the jeweler's saw. Saw out the area. File the edges smooth.

Chasing. A simplified chasing can be secured by outlining the design with liners while being careful to keep the tool in a straight or even line when pounding. (In planning the design, avoid narrow areas.) If the metal is reversed over a sandbag, the areas to be raised can be given a little additional height by hitting them from this side with a tool with a round end. A stippled background also gives a chased effect. Stipple as with leather; for higher designs and more complex work, heat and pitch block are needed.

Etching. Clean the metal with steel wool and avoid touching it. Trace the design using carbon paper. Paint the surfaces that are not to be etched with asphaltum varnish. Be sure to cover the back and the edge of the object. Allow to dry thoroughly.

Prepare a solution of nitric acid in a glass or porcelain container (use hydrochloric acid to etch aluminum). One-third acid to two-thirds water is an average proportion. If it seems weak, more acid can be added; if too strong, add more water. Pour the acid into the water and not the water into the acid as it might splash on the worker. Work at an open window or where air can circulate freely. Slide the prepared metal into the acid. Bubbles will form on the metal. If these are brushed off with a feather, the area eaten will appear smooth; if not removed, the surface will be pebbly. When the acid has eaten to the desired depth, remove the metal from the acid with wooden tools, immerse in cold water, and wipe dry. The asphaltum is removed with a cloth dipped in turpentine.

Stamping. Designs can be stamped on metal in the same way as on leather. Clearer designs are secured if the open spaces on the dies are not too tiny or narrow.

Finishing. All edges should be filed smooth. Surfaces should be cleaned with fine steel wool. After the cleaning, handle with tools or a cloth. Copper can be colored beautifully by heating; the color changes constantly as the heat increases. When a pleasing color is secured, remove immediately from the heat. An antique finish can be secured by covering the object with a liver of sulphur (potassium sulphide) solution. Rub with a clean cloth or steel wool, removing the solution from some areas but allowing it to remain in crevices.

Lacquer the cleaned article. Brush a thin coat of lacquer on quickly. Do not go over a wet stroke or the mark will show. Lacquer can be removed with lacquer remover.

PAPIER-MÂCHÉ

Papier-mâché, made from old newspapers and commercial paste (or one made of flour and water), can be used to make masks, marionette heads, bowls, trays, relief maps, and so forth. There are two procedures in making papier-mâché objects. One reduces the paper to a pulp; the other uses torn strips.

Pulp method. Tear (do not cut) newspaper, paper towels, or tissues into small pieces about one-fourth inch in size. Cover these with water (hot water hastens the process) and allow to soak for a day or so. Knead the paper thoroughly until mushy. Remove surplus water since just enough is needed for the mass to hold together. Add flour and knead again. Grease the object to be used as a mold so that the pulp will not stick to it, or spread cheesecloth over it by pressing it into the crevices (for masks on a clay base). Press a ball of the pulp over the surface, smoothing it out to an even depth. Add more pulp as needed, smoothing edges together securely. Allow to stand until dry. Remove thick pieces from the mold as soon as they are dry enough to handle so that drying will be more even. Otherwise, mold may form. If it does, wipe it off.

Torn strips. Prepare the mold as for pulp. Tear (do not cut) the paper into strips or small pieces. Dip the strip into a flour paste (cold or cooked). Apply it to the surface of the mold fitting it into crevices. For larger surfaces and objects, larger or longer strips can be used. For smaller objects or parts, smaller strips or pieces should be torn. After the form has been completely covered—with the strips or pieces overlapping—add a second layer. In order to be sure only one layer at a time is being applied, printed news sections can be alternated with colored comic sections. Do not add too many layers at a time. Allow to dry thoroughly and remove from the mold. More layers can then be added if desired.

If an unusually large form is to be made, it can be built over a chicken-wire frame, a mass of crushed paper, or a rolled paper or wooden frame.

Children can build papier-mâché animals over a wooden frame with a resulting figure strong enough to carry them.

Masks can be made over a silk stocking pulled over another person's head. Used gummed paper tape for the first layer. When this layer is complete cut the stocking up the back of the head, inserting the left hand between the stocking and hair so that no hair will be cut. Pull off the mask with a swift movement. Place crushed paper inside the mask and allow it to dry thoroughly before proceeding with more layers of paper. Wads of paper or cloth can be secured to the mask with paper strips in order to build up features, especially if grotesque ones are desired.

When enough layers have been added, sandpaper the form. Sandpapering can be done between layers for neater work. Paint the object with tempera paints and shellac or varnish. Remember that these finishes will change the colors.

Masks can be finished with such items as yarns, rope, and fur used for hair.

MARIONETTES

A head can be made of clay, papier-mâché, or even a dried apple. A cardboard tube or wooden dowel may be used for the neck.

A hand marionette requires only the hollow head and a dress with two sleeves fastened to it. The figure is manipulated by the index finger in the head, and the thumb and middle finger in the sleeves.

A string marionette can be quite simple or very complex. A simple one requires a body made of sticks or stuffed cloth with free-moving joints tied together with strings or leather thongs, or with cloth bodies stitched at the joints. To these attach the head, hands, and feet. After dressing, fasten strings to the head, hands, and knees. For convenience in manipulation, fasten the strings to sticks, the hand strings on one stick and the knee strings on another. With a little practice, the figures can be moved quite realistically. For more complicated movements, attach strings to the feet, elbows, and other joints.

FINGER PAINTING

Finger painting may be used to decorate book covers or linings, wrapping and other decorative papers, box tops, wooden bowls, bookends, and so forth. On wooden surfaces, shellac or varnish, applied quickly so as not to disturb the paint, will add permanency to the project.

Dip paper in water and lay it on a flat surface (a desk top, drawing board, or even the floor), smoothing out all wrinkles. Place a good teaspoonful of finger paint on the wet surface. Spread it over the surface using the hands. Designs are secured by wiping off the color down to the white paper if desired, by using the fingers, fingernails, palm, fist, or even the side of the arm. Cardboard strips with nicks cut on the side, combs, lids, and the like can also be used. Designs can also be made by patting with the finger tips, palms, and so forth.

Other colors can be introduced by wiping out areas of the first color and adding the new in its place.

As the paper curls when it dries, thumbtack it to a smooth surface for drying.

Although almost any paper may be used, the more absorbent papers do not permit much manipulation or experimentation. A cheaper substitute for finger paint can be made by adding powdered paint or tempera to boiled starch (after cooling). This can be made softer by adding soap flakes. This substitute, like substitute papers, restricts manipulation and experimentation because it dries more quickly.

CRAYONEX

Household articles, clothing, wooden objects such as boxes or screens, and the like can be decorated with wax crayon designs.

Cloth. Draw a design and transfer it to the material. Stretch and fasten the material to a drawing board. Fill in the areas with wax crayons, stroking in one direction and pressing firmly. Brush off any excess wax that comes off on the material.

Place a blotter on a board; put the waxed cloth, face down, on the blotter. Press with a hot iron. The blotter absorbs the melting wax. If blotters are not available, place the cloth between two sheets of clean paper to press.

Wood. Rub the wax crayon into desired areas. Brush off the excess. Wiping the object with a cloth dipped in turpentine gives it a nice finish. Also, brushing over the colored design with India ink gives it an interesting effect as the wax resists the ink which spreads into tiny spaces between the strokes.

BOOKBINDING

Simple sewed booklet of a few pages. Cut interior papers double size so that, when folded down the center, four pages result. Use a heavier paper for the cover. Cut it from one quarter to a half inch larger on

BOOKBINDING

Figure 29. Simple sewing

each side than the page papers so that it will project beyond these and will protect their edges. Fold all papers in the center.

Open all papers. Place them on top of each other as they will appear in the finished book with the cover projecting evenly on all sides and the edges of the pages meeting precisely.

Thread a needle with thread or cord. Pierce the pages and cover together on the fold at the center, also approximately halfway between the center and the edges. To sew together (Fig. 29), begin at the center hole on the outside and draw the thread to the inside allowing enough thread to remain on the outside for tying. Pass the thread through one of the other holes to the outside and bring it back to the inside through the third hole. Pass it through the center hole to the outside again taking care that the thread on the outside will come between the two ends. Tie the ends together securely and cut off any surplus thread. A bow makes a nicer finish than just a knot.

BLUEPRINTING

Blueprint paper must be kept wrapped and in a dark place when not in use. One must work quickly in a semidark room.

Cut paper to the desired size and lay on a board, colored side up. Place plants[1] or other objects on the paper in an interesting arrangement. Place the sheet of glass on top. Expose to the sunlight from one and a half to two minutes. Remove glass and plants and immerse in water until the blue color and white areas appear. Dry between blotters.

CANDLE MAKING

Dipped candles. Heat pieces of old candles until they are liquid in form. Cut a piece of cord to the desired length of candle plus six inches or so for handling. Tie this piece of cord to the center of a stick for convenience in drying. Dip the string into the wax mixture which

[1]For printing purposes, use plants of fine lines and not large areas.

should be deeper than the desired candle length. Remove and allow to cool. Dip again and cool. Continue until the candle reaches the desired thickness. To cool, the stick can be laid over two supports with the candle suspended between them.

Molded candles. Any metal mold, including original ones made from tin cans, can be used. Fasten the cord to a small piece of metal to weight it while pouring. Place it in the mold with the weight at the bottom of the mold. Hold the string upright by the left hand. Carefully pour a little of the melted mixture in the mold. Allow it to cool in order to keep the cord in place. Holding the cord upright again with the left hand (or tied over the center of a stick placed across the center of the mold), fill the mold by carefully pouring the mixture. When cool, remove from the mold by dipping the mold into very warm water. The heat will melt the wax next to the mold and the candle can then be turned out easily.

PAPER CRAFT—BEADS

Cylindrical beads. Cut strips of fairly heavy paper, such as wallpaper, art paper, or wrapping paper, as long and as wide as desired. The width of the bead is determined by the width of the paper strips; the thickness by the weight of the paper and length of the strips. Cover one side or back with paste. Beginning at one end of the strip of paper, wind it over a thin dowel or wire keeping the edges even and the sides smooth. Remove it from the wire to dry.

Round beads. Cut the strip into the desired width of bead at one end and taper it to a point at the center of the other end. Begin at the wide end to roll on the dowel.

Decoration. These beads may be painted with tempera paint and varnished. If so desired, simple designs of dots or bands, wavy or straight, may be applied before varnishing. The beads may be strung together or with other beads.

FELT

For figures such as toys, hollow forms are made by putting pieces of felt, either new or salvaged from old hats, together or by rolling the felt into tubular shapes and sewing or pasting. Except for very small figures, a stuffing of old cloth can be added for strength.

Forms such as flowers may be made by cutting the pieces and sewing them together. Decorations, either raised or flat, may be made in a similar way but sewed to a background such as a belt or purse. Flat pieces may be appliquéd. Embroidery can be applied to such pieces for additional decorative value.

YARN FIGURES

Animal or doll figures can easily be made of yarn and thread. Cut pieces of cardboard of varying lengths to the proportion of heads, arms, legs, body, and the like; if desired, head and body, both arms, or both legs may be measured together. Wrap the yarn around the length of the cardboard. Slip a piece of yarn under each end and tie the strands of yarn together securely before removing from the cardboard. The tied ends are kept at the ends of the sections. With another piece of yarn, tie around the neck, waist, elbow, etc. Tie arms and legs in their proper positions. Mark the eyes by sewing dark knots or beads in the proper places.

A young lady doll without legs can be made by cutting yarn at the bottom of the "body" so that yarn will spread out to form a skirt. A Dutch-trousered man can be made by tying at the waist while dividing the rest of the body into two sections for trousers and tying just above the ends to form the ends of the trousers and short feet.

Fluffy animal bodies can be made by wrapping yarn around the length of a cardboard strip made as long and as wide as the desired body. Hold a wire down the center and sew the wire to the wool catching all threads

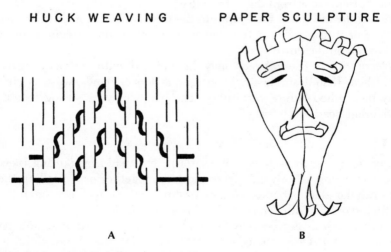

HUCK WEAVING   PAPER SCULPTURE

A   B

Figure 30. (a) **Huck weaving** (b) **Paper sculpture**

(on both sides) securely. Cut along the edges of the cardboard. The body fluffs out. Other parts of the body can be made in the same way and then fastened together.

NEEDLEWORK—HUCK WEAVING

Purses, towels, and bags may be made of huck towels decorated with colored yarns.

Use the wrong side of the towel. Sewing is done from right to left, running the yarn through the two prominent vertical threads for a stitch. Bands of varying colors may be made by sewing across the towel in straight rows. Designs may be created by catching threads on varying rows (Fig. 30a) to suit the worker and by varying the color in succeeding rows. (The threads will lie much closer together than the illustration indicates.)

There are many sewing and embroidery stitches that can be found in any needlework book and are therefore not repeated here.

PAPER SCULPTURE

Figures, masks, maps, Christmas-tree decorations, and the like can be sculpted from paper. Paper sculpture secures a three-dimensional effect by folding back pieces or sections, by cutting strips and curling over a pencil or scissor edge, and by bending and pasting parts. Objects may be freestanding or pasted to a background.

For instance, a mask (Fig. 30b) might be made from a triangular piece of paper folded down the center. The upper edge can be cut into strips and curled forward to represent hair. Strips treated in the same way can be pasted on the chin for a beard and openings cut for eyes. A strip of paper can be pasted above the eye (for an eyebrow) projecting from the surface in the center and curled on the end. Another triangular piece folded down the center can be pasted projecting out from the first fold for a nose. Other strips like the eyebrows are to be added for a mustache. A little practice and experimentation will result in many other forms and ideas. Yarns or other material may be added also if desired.

PYROGRAPHY

Wooden objects such as plaques, bookends, and boxes can be decorated with a woodburning pencil.

The pencil is allowed to get hot. Press the point along a line, drawing the blade over the wood. The blade burns the wood to a brown color. Be careful not to burn the wood too deeply. The design may be outlined only. If a stippled background is desired, the point can be touched to the surface at more or less equal intervals. A little practice will develop skill.

Pyrography can be applied to leather surfaces as well as wood.

PAPER AND CARDBOARD CONSTRUCTION

Figures, buildings, Christmas-tree decorations, etc. can be made of heavy paper or cardboard.

Cut pieces of cardboard or paper to the sizes desired. Where two pieces are to meet (as at a corner), allow an extra half inch on one piece and paste this to the inside of the other piece. Cellophane paper can be used for windows.

OILED PAPER

Various colored papers as well as colored Easter eggs can be made from oiled paper.

Draw a pan of water. Place a few drops of oil paint on the surface of the water. Stir with a stick. If more than one color is used, avoid stirring too much or the colors will combine and lose their identity.

The paper may be colored on one side or both. If only on one side, drop the paper on it when the stirred color makes an interesting pattern. Remove it immediately and lay it aside to dry.

Eggs should be held with a pair of tongs while dipping. There may be some difficulty in keeping them upright while drying.

SUPPLY SOURCES

American Handicrafts Co., Inc.
45–49 S. Harrison St.
East Orange, N.J.

American Reedcraft Corporation
130–132 Beekman St.
New York, N.Y.

Arts & Crafts Supply Co.
108–109 W. Mulberry St.
Baltimore 1, Md.

Fellowcrafters
64 Stanhope St.
Boston, Mass.

J. L. Hammett Co.
264 Main St.
Cambridge, Mass.

Horton Handicraft Co.
618 Capitol Ave.
Hartford, Conn.

Jackson Studio
104 Cedar St.
Oostburg, Wisconsin

Leisure Crafts
907 S. Hill St.
Los Angeles, Calif.

Magnus Brush and Craft Materials
108 Franklin St.
New York 13, N.Y.

Western Crafts and Hobby Supply Co.
213–215 Third St.
Davenport, Iowa

CRAFT–AGE CHART

	Pre-school	Primary grades	Inter-mediate grades	High school	Adult
Clay modeling	x	x	x	x	x
Stenciling		x	x	x	x
Silk-screen stenciling		x	x	x	x
Linoleum block printing			x	x	x
Stick printing	x	x	x	x	x
Weaving	x	x	x	x	x
Braiding		x	x	x	x
Square knotting		x	x	x	x
Basketry					
Raffia		x	x	x	x
Reed			x	x	x
Pine needles			x	x	x
Beadwork weaving			x	x	x
Chip carving			x	x	x
Woodwork	x	x	x	x	x
Carving			x	x	x
Plastics		x	x	x	x
Leather work		x	x	x	x
Metal work			x	x	x
Papier-mâché	x	x	x	x	x
Marionettes	x	x	x	x	x
Finger paint	x	x	x	x	x
Oiled paper	x	x	x	x	x
Crayonex	x	x	x	x	x
Bookbinding—simple sewed booklet		x	x	x	x
Blueprinting		x	x	x	x
Candle making					
Dipped	x	x	x	x	x
Molded			x	x	x
Paper craft—beads		x	x	x	x
Felt			x	x	x
Yarn figures			x	x	x
Needlework		x	x	x	x
Huck weaving			x	x	x
Paper and cardboard construction		x	x	x	x
Paper sculpture			x	x	x
Pyrography			x	x	x

MATERIALS AND CRAFTS

Beads—beadwork, paper craft
Blueprint paper—blueprinting
Candle ends—candle making
Cardboard—paper and cardboard construction
Clay—clay modeling
Cloth—stenciling, block printing, weaving, braiding, basketry, marionettes, crayonex
Colored ink—leather work
Cords—weaving, braiding, square knotting, candle making
Cork—woodwork
Corn leaves—basketry
Crayons—stenciling, woodwork, carving, crayonex
Crepe paper—braiding
Felt—felt
Finger paint—finger painting
Gesso—woodwork
Gimp—braiding
Grasses—basketry
Huck towels—needlework, huck weaving
Leather—braiding, woodwork, leather work
Linoleum—block printing
Metal—woodwork, metal work
Oil Paint—block printing, woodwork, oiled paper
Paper—stenciling, block printing, papier-mâché, marionettes, finger painting, oiled paper, bookbinding, paper craft, paper and cardboard construction, paper sculpture
Paraffin—carving
Pine needles—basketry
Plaster of Paris—clay modeling, carving
Plastics—plastics
Popsicle sticks—weaving
Poster paint—stenciling, woodwork, papier-mâché, finger painting, paper craft, block printing
Potato—block printing
Printer's ink—block printing
Raffia—basketry
Reed—basketry
Rush—basketry
Sculpstone—carving
Showcard paint—see poster paint
Soap—carving

Soap eraser—block printing
Sticks—block printing, marionettes, weaving
Stockings—weaving, braiding, papier-mâché masks, marionettes
Tempera paint—see poster paint
Textile paint—stenciling
Tin cans—metal work, woodwork, candle making
Toothbrush handles—plastics
Wood—chip carving, woodwork, carving, pyrography
Yarns—weaving, braiding, papier-mâché

SUGGESTED READINGS

Amon, Martha, and Ruth Rawson. *Handicrafts Simplified.* Bloomington, Ill.: McKnight & McKnight Pub. Co., 1961.

Benson, Kenneth. *Creative Crafts for Children.* Englewood Cliffs, N.J.: Prentice-Hall, Inc., 1958.

Erdt, Margaret. *Teaching Art in the Elementary School.* New York: Holt, Rinehart & Winston, Inc., 1962.

Griswold, Lester E. *Handicraft; Simplified Procedures and Projects.* Englewood Cliffs, N.J.: Prentice-Hall, Inc., 1952. Basketry, bookbinding, clay, weaving, block printing, leatherwork, metalwork, plastics.

Hall, E. T., F. P. Arnold, and B. E. Allen. *Let's Be Creative.* New York: The Girls' Friendly Society. Leather, felt, square knotting, braiding, woodwork, plastics, weaving, metal, chip carving.

McNeice, William, and Kenneth Benson. *Crafts for the Retarded.* Bloomington, Ill.: McKnight, 1964.

Mosely, Spencer, Pauline Johnson, and Hazel Koenig. *Crafts Design.* Belmont, California: Wadsworth Publishing Co., Inc., 1962.

Squires, John. *Fun Crafts for Children.* Englewood Cliffs, N.J.: Prentice-Hall, Inc., 1964.

Voss, Gunther. *Reinhold Craft and Hobby Book.* New York: Reinhold Publishing Corp., 1963.

Chapter 15

HOBBIES

Time is but the stream I go a-fishing in.—HENRY DAVID THOREAU

With our expanding leisure, increasing percentages of income uncommitted, and with an upgrading of the average number of years in school attendance, it is inevitable that hobby pursuits would assume a more prominent role in our lives.

Hobbies are favorite interests which are pursued during one's leisure moments for the satisfactions that accrue from taking part. Financial gain is of no consideration although people have been known to profit from hobby pursuits. They are not a stagnating repetition of the same but rather an ever-growing and widening sphere. Their rate of expansion depends on the individual's level of attainment and curiosity. They do not have to be very time consuming and costly. On the other hand, they can be pursued with all the zest and financial outpourings at one's command. The leader should guide the hobby enthusiast so that he will become the master and not the victim of his hobby.

It is difficult to account for the selections of hobbies. The selection of a hobby that provides a change or diversion from an individual's vocational life is easily explained. By the same token, we are intrigued by the sailor who spends part of his shore leave rowing in Central Park and by the house painter who paints landscapes and portraits during his leisure. Perhaps there is no accounting for tastes. Of real importance, however, is that we recognize that all of us possess tastes and drives that crave expression. What better outlet is there than a hobby?

ALL-FAMILY HOBBIES

Hobbies are too often thought of as activities for shut-ins or for individuals in the privacy of their attics. This concept is not necessarily true of all hobbyists. In fact, there are many possibilities very ripe for family participation. Hobbies that embody gardening, camping, picnicking,

196

sailing, collecting, construction, instrumental and vocal music, raising pets, hiking, photography, dramatics, nature lore, and other similar activities are adaptable for family participation.

An opportunity for the family to take part and enjoy activities as a unit will help to solidify it as a group. Our sociologists are concerned, with justification, over the dissolution of the American family. In many instances the home is but a place for feeding and sleeping. The need for added living, enjoyment, and participation in mutually agreeable activities is a real and attainable one. Travel lends itself admirably in this regard and is becoming increasingly popular. This is attested by the vast increase in motor, rail, plane, and ship travel. Camping, picnicking, and sailing are other activities that lend themselves to all-family participation.

RECREATIONAL PHOTOGRAPHY

Certainly one of the most popular of all hobbies is that of photography. One has but to look around to observe how tremendous has been the growth of this hobby. It is deserving of special mention in this chapter since it dovetails admirably with other interests. A few that come to mind are travel, camping, sailing, picnicking, mountaineering, and hunting. In fact, it lends itself so well to practically all other hobbies that it would border on the impossible to seek out an interest with which it clashes.

The fact that a greater variety of film speeds is procurable makes photography suitable for varying degrees of light. Also, the availability of a single film suitable for reproduction into either a colored picture, a colored transparency, or a black and white picture opens up new vistas in recreational photography. In addition, the simplification of camera equipment has kept pace with compact exposure meters that either attach to the camera or come built-in, thereby yielding simple clues for more accurate photography.

The do-it-yourself craze has been a part of photography for quite some time. However, a simplification of developing has been achieved through ready-mixed chemicals, lights, timers, enlargers, developing tanks, and the like. This phase of photography is captivating to young and old of both sexes, and it is all-encompassing whether on the active picture-taking and developing end or on the passive or viewing end. The challenge to further one's skill plus the pleasures resulting from viewing the photographs shortly after taking them with the "bonus" of viewing prized pictures for years to come make photography a hobby for one and all to enjoy.

CATEGORIES

There are countless hobbies, all of which can be categorized conveniently into collecting, learning, constructing, creating, and performing. The hobbyist will be interested quite often in more than one hobby. Even he who is concerned with a single hobby may find himself concerned with more than one category. For example, his interest in art may not only take the form of creating through painting, but may also entail constructing the easel, studying the mixing of colors, collecting postal-card-size reproductions of artistic works, and studying the styles of eminent artists by visiting museums, exhibits, and doing research on the subject. What follows is but suggestive of the categories or levels of hobby endeavor with appropriate examples:

HOBBIES CLASSIFIED

Collecting	*Learning*	*Constructing*	*Creating*	*Performing*
Leaves	Chemistry	Boat Building	Sculpture	Skeet
Butterflies	Fortune Telling	Model Building:	Drawing	Walking
Insects	Poetry	Aeroplane	Designing	Shooting
Coins	Classical Books	Aeroplanes	Pottery	Camping
Stamps	Music	Trains	Creative Writing	Band
Match Covers	Philosophy	Yachts	Papier-Mâché	Folk dancing
Bottles	Botany	Leather Tooling	Play Writing	Canoeing
Antiques	History	Soap Sculpture	Handicrafts	Sailing
Autographs	Interior	Clay Modeling	Block Printing	Fishing
Shells	Decorating	Radio Set	Model Furniture	Swimming
Dolls	Homemaking	Television Set	Dress Designing	Bowling
Buttons	Geology	Marionettes	Sewing	Archery
	Ornithology	Puppets		Dramatics
				Cooking

HOBBY QUESTIONNAIRE

In an effort to determine the interests and wishes of a group pertaining to hobbies, a questionnaire may be used. The following portion of a survey questionnaire was circulated throughout the public and parochial schools of Lock Haven, Pennsylvania.[1]

[1]Lock Haven Recreation Interest Survey conducted during 1947–1948 by the students of the State Teachers College, Lock Haven, Pennsylvania, under the author's direction.

Hobbies	Check the hobbies you take part in	Check your favorite hobby	Check hobbies you have never tried but would like to try
1. Stamp collection			
2. Collecting coins			
3. Collecting marbles			
4. Collecting flowers			
5. Collecting insects			
6. Collecting dolls			
7. Name any other collection you would be interested in			
8. Building models of			
a. Airplanes			
b. Boats			
c. Houses			
d. Furniture			
e. Trains			
f. Name any other			
9. Reading for pleasure			
10. Dramatics			
11. Arts and crafts			
a. Soap modeling			
b. Clay modeling			
c. Wood work			
12. Painting			
a. Oil			
b. Pastels			
c. Charcoal			
d. Finger painting			
13. Debating			
14. Marionettes			
15. Puppets			
16. Checkers			
17. Chess			
18. Photography			
19. Pets			

20. If there are any other hobbies not listed above but that you would like to take part in, please state here:

SUGGESTED READINGS

Baird, Forrest J. *Music Skills for Recreation Leaders.* Dubuque, Iowa: William C. Brown Company, Publishers, 1963.

Freeberg, William H., and Loren E. Taylor. *Programs in Outdoor Education.* Minneapolis: Burgess Publishing Co., 1963.

Haugen, Arnold O., and Harlan G. Metcalf. *Field Archery and Bow-hunting.* New York: The Ronald Press Company, 1963.

Hicks, Clifford B., and Richard Potts. *The World Above.* New York: Holt, Rinehart & Winston, Inc., 1965.

Kraus, Richard. *Recreation Today: Program Planning and Leadership.* New York: Appleton-Century-Crofts, 1966.

Wyler, Rose, and Eva-Lee Baird. *Science Teasers.* New York: Harper & Row, Publishers, 1965.

Chapter 16

DRAMATICS IN RECREATION*

The dearth of creative opportunities in our daily lives has been expounded by commentators of our time. Dramatics is one of the strong forces in recreation that offers a multiplicity of opportunities in offering meaningful situations that whet our thirst for creativity. Moreover, it helps to round out the need for cultural experiences in recreational programming.

The enthusiasm of the child for creative self-expression places in the hands of the recreation leader a strong tool for teaching new experiences in addition to providing fun and opportunities for worthwhile accomplishment. This desire is not limited to the child. The adolescent and the adult are increasingly finding enjoyment in dramatic activities in a recreational setting. To meet these and related needs, the recreation leader will encounter diversified activities in the field of dramatics. For convenience, the range of experiences may be extended from those appealing to primary-age children to that of adult participation. The leader might include creative play, pantomime, choric speaking, informal reading of plays, play festivals, reading festivals, puppetry, and formal play production. Debates, discussion groups, and lectures are found in the field of public speaking.

This chapter will concern itself primarily with the general techniques which might be helpful in handling creative and formal dramatics, puppetry, and choric reading. The media of debates, discussions, and lectures will be dealt with lightly.

CREATIVE PLAY

Creative play is a form of make-believe which centers around some experience with which the child is familiar. He pretends to be someone and to do things which are purely imaginary. The type of dramatic play is often suggested by surroundings, toys, people the child knows,

*This chapter was prepared by Dorothy W. Lynds.

and situations which arise out of subsequent activities. The recreation leader will therefore supply toys and materials which will stimulate creative play. A store, a house, or a train may be built from boxes or blocks. Furnishings for the home and train or stock for the store may be a stimulus to greater activity. One idea is the outgrowth of another until the children have set up a series of situations which will be recognized in creative play.

Short, simple stories read to children will motivate them to expression. This in turn may result in the dramatization of a story with scenery, costumes, and properties manufactured by the actors. The leader should encourage organization of scenes and dialogue by the children, guiding and suggesting, encouraging and praising, but not dominating. The scenes will be short and the dialogue sketchy with the probability that it will be changed every time it is played.

Children at this level tend to play in small groups. As they grow older the group is enlarged and the plays become more complex. From the mere suggestion of an idea, a simple plot with a definite scene and dialogue may develop.

DIRECTING OLDER GROUPS

Older children are interested in dramatizing familiar stories. Group discussion is suggested in order to arrive at an agreement on a clear picture of the story, its characters, and scenes. In presenting dramatizations the following steps are suggested:

1. Read the story to children or ask children to read parts.
2. Encourage children to discuss plot and characterizations.
3. Decide on important scenes.
4. Divide and group events in order to make a continuous and interesting series.
5. Plan properties and costumes.

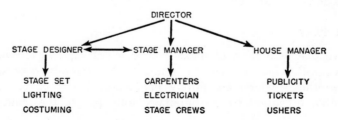

Figure 31. Organizational chart for children's productions

6. Have preliminary tryouts with children judging.
7. Arrange dialogue (probable revision later).
8. Rehearse and evaluate performance; making any changes necessary.

Criticism should come largely from the children themselves, while the director stands ready with advice when called upon. The leader may use pantomime with a reader supplying the background material. The creative play project may take the form of charades and guessing games of various kinds.

DIRECTING OLDER GROUPS

Adults in the recreational program are most interested in formal dramatics. They enjoy the challenge of interpreting a play already written. Here the leader will find that most of the planning will fall on his shoulders. "What about the actual performance?" "What type of play shall we produce?" "How is the cast chosen?" These and similar questions must be resolved with as much problem-solving relegated to the group as is expedient.

Selecting the play. The choice of a play depends on several factors:

1. The budget for production.
2. The type of audience for whom the play is to be given.
3. The talents of those who will make up the cast and production staff.
4. The talent of the director.

The question of the choice of a script may be decided by the group, which can be called upon to read plays and submit recommendations; a selected reading committee serving with the director may be employed.

The type of play to be produced has to depend largely on whether or not there is an adequate budget, especially if a royalty is quoted; this must be paid in advance of production. Nevertheless, there are good plays for which no royalty is paid. Then again, some publishers have budget plays and special scales of royalty. It would be wise for the director to have such a list. The director should also consider the following:

1. The elaborateness of the set.
2. The number of sets or scenes required.
3. The possibility of having to rent costumes.
4. The use of expensive lighting equipment.
5. The ability of the staff to handle intricate sets (hired stagehands may be needed.)

It is suggested that a tentative budget be made out before production begins. Every attempt should be made to fit probable expenses into the amount available.

The timeliness of the story should be kept in mind. Plays that have as their theme great human problems rarely become dated; but plays based on a specific national crisis such as war or political problems often lose their effectiveness within a few months or years. The audience is another factor in choosing a play. Age, interests, opportunities for seeing dramatic productions, financial status, and educations should determine the type of play you present for their enjoyment. A play must be chosen which can be set, lighted, and costumed within the capabilities and talents of the staff. Many interesting programs may be arranged using the one-act play or scenes from longer scripts.

Selecting the cast. The process of casting or choosing the players may depend on the group who will do the producing. Casting by type seems to be the safest method when public performance is involved. However, the recreation leader may find educational value in antitype casting, which is based on the theory that a person of reverse type should be given the part which takes him out of himself and provides experience in assuming the characteristics of another personality. Another method is by the standard of general ability and previous experience. The best method would be a combination of all those mentioned. Tryouts, readings, and interviews are used as a basis of selection. Again, this weeding out may be done by a group, a selected committee, and/or the director. The director should, however, have the final word.

The staff. The recreation leader, having assumed the duties of a dramatic director, faces the problem of organizing a staff, rehearsing the play and serving as a coordinator of all departments involved. He has undertaken the responsibility of the production. To aid him, he may appoint a staff of the stagehands, a wardrobe manager, lighting technician, make-up artist, scene designer, property man, and house manager, delegating to each specific duties. As his chief assistant, he will have a stage manager, who is responsible for scenery, properties, lighting, costumes, and make-up. The committees then work together for a unified and smooth-running production. Children and young people can handle these problems surprisingly well, although they need more supervision than adults. The director may appoint any additional assistants he may need.

Interpreting the script. How much the director interprets the script and his relationship with his actors is a matter of personal philosophy on the part of the director. Some schools of thought tend to believe that the director should train the actors in interpretation as he himself sees the part; others contend that the actors should be given a free hand in interpretation. Since a learning situation is desirable, the director should guide, encourage, and develop individual talent by allowing self-expression of each personality, with the fun in the doing of prime importance. The adult amateur may show surprising ingenuity and skill in interpretation if allowed to follow his own ideas. At no time should the director lose sight of the fact that all characterizations must fit together, blend, and supplement one another. The director should not insist on imposing his own ideas, but should rather give aid and direction where needed. Since he sees the entire production, he must regulate the mechanism of that production in order to produce an acceptable performance.

The rehearsals. In order to attain such a goal, a thorough plan for rehearsing is essential. It is suggested that, in general, the following steps of development be followed:

1. A complete knowledge of all aspects of the script by the director.
2. A thorough understanding of the plot and incidents in the story by the cast and production staff.
3. A decision as to the interpretation of point of view of the writer.
4. An understanding of the mood, theme, color and line, tempo and atmosphere of the plot.
5. An understanding of the structure of the play: the incentive incident, climax, falling action, and resolution of the plot.
6. A tentative interpretation of characters and action.

How this may be accomplished depends on the director. He may use any method which seems to answer his purpose. He may read the play to the cast; he may pass out scripts and ask the cast to study the play individually; or he may have a group reading in which the first interpretation comes from the actor. Parts may be changed around so as to allow some actors to read a variety of parts.

The director plans the rehearsal hours carefully to ensure maximum amount of work in the time allotted. In the early phase of the rehearsal, it is wise to block movement, that is, to organize and explain the movements and gestures necessary to supplement the plot of the play. For example, an actor may cross the stage to a chair, sit down, and pick up a letter in order to make the story clear to the observer. Each actor makes notes of any direction given. The stage manager also includes all notes in his prompt script. In this planning the director is governed by the fact that he is going to present a series of pictures, each independent, yet flowing naturally from one into another. It is suggested that the recreation leader read standard texts on play production before any attempt is made on a large scale.

The next phase of rehearsing is most important. This calls for the building up of characterizations. The actor begins to study his role, which involves not only memorization of lines, but vocalization, gesture, and business. The actor must speak clearly enough to be easily heard and understood by all those in the audience. The lines must be read with intelligent understanding in keeping with the character portrayed. Business is any behavior that is used to interpret the character. An old man may limp, a nervous girl may pick up and drop articles on stage, or a near-sighted person may adopt a peculiar posture. Gesture is, generally speaking, any movement of a part or the whole of the body to express an idea or an emotion.

As the rehearsal progresses, the director begins to see the finished product. He uses the last few rehearsals to polish the lines and actions and checks the tempo to prevent the play from dragging. He will watch again for clarity of the story, the building up of the climax, and the development of incidents leading to the conclusion. He will recheck movement and business to be sure they are important to the plot and that they flow smoothly together to give an illusion of reality.

The dress rehearsal. The dress rehearsal should be as complete and as much like the first performance as possible. All stage sets, costumes, properties, and make-up for character parts should be as they will appear before an actual audience. A sample audience of a few friends for the dress rehearsal would serve as sound practice for amateur players.

The organization backstage is quite as important as that on the other side of the curtain. The director should rehearse the stage manager and the stage crew in the job of changing sets or moving stage properties. The actors should know their stage positions for entrances and their off-stage waits. The director should arrange for curtain calls and place the actors in a pleasing group, not allowing a stilted, stiff line to greet an appreciative audience.

Situating the director. Whether the director will be on the stage during the actual performance or in the audience is a matter for the director to decide. With young amateur players, it is perhaps better for him to be backstage within call to deal with any emergency situation. If he plans to do this, he should view the final rehearsal from the house

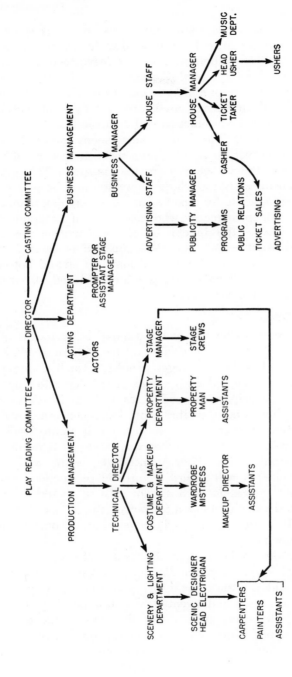

Figure 32. Organizational chart for adult productions

so that he may make suggestions and check any weak spots in the performance or the staging. If he feels that his cast is competent and would profit from the experience, he may leave them to handle the entire performance. It is probably better that no last-minute changes be made in staging or interpretation unless absolutely unavoidable. The director should remain calm, poised, and quietly confident to help assure the others that the production will be a success.

House management. The house management should be checked by the director. However he should leave the actual work of this department to the committees selected for that purpose. This group usually includes a general manager whose assistants may be a box-office manager, who is responsible for ticket sales, an advertising man, and a press agent, and the house manager who takes care of programs and ushers. It would be wise for the director to ask for a written report of all departmental expenditures and to check the budget carefully to be sure that all bills can be met. The general manager should not consider his job completed until all bills and taxes are paid and all written reports are in the hands of the director.

CHORIC READING

The recreational leader has at his disposal other means of encouraging dramatic expression for learning and fun. Choric reading is popular with older as well as with younger people. In such a corporate experience, a definite social, educative, and artistic contribution is enjoyed by those who participate in reading as well as by those who listen. The speaking choir is not a singing choir, but is concerned with the study and appreciation of poetry through speaking it aloud. It is a balanced collection of voices reading together with unity as a result of thinking and feeling as one person. They, of necessity, learn such techniques of speech and voice as will assure an artistic production. There are no "special-quality" voices in such a choir. There should be no artificial tones. A natural voice developed for power, range, and flexibility is necessary to do full justice to the infinite varieties of content and interpretation in fine poetry.

The verse choir. What is the right number of people in a verse choir? In organizing a verse choir, the director chooses a number not too large for handling and yet large enough to give tonal quality and power to readings. Between ten and twenty-two voices is adequate for two-part arrangements. However, since one of the aims of the choir is to give opportunity for oral expression to as many people as possible, the director should be willing to work with a large group.

After the choir has had experience in reading together, the voices may be divided into two general groups, dark or heavy voices and light voices. If the director wishes, the voices may be divided into three sections—dark or heavy, medium, and light. This division applies to adult rather than to children's voices. The voices may be grouped so that the heavy voices are to the left of the director, light to the right, medium in the center, or any other arrangement which seems best. They may stand in a half circle on levels, in a V-formation, or any way which seems attractive and functional. They should stand in such a manner that they may hear each other easily and see the director, if there is one.

Techniques of group speaking. In the techniques of speaking together, the director, with the group, should decide on some basic rules. The following are suggested:

1. Clean-cut articulation of vowels and consonants.
2. Adequate breath control, with easy, relaxed, but controlled posture.
3. A pleasing natural tone, with range, flexibility, and control.

To read together successfully, the members of the group must come to an understanding of the thought and interpretation of the material. Each individual may have a slightly different concept, but fundamentally the group agrees on meaning, mood, tempo, phrasing, and intonation. A conductor is necessary at the beginning of the choir's career to signal the start, indicate pauses, and emphasis. However the conducting should be unobtrusively done. After considerable training, the choir may become skillful enough to read without a director, or use a member of the group to indicate the starting and pausing in speaking.

Materials available. The material which may be used in choral reading is varied. The group may include Bible passages, sacred themes from other books, old and modern ballads, nonsense verse, modern poetry, Greek or modern choric drama, and children's poetry. It is less effective to use material of personal thought and emotion, since this type cannot be well expressed by a group. Poetry and prose of a universal theme is more suitable. The director should avoid the use of mediocre verse.

There are several methods of arranging material for the choir:

1. The entire group may read together as one unit.
2. A solo part may be used by one voice, with the choir reading the explanatory selections as a background.

3. Antiphonal or two-part alternate reading, which uses alternate voices, one section reading a line or lines and another section reading the responses. This method is sometimes found in church services, with a leader reading one line and a choir responding with the next line.
4. Numerical cumulation and reduction is the arrangement by which voices or groups of voices are added or subtracted from the whole. Group 1 may read two lines, Group 2 join them on the third line, Group 3 join 1 and 2 on the fifth line. In the same manner they may reduce the number speaking.
5. Sequential reading is the speaking of successive images by successive speakers. The selection to be read is divided into lines or words suggesting individual images or pictures with a series of voices speaking the words in succession. Groups of voices may be used in the same way.
6. Simple refrain is the arrangement of a solo voice reading the main verse and the entire choir joining on the refrain. A group of three or four voices may take the place of a single voice with the remaining choir supplying the refrain.

The director should avoid detracting from the beauty of the poetry by a too elaborate scheme of orchestration. Choric reading is not restricted to adults. It may be used for children of all ages. The material must be chosen in their fields of interest and adapted to their talents. For children, the same procedure is followed as for adults, although in a more simplified manner.

Other media. Reading festivals including material from prose, poetry, and plays may interest adults who haven't time to spend in long group rehearsals. The selections are prepared individually and then presented to the audience. A festival requires a very simple stage set of colorful screens or a curtain, maybe flowers, and a reading stand. The pure enjoyment of reading and the desire to share such an experience should motivate this type of program with no thought of competition.

Another type of informal social recreation is found through debates, discussions, or lecture series on a variety of subjects. Individuals or a committee group may use problems on current events, community affairs, or hobby interests. Such a program provides a means of self-expression to large or small groups and requires relatively little planning on the part of the recreation leader. This does not imply that such a series of events materializes by chance. A competent chairman may be chosen to organize and carry out the project with the general help of the recreation leader. This delegation of responsibility is suggested for young people as well as for adults. It is obvious that such a technique helps to develop leadership qualities, especially in the young people, which enhances the value of the undertaking.

SHADOW PLAYS, PUPPETRY, AND MARIONETTES

When planning recreation for younger children, the director may use shadow plays and puppetry as a means of stimulating creativeness. Shadow plays are particularly fascinating to children. A sheet is mounted in a rigid frame and a strong light placed behind it at a distance which permits actors to work between it and the screen. Real properties and costumes are not needed because the outline shadow is all that is required. Cardboard cutouts, drapes, boxes, or anything that suggests the scenery may be used.

If the children don't want to take the part of characters, paper dolls fastened on a long stick may be used behind a small screen mounted above the eye level. The child stands behind the screen as he moves his figures.

Marionettes and puppets provide another avenue of creativeness. To make the marionette, dress it, build and paint scenery, and manufacture properties and furniture for the miniature stage will provide motivation for long hours of meaningful play. The stage may be simple or elaborate. A table turned upside down with a curtain hung around three sides with the fourth drawn for the front, will answer the purpose. A box with the opening cut for stage front at one side will also do.

The simplest marionette has one string from the head which even the smallest child can handle. Anywhere from three to fifteen or more strings may be used in the more elaborate figures. After awhile, children become very adept at handling their marionettes. Any book on the subject will give directions for making cloth, wooden, or modeled dolls.

Very simple hand or fist puppets can be made and pulled over the hand, using the fingers to move the arms and head. The head is hollowed to allow the fingers to be inserted while the body part covers the hand. A three-way screen with a square opening and draw curtain on the center panel serves as a portable stage. Paper dolls' heads with faces already painted may be used in the same manner.

Planning a common project and working it through to a successful conclusion is a cooperative and creative enterprise in real living. The thrill of seeing one's ideas come to life, understood and enjoyed by others is a soul-satisfying experience. The astute recreation leader can provide opportunities for learning these new skills while having fun in their execution.

SUGGESTED READINGS

Anderson, Paul. *Story-telling with the Flannel Board.* Minneapolis: T. S. Denison & Co., Inc., 1963.

Cummings, Richard. *101 Hand Puppets, A Guide for Puppeteers of All Ages.* New York: David McKay Co., Inc., 1962.

Deason, Myrna, *et al. The Modern Skit and Stunt Book.* Minneapolis: T. S. Denison & Co., Inc., 1963.

Eisenberg, Larry, and Helen Eisenberg. *The Handbook of Skits and Stunts.* New York: Association Press, 1953.

Gilbert, Margaret Wardlow. *Plays That Sing.* New York: The John Day Company, Inc., 1963.

Howard, Vernon. *Puppet and Pantomime Plays.* New York: Sterling Publishing Co., Inc., 1962.

Stahl, Leroy. *Simplified Stagecraft Manual.* Minneapolis: T. S. Denison & Co., Inc., 1963.

Walker, Pamela. *Seven Steps to Creative Children's Dramatics.* New York: Hill & Wang, Inc., 1957.

Chapter 17

INDUSTRIAL RECREATION

Industrial recreation constitutes an organized attempt at helping to assure a satisfied and efficient worker. The complexities of day-to-day living and the multiplication of wants often contribute toward untold frustrations, anxieties, and tensions. By fragmenting the contribution that each worker makes toward the finished product, this situation has become even more pronounced. The greater part of this dilemma is traceable to the mechanization of industry and specialization of labor. In addition, urbanization and the attendant crowded living conditions are additional factors that point up the need for contributing toward one's emotional and spiritual make-up. To help alleviate this state, wholesome recreational outlets for the worker have been found to contribute greatly toward balanced living.

The monotonous repetition of minute operations deprives the worker of the satisfactions that used to be achieved by seeing the task through from the raw material to the completed product. This failure to whet the urge for creativity and to realize the satisfactions in carrying a task through to completion must be compensated for somehow. Do we find a partial answer in the vast increase in alcoholic beverage consumption throughout the land? Hasn't the machine created a challenge as to what to do with the time saved through its constantly increased use by industry?

That this problem faces society with constantly growing force is indeed a fact. At that, it is too large to be handled by any one agency. We shall be concerned in this chapter with the role industry can assume in this growing problem. At the outset, we should recognize that industrial recreation does not call for any special activities or events as distinct from public recreation. Rather, it is charged with the problem of attempting to meet the needs of the workers in each plant, based on individual interests and drives. Recognition should be given to the truism that the average worker of today is less tired physically than mentally, with nervous fatigue and boredom usually in evidence. Furthermore, the void created by the monotonous repetitive tasks and the crowded conditions of city living under which the majority in industry live call for positive steps.

SURVEYING INTERESTS

The focal point of the industrial recreation program is the interest level at which the employees are found. This information can be discerned by questioning each employee via a questionnaire; the interview technique may be used to augment the questionnaire or as an alternative. Certainly, both employer and employee groups should be consulted before a final decision is made; an advisory committee that includes representation from these two groups should be organized and consulted.

A sample industrial recreation survey[1] follows:

1. Men employees are to place a check mark in the column marked "M" opposite the activities in which they would like to participate. Wives of employees or women employees check their preference in the column marked "W."
2. Place a circle around the number in front of the activities in which you have had experience and which might qualify you for leadership authority.
3. Place a "C" before activities in which your children would be interested.
4. Please take this form home, fill it out carefully and return it to: _____

Physical Activities

	M	W			M	W
1. Archery				19. Handball		
2. Archery golf				20. Hockey, Ice		
3. Badminton				21. Hockey, field		
4. Baitcasting				22. Horseback riding		
5. Baseball				23. Horseshoes		
6. Basketball				24. Indoor tennis		
7. Bocci				25. Lacrosse		
8. Bowling				26. Paddle tennis		
9. Boxing				27. Polo		
10. Calisthenics				28. Pool and billiards		
11. Croquet				29. Ping-Pong		
12. Dart baseball				30. Quoits		
13. Dart bowling				31. Riflery		
14. Deck tennis				32. Roller skating		
15. Fencing				33. Shuffleboard		
16. Football				34. Soccer		
17. Golf				35. Softball		
18. Gymnastics				36. Speedball		

[1]Recreation-Interest Finder, National Recreation Association, 20 N. Wacker Drive, Chicago, Illinois, 60606.

Physical Activities

	M	W			M	W
37. Squash			43. Track and field			
38. Swimming, diving			44. Tumbling			
39. Target shooting			45. Volley ball			
40. Tennis			46. Water polo			
41. Tether ball			47. Weight lifting			
42. Touch football			48. Wrestling			

Social Activities

	M	W			M	W
49. Bingo			55. Dominoes			
50. Cards			56. Folk dancing			
51. Checkers			57. Smokers			
52. Chess			58. Social dancing			
53. Cribbage			59. Social parties			
54. Dinners			60. Square dancing			

Outing Activities

	M	W			M	W
61. Bicycling			69. Nature and astronomy study			
62. Boating						
63. Bobsledding			70. Picnicking			
64. Canoeing			71. Sailboating			
65. Fishing			72. Skeet and trap shooting			
66. Hiking						
67. Hunting			73. Skiing			
68. Ice skating			74. Speedboating			

Cultural Activities

	M	W			M	W
75. Amateur shows			92. Drawing			
76. Band			93. Embroidery			
77. Chorus			94. First aid			
78. Dramatics			95. Gardening			
79. Forums			96. Glass collecting			
80. Glee clubs			97. Homemade games			
81. Clubs—art			98. Kite making			
82. Airplane			99. Leather craft			
83. Basketry			100. Linoleum block printing			
84. Bible study						
85. Camera			101. Metal craft			
86. Coin collecting			102. Model making			
87. Cooking			103. Library			
88. Crafts			104. Needlecraft			
89. Crocheting			105. Printing			
90. Debate			106. Pottery making			
91. Dogs			107. Puppetry			

Cultural Activities

	M	W		M	W
108. Quilting			118. Lectures and		
109. Radio (shortwave)			concerts		
110. Sculpturing			119. Movies, educational		
111. Soap carving			120. Movies, feature		
112. Stagecraft			121. Newspaper staff		
113. Stamp collecting			122. Orchestra		
114. Science			123. Trips to zoos, etc.		
115. Women's			124. Opportunity for		
116. Wood working			study in		
117. Writing					

What Activities Do You Prefer?

Man—1st choice _____

Man— 2nd choice _____

Man—3rd choice _____

Woman—1st choice _____

Woman—2nd choice _____

Woman—3rd choice _____

ORGANIZED INDUSTRIAL RECREATION

The National Industrial Recreation Association was first established in 1941. Currently, it serves over eight hundred industrial members. National tournaments, under N.I.R.A. sponsorship, are conducted in riflery, pistol shooting, bridge, golf, bowling, fishing, deer hunting, archery, and skeet and track shooting. As an added service, it publishes *Recreation Management*. In 1961, N.I.R.A. worked out a certification program for qualified industrial recreational administrations. As of this date, 159 have been certified. In recognition of the growing importance of employee tours, it organized in 1957 the National Industrial Travel Council consisting of carriers, hotel chains, and tour operators.

In 1964, the National Industrial Recreation Research and Educational Foundation was incorporated to receive and designate funds for industrial recreation research and to establish a national scholarship program. N.I.R.A. annually awards a scholarship to a student in recreation or an allied field. The Helms Athletic Foundation, in cooperation with N.I.R.A., has made since 1959 an annual award to the most outstanding company recreation program in N.I.R.A.'s five membership categories.

The organization of industrial recreation should be a cooperative undertaking. This state of affairs is readily explained when one recognizes that both sides stand to gain from this enterprise. Through a survey in Pennsylvania[2] it was revealed that forty per cent of the industrial recreation programs were administered by employees, thirty-seven per cent by joint employee-management; a total of fifty-seven per cent was administered either by management or joint employee–management. This study also uncovered that where the programs were supervised by employees or joint employee–management, the employees had more administrative independence. In a national study completed in 1949 by the National Industrial Conference Board which covered 264 companies, approximately thirty-five per cent were controlled by employer management, forty-six per cent by the employees themselves, and nineteen per cent by the company management and employees jointly. In summation, industrial recreation can be operated under one of three possible administrative setups: employee, employee–management, or management.

A committee representing the employer and/or the employees should be organized to institute preliminary plans and procedures to be followed. A questionnaire adapted to industry's needs is to be formulated. Upon the issuance and completion of the questionnaires, they are to be tabulated. The next step is to analyze the findings, whereupon a tentative program of activities can be arranged. Concurrent with or shortly after this the various responsibilities are to be delegated to subcommittees, such as:

1. Membership
2. Finance
3. Facilities
4. Physical Activities Program
5. Social Program
6. Arts and Crafts Program
7. Musical Activities Program
8. Hobby Activities Program
9. Family Activities Program

The philosophy of the greatest good to the greatest number should prevail. Only after this is assured should the wishes of smaller activity groups be met.

Survey of facilities. The facilities available for use by the employees should be ascertained. The play areas for recreational use on the company's grounds might well serve as the point of departure. Among the

[2]Fred M. Coombs and Allen E. Weatherford, "Survey of Industrial Recreation in Pennsylvania" (Pennsylvania State College, unpublished, 1950).

companies that have developed their own facilities are 3-M, National Cash Register, and General Electric of Cincinnati. This practice reduces the likelihood of overcrowding. Moreover, it helps to assure the completion of tournament play during the designated time intervals. In addition, community parks, playgrounds, "Y"'s, indoor centers, school play areas, auditoriums, gymnasiums, swimming pools, golf courses, tennis courts, church recreation areas, and private recreation areas are among the facilities to be explored.

Next in order should be an evaluation of the facilities available in relation to the needs as determined by the interest questionnaire. The need for added facilities to be constructed by the plant may be an outgrowth of this investigation. Quite often, the existing facilities in the community may prove to be adequate to get the program under way.

Attracting the novice. Perhaps the fear of failure or of embarrassment deters more people from partaking of recreational activities than any other factor. This can be obviated somewhat by classifying participants according to ability. There is less apt to be embarrassment when all learners find themselves on a similar level of ability. Furthermore, by offering a variety of activities, more workers are bound to be stimulated by some phase of the program. The use of unusual activities can also serve as an attracting force.

Lockheed Aircraft Corporation employs a slow-pitching softball league for players of forty-five years of age or beyond. Briggs Manufacturing Company conducts a Kings and Queens Bowling League for employees and their wives; twenty leagues have been operating for twelve years. By including the workers' children in the program, the interest of the worker himself may be enhanced. For example, Goodyear Tire and Rubber Company offers Kid's Basketball, Kid's Visitation Days, and a Youth Band. Father and son (mother and daughter) affairs are also suggested to attract the hard-to-get employee into the recreation fold.

Scheduling of program. It is safe to say that the industrial recreation leader is charged with the responsibility of arranging activities whenever the workers desire them. As a starting point, the lunch period offers the most likely time, if but for an abbreviated period. The interval between the close of the working day and dinner time is a very popular period throughout the country. Next comes the evening, wherein the sated and cleansed worker is ready for an evening of fun and relaxation. This time also lends itself to the inclusion of members of the worker's family. The vacation period is also a very suitable time for organized recreational pursuits under industrial auspices. Opportunities for camping, fishing, hunting, hiking, and picnicking are offered by some industrial concerns at their company-owned lodges and camps.

Miscellaneous provisions. In addition to organized activities, industries quite often provide opportunities for breaks from work by devices that border on the recreational. The use of rest periods offer an opportunity for a smoke, chat, or just resting. Many plants have found that the use of tea and cookies during the midmorning and midafternoon give a lift to waning energies and result in a less tired worker. Musical programs piped through the public address system tend to make a pleasanter working day and ease tensions.

Lounges where employees can relax during their rest periods and lunch hour are also popular; opportunities to listen to records of their own choice, radio and television programs, to read, or merely to chat are the choices at their disposal. Tournaments, league play, socials, dances, banquets, picnics, and rod and gun clubs are added activities wherein the worker and his family can re-create. All of these measures are based on the realization that steps that succeed in making the workers' day more pleasant and relaxing contribute toward a healthier, happier, and more productive employee.

Leadership qualifications. All too often, industrial recreation leadership is taken from the personnel office. There is no brief for a condemnation of this procedure per se. Industry is usually interested in securing the best man for the job. This criterion, though, is often slighted when the problem of selecting a recreation leader arises.

A former athlete is often chosen from the employee group without regard for the exacting demands the position often makes. The qualifications for general recreation leadership are discussed elsewhere at length. That industrial recreation is a field of endeavor that warrants specialized training is proved by the specialized courses offered by colleges and universities to help prepare candidates for this field. The recreation major incorporates sufficient training to qualify for the average industrial recreation position. As stated previously, specialization is to be acquired during graduate study.

VALUES OF INDUSTRIAL RECREATION

It is indisputable that mechanization of industry has increased the productivity of each worker and has contributed to the shorter working day; the increased leisure can be used for naught, for good, or possibly for damaging interests. Industrial recreation can help to provide the worker with wholesome outlets for his leisure. For some time, industry has recognized that sound use of one's leisure can contribute toward a more efficient worker and do much toward reducing absenteeism. After all, a well-adjusted and contented worker is an asset to his employer.

Industrial recreation affords the worker opportunities to express himself and to achieve satisfactions while participating with his co-workers. Heightened morale and *esprit de corps* are likely to result as well as restoration for the next day's work. The latter outcome is particularly necessary to obviate the tension and boredom which often arises. The recuperative effect of a game of badminton or a game of horseshoes for a harried office worker becomes readily apparent. A relaxed and happy worker is bound to be a more productive one. Moreover, a well-conceived and effectively administered recreation program for employees can enhance, as no other venture, employer–employee relationships.

TRENDS

The shorter working day and week and vacations with pay have contributed toward the most abundant leisure for the worker in the history of man. Scientific and medical advancements have extended the worker's life expectancy, while at the same time, helping him to retain a more functional and agile human machine. All of these have contributed toward a more receptive worker for recreational planning that may be planned for his welfare.

Industry has recognized for some time that all-family recreational activities serve to strengthen family solidarity, thereby contributing toward a happier and more effective worker. Rather than emphasize interplant sports exclusively, the trend is unmistakably toward varied activities which encompass all age groups and passive as well as active interests. Not only are the activities conducted during the lunch hour and after working hours during the week, but also during the workers' days off and weekends.

Still another welcome addition to industrial recreation programs is that of employee travel. Charter plane travel has become an important addition of the opportunities available to the worker. With the advent of longer vacation periods and the likelihood that the sabbatical will spread from steel to other industries, charter plane travel both here and abroad will take over in greater force. For example, Owens-Illinois Co. has arranged flights to Hawaii, Mexico, Sweden, and Norway.

In view of the earlier retirement age with the worker's vigor still intact, industries are displaying added concern for their former workers who have retired. Programs geared to the needs of those past retirement are in evidence in industries throughout the land. This has helped to ease the suspicion held by some that industrial recreation is concerned exclusively with increased productivity.

In all, industrial recreation is gaining adherents annually. It constitutes a force that is not only a great contribution to industrial life but also a contributant that overflows and adds toward community-wide recreational offerings.

SUGGESTED READINGS

Anderson, Jackson M. *Industrial Recreation*. New York: McGraw-Hill Book Company, 1955.

Carlson, Reynold, *et al. Recreation in American Life*. Belmont, California: Wadsworth Publishing Co., Inc., 1963.

Diehl, L. J., and F. R. Eastwood. *Industrial Recreation, Its Development and Present Status*. Lafayette, Indiana: Purdue University, 1940.

Duggins, G. H., and F. R. Eastwood. *Planning Industrial Recreation*. Lafayette, Indiana: Purdue University Studies, 1941.

Jenny, John. *Introduction to Recreation Education*. Philadelphia: W. B. Saunders Co., 1955.

Kraus, Richard. *Recreation Today*. New York: Appleton-Century-Crofts, 1966.

Meyer, Harold D., and Charles K. Brightbill. *Community Recreation*. Englewood Cliffs, N.J.: Prentice-Hall, Inc., 1964.

Petrill, Jack. *After the Whistle Blows*. New York: William-Frederick Press, 1950.

Chapter 18

SOCIAL RECREATION

Man is a highly social being; people like people; people like to be with people. Moreover, people stand to benefit from sharing experiences with others. Consequently, social recreation is in high regard as a phase of recreation. Consequently, there is a growing realization on the part of parents, teachers, and leaders that our youth and adults have much to benefit from socializing and partaking of wholesome recreational activities at gatherings, parties, and the like. This applies particularly to social affairs wherein members of both sexes are represented. Opportunities for fellowship and situations wherein one's ability to get along with others is fostered have much to contribute toward one's poise, personality, and maturity.

Colleges that prepare recreation leaders often make equipment and student leaders available for church, service club, and organizational parties and functions. This service not only builds good will but also offers opportunities whereby the student leaders benefit from meaningful laboratory experiences.

In our society with its constantly increasing leisure, there exists a growing need for wholesome recreational outlets. Our complex civilization requires long periods of schooling in the preparation for careers. In many professions, pretraining requirements are imposed after high-school graduation prior to entrance into such professional schools as law, medicine, dentistry, and the like. Financial independence is postponed until the midtwenties and quite often even later.

At the same time, interest in the opposite sex becomes pronounced at about the age of eleven or twelve in girls and thirteen or fourteen in boys. That plus the stimulations provided by the movies, magazines, radio, and television account, if but in part, for the bewildered state many of our youth find themselves in today. This situation ought to challenge the best thinking of our leaders in the field. Cheerful, properly furnished centers where our boys and girls, men and women, may go for wholesome social activities under properly trained leadership are of prime importance. Otherwise, commercial recreation will continue to make in-

222

roads, with its emphasis on profits and low, if any, standards of social behavior.

CO-RECREATION

With the bolstering of human relationships assuming greater importance in education, the fostering of recreational opportunities for both sexes is in direct line with this objective. As a matter of fact, it provides a fundamental step. Basically, co-recreation emphasizes playing with members of the other sex rather than against. The range of co-recreational activities encompasses the whole of recreation, with the exception of competitive sports involving body contact, which are very popular during early and late adolescence.

It is noteworthy that, especially prior to and during adolescence, our youth need wholesome experiences on an informal plane with the opposite sex. Co-recreational activities involving dancing, music, dramatics, arts and crafts, parties, and picnics, among others, are accompanied by situations wherein the give and take of human relationships can take place under trained guidance. Also, countless opportunities are afforded for development of the social graces. These incidental learnings are possible while the participants enjoy wholesome relationships.

SOCIAL BENEFITS

The benefits to be secured from social recreation are but limited by the preparation and ingenuity of the leader in charge. Basically, it offers an opportunity to have a good time via wholesome activities. While that should be justification enough, there are other valuable outcomes. Opportunities are afforded for finding oneself through the activities for social betterment, for improving one's ability to get along with others, for self-expression, for developing new interests while nurturing the gregarious impulse, and for socializing with the opposite sex.

Indirectly, these outcomes will contribute toward a more amiable and happy group. What is perhaps of greater importance, it can help to contribute toward better adjusted and socially competent individuals. At a time when more beds are occupied in hospitals by the mentally ill than for all other ailments combined, who can venture to say that social competence ought not to become the leading objective of recreation and even education?

LEADERSHIP AIDS

A spirit of fun and friendliness should permeate the entire program. Each participant should be made to feel that you are glad he came and

that the party would not be complete without him. Ought we not to borrow the technique of the bowling alley owner or the bartender who
extends a very cordial greeting to each customer as though he were his
long-lost cousin? It is a good psychological approach which helps to build
up the ego and nourishes the feeling of being wanted and welcome.

The use of decorations, flowers, freshly marked courts and lines, and a
clean area help to add to the participants' enjoyment. Moreover, it
indicates you were so pleased to have them that you made special
preparations to assure them a good time. All too often, leaders give the
impression that the members of their groups are a necessary nuisance,
which belies the fact that their very livelihood depends on them.

PROGRAM PLANNING

The planning of a social recreation program should be a cooperative
venture. If possible, committees (planning publicity, entertainment, refreshment, decoration, clean-up) representing those who will participate
can be of inestimable assistance to the leader in his program planning.
To be sure, the leader should be in a position to present a tentative program with an alert eye for any suggestions cast his way. This grass-roots
approach can pay off in avoiding failures which are often reflected by
using games that are beyond the interest or attainment level of the
group. An underestimation of the group's ability may also cause the program to fall short of success.

Holidays, celebrations, and special occasions help to give meaning to
the program and provide the focal point around which the planning can
center. The facilities and equipment should be given prime consideration in the planning. Of great importance should be the selection of a
familiar and highly successful activity to start off the program as well as
a splendid closing activity to send the group home in a buoyed and
cheerful mood. Refreshments should not be served until two thirds or
three quarters of the time has elapsed. Remind all that the best is yet to
come.

THE SCOPE

Here again, the scope of social recreation activities are limited only by
the imagination and ingenuity of the leader. Whenever feasible, the activity should stem from the needs and interests of the group. Likewise,
community needs and interests are distinct and often differ from those
of even neighboring communities. The adroit leader will therefore be on
the alert to detect and allow for these differences.

What follows is but a suggestive list of possible activities with the exact prescription to be written by the leader after careful analysis. Various social games may be included as part of these events.

Social Recreation Events

Parties and Dances	Entertainments	Eating Events	Celebrations	Miscellaneous
Birthday	Stunt Night	Picnics	Holidays	Record Hour
Graduation	Amateur Night	Dinners	Birthdays	Hay Rides
Costume	Fun Night	Tureen Suppers	Anniversaries	Square Dancing
Holiday	Dramatic Exhi-	Banquets	Class Reunions	Barn Dance
Sadie Hawkins	bitions	Fishfrys	Alumni—	Record Dance
Masquerade	Vocalists	Clambakes	Alumnae	Gatherings
Splash	Instrumentalists	Breakfasts	Festivals	Treasure Hunts
St. Valentine	Monologues	Marshmallow	National Heroes	Teas
Card	Imitations	Roasts	Brotherhood	Father and Son
Get Acquainted	Whistling	Wiener Roasts	I Am an Amer-	Night
Game	Harmonica	Basket Lunches	ican	Mother and
		Barbecues		Daughter
				Night

TRENDS

The growing impact of the machine on industry, the farm, and the home is almost incredible, with the result that the worker, farmer, housewife, and youth are less physically exhausted by their jobs and chores. This increasing energy reserve and leisure provide the nucleus for the recreation movement in general and social recreation in particular. This is reflected by constantly growing expenditures for the construction of recreation areas and leadership. Training programs are on the increase in our colleges, extension divisions, recreation institutions, and 4-H clubs. While much emphasis is being placed on the needs of rural areas, the need is equally great in urban areas.

Lay leaders, who volunteer their services, are being used in increasing numbers, with the growing realization that they need special training. More extensive use is being made of schools and churches in addition to the construction of special recreation areas. Greater stress is being placed on social recreation and co-recreation to help foster wholesome recreational participation on the part of both sexes. Finally, state and local laws are being passed so that recreation can be supported through taxation.

PARTY GAMES

Following are examples of activities that are suitable for inclusion in social recreation; others are to be found in the chapter, *The Picnic,* wherein a progressive games party involving ten components is incorporated. In addition, reference is made to lawn games and novelty games. Moreover, suitable activities may be found in the chapter, *Music in Recreation.*

Who Am I? This game is played in pairs. Each contestant attempts to guess the name of the prominent public figure or sports celebrity pinned on his back. They are to alternate, asking questions of each other with the answers restricted to a "yes" or a "no." Each participant keeps a tally of the number of questions asked of him on a sheet handed him; the name and picture number is included on the sheet as well as the instructions for the game. As soon as one correct name is guessed, both are to go to the judge's stand to register. The contestant with the least number of questions asked before guessing correctly becomes the winner.

Tie Escape. Use two pieces of twine about eighteen inches long for each pair taking part. Join the wrists of each one with a separate piece of twine through that of the one paired off with him. They are then instructed to try to get apart. After they have struggled for awhile, reveal the solution. Take the center of one string and pass it through the loop under his partner's wrist and then over his hand. They will then be separated.

Occupations. One or more who know this game should be spotted in the group; upon hearing the leader ask for volunteers, one of those "in the know" sheepishly steps forward. While he is out of the room, the group selects an occupation. Upon being ushered back into the room, the leader asks "Is it a plasterer?" "No." "Is it a bricklayer?" "No." Is it a peanut vender?" "No." "Is it a lawyer?" "No." "Is it a mason?" "Yes." The clue is to select the trade that follows a profession (lawyer).

MIXERS

Remember Me? If feasible, have the group seated or standing in a semicircle so that all can see one another. The first person gives his name to the second whereupon he mentions the name of the first and his own to the third. The third mentions the names of the first two and his own to the fourth and so on down the line. This is continued until someone misses, whereupon he is eliminated and becomes a spectator.

Pig in a Poke. Each participant is handed a paper bag large enough to cover his head, a small index card, a pencil, and a numbered tag registered with his name. The tag is pinned on his chest and holes are torn in the bag so that he may see through it after placing it on his head.

While trying to keep others from recognizing him, he records the names and numbers of those he believes he knows. Upon checking numbers and names, the one who has guessed the greatest number correctly is designated the winner.

How Do You Do! Have the group line up in concentric circles evenly divided. As the music starts or as the whistle is blown, the inner circle starts marching clockwise with the outside circle going counterclockwise. When the music stops or a double whistle is sounded, the circles face each other with introductions and conversation taking place between those opposite each other. This is continued until all have had a chance to meet.

RHYTHMICAL PLAY

Grand March.[1] The boys and girls form separate lines on opposite sides of the room, facing the leader. The boys stand at the leader's left, the girls at his right. March music is played, but if no instrumental music is available, any good marching song may be sung.

The lines march forward, then toward each other, the boys passing behind the leader and outside the line of girls, while the girls go in front of the leader and inside the line of boys. When the lines meet at the opposite end of the room or hall, the marchers come up the center in twos with arms locked.

The first couple goes to the right, the second to the left, the third to the right, and so on, continuing around the room until the lines meet and the marchers come up in fours.

The leader divides the fours into couples and again sends the lines around as before. When they meet at the other end of the hall, each couple in the left line joins hands and raises them to form a bridge. The right line passes under the bridges. Both lines continue to march during this figure. When the lines meet at the upper end of the hall, the right line forms bridges and the left passes under.

When the lines meet at the lower end of the room, the first couple in the left line makes a bridge, while the first couple from the right line goes under. The second right couple makes a bridge under which the first couple from the left passes. Thus the couples alternately make bridges or go under them. The figure should be repeated at the other end of the hall. This is rather difficult and should not be attempted until a group is accustomed to marching; it is pretty and popular, however.

[1]Ella Gardner, *Handbook for Recreation Leaders*, Children's Bureau Publication 231 (Washington, D.C.: Federal Security Agency, 1948), pp. 24–25.

At the end of the bridge making the marchers come up from the lower end of the hall in fours with arms locked. The first four go to the right, the second to the left. They return in eights. If the room is wide enough and the crowd is larger than fifty, the eights may go around again and return in sixteens.

As the grand march is frequently first on the program, now is a good time to introduce the players to one another, if introductions are needed. A song such as the following, which may be sung to the tune of "Auld Lang Syne," performs the ceremony easily:

> We're always glad to meet new friends,
>   Our greetings are to you:
> We can not all shake hands, you see,
>   So here's our "How d'ye do."[2]

During the last line each person shakes hands with himself high over his head. A state, school, or organization song will fit in here just as well.

Each player in the eight (or sixteen) takes the hand of his neighbor on each side. The player on the left end of each line looks back of him to the player at the right end of the line behind—whose hand he presently will take. To start the figure the leader takes the hand of the player at the right end of the first line and leads that line behind itself, in front of the second line. When the last player in the first line is about to pass the player at the right end of the second line, he takes this person's hand and the rest of the second line fall in. The leader marches on, going now behind the second line and in front of the third. The boy at the end of the moving line always takes the hand of the girl on the right-hand end of the line behind him. This continues until the whole group is in one long winding line, which then is led into a single circle. This figure is called the serpentine. It leaves each player standing beside the partner with whom he has marched; and these partners can be retained for succeeding games.

Balloon Ankle Dance. Any number of dancing partners can take part. An inflated balloon is tied around each female's ankle. Once the music gets under way, the male dancing partners attempt to burst the balloons of the competitors while protecting those of their own partners. The couple ending up with an inflated balloon is designated the winner. Either fox-trot or waltz music may be used.

---

[2]These words are by George L. Farley, state 4-H Club leader, Amherst, Massachusetts.

Broom Dance. The group is paired off as couples with an odd player dancing with the broom as the couples dance to fox-trot or waltz music. The music is interrupted as the lone dancer drops the broom and rushes for a partner; all dancers have to change partners each time the dancing stops. Music is resumed with the new odd player wielding the broom.

Musical Chairs. Use one less chair than the number of participants. The chairs are to be lined up side by side so that the seat portion of one chair is in line with the back of the one next to it. By so alternating the front and back of each chair, the participants will be able to "land" on every other chair as they parade in a circle around the chairs. When the music stops or a whistle is blown, the players are to scramble for a seat. Since there is one less chair than participants, the one left without a seat is eliminated. Before resuming play, a chair is removed each time so that the number of participants may be reduced until there is a lone survivor.

Virginia Reel. Employ sets of six couples with boys in one line facing the girls in the other. "Turkey in the Straw" (Victor LPM-1623) or any 4/4 music will prove adequate. The leader should call, as follows:

First: "Forward and bow"—each dancer takes three steps forward, bows to partner, and takes three steps backward.

Second: "Right hand to partner"—partners turn with right hand clockwise and return.

Third: "Left hand to partner"—partners turn with left hand and return.

Fourth: "Both hands to partner"—partners turn with both hands and return.

Fifth: "Do-si-do-right"—with arms folded, partners pass around each other, right shoulders close, and return stepping backward.

Sixth: "Do-si-do-left"—the same maneuver is repeated to the left.

Seventh: "Head couple slides to the foot and returns halfway"—couple nearest to the caller clasps hands, slides to the foot, and returns to the middle.

Eighth: "Head couple reel"—turn partner with right hand so that the boy faces the girls and the girl faces the boys. They offer left hands to the foot girl and head boy, respectively, turn them once and return to each other by turning with their right hands joined. They then proceed to the second in line and so on until all have had a chance to turn. The head couple then turns at the middle so as to return to their own side and skip to their positions at the head of the line.

Ninth: "Head couple goes down"—the boy and girl of the head couple turn to the left and right, respectively. The head boy turns and leads the other boys to the left and the head girl does the same to the right as they skip outside their lines clapping. As the head couple meets, they form a bridge with their hands. The others skip through the bridge with the former second couple thereby becoming the head couple. The dance is completed when each couple has served as the head couple.

NOVELTY GAMES

Cigarette Blowing. Each participant—as many as space will allow— is handed a cigarette and asked to line up in a kneeling position behind the starting line. The cigarette is placed on the line. At the signal, each player is to try to blow his cigarette until it crosses the finish line about fifteen yards away. (Beverage straws or table tennis balls may be substituted.

Note: The use of one's hands after the starting whistle is blown disqualifies a player.

Balloon Blowing Contest. The participants—from six to eight are usually best—are to line up with one hand behind their backs. The players are to blow until the balloon bursts. First place is given to the one whose balloon bursts first.

Note: Caution the players not to stretch their balloons since this makes them easier to inflate. This can be avoided by handing out the balloons after the players have followed the instruction to keep one hand behind the back.

Shoe Scramble. An unlimited number of players place their shoes in a pile at a spot designated by the leader. At a given signal, they all run a required distance to the pile, pick out their own shoes, and return to the starting point with the shoes in their hands.

Note: This provision aims to avoid the advantage those with laceless shoes might have over the others.

"Beer" (Milk) Drinking Contest. Four-ounce baby bottles are filled with milk and capped with nipples. The one who empties the bottle first is the winner. This game is best when played with from six to eight contestants.

Note: Baby bonnets can add to the hilarity of the event. Caution the participants that they will be disqualified for biting holes in the nipple to make the milk pour more easily.

Indoor Track Meet. Events: Give ten points to the one who excels in each event.

1. Shot Put—use a balloon, table tennis ball, or roll of cotton.
2. Javelin—use a straw or wooden applicator with cotton on the end.
3. Discus—use a paper plate.

4. Standing Broad Jump—heel the starting line and jump backward.
5. Mile Stretch—have any number of teammates (same number from each team) touch the line and the rest lie from toe to head in any manner. The team with the longest line wins.
6. Air Relay—teams in shuttle formation at the start with an even number on each side. Put crackers on floor bench in front of each player. One cracker is to be handed each player. Start by having the first person of each team run to the other side, eat the cracker, and then whistle. The next person on each team repeats the performance until all have participated.

QUIET GAMES

Charades. This game is not limited insofar as contestants are concerned. The players may be broken up into two groups or, if a large number is involved, into several smaller groups. The groups take turns at acting out the words that were chosen; the words should be broken down into syllables, groups of syllables, and lastly into motions descriptive of the entire word.

Should a member of the opposing team(s) guess correctly, then a point is scored for his side. If no one guesses right, then the team that performed the charade presents another. The winner is the team scoring the most points after all have had an equal number of tries.

"Silly Tillie." The leader begins by saying "Tillie is silly, funny, and odd, but not peculiar." Then again the leader may give another example by saying, "Tillie likes yellow, but not blue, she likes glass, but not windows." A few who know the game can add to the curiosity of those who do not. By proceeding around the room, you will find out who is familiar with the game and who is not.

Those who are unfamiliar with Silly Tillie are advised to be observant and to guess just what is happening. Since what Tillie "likes" or "is" must be made up of double letters, persons knowing the game may throw suggested hints by emphasizing the double letters: "Tillie likes the *Mississippi*, but not the Ohio River." A person may give up, but should not be told what is happening until everyone has caught on or until all have given up.

Marshmallow-Eating Contest: About five or six couples are usually best for this game, although many more can take part. Have two marshmallows for each person in the game, enough powdered charcoal to cover the marshmallows with a thin coating (this can be purchased at the drug store), one paper bag for each couple, and a blindfold for each person in the contest. All watch the leader place four marshmallows in each paper bag to be shared by two contestants. However, the leader does not let the people in the contest see the charcoal in the bag which will cover the marshmallows and blacken them. All contestants are blind-folded and instructed to hold the edge of the bag with the left hand. They are told to feed each other with the right hand when told to "go." When it is over, the contestants will get as big a laugh as the rest when they discover their faces are covered with the black charcoal.

Variation: If you wish, the leader can put charcoal in only one bag, thereby restricting the joke to one couple.

Concentration. Each participant—as many as thirty may play—sits in a chair that is situated in a semicircle. Beginning with the first chair and going around from left to right, number each chair consecutively. Each player assumes the number of the chair in which he sits.

The game is started by the number one player. He begins a rhythm by slapping his thighs twice and clapping twice. As he is clapping his hands he repeats his own seat number and the number of another player. The player whose number is called must repeat his own number and give a number of one of the other participants while repeating the motions and retaining the rhythm.

If the player whose number is called cannot repeat his number and another number in the clapping part of the rhythm, he moves to the last chair of the semicircle. All players from this player to the end of the circle move up one chair and as a result obtain a new seat number.

The object of the game is to sit in the first chair at the end of a certain period of time. The player who gets this chair will be declared the winner.

Strategy: Call, as often as possible, the number of those players sitting in the first few chairs so that they will make an error and will have to move. In this way, more people assume new numbers and more confusion results.

Airplane. Small groups of twenty-five or less are best for this game. All the players sit around in a close circle. The object is to pass the sound of an airplane or a dog's bark (harumph) around the circle, either direction at any time, without breaking the chain. If you should laugh when it is your turn to pass the sound along and break the rhythmical chain, the leader will put a D after your name. Each time a person misses, letters are added after his name until the word D–O–N–K–E–Y is spelled.

Categories. For this game the number of participants may be unlimited although fifteen to twenty in a group is preferable. The people are seated in a circle with everyone facing the center. A rhythmic pattern is started by everyone's slapping their knees twice with both hands, then raising their hands overhead and snapping their fingers twice. On the rhythmic finger-snapping count, the leader says, "Categories." The next person in line must name a category on the next rhythmic count. The third person in line then must name an object in this category and so does everyone that follows until one person misses. An example of a category is "automobiles" followed by naming Ford, Dodge, and so forth. The penalty for missing one of the categories is to drop out of the game —or, if a point system is used, the person who misses scores a point; the winner of the game is the person with the fewest points.

Note: The category that is selected has to be familiar enough so that the one who names it can present five samples, if challenged.

Sniff. Any number can play this game. Cigarette paper or similar thin pieces of paper are used. Have everyone sit close together in a circle. If both sexes are represented, have them alternate around the circle. Start the game by placing the paper under the nose while inhaling so that the paper will adhere to the nostril. Then turn to the person on the left who is responsible for taking the paper by inhaling and to pass it on to the next player. This is continued around the circle.

When a person misses or drops the cigarette paper you may either eliminate him from the game or keep him in the game until he spells out D–O–N–K–E–Y.

LEADERSHIP AIDS

The following statements will prove of tremendous help when leading social recreation:

1. Endeavor to anticipate the problems you may meet in leading a group that is unfamiliar to you.
2. Try to secure information as to:
   a. The type and number of participants.
   b. The size of the area where the function is to be held.
   c. If possible, try to determine the degree of "recreational literacy" of the group to be led.
3. Provide activities for the early arrivals.
4. The group may be "warmed up" by group singing and/or "ice breakers."
5. If the occasion lends itself, try to build the program around a holiday or special celebration such as parents' night, father and son, boys' week, Columbus Day, Thanksgiving Day, and the like.
6. Everyone likes to play. Try to remove any "play resistance." Since the play spirit is contagious, try to interest as many as possible in each game.
7. Start off with a "sure hit" game. A strong beginning and an equally successful final game provide an ideal setting for a successful program.

8. In teaching a game, it may help to do the following:
   a. Name the game—it may help to coin original names such as Hot Potato, Bronco Buck, and so forth.
   b. Explain the game.
   c. Repeat the explanation while demonstrating it.
   d. Ask for any questions.
   e. Start play.
9. The leader can instill enthusiasm in the group. A sense of humor can do much to brighten the occasion.
10. Prizes from the "five-and-dime" with the fun element in them can add interest to the affair.
11. Look for signs of waning interest—"kill the activity before it dies."
12. Decorations help provide a festive atmosphere.

SUGGESTED READINGS

Burns, Lorell Coffman. *Instant Fun for All Kinds of Groups.* New York: Association Press, 1964.

Carlson, Adele. *4 Seasons Party and Banquet Book.* Nashville, Tenn.: Broadman Press, 1965.

Harbin, E. O. *The Fun Encyclopedia.* New York: Abingdon-Cokesbury Press, 1940.

Hindman, Darwin A. *Complete Book of Games and Stunts.* Englewood Cliffs, N.J.: Prentice-Hall, Inc., 1956.

Ickis, Marguerite. *The Book of Patriotic Holidays.* New York: Dodd, Mead & Co., 1962.

Millen, Nina. *Children's Festivals from Many Lands.* New York: Friendship Press, 1964.

Wackerbarth, Marjorie, and Lillian Graham. *Successful Parties and How to Give Them.* Minneapolis: T. S. Denison & Co., Inc., 1962.

Chapter 19

MUSIC IN RECREATION

"Such sweet compulsion doth in music lie."—JOHN MILTON

Music is a form of human expression of pleasing and melodious combinations of tones. It is the language of the spirit and a release of thoughts that are inexpressible. Music can "soothe the savage breast" with a ballad, it can be used to arouse patriotic fervor by a march. It can also be diverting to the mind, as in lilting melodies, and the source of inspiration, as in the *Finlandia* type of tone poem. Listening to an opera in Brussels so inspired the people that they rushed out on the street and began the revolt which resulted in the separation of Belgium from Holland.

Music can serve to complement a program by enriching it and helping to round it out. Moreover, it can act as an "ice breaker" or remover of barriers that often exist within a newly organized or "cold" group. When it comes to means of expressing oneself, there are few media that can compare favorably with music. Music with its myriad outlets may well be considered when other steps to "reach" an individual have fallen short of success. Greater realism is achieved with stereo.

THE VALUE OF MUSIC

Music can be the source of vast pleasures, whether one merely listens or takes part actively through playing or singing. It is noteworthy that much of life is symbolized by rhythmical behavior. Just as the human mechanism operates most efficiently within a rhythmical pattern by eating and resting at regular intervals, so does the mind find rhythmical expression highly gratifying; the various means of expression as they apply to the field of recreation are considered later in this chapter.

Medicine is discovering the worthwhileness of music as an adjunct therapeutic measure in the relatively new field of music therapy. Just as psychiatry finds music effective for the mentally ill, so does industry observe increased production through its aid to morale and influence on

235

boredom. Restaurants lay claim to the plausible belief that appropriate music favorably influences the appetite and ultimate digestion.

The physiologist reminds us that the greater part of what we refer to as fatigue is most often mental rather than physical and symptomatic of boredom rather than muscular tiredness. Perhaps the Volga boatman was indirectly aware of this concept when he resorted to his famous chant to ease his labor, thereby diverting his attention toward song. Work songs were used likewise by our Indians. Songs of the railroad, canal, and other American songs of this type attest to the fact that music has proved its worth in lightening one's burden.

MUSIC—RECREATIONAL OR OTHERWISE

The question may arise as to how recreational music differs from the more formal brand of music. For one, it readily becomes apparent that a more informal approach in handling the individual or group is used. Less stress is placed on excellence, although skillful performance need not be ruled out as a phase of recreational music. Although effective performance may be sought, it need not be at the expense of the satisfactions which should be uppermost in the minds of recreation personnel; the joy of singing or playing is of prime importance, with technical excellence to be relegated to a minor role. In addition, the element of choice rather than a fixed program should also be emphasized. The overall aim is to show how much better and richer life can be through the influence of music rather than to produce polished musicians; that is the recreational approach.

Recreational music applied. In recreation, the various forms of musical expression can be distinct activities or they can be correlated with other activities. Instances of correlated activities are to be found in singing games; in folk dances, which include folk songs; in pageants and dramatics, through musical interludes and ballads; and in arts and crafts, by constructing the instruments to be played.

Music is an integral part of the child's play realm. We often associate a tune with a vivid experience. Herein, the play leader has an opportunity to enrich the experiences of his charges with musical accompaniment. The added enjoyment of singing during play will add to the worthwhileness of the activity and may result in a more joyful experience. Added exposures to rhythmical patterns of melodies should contribute to the development of the child's rhythmical sense. Furthermore, music can offer an added means of self-expression, thereby enhancing the possibility of finding oneself through this form of play.

APPRECIATION OF MUSIC

A taste for music can best be cultivated through a graduated approach. Just as the pediatrician will prescribe a very small quantity of a vitamin for an infant and slowly increase the dosage, so ought the leader to start off with a minimal exposure to this new art. It is fundamental that the leader be interested and enthusiastic about that which he is to impart to others. He should not overlook an element of sound teaching often referred to as apperception, which calls for starting with a subject on the level at which you find him; the educational aphorism to proceed from the known to the unknown should be heeded.

The objective is to acquire a taste for the best in music, whether it be of the classical or popular kind; an enrichment and elevation of taste is to be sought. Since jazz and swing dominate the airwaves and movies and account for the lion's share of the recording studios' output, more stress should be placed on classical music. For this activity to be truly recreational, the leader should constantly "feel the pulse" of his group so as to guard against making it too highly instructional. He ought never to lose sight of the fun element which calls for enjoying every phase of the experience, and he should adapt the program to the interest level of his charges.

Acknowledging that music is an art, it warrants distinct treatment. In referring to the appreciation of music, Dickinson reminds us "that music, like all art, is intended for the gratification merely of the intellect and the physical senses."[1]

INFLUENCE OF RADIO AND TELEVISION

Perhaps the leading contributor toward furthering interest in music is radio. It has transferred the influence of the concert hall, opera, and stage into the home. It is deserving of much acclaim for this feat despite the fact it often relegates its all-too-few musical concerts to periods when audience ratings prove them to be poorly attended. If the potential of television is but partially realized, it ought also to contribute much toward raising the musical tastes of the young and old alike; an opportunity to see as well as hear the opera that opened the Metropolitan Opera season or to observe an outstanding conductor direct a highly skilled symphony orchestra can spur on efforts at acquiring this joyful diversion.

The increased popularity of classical music reflects the trend toward

[1] Edward Dickinson, *The Spirit of Music* (New York: Charles Scribner's Sons, 1931), p. 39.

the elevation of our musical tastes. Radio has made extensive use of recordings and transcriptions and has through this means exerted much of its influence. Record hours are growing in popularity throughout the nation and are well attended in settlement houses, community centers, libraries, playgrounds, as well as in schools and colleges.

CONCERT OFFERINGS

In the realm of "live" music, we find outdoor concerts in greater evidence and remarkably well attended. It is a common sight to see as many as twenty thousand persons in attendance at New York's Central Park Mall band concerts. Capacity audiences are also the rule in Philadelphia's Robin Hood Dell, Chicago's Grant Park, and the Hollywood Bowl. Needless to say, appreciation of our finer music can best be achieved through myriad opportunities to listen and enjoy.

Renewed emphasis on high-fidelity recording machines and collections, the increase of frequency-modulation (FM) radio stations, and television's concert presentations have contributed toward increased opportunities to elevate one's musical tastes. Concert offerings are making indelible impressions on the public. The Community Concerts Series throughout the country and record-lending libraries are also making inroads on our listening habits.

SUGGESTED ACTIVITIES

MOVIES

1. *The Symphony Orchestra.* A sound film by Erpi, 1938, which reveals the part played by the members of the orchestra and the director while interpreting a score, and the appearance and sound of each instrumental family. An aid in stimulating interest in symphonic music and instrument playing.

2. *The Brass Choir.* A sound film by Erpi, 1937, which shows the differences between the various brass instruments of a symphony orchestra and demonstrates the techniques of playing them. Useful in stimulating interest in symphonic music and instrument playing.

3. *Instruments of the Orchestra.* A sound film by Eastin Pictures Co., Davenport, Iowa. Helpful in developing an audiovisual conception of the sounds of musical instruments.

RECORDINGS

1. *The Ballad Hunter.* These recordings of American folk songs are highlighted by interviews with the singers. Five sixteen-inch 33⅓ rpm

recordings. Regarded as one of the finest albums of American folk songs. Procurable from the Federal Radio Education Committee, U.S. Office of Education, Washington, D.C.

2. *Contributions to Music.* This is a dramatization of the Negro's contribution to American musical life through thirty-nine minutes of celebrated Negro musical artists. Recorded at 33⅓ rpm and procurable from the Federal Radio Education Committee, U.S. Office of Education, Washington, D.C.

3. The RCA Victor *History of Music in Sound* and *Adventures in Music* merit review for possible adoption.

4. *The Rhythmic Activities Series.* Produced by RCA Victor and highly recommended. Volumes 1, 2, and 3 are designated for the primary grades and 4, 5, and 6 for the upper grades. They were originally issued in 1947 and contain suggestions for listening, with descriptive notes. In addition, they offer suggestions for imitative play, story and dramatization, rhythm instrument play, and free expression (hopping, leaping, jumping, clapping, and the like) for the primary grades.

Volumes 1, 2 and 3 are E-71 or WE-71 (78 rpm or 45 rpm); E-72 or WE-72 (78 rpm or 45 rpm), and E-73 or WE-73 (78 rpm or 45 rpm), respectively. Volumes 4, 5 and 6 are E-74 or WE-74 (78 rpm or 45 rpm); E-75 or WE-75 (78 rpm or 45 rpm), and E-76 or WE-76 (78 rpm or 45 rpm), respectively.

MISCELLANEOUS

1. *Music Appreciation Period*—how to listen to and appreciate music. Examples of music that are suited to the type of composition are as follows:

THE DANCE. Debussy's "Golliwog's Cakewalk," Dvořák's "Slavonic Dance No. 1 and 8," Bach's "Sarabande," Chopin's "Waltz in C-Sharp Minor," de Falla's "Ritual Fire Dance," German's "Merrymakers' Dance," Saint-Saëns' "Henry VIII: Gypsy Dance," and Khatchaturian's "Saber Dance."

THE ART SONG. Grieg's "Ich Liebe Dich," Tchaikovsky's "None But the Lonely Heart," MacDowell's "To the Sea," Moussorgsky's "Song of the Flea," Schubert's "Serenade," Cadman's "At Dawning," Nevin's "The Rosary," Foster's "Old Black Joe," and Jacobs-Bond's "A Perfect Day."

THE SUITE. Khatchaturian's *Masquerade Suite,* Mendelssohn's *Midsummer Night's Dream Suite,* Tchaikovsky's *Nutcracker Suite,* Grieg's *Peer Gynt Suite,* Taylor's *Through the Looking Glass Suite,* and MacDowell's *Woodland Sketches* and *Suite No. 2 for Orchestra.*

THE OPERA. Verdi's *Aida,* Gounod's *Faust,* Bizet's *Carmen,* Leoncavallo's *I Pagliacci*, Rossini's *Barber of Seville*, Mascagni's *Cavalleria Rusticana*, Wagner's *Tristan and Isolde*, Donizetti's *Lucia di Lammermoor*, Thomas' *Mignon*, and Strauss' *Salome*.

THE OPERETTA. Sullivan's *H.M.S. Pinafore*, Romberg's *The Student Prince*, Kern's *Show Boat*, Gershwin's *Porgy and Bess*, Herbert's *Babes in Toyland*, Balfe's *The Bohemian Girl*, DeKoven's *Robin Hood*, and Friml's *Rose Marie*.

THE BALLET. Ravel's *Daphnis and Chloe*, Tchaikovsky's *Swan Lake*, Borodin's *Prince Igor*, Debussy's *Afternoon of a Faun*, Stravinsky's *Petrouchka*, Rimsky-Korsakoff's *Scheherazade*, Gliere's *The Red Poppy*, and Copland's *Billy the Kid*.

THE TONE POEM. Sibelius' *Finlandia*, Saint-Saëns' *Danse Macabre*, Dukas' *The Sorcerer's Apprentice*, Moussorgsky's *Night on Bald Mountain*, and Rachmaninoff's *The Isle of the Dead*.

THE SYMPHONY. Franck's *Symphony in D Minor*, Tchaikovsky's *Symphony No. 5*, Haydn's *Surprise Symphony*, Beethoven's *Symphony No. 5*, Mozart's *Jupiter Symphony*, and Brahms' *Symphony No. 2*.

THE OVERTURE. Tchaikovsky's *1812 Overture*, Beethoven's *Egmont Overture*, Rossini's overture to *William Tell*, Offenbach's overture to *Orpheus in Hades*, von Suppe's overture to *The Light Cavalry*, and Mozart's overture to *The Magic Flute*.

THE CONCERTO. Beethoven's *Piano Concerto in G Major*, Tchaikovsky's *Piano Concert in B-Flat Minor*, Brahms' *Violin Concerto in D*, Schumann's *Concerto for Piano in A Minor*, and Mendelssohn's *Concerto in E Minor*.

2. *Record Hour*—recorded music with comments about the composer and his work.

3. *Concerts*:

a. Community band and orchestra may gladly give concerts on a regular basis in the playground, community center, or some such place.

b. The American Federation of Musicians has a fund through which it may be possible to secure the services of professional musicians at little cost to the recreation department.

c. Playground or center band consisting of those who frequent the recreation area.

d. City-wide band for larger communities wherein representatives from each recreation area may have an opportunity to play with a larger aggregation.

4. *Record Library*—a small sector of the indoor center or library where one can borrow some records. Also, a place should be set aside for listen-

ing with earphones so as not to disturb others who similarly want to listen to recordings of their own choice. This type of setup is to be found in many public, college, and public-school libraries. Its suitability for inclusion in the recreation program becomes readily apparent.

VOCAL MUSIC

Long before a child can display signs of humming or singing a tune, he imitates sounds. This is preliminary to later attempts at vocalizing and should be recognized as such. Vocal music is at its simplest when one attempts to hum or sing while working or playing. We then find it cropping up in the informal singing group with its usual locale about the piano. Later we note its appearance as community singing with a leader and musical accompaniment prominent. This is followed by singing on the part of small groups, such as Barber Shop Quartets.[2] Choral work comprising men's, women's, and mixed choruses is the acme of vocal music. Since group singing is most common in recreation programs, more detailed consideration will be given to this fundamental musical activity.

GROUP SINGING

To begin with, the church can be credited with the inauguration of group singing in the form of hymns and spirituals. During the days of ancient Greek drama, the chorus consisted of a number of people on the stage who either explained the action of the play or commented in song on the events portrayed.

Of more recent times, we have the influence of World War I with the masses singing doughboy songs of the "Johnny Get Your Gun" and "Over There" type. The public schools have contributed their share by furthering interest in group singing, as have the Sunday Schools, the settlement houses, the community centers, the camps, and the playgrounds. The influence of the family piano should not be overlooked with the familiar crowding of the makeshift harmony group. In addition, the contributions of the radio and theater organ sings help to round out the picture.

Should it be necessary to justify community singing in the recreational program, one can start by stating that it offers a simple and effective means of musical expression. It imparts to the singer an exhilarating and emotionally satisfying feeling belonging to this form of musical expres-

[2]Fostered in the United States and abroad by the Society for the Preservation and Encouragement of Barber Shop Quartet Singing in America.

sion. It provides an engaging activity where one can "lose oneself," thereby tending to refresh the participant both from and for his daily occupation. It also provides a contrasting activity for most, which increases its re-creative value.

Although practically everyone likes to sing, there is still a certain degree of timidity and shyness toward singing alone; group singing overcomes this obstacle. Community singing also tends to permeate the group with a congenial and binding spirit. In addition to being suitable as a program in itself, it can be employed as an opening feature at assemblies, rallies, town meetings, and similarly suitable events. Herein, it acts as a socializing and integrating force, tending to "warm up" the group for the activities to follow. Nor is it fantastic to believe that the ability to sing harmoniously in a group, to blend one's voice with those of others, can contribute toward harmonious living with our associates.

Importance of song selection. Moreover, the selection of songs has undergone a marked transformation. Whereas previously such songs as "Tenting Tonight," "Old Black Joe," and "Auld Lang Syne" were used exclusively in sing programs, the trend has shifted toward tunes of a more popular vein.

This thought was expressed graphically by a *New York Times* reporter. "As the program progressed, one thing was painfully apparent: Standbys such as 'Old Folks at Home,' 'When You and I Were Young Maggie,' and 'Peggy O'Neil,' were less popular than swingy 'Joseph, Joseph' and the intricate 'Oh, Ma-ma' music of the modern genre."[3] It is important to note that community singing has lagged behind the trend toward including popular tunes in its programs. This snubbing of songs that the majority are singing on their own is accountable, to a great extent, for retarding the community-sing movement.

What is sought is musical expression through song and not superimposed programming without regard to the group's interests. This need not imply the exclusion of the immortal tunes from our sing programs. On the contrary, once our groups are organized our opportunities to teach such songs are enhanced. Furthermore, it is essential that we accept the so-called popular tunes as desirable forms of musical expression which are increasingly losing the stigma of being musical trash; they are now recognized as a modern form of American music.

This is further evidenced by the fact that both Paul Whiteman and Benny Goodman have successfully presented their bands at the musically exclusive Carnegie Hall. The music of Gershwin, Kern, and Berlin is

[3]H. D. Corbin, "Everybody Sings," *Journal of Health and Physical Education* (May 1939), p. 287.

not really displacing that of Beethoven, Wagner, and Tchaikovsky. It is merely illustrating a transition in American musical life.

Interest and song selection. The matter of interest should always be considered in selecting the song program. Since interests vary with the type of audience, it is essential that the leader determine as far as is possible, the interests of the group he is to lead. The age, experience, and musical literacy of the group are to be considered. If it is a regularly scheduled group, the leader will get to know the song tastes of the group. Even though thorough planning is vital for the success of a sing, it should be concealed so as not to mar the spontaneity of the program. While a group at a parents' meeting would be interested predominantly in folk songs and ballads, youngsters in a playground prefer, in addition to popular tunes, play songs like "Old McDonald Had a Farm" and "The Monkey and the Zebra." At a public gathering or assembly, the singing of patriotic songs such as "The Star Spangled Banner," and "America, the Beautiful" is appropriate. The above examples are intended to illustrate that songs can be selected to suit the occasion.

To further exemplify this point, let's look at the program selected for the dedication ceremonies given by the Brooklyn Department of Parks for the elephant, Astra. As part of the celebration, a circus program was planned, with speeches by such celebrities as Alfred E. Smith and Freddie Bartholomew, plus group singing by the guests. As will be exemplified, it is often possible to add zest to a special occasion by selecting song titles suggestive of the event. Although one may not always find it feasible, it is surprising how often the effort will be amply rewarded. The songs selected for the occasion and their suitability are as follows:

SONG	SUITABLE FOR
1. "Alexander's Ragtime Band"	General opening number
2. "The Old Gray Mare"	The circus
3. "The Man on the Flying Trapeze"	The circus
4. "Little Annie Rooney"	Alfred E. Smith
5. "East Side-West Side"	Alfred E. Smith
6. "Pack Up Your Troubles in Your Old Kit Bag	General closing number

When there is no special occasion a program of a more general nature is in order. The alternating of a popular tune with an "old timer" is suggested to help meet the varied interests of all age groups. It certainly merits consideration for groups whose interests are unknown. The use of request numbers for a portion of the program is bound to be a satisfactory means of rounding out the program. It is advisable to alternate slow with vigorous tunes, so as to avoid possible boredom; an overdose of slow tunes may lead to lethargy, while an excess of fast tunes may be enervating.

ROTE TECHNIQUE OF SONG TEACHING

It is well to be versed in the methods of instructing a song by rote; there is no telling when song books or song sheets are not available. For one, the song should be one that is simple and that can be learned readily. The group may be motivated by an explanation of the background of the song, the circumstances attending its writing, and the period or year it was written, with something of the customs of the time.

The following steps are suggested:

1. The group should hear the words and music sung by the leader.
2. Then the song is divided into phrases, with the group repeating each phrase after it is sung by the leader.
3. This procedure is followed until the entire song is covered.
4. It is then sung in its entirety by the leader.
5. The group should sing it through on its own, thereby completing the technique.

Furthermore, recorded music can be used as an audio aid for song teaching. Decca Records features Frank Luther in the twenty-four songs of *Children's Corner*. Singing activities for primary grades and upper grades are contained on RCA Victor records: E/WE-83 (primary grades) and E/WE-84, E/WE-85, E/WE-86 (upper grades).

Leader's ability to sing. While it is not an absolute necessity, acceptable ability to sing on the part of the leader can do much toward adding to his effectiveness. It can serve as a cohesive force that may carry the group over the rough spots and possibly stimulate it toward greater effort. The author arrived at this conclusion when he led community singing in Brooklyn's Prospect Park. Laryngitis revealed beyond doubt that a much better response was realized when his voice was more audible to the singers.

Musical terms. The inexperienced leader may not be certain as to whether he is interpreting the song in the exact tempo as indicated by the composer. He should therefore be guided by the principle that it is better to err by being too rapid than too slow in tempo; a tune that drags becomes almost intolerable. Quite often, one will run into English designations for the tempo of a tune. On the other hand, it is well to become familiar with the Italian musical terms, for they are used frequently.

GLOSSARY OF MUSICAL TERMS

Adagio—slowly, leisurely
Allegro—quick, cheerful
Andante—slow, a walking tempo
Animato—spirited, with animation
Cantabile—flowing, in a singing style
Common time—4/4
Cut time—2/2
Crescendo—gradually louder
Diminuendo—gradually softer

Dolce—sweet, soft
Forte (f)—loud
Largo—very slow, broad
Mezzo forte (mf)—moderately loud
Moderato—in moderate tempo
Piano (p)—soft
Pianissimo (pp)—very soft
Valse—a waltz
Vivace—lively, quick

Adding spice to the program. To add variety to the sing, have the group whistle, hum, or la-la designated portions of tunes. In fact, when a request is made for a song to which there are no mimeographed lyrics available, the leader can suggest that those who are unfamiliar with the words simply hum or la-la the tunes.

Another device to stimulate interest is to select a better than average singer to serve as a soloist. He can be chosen to sing the solo parts of such songs as "Shortnin' Bread" ("Put on de skillet" to "coffee too") while the rest chime in at the chorus portion ("Mammy's little baby loves shortnin' . . ."). Such numbers as "Darling Nellie Gray" and "Home on the Range" also lend themselves to this type of treatment.

Still another variation is that of using a vocal soloist while the rest hum. Sentimental tunes of the "Carry Me Back to Old Virginny," "Swing Low, Sweet Chariot," and "Beautiful Dreamer" type are among those that are suited for this variation.

Novelty songs. Spice can also be added to the program by singing novelty songs such as "Row, Row, Row Your Boat," "Are You Sleeping?," "Old McDonald Had a Farm," and "John Brown's Body" to mention but a few. For the round-type tune, "Row, Row, Row Your Boat" will be used as an example. The group is to be divided into three sections. As the first section starts to sing, "Row, row, row your boat" the others are silent. When the word "boat" is reached, the leader signals the second section to start to sing "Row . . ." as the first sings "gently. . . ." The same procedure is followed by the other sections. "Are You Sleeping?" is also a round and can be used similarly. "Lovely Evening," "Three Blind Mice," and "Are You Sleeping?" are four-part rounds.

Original words. Another novelty song is "My Hat It Has Three Corners." Sing it as written the first time. For the second time, omit the word "hat" but motion as though you were tipping your hat. The third time, do as before also leaving out "three" and holding up three fingers.

The next time, repeat the previous omissions and exclude "corners" as you touch your elbow. Finally, omit "my" and point at yourself.

Combining songs. The combined use of "There's a Long, Long Trail" with "Keep the Home Fires Burning" can be used to instill the competitive spirit in song. After the group is divided into halves, the group that is to sing "Keep the Home Fires Burning" does not start until the other has completed the first two words, "There's a."

Other combat songs that can be used are "It's a Long Way to Tipperary" with "Pack Up Your Troubles" and "Are You Sleeping?" with "Three Blind Mice." Since "Are You Sleeping?" and "Three Blind Mice" are four-part rounds as well, the division of each group into four parts will make possible an eight-part round.

Action songs. The inclusion of songs that entail body movement are exceedingly popular with audiences. So much so, that they are a must in a well-rounded sing program. They hasten the warming-up process of the group and they add the satisfaction of physical release to the other benefits of singing. Suitable examples are "Down by the Old Mill Stream," "The Laugh Song," and "The Queen's Navy."

"Down by the Old Mill Stream"

Down by the old (*stroke beard*) mill (*circular motion with hands*) stream (*sweeping motion of arms while giving ripple effect with fingers,*
Where I (*motion to self*) first met (*shake hands with self*) you (*point at neighbor*).
With your (*point at neighbor*) eyes (*point at own eyes*) so blue (*point at sky*),
Dressed (*sweep over clothing*) in gingham too (*display two fingers*).
It was there (*point away from self*) I (*point to self*) knew (*point at brain*),
That you (*point at neighbor*) loved (*embrace self*) me (*point to self*) true.
You (*point at neighbor*) were sixteen (*display both open hands—ten, then open one hand—five, then display one finger to total sixteen*).
My (*point at self*) village queen (*circular motion over own head to signify a crown*),
Down by the old mill stream (*motions as above*).

"The Laugh Song"
(*Tune*: "John Brown's Body")

It isn't any trouble just to l-a-u-g-h,
It isn't any trouble just to l-a-u-g-h,
So laugh when you're in trouble
It will vanish like a bubble
If you'll only take the trouble
Just to l-a-u-g-h.

2nd verse: *Rollicking laughter to the musical*
accompaniment.

For the second time, repeat the musical accompaniment alone while the group laughs heartily throughout.

"The Queen's Nivy"[4]
(*Tune*: "The Old Gray Mare")

Oh, I don't want to march with the infantry (*keep time with foot*),
Ride with the cavalry (*riding motion, holding reins*).
Shoot with artillery (*aim gun*).
Oh, I don't want to fly over Germany (*flap arms*),
#I'm in the Queen's Nivy (*stand up and salute*),
I'm in the Queen's Nivy (*salute*), I'm in the Queen's Nivy (*salute and sit down*).
Return to the beginning and sing to end of line marked #.

Competition in song. By dividing the sing audience into any of a number of possible divisions, added interest and a more willful response may be secured. This measure is particularly suited to a group that does not respond sufficiently. Challenge the females in the group to compete with the males by requesting that each group sing a chorus alone. Have both groups join in for the third chorus. At the conclusion call it a "draw," reminding them that although they both sang well on their own they sounded much better together. The seating arrangement may lend itself toward competition between odd-numbered rows (1, 3, 5 and so forth) against the even-numbered ones (2, 4, 6, and so forth). If the seats are numbered, then the even-numbered seats can compete against the odd-numbered ones; the same can hold true for the aisles.

There are numerous other possibilities which are adaptable to the occasion. Harry Robert Wilson capably illustrates some of these measures when he states, "Divisions can be made in the following ways, many of which offer some jovial good fun: . . . married, single; everyone over thirty-five years of age, everyone under thirty-five years of age; everyone who is happy, everyone who is unhappy; everyone who went to church last Sunday, everyone who did not go to church last Sunday; Democrats, Republicans; sopranos, altos; tenors, basses; freshmen, sophomores, juniors, seniors (in schools); students who expect to get their degree or diploma, students who never expect to get their degree or diploma (college and high school); everyone in the balcony, everyone on

[4]Harry Robert Wilson, *Lead a Song* (Hall & McCreary Company), p. 90. Used by permission.

the main floor; all those who help their mothers wash the dishes, all those who do not help their mothers wash the dishes (for children)."[5]

How to lead. Of basic importance in community singing, as in all other recreational activities, is leadership. It is essential that the leader should possess an elementary knowledge of music. He should be familiar with the accepted hand movements that are used to lead songs written in the various tempi. In addition, ability to sing well enough to lead the group by his voice as well will prove helpful.

The following are the more common tempi and the simplified methods of leading them:

A. Two-four time (2/4)   —Two beat

B. Three-four time (3/4)   —Three beat

Note: Music written in 3/8 time can be led as though the music were written in 3/4 or waltz time.

C. Four-four time (4/4)   —Four beat

Note: Many songs written in 4/4 time, especially those in the more popular vein, are played and sung in 'cut time' or 2/4 time. Even though some songs may be written in cut time (C2/2) they may be beat out in 4/4 time if of a slow tempo. Experiment beforehand to see which is most advisable.

D. Six-eight time (6/8)   —Six beat

Note: When leading marches in 6/8 time, the two-beat method should be used.

In leading, the movements of the leader should be clear-cut so as to indicate precisely what is meant. The movements of the right hand usually designate the tempo, whereas those of the left hand signify increase in volume with the palm upward or decrease in volume with the palm downward. An abrupt and angular motion can be used to denote a snappy, majestic beat, whereas a curved beat indicates a melodious song.

[5]Wilson, *Lead a Song,* p. 74.

Some song leaders secure the desired effect by motioning downward while emphasizing each syllable. This also spares the song leader the need to distinguish whether a song should start with the downbeat or upbeat.

Progressive leadership steps. As a supplement, let us consider how to organize and conduct a community sing in progressive steps.

1. Secure adequate publicity through the newspapers, bulletins, posters and the like.
2. If there is to be a large audience, it will be of advantage to use an amplifier or public address system.
3. It is essential that each member of the audience be given a copy of the words to each song. Do not take for granted that the lyrics are known, since the least bit of uncertainty as to the exact wording will definitely cause a decrease in volume. The simple expediency of mimeographing or using any other reproducing method will enable the leader to select a varied program. There is no published song book on the market that can possibly embody the lyrics of both old and up-to-the-minute song hits.
4. When the program is conducted during the evening or in an enclosed area where the procuring of adequate light is a problem, it is advisable to use a projector by means of which the words can be cast on a screen. An opaque projector is a great aid for this purpose.
5. The leader should stand in a position so that his movements can be easily seen by everyone.
6. As a variation with some groups, it may be advisable for the leader to walk among the members of his audience while leading them. This method will often improve the leader–audience relationship and increase the response.
7. All participants in the community sing, whether seated or standing, should be close together as a unit. This will make possible a better blending of voices and facilitate the spreading of enthusiasm. It will also assist the group in keeping time with the music.
8. Musical accompaniment is an essential aid. A piano, accordion, organ, or a similarly appropriate musical instrument can be used.
9. The playing of a few bars of each song prior to its singing is recommended so that the group will hear a sample of the key and tempo of each song. It will also serve to refresh the memory of those who may not be very familiar with the tune.
10. Impress the audience with the fact that community singing differs from other forms of audience entertainment in that each singer contributes toward the enjoyment of the others; the best results are secured when all sing in unison. Seek their wholehearted cooperation and participation on this basis.
11. The leader and accompanist should select a key suited to the majority of the group. Use a pitch pipe if a piano is not at hand.

12. To add variety to the singing, have the group whistle and hum designated portions of songs.
13. Interject phrases of encouragement such as "That was great!" and "Let's try to make it perfect!" When a song is sung poorly, it is usually desirable to repeat it, while at the same time pointing out the shortcomings in a good-natured manner.
14. Should the program be scheduled to last an hour or more, one must guard against tiring the singers' voices. An intermission is suggested during which some form of entertainment might be provided. This can take the form of amateur singing, harmonica playing, instrumental recitals, and so forth. An intermission program of this sort will serve the dual purpose of entertaining the audience, while at the same time enabling its members to rest their voices.
15. Just as the public speaker finds it invaluable to practice his speeches before a mirror, so can the sing leader benefit by seeing himself as he appears to the audience.
16. Another means of improving the performance is to have a close friend take notes of the sing session as an impartial observer and make a list of the obvious faults; then the leader should take every opportunity to make the needed corrections.
17. Sincere enthusiasm and naturalness in speech on the part of the leader will improve his standing with the audience. Opportunities to employ humor will often arise. One can use these to good advantage providing they are not overdone.

These suggestions are intended to help overcome as well as obviate the common problems associated with community singing. Nevertheless, one must acknowledge that all the advice in the world cannot serve as a substitute for the actual experience. It will indeed be startling to observe how polished the performance will become as the sessions progress.

RHYTHMICAL DEVELOPMENT

The basis of all music is rhythm which finds an outlet through the body. Rhythm must be felt inwardly by the individual before it can be reflected in the individual's behavior. The development of a person's rhythmical sense should be started as early in life as possible, preferably in early childhood. Even the simple act of keeping time is pleasurable.

In order to effect the child's physical reactions to rhythm, he should be exposed to the following simple rhythmical motions to appropriate musical accompaniment: walking, galloping, hand clapping, tapping with hands or feet, head swaying, total body swaying, jumping, skipping, and marching.

The child may respond to any one or a group of beats in a measure whether it is two-four, three-four, or six-eight. Through these activities, he may develop the wherewithal to coordinate his body reactions via rhythmical and emotional responses. Some children are lacking in the ability to react with suitable rhythmical responses. This shortcoming can usually be overcome through experience with rhythm. It is advisable to guard against employing the same musical numbers for an extended period since the learned responses may then be restricted to *songs* rather than to the rhythm itself:

Suggested Records[6] for Rhythmical Development
Body Rhythm

Volume I   78 RPM E-71   45 RPM WE-71

1. "Gnomes"—Reinhold; "Dwarfs"—Reinhold; "Fairies"—Scherzo—Schubert; "Clowns"—*Midsummer Night's Dream*—Mendelssohn

2. "Sparks"—Moszkowski; "Etude Joyeuse"—Kopylow; "Barcarole"—Rubinstein; "Valsette"—Borowski; "Valse Serenade"—Poldini; "Love's Dream"—Czibulka

3. "March in F Major," "Theme for Skipping," "Flying Birds," "Wheel Barrow Motive," "Plain Skip," "Tiptoe March," "Military March," "Galloping Horses," "Running Horses," "High Stepping Horses," "Skipping Theme"—Anderson

4. "Gigue in A"—Corelli; "Jaglied"—Schumann; "Sicilienne"—Gluck; Ballet—Gluck; "Adagio"—Corelli

Volume II   78 RPM E-72   45 RPM WE-72

1. "Soldier's March"—Schumann; "March in D Flat"—Hollaender; "March"—*Nutcracker Suite*—Tchaikovsky; "March"—*Alceste*—Gluck

2. "Boating on the Lake"—Kullak; "Skating"—Kullack; "Walzer"—Gurlitt; "March"—Gurlitt; "La Bergeronette"—Burgmuller; "Waltz"—Schubert; "Scherzo"—Gurlitt; "L'Arabesque"—Burgmuller; "Tarantelle"—Saint-Saëns

3. "Run, Run, Run"—Concone; "Jumping"—Gurlitt; "Running Game"—Gurlitt; "Air de Ballet"—Jadassohn; "Waltzes Nos. 1, 2 and 9"—Brahms.

4. "Praeludium"—Jarnefelt; "Les Pifferari"—*The Pipers*—Gounod; "Happy and Light of Heart"—*Bohemian Girl*—Balfe; "Tarantelle"—Mendelssohn

[6]All records are by RCA Victor unless otherwise indicated.

Volume III   78 RPM E-73   45 RPM WE-73

1. "Northern Song," Op. 68, No. 31—
   Schumann; "Song of the
   Shepherdess"—Weber; "March—
   Bach–MacDowell; "Papillons,
   No. 8"—Schumann; "Dance of the
   Moorish Slaves"—*Aida*—Verdi;
   "Slavonic Dance No. 1"—Dvořák;
   "Siciliana"—*L'Allegro*—Handel

2. "Polly, Put the Kettle On"—English
   Folk; "Lavender's Blue"—English
   Folk; "Waltz", Op. 9a, No. 3—
   Schubert; "Come Lasses and Lads"
   —English Folk; "John Peel"—Old
   Hunting Song; "Marche Militaire,"
   Op. 51, No. 1—Schubert

VOLUME III   78 RPM E-73   45 RPM WE 73

3. "Cradle Song"—Houser; "The
   Blacksmith"—Brahms; "Dolly's
   Funeral"—Tchaikovsky;
   "Tarantelle," Op. 46, No. 7—
   Heller; "Berceuse"—Ilyinsky;
   "Silhouette"—Reinhold; "Valse
   Gracieuse"—Dvořák

4. "Mirror Dance"—Gounod;
   "Elfenspiel"—Kjerulf; "The Witch"—
   Tchaikovsky; "March of the Tin
   Soldiers"—Tchaikovsky; "Knight of
   the Hobby-Horse"—Schumann;
   "The Clock"—Kullak; "Postillion"—
   Godard; "Peasants' Dance"—Schytte

Childhood Rhythm Records
Fundamental Rhythms

Name	Record Number
"Ducks, Camels, Horses, Elephants"	RE 103
"Trains, Soldiers, Tops, Airplanes	RE 104
"Swings, Seesaws, Rowboats, Bicycles"	RE 105
"Fairies, Witches, Giants, Dwarfs"	RE 106

The rhythm band. An especially effective way to further rhythmical expression is through the rhythm band. It offers a progressive learning situation for those who have advanced from the body rhythm state
and provides a basic exposure to instrumental music. The instrumentation
consists of small percussion instruments which are played in a social setting with other members of the same age group. We are reminded that
"Percussion instruments are but extensions of patting feet, clapping hands,
and snapping fingers."[7] More careful listening may result from accompaniment with percussion instruments.

Control over the child's rhythmical reaction can be developed so
that he can react precisely to the set rhythms which comprise a song.
During rhythm band play, the child has to confine his response to the
beat he is instructed to play. Recorded or piano music is essential to accompany a rhythm band. Moreover, music that is familiar to the children should be used for accompaniment at the outset. Marches, Mother

[7] L. B. Pitts, M. Glenn, and L. E. Walters, *The Kindergarten Book* (Boston: Ginn
and Company, 1949), p. 137.

Goose melodies, and other familiar tunes are suggested. Whenever possible, emphasis is to be placed on individual interpretation.

The small percussion instruments that are employed in a rhythm band need not be restricted to a stereotyped list. To be sure, most bands of this type use a few of the following common pieces:

Triangles	Cymbals	Bird whistles	Swiss bells
Tambourines	Wood blocks	Shepherds pipes	Castanets
Drums	Sand blocks	Bazookas	Maracas
Rhythm sticks	Ocarinas	Kazoos	Rhythm-tone gourds
Sleigh bells	Marimbas	Jingle clogs	

Organization of a rhythm band. It is advisable that the children be prepared for the advent of the rhythm band. An opportunity to observe an organized rhythm band in action can do much toward stimulating interest in the activity. Preliminary rhythmical development through body rhythm activities is very desirable although not absolutely essential.

At the start, each instrument should be played before the group. This demonstration is to be followed by affording each child an opportunity to play a familiar tune. The instruments ought to be rotated to expose each child to the experience of playing each instrument. To facilitate more effective responses, all instruments of one type should be kept in a distinct section.

In presenting a new tune, the music should be played at least once to familiarize the children with it. Thereupon, the band is to play with each child interpreting the music in his own fashion. The guiding hand of the leader ought to make its presence felt, but not at the expense of spontaneity and enjoyment. Each child is to be encouraged to lead the band. This feature may aid the child to acquire leadership traits, better insight into the importance of cooperation, and enhanced musical ability. Whenever feasible, the children are to be allowed to play numbers of their own choice. They are to be given an opportunity to suggest the instruments most desirable for each phrase once they become familiar with the music. Once the band is well established, the reading of rhythmic symbols can be taught with greater emphasis to be placed on shading of tone, proper phrasing, and rhythm.

Suggested Music for Rhythm Bands

(RCA Victor Recordings)

Elementary Grades   78 RPM E-90   45 RPM WE-90

1. "Amaryllis"—Old French Rondo— Ghys; "Minuet in G"—Paderewski

2. "Le Secret"—Intermezzo—Gautier; "Pirouette"—Finck

3. "Gavotte"—*Mignon*—Thomas;
   "Rendezvous"—Intermezzo—Aletter

4. "Rataplan"—Donizetti; "Serenata"—
   Moszkowski; "Waltz No. 5"—
   Koschat; "With Castanets"—
   Reinecke; "Shadows"—Schytte

Novelty instruments. In the development and nurturing of the rhythmical sense in the child, much originality can be exercised. Experiments can be carried on by striking all subjects. The sounds that will emanate from the most unexpected sources are often astounding.

Glass objects are simple and fruitful sources of sound. For example, soda bottles of varying sizes may be used. Shading of tone can be achieved by adding water to the bottles until the desired note is secured. Similar effects can be obtained by using drinking glasses of different sizes with water added as needed. Each glass can have a different color by adding water colors so as to simplify the identification of each desired note; this device may be especially helpful to the very young child. In a similar vein, each glass or bottle may be numbered so that tunes may be played simply by following written numbers instead of notes.

For the drum effect, gourds, butter tubs, hollow stumps and kegs (covered with aviator's linen coated with shellac for a drum skin) are advocated; wet sheepskin stretched across a rim with thumbtacks to hold it in place plus tiny sleigh bells attached to the rim is suggested for a tambourine.[8] Other rhythmical instruments can be made by using "horseshoes or railroad spikes for triangles; round cereal boxes for drums, . . . combs with tissue paper to carry melody hummed on them."[9] A xylophone can be made from strips of wood of varying lengths for each note; the strips are then nailed to and suspended from a rope.

Imparting knowledge of instruments. As an added means of furthering the child's awareness and knowledge of instruments, we can expose him to recordings that emphasize solo performances of various orchestral instruments. The following RCA Victor records (with serial orchestral instruments. The following RCA Victory records (with serial numbers) may prove helpful:

Volume I   78 RPM E-77   45 RPM WE-77

1. "Lullaby"—Brahms; "Little
   Sandman"—Brahms; "Hush My
   Babe"—Rousseau; "Lullaby"—
   Mozart; "Cradle Song"—Schubert;
   "Sweet and Low"—Barnby

2. "March of the Little Lead Soldiers"
   —Pierné; "March" (Trumpet and
   Drum) and "Impromptu" (The Top)
   —*Petite Suite*—Bizet

[8]S. N. Coleman, *Creative Music for Children* (New York: G. P. Putnam's Sons, 1922), pp. 40–42.

[9]Nicoletta Uriuoli, "Music and Drama in Program," *Recreation Magazine* (December 1949), p. 442.

3. "Badinage"—Herbert; "Legend of the Bells"—Planquette; "Humoresque"—Dvořák; "Scherzo"—Third Symphony—Beethoven; "Minuet"—Paderewski; "Gavotte"—Popper; "Minuet"—Beethoven; "Rock-a-bye Baby"—Traditional

4. "Run, Run"; "Ring Around the Rosy"; "March Little Soldier"; "Sleeping Time"; "Hobby Horse"—*Memories of Childhood*—Pinto

Singing games and folk dances. The child's rhythmical and musical development can be enhanced by the traditional singing games. Folk dances can lay claim to these contributions as well. It is therefore significant that Hood and Schultz[10] present the music and play directions for such simple dances and games as "Shoemaker's Dance," "Chimes of Dunkirk," "I See You," and "Skip To My Lou" in their outstanding book.

Recordings are available from RCA Victor for other worthwhile singing games and folk dances. They are listed below, along with their issue numbers.

Singing Game and Folk Dance Recordings
Singing Games

Primary Grades   78 RPM E-87   45 RPM WE-87

1. "The Big Gray Cat," "Hippity Hop to the Barber Shop," "Ten Little Indians," "Yankee Doodle," "The Snail," "Sally, Go Round the Moon," "A-Hunting We Will Go," "The Thread Follows the Needle"

2. "London Bridge"—English; "Here We Go 'Round the Mulberry Bush"—American; "Soldier Boy"—American; "The Muffin Man"—American

3. "The Farmer in the Dell"—American; "Did You Ever See a Lassie?"—American; "Way Down in the Paw Paw Patch"—American; "Old Pompey"—American; "Skip to My Lou"—American

4. "Looby Loo"—English; "Oats, Peas, Beans and Barley Grow"—English; "The Needle's Eye"—American; "Jolly is the Miller"—English

Folk Dances

"Bean Porridge Hot"
"Carrousel"
"Bluebird Through the Window"
"Children's Polka"
"Jump Jim Crow"
"Nixie Polka"
"Thread Follows the Needle"
"Yankee Doodle"

"Indian War Dance"
"Jolly is the Miller"
"Rig-A-Jig-Jig"
"Skip to My Lou"
"Swiss May Dance"
"Ten Little Indians"
"Hot Cross Buns"
"Csebogar"

Bowmar, No. 3

[10]M. V. Hood and E. J. Schultz, *Learning Music Through Rhythm* (Boston: Ginn and Company, 1949), pp. 18–23.

American Folk Dances

"Captain Kinks"   "Schottische"
"Sicilian Circle"   "Polka"
"Patty Cake Polka"   "Varsovienne"
"Virginia Reel"   "Oh, Johnny"

Bowmar, No. 5

Folk Dances—Lower Grades

"Bleking"—Swedish   "Seven Steps"—German
"Bow-Bow-Belinda"—American   "Danish Dance of Greeting"
"Donkey Dance"—Mexican   "Chimes of Dunkirk"—Belgium
"Children's Polka"—German   "Carrousel"—Swedish

Burns-Evans-Wheeler, Album I

"Put Your Little Foot"—American   "Heel and Toe Polka"—American
"Kolos"—Serbian   "Swedish Clap Dance"
"Oh! Susanna"—American   "Corsican"—French, Parts I and II
"Csebogar"—Hungarian

Burns-Evans-Wheeler, Album II

RCA Victor's Folk Dance Series incorporates Festival Folk Dances (LPM-1621), Happy Folk Dances (LPM-1620), Special Folk Dances (LPM-1619), First Folk Dances (LPM-1625), Folk Dances for Fun (LPM-1624), All-Purpose Folk Dances (LPM-1623), and Folk Dances for All Ages (LPM-1622).

Note: See Appendix B for square dance record sources.

MUSICAL PARTY

The scheduling of a musical party can be a most enjoyable and stimulating event. Here again, the program should be geared to the musical interests and aptitudes of the group. The features of a musical party conducted by a musical club[11] are suggestive of the events to be included for such an occasion. The means of scoring and the awards, if any, can be worked out by the party committee in keeping with the local setting.

PARTY PROGRAM

Theme: Music is Fun!

Haste thee, Nymph, and bring with thee
Jest and youthful Jollity,
Quips and cranks and wanton wiles,
Nods and becks and wreathed smiles,
Such as hang on Hebe's cheek,
And love to live in dimple sleek,
Sport that wrinkled Care derides,
And Laughter holding both his sides.

—JOHN MILTON

Let's Relax (introductory remarks)
Let's all sing (group singing)
Anecdotes

[11]Musical party tendered by the Music Club of Lock Haven, Pennsylvania.

Sonata before dinner. A hostess was mortified. A distinguished assemblage had convened at her house for a dinner party and a series of unfortunate accidents had delayed the announcement of dinner. In an effort to entertain the guests, she seated herself at the piano and played a Chopin nocturne for them. Still dinner was not ready, and another awkward pause loomed. Turning to an elderly gentleman on her right, she asked sweetly, "Would you like a sonata before going to dinner?" He replied briskly: "Why, yes, thanks! I had a couple on my way here, but I could stand another."[12]

Kreisler and his violin. A society woman who invited Fritz Kreisler to dinner added to her note: "P.S. Please bring your violin." Mr. Kreisler was equally polite and wrote a note accepting the invitation. He too had a postscript: "P.S. My violin never dines out!"[13]

"Leonore Overture" and Stokowski. It was a memorable night when Stokowski was conducting the Philadelphia Orchestra in Beethoven's "Leonore Overture No. 3" and the off-stage trumpet call twice failed to sound on cue. Directly the last note of the overture had been played, the apoplectic Stokowski rushed into the wings with murder in his heart. He found the trumpeter struggling in the clutches of a burly watchman. "I tell you you can't blow the damn thing here," the watchman kept insisting. "There is a concert going on inside."[14]

Gershwin and Stravinsky. The Russian composer Stravinsky tells the story of an exchange between Gershwin and himself when Gershwin was visiting Paris in the spring of 1928. "How much will you charge me for a few lessons in orchestration?" Gershwin asked. "How much do you make a year?" retaliated Stravinsky. "$100,000," answered Gershwin. There was a short silence and then Stravinsky said, "How about you giving me lessons?"[15]

"The Scheherazade Suite." Then there's the story of the buck announcer whose first assignment was to cover a program of classical music. Finding a handy corner, he utilized both space and time for a brief rehearsal. He thereupon announced, "First the orchestra will play the Ave Maria by Bach–Gounod." An observant musician tapped him on the shoulder and explained that when you see a dash in an attribution it means that the composition was written by the first man and arranged by the second. The announcer was appreciative. Full of knowledge and its accompanying courage, he introduced the final number as "the

[12]Ted Cott, *Victor Book of Musical Fun* (New York: Simon and Schuster, Inc.), 1945. Used by permission.
[13]*Ibid.*, p. 33.
[14]*Ibid.*, p. 55.
[15]*Ibid.*, p. 87.

Scheherazade Suite," composed by Rimsky and arranged by Korsakov.[16]

Alec Templeton. The things which Alec Templeton, famous British pianist, has done to the classics and the composers of the classical music are enough to cause these composers to whirl in their graves. The following are some of his concert references:

"Debussy at Dubuque"   "Mendelssohn Mows 'Em Down"
"Corelli at the Corral"   "Haydn Takes to Ridin' "
"Mozart Matriculates"   "Handel with Care"
"Bach Goes to Town"

VOCAL DUETS EXTRAORDINARY

Each individual is presented with one half of a song sheet. The person who has the other half that matches the one held by any participant becomes his duet partner; the two are then to sing the music on their joint song sheet. (This feature may be used also as an "ice breaker.")

CAN YOU ANSWER THIS ONE?[17]

One word each for the answer to these questions, please, the words being common musical terms.

What do you open a lock with?   *A key*
How does the photographer tell you to look?   *Sharp*
What tragedy can happen to your car tire?   *Flat*
What does your tailor take, first of all?   *Measure*
If as an Army captain, you get a promotion, what is your new rank?   *Major*

In practically every concerto, at one point (usually toward the end of the first movement) the orchestra leaves off and the solo instrument plays an extended passage in free style, soloist and orchestra presently coming together to bring the movement to a close. What is such a passage called?   *Cadenza*

Genius has had its handicaps and penalties; composers have gone deaf, blind or mad. Can you name two in each category?

Blind	*Mad*
Delius	Smetana
Bach	Hugo Wolf
Handel	Schumann

In what opera does a mechanical doll sing?   *"Tales of Hoffman"*

[16]*Ibid.*, p. 45.
[17]*Ibid.*, *passim.*

What orchestra instrument gives the others the pitch? *Oboe*

What have the following in common: Minuet, sarabande, bourree, courante, galliard? *Dances*

Everybody knows that Beethoven's "Sixth Symphony" is nicknamed Pastoral. Can you recall two other works each of which is also called Pastoral Symphony? The oratorio, *The Messiah*, by Handel; *The Second Symphony*, by Vaughan Williams.

Reginald DeKoven has composed a song that has become practically the national anthem of the bridal service itself. What is its title and for what operetta was it written? "Oh Promise Me," *Robin Hood*.

Which composers wrote the two most popular wedding marches? *Mendelssohn, Wagner*

To which of these does the bride march up the aisle to be married? Wagner's "Bridal Chorus" from *Lohengrin*

To which one does she come down the aisle with her husband? Mendelssohn's "Wedding March."

MATCHING MUSICAL TERMS[18]

1.	A slang term applied to "the four hundred"	*Swells*
2.	The prohibition law did away with them	*Bars*
3.	A derogatory term applied to lawyers	*Sharp*
4.	Terms related to our national game	*Base and Run*
5.	A part of a fish	*Scale*
6.	Something used by a shepherd	*Staff*
7.	That which betrays one's birthplace	*Accent*
8.	Something related to railroads	*Lines and Ties*
9.	Something to take when tired	*Rests*
10.	The name of a girl	*Grace*
11.	Two parts of a dollar	*Quarters and Halves*
12.	A portion of a sentence	*Phrase*
13.	An unaffected person	*Natural*
14.	A reflection upon character	*Slur*
15.	A plant for seasoning	*Time (thyme)*
16.	Obtainable from a bank	*Notes*
13.	An unaffected person	*Flat*
18.	Found on a check	*Signature*
19.	It is free at gas stations	*Air*
20.	Used for bundling	*Cord (chord)*
21.	Something used by a seamstress	*Measure*
22.	A telegraph operator uses it constantly	*Key*
23.	An important officer	*Major*
24.	Related to a policeman	*Beat*

[18]Charles F. Smith. *Games and Game Leadership*. Reprinted by permission of Dodd, Mead & Co. Copyright 1932 by Charles F. Smith.

SUGGESTED READINGS

Baird, Forrest J. *Music Skills for Recreation Leaders.* Dubuque, Iowa: William C. Brown Company, Publishers, 1963.

Best, Dick and Beth Best. *The New Song Fest.* New York: Crown Publishers, Inc., 1963.

Carabo-Cone, Madeleine. *The Playground as Music Teacher.* New York: Harper & Row, Publishers, 1959.

Leonhard, Charles. *Recreation Through Music.* New York: A. S. Barnes & Co., Inc., 1952.

Lomax, Alan, and Elizabeth Preston. *The Penguin Book of American Folk Songs.* Baltimore: Penguin Books, Inc., 1965.

Music Therapy, Third Book of Proceedings of the National Association for Music Therapy, Lawrence, Kansas: Allen Press, 1953.

Nye, Robert, *et al. Singing with Children.* Belmont, Calif.: Wadsworth Publishing Co., Inc., 1962.

Ottman, Robert W. *Music for Sight Singing.* Englewood Cliffs, N.J.: Prentice-Hall, Inc., 1965.

Zanzig, Augustus. *Starting and Developing a Rhythm Band.* Washington, D.C.: National Recreation and Parks Association, 1951.

Chapter 20

THERAPEUTIC RECREATION AND PLAY THERAPY

One out of every twelve is a handicapped person. This accounts for approximately 16,500,000 individuals, whose conditions are usually not fully understood. Invariably they have similar wants, interests, appreciations, and feelings for recognition, acceptance, expression and self-realization. That they are often deprived of these opportunities goes without saying.

The need for leaders in therapeutic recreation is nowhere near being met. In fact, there is no evidence that this gap is being narrowed or about to be in the immediate future. This shortage of personnel is critical and warrants a many-pronged attack. Aside from the efforts of outstanding professionals in the field, the resort toward scholarships has proved very advantageous. In the state of Indiana, the scholarship program of the Department of Mental Health provides the undergraduate with tuition plus a stipend of two hundred dollars per month during the time in school. In return for this financial assistance, the student agrees to work in a mental hospital for a period commensurate with the financial support.

Terms defined. The recreation leader may find himself bewildered by the seemingly interchangeable use of therapeutic recreation, play therapy, and occupational therapy. Actually, they are not one and the same. On the other hand, they are all related in that they employ the tools of recreation as a phase of their treatment. Therapeutic recreation makes use of play media to provide the mentally and/or physically ill with satisfactory interests and outlets in conjunction with the other therapeutic means at hand. It is suited for all age groups and is used as adjunctive therapy to promote general well-being and develop social skills as therapy progresses. It is general in nature.

In play therapy, we observe techniques that are utilized primarily on children. They are afforded opportunities to "play out" their troubles. They express their innermost feelings while being figuratively carried away by the play situations. Children may act out their suppressed aggressions by reacting against such parental substitutes as the therapist, dolls, or clay models without subsequent guilt feelings. The play materials become symbols of the child's anxieties and perplexities. According to Gardner[1] "The outstanding feature of the play is his endless replaying of the same activity in precisely the same manner. There is no great deviation in the pattern and he never seems to tire of it.'"

By means of occupational therapy, an emphasis is placed on the use of handicrafts to help to restore the patient to a state of restored confidence and vocational competence. While all are superficially similar, there is a closer relationship between recreational and occupational therapies than between either of these and play therapy.

HISTORICAL GLEANINGS

In primitive times, the crippled were treated inhumanely. Infanticide was commonly practiced by the Spartans. The Roman considered a crippled child an "ill omen" upon his household. This, coupled with the fact that during certain periods of the Roman era the father possessed the right to destroy his offspring, makes very apparent the depths from which we have risen.

The use of play activities as means of helping the emotionally disturbed, the psychotic, the crippled, the problem child, or the convalescent has been given added emphasis in the last thirty years. However, the birth of recreational therapy antedates the Christian era. Of more recent date, the physician Pinel resorted to work-through-play as a mental therapeutic device. Dr. Benjamin Rush recognized the need for relaxation to prevent abnormalities brought on by tensions.

While this has not been true for long, the leader of professional medical recreation currently has the educational background and skills for directing programs in a hospital setting. These are aimed at working in concert with the psychiatrist to help meet the needs of the individual patients. This can now be judged for its direct therapeutic outcomes. He is a respected member of the therapeutic team.

As in any professional endeavor, there is genuine concern for the values in each activity and their carry-over into their lives upon leaving the institution. The fact that they were hospitalized in the first place is an indication of a weakness in making sound use of their leisure potential. Hence, the need for direct effort at filling this void with meaningful

[1]George E. Gardner, "Recreation's Part in Mental Health," *Recreation Magazine* (January 1952), p. 447.

skills and appreciations of a significant number of recreational pursuits. The appropriateness of Mabel Palmer's *The Social Club: A Bridge from Mental Hospital to Community* bears particular mention and relatedness at this juncture.

RELEASE THROUGH PLAY

The presence of the patient in the hospital setting reflects an inability to reside satisfactorily in the outside world. Hence, the psychiatric hospital staff and activities are aimed at "guiding, teaching and directing the patient"[2] toward what Dr. Karl Menninger has termed "living and learning." Adjunctive therapy and the adjunctive therapist have essential roles to play in this "living and learning," involving activities, work, or play to aid in the patient's rehabilitation. The therapists referred to are specialists in recreation, music, art, occupational therapy, and the other therapies in the hospital activities program. Pratt thereupon groups the diverse activities under the four aspects of work, play, education, and creative activities. In this regard, the recreation therapist is a vital member of the therapy team with a basic concern for the areas of play and creative activities.

Play affords the individual a safety valve through which he gives vent to his feelings which might be damaging or undesirable. The game provides an outlet under the bonds of rules, boundaries, and officiating which parallels life. It can constitute a form of therapy while helping the patient become restored and sense fulfillment; moreover, it approximates conditions he will encounter on the outside and provide him with a carry-over of interests and pursuits.

VALUES

Today, we recognize the importance of aiding each individual toward an optimum adjustment despite his handicaps. To help the patient achieve joyful participation within his capacity to participate is recognized as a desirable adjunct to whatever medical or psychiatric treatment is indicated. The acceptance of psychosomatic medicine probably ushers in a period of even greater emphasis on recreational therapy. Certainly, the roles of satisfactory adjustments, emotional outlets, and socializing influences loom large in a well-conceived recreational program.

Starting with the needs of each individual, wholesome opportunities for restoration of muscular strength and circulatory efficiency can be

[2]James F. Pratt, "Learning to Work and Play Again," in *Recreation in Treatment Centers*, Vol. III, September 1964, p. 18.

provided through play situations. The vital part the will to get well can play in one's recovery is not to be underestimated. An effective recreation program may contribute greatly toward bolstering a patient's morale and making him happier and more cooperative, thereby supporting the other measures leading toward a speedier recovery. As a result, recreational therapy is an accepted branch of the healing art in federal, state, and local hospitals throughout the country.

The need for recreation is omnipresent in all people. Although it fills a vital need in the normal individual's life, it is even more necessary for the infirm in helping to mitigate the confining existence of being hospitalized. The tendency to become morbidly concerned about one's welfare and preoccupied with fantasy rather than reality can be obviated by recreational therapy. In regressive cases, these contacts with reality can serve as opening wedges through which the patient can be reached and help support the other therapeutic measures.

OBJECTIVES

Mitchell and Mason[3] inform us: "It is doubtful if any of the manifold contributions of play in other areas of human life, not even its contributions to physical development, exceeds that which it makes to mental health." That it can serve as a preventive as well as a therapeutic force holds true indeed. For the normal individual, the activities are primarily recreational with such associated outcomes as cultural growth, character development, and social adaptability. For the atypical, play can fortify the other therapeutic measures so that regression, if any, will cease and contact with reality can be furthered. The mentally ill often feel that they are misunderstood, their abilities unappreciated. Opportunities wherein the patient can take part and perform successfully, prompting approval and praise, can help to integrate him. These pleasurable experiences will evoke further responses in keeping with the Law of Effect which states, in a positive vein, that we learn more quickly and repeat more willingly those responses which we find to be satisfying. By placement of his responses on a volitional level, the patient is likely to progress more rapidly.

VARIED NEEDS

If properly executed, recreational therapy can meet varied situations. The amputee has need for reeducation so that he may learn to participate

[3]Elmer D. Mitchell and Bernard S. Mason, *The Theory of Play* (New York: A. S. Barnes & Company, Inc., 1948), pp. 257–262.

in a variety of recreational activities despite his disability. The psychotic and postpsychotic require a restoration of self-confidence and acceptance by others. To the convalescent, pleasing recreational outlets may relieve the monotony and possibly restore him to normal living in a minimum of time. For the maladjusted, the play therapy can help reduce the tensions caused by conflicts.

The asocial individual will have need for socializing influences in the form of parties and group activities. By the same token, the underactive patient may require progressively more strenuous activity whereas the overactive one may have need for outlets that are quieting and tend to retard his overactive tendencies. To restore confidence in the self is of vital import. Ultimately, a restoration of physical, emotional, mental, and social well-being may take place.

Recreation on the therapeutic level holds out these possibilities for those who are skilled in this specialty.

PLAY THERAPY

Play therapy is divided by Axline[4] into the "directive" type wherein the therapist leads and interprets and the "nondirective" in which the therapist may leave the responsibility and direction to the child. Even in nondirective therapy, the situation may be "structured" by the therapist so that the desired opportunities arise. This classic on the subject emphasizes the nondirective approach and the striving within each person for "self-realization" through acceptance by others as well as by himself; the well-adjusted individual is usually so constituted. Maladjustments arise when self-confidence wanes accompanied by vicarious rather than direct growth in self-realization. Symptoms of maladjustments are day dreaming, identification, withdrawal, regression, and projection.

Play offers the child a natural medium for self-expression so that he may "play out his accumulated feelings of tension, frustration, insecurity, aggression, fear, bewilderment, confusion."[5] He can thereby bring them forth so that he may face, control, or shed them. Through this emotional release, he strengthens his self-understanding and achieves renewed confidence to think and act. In the play-therapy room, such play items as clay, hand paints, or puppets are his to do with as he pleases without influences or restraints. The bolstering of his ego and self-esteem

[4]Virginia M. Axline, *Play Therapy* (New York: Houghton Mifflin Company, 1947), pp. 9–14.
[5]Axline, *Play Therapy*, p. 16.

are natural consequences. This therapy can be effected individually or in a group situation.

Another authority[6] informs us that small or inanimate objects make it possible for the child to master situations which threaten him. Through his play, the child tends to repeat spontaneously those events that created the tensions. We are told, for example, that fear of a fire engine may bring forth in the child's play an attempt to bury his toy fire engine so that it will have less power to frighten him. In the secure atmosphere of the play-therapy room, the child can rid himself of this tension. When anxieties are attributable to difficulties in the home, the problem is more complex. Solomon goes on to say, "reenactment of these events in effigy has therapeutic value. In such situations the actual content becomes of major importance and the desensitization to the traumatic experience can take place by releasing the dammed up surplus affect."[7]

CLINICAL TECHNIQUES

In discussing the clinical approaches for different types who have need for therapy, Solomon categorizes and describes them as follows:[8]

Aggressive—impulsive group. This group displays overt signs of hostile or affectionate behavior. They show deficient "development and integration of the superego." Their aggressions reflect quite successful defenses against anxiety. They are potential delinquents. The therapy must be handled firmly. Should property be damaged or the therapist attacked, the child should be stopped without "anger or vindictiveness."

Anxiety—phobic. This group shows a "predominant emotional tone of fear" and displays "extreme emotional responsiveness and invites emotional reactions from others. In phobic cases the fears are attached to objects or situations whereas in the anxiety cases the fears are more generalized. The punishment or guilt factor for their strong instinctual urges is provocative of the symptomatology." Repressive measures are contraindicated. The therapist must be a stabilizing force.

Regressive—reaction. In this type, "original anxiety is replaced to a great extent by various types of defense mechanisms." They veer away from tensions by "retreating into infantile forms of behavior or to actions which are opposite in trend from the original emotional reaction." They are more occupied with things than with other people. The therapist is to express warm interest in the child and his creativeness, using

[6]Joseph C. Solomon, "Play Technique," *American Journal of Orthopsychiatry*, 18 (July 1948), 402–413.

[7]*Ibid.*, p. 403.

[8]*Ibid.*, pp. 408–410.

finger paints, clay, crayons, or any other means of invading the "child's fantasy world."

Schizoid—schizophrenic. This condition represents a disintegration of the ego. The patients may become so "completely unemotional in relation to reality that they appear as little robots." They range from slight withdrawal to complete disorganization of personality. The therapist plays with the child in order to invade his world. Through this means an "affectional relationship" can develop so that the child can approach reality. Overwhelming emotions were responsible for his "retreat from reality." An "ego structure" must be developed to return the patient to reality.

THE RECREATION THERAPIST

The recreation therapist is a member of a team of therapists who minister to the needs of the patient. He is to work closely with the physician, psychiatrist, or psychologist in charge. The range of the recreational therapy should be geared to the patient's needs as they are revealed by all therapists assigned to the case. The recreation therapist should be cognizant of the treatment objectives, the patient's needs, his physical limitations, and any precautionary steps that might be required. In addition, he should have a thorough knowledge of all aspects of suitable recreational activities. These can serve to prevent recurrences as well as to assist in restoring the patient to reality. It is noteworthy that the poorly adjusted requiring psychiatric care are deficient in recreational skills and appreciations. Hence, the need exists for steps to assure outcomes that extend beyond the immediate needs so as to include activities with carry-over into day-to-day living upon release from the institution.

It is of great importance that the therapist possess an approach that is sincere so that the patient can readily warm to him and regard him highly. The ability to establish rapport and to make the patient feel at ease is also very essential. By imbuing the patient with a feeling of confidence, created in part by graduated successes, even prolonged periods of therapy will not bring a loss of cooperative effort. A growing recognition of the contribution that the recreation therapist can make to the patient's recovery has done much toward instilling regard for this important position among the therapies.

POSSIBLE ACTIVITIES

Familiarity with the therapy situation will unearth numerous activity possibilities. Needless to say, the level at which the patient is found should be the point of departure for that individual. Progression from individual to group activities are to be encouraged whenever suitable. The use of socials, parties, dances, teas, and picnics are to be utilized in this regard. Invitations, decorations, planning, and social games offer opportunities for related activities.

Swimming is a splendid activity for most since it offers a pleasurable outlet for the crippled and stimulates the psychotic to action. The universal appeal of a ball's bounce or the challenge that comes with trying to catch a ball in flight can also serve to interest the patient. The ravages of atrophy can be mitigated by calisthenic exercises. Games and sports afforded interesting play situations; quoits, horseshoes, bowling, shuffleboard, volleyball, paddle tennis, tennis, golf, softball, basketball, and even low organized games may be used. In the realm of play therapy, in addition to low organized games suited for small groups, we find finger painting, doll play, clay modeling, puppets, and hand painting.

MENTALLY RETARDED

Recreation has assumed a more positive and accepted role in the lives of the mentally retarded. It is recognized as a vital adjunct to the other educational and therapeutic measures taken. The personal satisfactions and self-fulfillment ready him for the other therapies and provide stimulation for his other accomplishments. The fundamental aim is to advance each participant toward greater self-reliance and achievement levels. Recreational and play activities yield, aside from physical well-being, emotional and social benefits.

By and large, the mentally retarded child behaves like other children of the same mental level. Hence, the activities taught can be similar to those taught normal children. The difference shows up markedly when new skills are taught.

They encounter difficulties in their readiness for learning as well. According to Dunsing and Kephart, it is "a hierarchical buildup of generalizations which allows the child to deal increasingly effectively with his environment. Learning disabilities may be viewed in terms of difficulties in this developmental sequence. When such difficulties occur, then there are gaps in the sequence which will affect future learning either by limiting or distorting it."[9]

Most retardates are slow in learning new skills due to reduced mental

[9]Jack D. Dunsing, and Newell C. Kephart, *Motor Generalizations in Space and Time,* chapter in *Learning Disorders,* Herome Helmuth (Seattle, Washington: Special Child Publications, 1965), p. 81.

ability. Their difficulty in conceptualizing calls for different teaching techniques. They, therefore, need to be taught to play. This may require, at the lower levels, that they be taken "by hand" to react to the desired body movements.

Every encouragement is to be given to provide carry-over into family situations. Properly directed opportunities to take part in family fun will lend encouragement and follow through. Greater self-assuredness and elevation of the self-image are likely outcomes. In this vein, community-wide efforts are to be enlisted to provide suitable programming. "Y's," public schools, community centers, and other municipal recreation agencies are to be utilized in this effort.

ACTIVITIES

The difficulty the retardate has to conceptualize points up the need for methodical and graded skill teaching. What follows are a few examples which are suggestive of the range of activities within each area.

Physical fitness: Calisthenics, combatives, medicine ball play, tug-of-war, running, obstacle course, stick activities, self-testing activities.

Stunts, tumbling, and apparatus activities: Dual stunts, individual stunts, tumbling, self-testing activities, pyramid building, balance beam, stall bars, trampoline, weight training.

Musical activities: Rhythm bands, toy symphonies, vocal music, in-instrumental music, singing games, harmonica, autoharp, flutophone, recorded music, concerts, folk music.

Rhythmic activities: Marching, rhythmical games, folk dancing, grand marches, rope jumping, social dancing, square dancing, gymnastic dancing, modern dancing, basic rhythms.

Aquatics: Swimming, synchronized swimming, wading pool activities, water safety activities, rowing, canoeing, sailing, diving, fishing, surfing, paddle board play.

Games and sports: Games of low organization, games of high organization, lead-up games, stickball, softball, soccer, basketball, relays, speedball, paddle ball, boccie, croquet, billiards.

Individual sports: Hiking, skiing, weight training, bicycling, horseback riding, ice skating, diving, bait casting, kite flying, punching bag, baton twirling, fishing.

Outdoor recreation: Nature lore, astronomy, Indian lore, picnicking, hunting, fishing, explorations, spelunking, field trips, collecting (stone, insect, etc.), mountain climbing.

In addition to the above activities, reference is made to the following chapters: *Arts and Crafts, Special Events, Active Games, Social Recreation, Club Organization, Tournaments, Hobbies, Music in Recreation, Tell Me a Story, Toy and Child Play,* and all of Part Five involving outdoor recreation.

TRAINING

Recognizing that training in general recreation is to be the concern of the undergraduate level, a recently conducted conference[10] recommended that graduate programs concern themselves with curricula designed to care for the mentally ill. It endorsed the "Content Areas for Hospital Recreation Curriculum" recommended by a previous conference[11] which allocated forty per cent to core curriculum, fifteen per cent to professional specialization (evaluation to be added), thirty per cent to related professional fields (psychodynamics of mental illness should replace abnormal psychology), and fifteen per cent internship.

The curriculum is to include: (1) understanding illness and its psychological effects; (2) medical and psychiatric information; (3) recreation program planning skills incorporating needs, interests, and the hospital situation; (4) effective use of community resources; (5) knowledge and practice as recreation leader, as member of the hospital team and psychiatric staff; (6) development of proper attitudes; (7) interpretation of job responsibilities; (8) knowledge and practice in group processes and dynamics; (9) applied understanding of behavioral sciences; (10) research and evaluation; and (11) comprehension of psychological aspects of leisure.

PROFESSIONAL ORGANIZATIONS

Among the existing organizations for the ill and the handicapped, the Hospital Section of the American Recreation Society is the oldest. It came into being in 1948 and has disseminated the efforts of its working committees and others via the A.R.S. quarterly publication, *The Bulletin,* and a newsletter.

The merger executed in 1965 involving the American Recreation Society, National Recreation Association, *et al.* into the National Recreation and Park Association has created the need for a redefinition and restructuring of the professional efforts in behalf of the ill and handicapped.

[10]Conference on Recreation for the Mentally Ill, Washington, D.C.: American Assn. for Health, Physical Education & Recreation, 1958, pp. 22, 23.

[11]Conference on Professional Preparation of Recreation Personnel, Washington, D.C.: American Assn. for Health, Physical Education & Recreation, 1957, pp. 33, 34.

To be sure, the Section of the Ill and Handicapped within the state associations of park and recreation are continuing their efforts in this direction. The Indiana Park and Recreation Association is a case in point of effective efforts on the state level.

To help expedite united effort, these three groups sent two representatives to Washington, D.C., in November 1953 to set up tentatively the Council for the Advancement of Hospital Recreation. Through continued support, the Council has created a plan of "voluntary registration for qualifying personnel" based on standardized qualifications for hospital recreation director, leader, and aide.

PERSONNEL STANDARDS

The voluntary registration plan of the Council for the Advancement of Hospital Recreation has since 1957 brought about the registration of over 300 individuals.

One of the professional obstacles in the path of therapeutic recreation is the shortage of personnel aspiring to enter the field. Here again, effective and energetic recruitment is to be pursued in order to help achieve long-range objectives. All applications have to be cleared initially through the applicants' professional affiliate. The standards for the Hospital Recreation Director, the Hospital Recreation Leader, and Hospital Recreational Aide according to the Council for the Advancement of Hospital Recreation are as follows:

PROFESSIONAL

Hospital Recreation Director

1. Master's degree from an accredited college or university with a major in hospital recreation, recreation in rehabilitation, or recreational therapy and one year of successful full-time, paid experience in recreation for the handicapped in a medical setting (the required clinical experience for the master's degree may be substituted for an equal portion of successful full-time, paid experience); *or*
2. Master's degree from an accredited college or university with a major in recreation and two years of successful full-time, paid experience in recreation for the handicapped in a medical setting; *or*
3. Master's degree from an accredited college or university with a major in a professional field closely allied to recreation and applicable to recreation for the handicapped in a medical setting and an undergraduate degree from an accredited college or university with a major in recreation or its equivalent (twenty-four college credits in professional courses in recreation), and two years of successful full-time, paid experience in recreation for the handicapped in a medical setting.

Note: It is estimated that there are 2800 employed full time in recreation programs in a medical setting. There are 273 registered at the Director's level with the Council for Advancement of Hospital Recreation and 105 at the Leader's level; 38 were registered as Recreation Aides.

Hospital Recreation Leader

Bachelor's degree from an accredited college or university with a major in recreation or in a field of study appropriate to a specialized recreation function within the hospital recreation program, *e.g.*, music, sports, drama, dance.

SUBPROFESSIONAL

Hospital Recreation Aide

Diploma from an accredited high school and three years of successful full-time, paid experience under direct supervision of a qualified hospital recreation director or leader or 400 clock hours of approved in-service training under the direct supervision of a qualified hospital recreation director or leader. (A combination of appropriate experience and in-service training may be substituted.)

SUGGESTED READINGS

Axline, Virginia M. *Play Therapy.* New York: Houghton Mifflin Company, 1947.

Baruch, Dorothy W. *One Little Boy.* New York: Dell Publishing Company, Inc., 1964.

Chapman, Frederick. *Recreation Activities for the Handicapped.* New York: The Ronald Press Company, 1960.

Haun, Paul. *Recreation: A Medical Viewpoint.* New York: Columbia University Bureau of Publications, 1965.

Hunt, Valerie. *Recreation for the Handicapped.* Englewood Cliffs, N.J.: Prentice-Hall, Inc., 1955.

Linn, Louis, Leonard A. Weinroth, and Rugh Shama. *Occupational Therapy in Dynamic Psychiatry.* Washington, D.C.: American Psychiatric Association, 1962.

Palmer, Mabel. *The Social Club.* New York: National Association for Mental Health, 1966.

Pearson, G. H. *Emotional Disorders of Children.* New York: W. W. Norton and Company, Inc., 1949.

Pomeroy, Janet. *Recreation for the Physically Handicapped.* New York: The Macmillan Company, 1965.

Stone, Alan A., and Sue Smart Stone. *The Abnormal Personality Through Literature.* Englewood Cliffs, N.J.: Prentice-Hall, Inc., 1966.

Therapeutic Recreation in the Community: Compilation of Papers Presented at First Indiana Institute of Therapeutic Recreation in the Community. Bloomington, Indiana: Indiana University Press, 1962.

Chapter 21

TELL ME A STORY*

Story Hour! Like a key these magical words unlock the fascinating gates to strange worlds for the story teller and his audience. Adventure, travel, suspense, beauty, old friends, endless surprises—these are the treasures enjoyed by all. Whatever the season or time, wherever the place, the story hour reigns supreme.

Through countless ages man has told his tales. In jungled Africa early tribal lore stilled the fears and glorified the deeds of stalwart tribesmen. The hamlets and villages of the Far East sheltered the story tellers of the Orient. Blind Homer sang of the greatness of Greek heroes.

Universal is character, the story hour reached new regions with the migrations of people. Women compelled to marry into alien tribes related familiar tales to the members of their new household. Through the lowly slave or captive prisoner of war, the tales of one region became fused with the culture of the conquerors. Seafaring sailors, battle-scarred soldiers, traveling crusaders carried them into the far-flung areas of their wanderings and gathered new material in return.

Widening in its course of rambling during the Middle Ages, the stream of storytellers drew the Icelandic bards and the welcomed minstrels of old England. In banquet halls the latter group sang of the exploits of King Arthur or the daring of Beowulf. In faroff thatched roof cottages of Ireland, the old Granny wove her magic while an Iagoo enthralled his listeners as they sat around winter fires in the New World.

These were the masterful tellers of tales, spinning their wondrous stories of gods, men, and beasts. Conceived and fashioned throughout the ages, this folk art has been transmitted to the inheritors of today's story hour. Through a spiritual affinity with the recorded and verbal expressions of the past and present, the storyteller continues to bring pleasure and adventure to eager listeners as he lives his story and makes it live.

This spiritual relationship enables the teller to acquire an understanding of his art and an ability to transmit this understanding to his listeners. It permits him to bring his eager followers, figuratively speak-

*This chapter was prepared by Spencer G. Shaw.

273

ing, over the drawbridge and up to the threshold of the castle. From this vantage point children explore by themselves as they listen to the stories. Mentally, they push back, undisturbed, the boundaries of their circumscribed life. They outrun the limitations imposed upon them by social forces and the standards of a commonplace world. Experiencing anew, one of the most precious gifts of childhood, children soar, glide, or even take seven leagues at one step with their hero or heroine of storied adventure. Once again, story hour assumes a familiar role.

THE PURPOSES OF STORYTELLING

Ever since man first used this art form as a means of recording his needs or explaining the mysteries of life, countless reasons for storytelling have been advanced. Today, new interpretations for their use have emerged, depending upon the situation in which a story is told. The librarian, school teacher, camp director, playground supervisor—all have story hours in their respective programs. Whatever the situation, time, or place where stories are told, certain broad, fundamental objectives are apparent.

Through storytelling the *primary* purpose is achieved: *to provide entertainment for children in a wholesome recreational and educational activity.* Presented with artistic restraint and dignity, story hour offers a positive form of recreational activity which permits group sharing of fun and pleasure. The young listeners discover new worlds beyond the law of cause and effect. Identifying themselves with their storied friends, they take imaginative journeys with little Sal and her mother in *Blueberries for Sal*[1] or dance gaily with *"The Twelve Dancing Princesses."*[2] The riddle-conscious youngsters find appeal in the wonder and magic of the farmer in *"Doctor and Detective, Too"*[3] or in the cunning of the simple Turkish priest, Nasr-el-Din Hodja, who confounds three learned priests in one of the Hodja tales, *"Three Questions."*[4]

Almost a corollary to the first purpose is this *second* objective of storytelling: *to satisfy the play spirit of childhood.* Covering every mood and range of feeling, the stories may reflect the humor in living or abound in exciting action. Listening to the tale, *The Cow in the Kitchen,*[5] youngsters will always give squeals of delight to the growing predicament of

[1] Robert McCloskey, *Blueberries for Sal* (New York: The Viking Press, Inc., 1948).

[2] Jacob and Wilhelm Grimm, *Grimm's Fairy Tales* (several editions).

[3] M. C. Hatch, *Thirteen Danish Tales* (New York: Harcourt, Brace & World, Inc., 1947), pp. 94–106.

[4] Alice G. Kelsey, *Once the Hodja* (New York: Longmans, Green & Company, 1943), pp. 100–108.

[5] Jane Flory, *The Cow in the Kitchen* (New York: Lothrop, Lee & Shepard Company, Inc., 1946).

the old farmer who tries to please a nagging wife. Absorbed in the adventure of *"The Three Little Pigs,"*[6] small children will invariably puff their cheeks and "huff and puff" as the wolf tries to blow the houses down. Even *"Rumpelstiltskin"*[7] spinning straw into gold draws forth appropriate body motions from the group. And when older boys and girls respond with shouts of laughter to the exploits of the tall-tale hero, *"Pecos Bill and His Bouncing Bride,*[8] I know that they are living the story.

Thus, with its effects heightened by such group responses, the related tales provide the young listeners an opportunity to satisfy a basic need. Exercising a self-active inner impulse, they are able to find expression in uninhibited body movements or sounds and share, vicariously, the pleasures of others.

A *third* fundamental purpose of story-telling is a natural outgrowth of this folk art: *to introduce children to the inexhaustible store of literary wealth.* Through oral interpretations of an author's creation, a weaver of magic brings life to the words of the printed page. Following the traditional paths, he gently, but persuasively, leads his young followers through the slowly opening doors while relating to them old and modern tales. There unroll before their watchful eyes the wonders of the past, the strongly etched emotions of man, the great adventurous spirit of the different ages.

Fashioning mental images of the experiences of a *Dick Whittington,*[9] "thrice Lord Mayor of London" or the dangerous wanderings of *Little Red Riding Hood,*[10] children become aware of the moving power of the printed word. The world of Robin Hood or the ageless messages contained in Bible lore become meaningful with a retelling of such significant events as the dauntless bravery of Daniel[11] or the devotion of Ruth and Naomi.[12] Bringing such treasures to children in a properly motivated activity, the storyteller may help to create and stimulate their appreciation for the vast store of literature. What a cherished moment for the young listeners when they proceed, alone, along the literary pathway.

---

[6]Veronica Hutchinson, comp., *Chimney Corner Stories* (New York: G. P. Putnam's Sons, 1925), pp. 54–62.

[7]Jacob and Wilhelm Grimm, *Grimm's Fairy Tales.*

[8]James Bowman, *Pecos Bill, the Greatest Cowboy of All Time* (Chicago: Albert Whitman & Co., 1937), pp. 238–59.

[9]Marcia Brown, *Dick Whittington and His Cat* (New York: Charles Scribner's Sons, 1950).

[10]Feodor Rojankovsky, *The Tall Book of Nursery Tales* (New York: Harper and Brothers, 1944), pp. 7–11.

[11]Nancy Barnhart, *The Lord Is My Shepherd* (New York: Charles Scribner's Sons, 1949), pp. 165–72.

[12]*Ibid.*, pp. 97–100.

Wonderingly, they may select a book while endless questions fill their minds:

> Here's an adventure. What awaits
> Beyond these closed, mysterious gates?
> Whom shall I meet, where shall I go?
> Beyond the lovely land I know?
> Above the sky, across the sea?
> What shall I learn and feel and be?
> Open strange doors, to good or ill!
> I hold my breath a moment still
> Before the magic of your look.
> What will you do to me, O Book![13]

Creating an appreciation for literature is just the initial step. Full awareness of its latent values cannot be recognized until children experience a sense of responsiveness to the tale. Thus, *a fourth* purpose of storytelling emerges: *to help develop within our young audience a feeling of social sensitivity to life and people of the past and the present.*

This social sensitivity is an awareness of some of the motives of human behavior. Moreover, it is a growing realization of some of the forces which motivate personal conduct in relation to others about us. Through this humanizing process children may find in some of the story situations or character delineations an emotional experience which may ease the cravings of a personal, social, or spiritual need. They will be able to discern purposes in a storyteller's art other than the ability to entertain. Mutually sharing their literary treasures, the teller of his young friends will realize that the related stories also *educate, inform, illustrate,* and *inspire.* In order to illustrate more fully this concept of storytelling, a list of suggested selections relating to each of these functions is presented here:

SUGGESTED STORIES TO HELP DEVELOP A FEELING OF SOCIAL SENSITIVITY

To Entertain (provide enjoyment)

1. *Curious George Gets a Medal.* H. A. Rey
2. *The Emperor's New Clothes.* Hans Christian Andersen

To Educate (provide personal, social, and intellectual guidance)

1. *Thin Ice.* Jerrold Beim
2. *The Hundred Dresses.* Eleanor Estes

[13]Ralph Henry and Lucile Pannell, *My American Heritage* (Chicago: Rand McNally & Co., 1949), p. 19.

*To Inform (provide information of local interests, acquaint listeners
with life and ideas strange to them)*

1. *Fly High, Fly Low.* Don Freeman
2. "Ah Mee's Invention" in *Shen of the Sea.* A. B. Chrisman

*To Illustrate (provide worthwhile concepts
without moralizing)*

1. *The Poppy Seeds.* Clyde Bulla
2. "The Paradise of Children" (Pandora) in *Wonder Book, and Tanglewood
Tales.* Nathaniel Hawthorne

*To Inspire (provide ethical, moral,
and spiritual values)*

1. "The Juggler of Notre Dame" in *The Way of the Story-Teller.* Ruth Sawyer
2. *David and Goliath.* Bible Story

But, one may ask, are children usually aware of this humanizing process? In all likelihood they are completely ignorant of this purpose of
storytelling. Such matters as lessons in living or value concepts are not
the dominant factors of consideration. For them it is, rather, the opportunity of sharing together a recreational activity that permits imaginative
wanderings and endless joys.

This approach of the children to story listening should not deter the
teller from his task. Unlike some of the weavers of tales who filled their
lore with lessons of morality and didacticism, a storyteller of today hopes
that any attainment of social sensitivity may be reached through an
assimilative process on the part of his audience. Thus, through the telling of myths, legends, folktales, and modern narratives we help our
young listeners to achieve this goal.

The storyteller also has an obligation to the art form which he employs. This is implicitly stated in the *fifth* major purpose of storytelling:
*to add to a richly endowed folk art; to transmit its gifts and its living
force to those who follow.* Spinning their tales from the fabrics of life
around them, storytellers have gladly shared their wondrous gifts.
Traveling from tribe to tribe, from inn to castle, a wrinkled Nokomis or
a welcomed bard stirred the imagination of their friends and gave added
treasures to those who followed.

Fused into a beautiful, always changing pattern, these tales became
our heritage from the past; the art of telling them is our obligation to the
present. Perhaps, as never before today's storyteller finds his task increasingly difficult. This is nothing new, for with each advance in the

development of communication, other outlets have been devised to spread the folklore of mankind.

The crude markings on the walls of the caves, depicting the glowing deeds of early heroes, supplemented the oral descriptions. The lays of the wandering minstrels gave way to the printed word. Forlorn and alone, these weavers of tales became immortalized in Sir Walter Scott's, *"The Lay of the Last Minstrel."* And now, within the last century, technology has produced new media of communication—the phonograph, films, radio, and television. Each in its own way has made inroads upon the folk art of the storyteller. In one respect the advance of mankind has limited his horizons; in another, it has enlarged his worlds to conquer, if only vicariously. The storyteller, far from being repressed, is needed today, more than ever, to keep alive the cultural gifts of the past and to add today's meaningful tales.

Who is better able than the storyteller to open the locked doors to the simple tales of Grimm or the dramatic sagas of Iceland? Through what other medium may we learn of the eternal truths of some of the Tolstoy stories or the delightful tales of a Padraic Colum? By what other means may children learn of the majestic sweep of Biblical lore or the intense feeling of a Hawthorne, a Dickens, or a Poe? In today's world who is better equipped than the storyteller to reveal the beauty in Leo Politi's *The Song of the Swallow* or the laughter contained in Claire Bishop's *The Five Chinese Brothers*? How will the printed story come alive? Only when it is expressed in the spoken word of the storyteller.

Mechanical in form, the new media of communication are devoid of any feeling or sound until utilized by man. The spoken word is alive, pulsating with emotion and capable of bringing together something ancient, something modern, and something timeless. It is, therefore, the teller's task to interrelate the different media wherever possible. As long as children express this thought, the duty of the storyteller remains clear:

"I think there should be more men in the world like you to take time out to tell us children stories."[14]

TECHNIQUES OF STORYTELLING

In developing the first principle, the art of selecting stories, a storyteller is guided by an appraisal of several factors: purpose, situation, audience, types of stories.

[14]Letter (excerpt) from pupil, Brooklyn elementary school, 1950.

Purpose for telling stories. To tell a story merely for the sake of telling indicates a sense of aimlessness which makes any story ineffectual. We have already discussed the rather broad objectives of storytelling which are fundamental to most story hours. However, one must be cognizant of the more specific purposes which grow out of the needs of a particular audience or situation. Remembering this fact and the purposes of storytelling, as stated earlier, the teller should plan the course upon which he will take his young friends.

Situation for telling stories. Since this will vary according to the locale of the story hour, the following chart will merely indicate a few of the places and situations where storytelling can be utilized:

DETERMINE THE SITUATION FOR TELLING STORIES

Home	*School*	*Library*
1. Before bedtime	1. After rest or lunch periods	1. Browsing periods
2. Confinement because of illness	2. Assembly programs	2. Class visit to library
3. Parties	3. Holiday observances	3. Holiday observances
4. Rainy days	4. Library periods	4. Special programs (*i.e.,* Book Week, puppet shows)
5. During long trips	5. Relaxation after tests or study periods	5. Story of picture-book hours
6. When problem arises in behavior pattern or in display of negative social attitude	6. With units of study	6. Same as *Number 8* under *School*
7. Other	7. During inclement weather	7. Other
	8. When problem arises in group or individual behavior pattern or display of negative social attitude	
	9. Other	

Community Center	*Camp*	*Church or Synagogue*
1. Correlate work and activities (*i.e.,* crafts, trips)	1. Bedtime—each group in own tent	1. Holiday observances (*i.e.,* Easter, Purim, Christmas, Hanukah)
2. Club groups	2. Campfire	2. Part of worship service (*i.e.,* in Junior Church)
3. During inclement weather	3. Confinement in infirmary	3. Special programs
4. Holiday observances	4. Correlate with arts and crafts, nature lore, hikes	4. With units of study
5. Indoor fireside entertainment	5. Inclement weather	5. Same as *Number 8* under *School*
6. Playground activity	6. Worship services	6. Other
7. Special programs	7. Special programs	
8. Stay-at-home camp	8. Regular story hour	
9. Regular story hour	9. Travel to or from camp	
10. Same as *Number 8* under *School*	10. Same as *Number 8* under *School*	

Knowledge of audience. Knowing your audience is an important consideration which embodies three essentials—composition, size, and peculiarities of group. A complete disregard in noting such an elemental factor as the composition of the audience may cause problems when you actually present the story. Mutual interests as well as widely divergent likes and dislikes are common among your youthful friends. A group of seven-year-old girls and boys may find equal enjoyment in Wanda Gag's *Millions of Cats*.[15] However, an older group of boys will yearn for the exciting tale of Robin Hood and Little John[16] while their hair-ribboned companions of the same age may still request the old fairytale favorite, "The Shepherd's Nosegay."[17] It is a poor storyteller who thinks any story will fit all ages of all children. Therefore, story selection has to be considered on the basis of the sexual composition of the audience and the changing interests of the various age groups.

The size of the audience. Predetermined from gathered information, this essential knowledge will remove another deterrent from the success of a story hour. Obviously, a smaller group is more desirable. It affords the children a closer, personal relationship to the teller and his story. If you are using a picture book for young readers (*Make Way for Ducklings*[18] by Robert McCloskey or *Madeline*[19] by Bemelmans), the showing of the illustrations is necessary in telling the story. For this reason the size of the group should be small.

To tell a story before a large group places a great strain upon the storyteller. Called upon to exercise the highest talents of his folk art, the teller may find that any story appeal is dependent upon mass appeal and mass response. The high degree of personal relationship maintained in a smaller group is lessened as the audience increases in size. Story selection, therefore, has to be governed, at least in part, by a consideration of its effect in telling to a large group.

The peculiarities of the audience. The storyteller has to discern any characteristics which may be peculiar only to the particular group to whom stories are being told. These include such factors as races, creeds, nationalities represented, and language difficulties of the listeners. It will aid in selecting stories for a group who may wish to hear those tales

[15]Wanda Gag, *Millions of Cats* (New York: Coward-McCann, Inc., 1928).

[16]Howard Pyle, *The Merry Adventures of Robin Hood* (New York: Charles Scribner's Sons, 1946).

[17]Phyllis Fenner, *Princesses and Peasant Boys* (New York: Alfred A. Knopf, Inc., 1944), pp. 128–37.

[18]Robert McCloskey, *Make Way for Ducklings* (New York: The Viking Press, Inc., 1941).

[19]Ludwig Bemelmans, *Madeline* (New York: Simon & Schuster, Inc., 1939).

native to their culture. Notice the happy, proud look on the faces of the Puerto Rican children when you preface your story with these words: "Now, we are going to take a journey in storyland to the faraway country of Puerto Rico. There, we will meet a girl who disobeyed her mother and went swimming in a haunted river. What happened to her? Listen, as we hear one of the children's favorite stories, 'The Earrings,' taken from the book *The Tiger and the Rabbit, and Other Tales.*"[20]

In addition to bringing the cultures of other lands to young listeners through such story selection, you will also become more discriminating in choosing your material. Such story elements as dialect or national, religious, and racial stereotypes will be carefully studied and analyzed before approval will be given to use the narrative. If you know your audience, you will be careful in selecting any material which may offend directly or through inference any member of the story-hour group. As a storyteller you are obligated to bring to the audience only those narratives which interpret honestly the motives, conduct, and customs of any people. Does this mean the avoidance of stories with dialect? It does if you are not proficient in using such dialect. If you interpret it poorly in your telling, you may indicate to your listeners, by inference, a desire to ridicule. Also, refrain from using stories about a particular group toward whom you may have some preconceived stereotyped misconceptions. Never select a story which does little to increase the respect of others for those individuals who are of the same race or religion as the storied characters. Thus, avoid such tales as the Inez Hogan stories of Nicodemus or Elvira Garber's *Ezekiel Travels.*

THE MATERIAL FOR STORYTELLING

Having concerned ourselves with the purpose, the situation, and the audience for whom the story is intended, we are now ready to consider the story itself. In our selection of materials we need to know:

Types of stories. As storytellers continually selected their tales and handed them on to succeeding generations, there eventually emerged certain kinds of stories. These were flexible in their classification, however, and were grouped in different categories mainly for convenience. In the table below are given some of the possible classifications of such stories with examples illustrative of each class. The types of stories indicated are relative and the material included under each may be inserted in one or more of the categories listed.

[20]Pura Belpre, *The Tiger and the Rabbit, and Other Tales* (Boston: Houghton Mifflin Company, 1946), pp. 21–28.

CLASSIFICATION OF STORIES FROM A STORYTELLER'S PACK

Adventure

"The Adventures of the Giant Squid of Chain Tickle" in E. Johnson, *Anthology of Children's Literature*, pp. 824–27.

"Fatal Coils" in T. Waldeck, *Treks Across the Veldt*, pp. 142–50.

Animal

Beatrix Potter, *The Tale of Peter Rabbit*.

Rudyard Kipling, *How the Rhinoceros Got His Skin*.

Biography

"George Washington Carver" in A. Fauset, *For Freedom*, pp. 105–20.

"Creating Opportunities for Work" in E. McGuire, *The Growth of Democracy*, p. 244.

Epic

"Robin Hood and Little John" in H. Pyle, *Merry Adventures of Robin Hood*.

"Beowulf's Encounter with Grendel" in S. Riggs, *The Story of Beowulf*.

Fable

"The Tortoise and the Hare" in *Aesop's Fables*.

"The Town Mouse and the Country Mouse" in *Aesop's Fables*.

Fairy Tale

"Sleeping Beauty" in *Grimm's Fairy Tales*.

"The Apple of Contentment" in H. Pyle, *Pepper and Salt*.

History

M. Andrews, *The Perfect Tribute*.

"The Star-Spangled Banner" in Lyons, *Stories of Our American Patriotic Songs*.

Holiday

O. Wilde, "The Selfish Giant" in W. Harper, *Easter Chimes*.

"David Comes Home: a Hanukah Story of Today" in Assoc. for Childhood Educ., *Told Under the Christmas Tree*.

Humor

"Three Fridays" in A. Kelsey, *Once the Hodja*.

"To Your Good Health" in P. Fenner, *Princesses and Peasant Boys*.

Modern Fanciful

Wanda Gag, *Millions of Cats*.

Dr. Seuss, *The 500 Hats of Bartholomew Cubbins*.

Myth

Androcles and the Lion.
"Ulysses and the Cyclops" in A. Church, *The Odyssey of Homer*, Chap. 1.

Parable

"The Good Samaritan" in *Bible (New Testament)*.
The Prodigal Son in *Bible (New Testament)*.

Picture Book

M. Flack, *Wait for William.*
Leo Politi, *Song of the Swallows.*

Proverb

My Mother Is the Most Beautiful Woman in the World, Reyher.
"Crow's Nest" in Sawyer, *Picture Tales from Spain.*

Structural characteristics of a story. A keen sense of appreciation for the aesthetic elements in the story material will enable you to make wise selections for reading or telling. Thus, a teller analyzes such structural essentials as (1) the beginning, (2) the body, (3) the conclusion, (4) the style, and (5) the characters.

The beginning of a story for telling is brief and includes such basic factors as time, place, theme or problem to be solved. Usually, the beginning may also introduce one or two of the characters in an interesting situation.

Once on a time there was a king who had a daughter, and she was such a dreadful story-teller that the like of her was not to be found far or near. So the King gave out, that if anyone could tell such a string of lies as would get her to say, 'That's a story,' he should have her to wife, and half the kingdom besides. . . .[21] (From "Boots, Who Made the Princess Say, 'That's a Story.' ")

In a few sentences the author has established time ("Once on a time"), place (a royal kingdom), and even some of the characters in the story (the king and his daughter). Also indicated in a strong, understandable manner is a central theme—how to overcome the princess' bad habit of storytelling. Etching very vividly the central idea of the tale, the theme is sometimes contained in the story title, for example, "Why the Sea Is Salt," "How the Camel Got His Hump." The theme may also reveal an element of contrast. Recall John Ruskin's story *King of the*

[21]George Webb Dasent, from *East o' the Sun and West o' the Moon.* Courtesy G. P. Putnam's Sons.

Golden River.[22] Hans and Schwartz, "The two older brothers, were very ugly men" who received "from all those with whom they had any dealings the nickname of the 'Black Brothers.' "[23] Their younger brother, Gluck, was small and good.

The body of the story elaborates upon the theme and contains the development of the plot. For our purposes the latter must be logical and plausible. If the story unfolds in a plausible manner, the outcome will be consistent with the state of affairs preceding it. Furthermore, a logical development will permit the hero or heroine to triumph only after there have been some failures and elimination of obstacles. From such experiences the characters should have some gainful learnings.

In addition to a logical and plausible plot development, the body of the story should have a unity of interest. This is best attained when the author maintains a continuous relationship with his central theme. Such attention to this detail will give directness and a heightened dramatic effect to the story. In the delightful story *Angelo, the Naughty One*, by Helen Garrett,[24] this study is well marked. The theme reveals Angelo's dislike for water and for baths. In the story development unity of interest is maintained as the author carries her young hero from one episode to another in his fruitless efforts to avoid having a much-needed bath.

Another prerequisite of plot development is an economy of incidents. Giving proper balance to the narrative, this element is best exemplified in the old folktales. These usually have a definite number of tasks, riddles, or trials for the hero or heroine to perform before attaining success or suffering defeat. Thus, the wolf had to try three times in "The Three Little Pigs" before he met his fate. Yan, the prince in disguise, evaded the princess three times in "The Shepherd's Nosegay"[25] before she could win him in marriage. Unfortunately, many stories disregard this essential. They either abound in endless digressions or go off on numerous tangents. Unless a storyteller is skilled in adapting such tales, he has to leave them behind.

The conclusion to a story becomes effective and dramatic if the events preceding it have a logical development, unity of interest and economy of incidents. Once the climax is reached, the storyteller has to notice

[22]John Ruskin, *King of the Golden River* (Yonkers, N.Y.: World Book Company, 1946).
[23]*Ibid.*, pp. 15–17.
[24]Helen Garrett, *Angelo, the Naughty One* (New York: The Viking Press, Inc., 1944).
[25]Fenner, *Princesses and Peasant Boys*, pp. 128–37.

the ending of the narrative. It must follow the climax very quickly. It should reveal a plausible solution to the problem and be consistent with the theme of the story. The teller should avoid stories which end with a moral. Remember, any moral appeal which is contained in a story will be recognized without having it made obvious. In story selection we are guided by the principle: *a child listens for the sake of enjoyment* and *"not to be developed."*

The author's style of writing has to be carefully studied by the storyteller. There will be qualities of expression which are peculiar only to a particular writer. For example, the careful selection and phrasing of words in a Kipling story help to establish for these tales an atmosphere all their own:

In the High and Far-Off Times the Elephant, O Best Beloved, had no trunk. He had only a blackish, bulgy nose, as big as a boot, that he could wriggle about from side to side; but he couldn't pick up things with it. But there was one Elephant—a new Elephant—an Elephant's Child—who was full of 'satiable curiosity and that means he asked ever so many questions. And he lived in Africa, and he filled all Africa with his 'satiable curiosities."[26]

The poetic prose of Hans Christian Andersen gives a matchless beauty to the stories which few authors have been able to emulate. In a Howard Pyle story or a Richard Chase folktale from the mountains of North Carolina and Virginia, the mood and temper of the narrative are ably set forth because of the unique selection and use of words. The style of writing may also reflect an author's conception of a proper balance of description and action. Stories which contain long, descriptive passages are difficult to tell and should be approached cautiously. This does not mean the avoidance of all description; rather, the teller has to plan a careful adaptation of such material. By eliminating extraneous ideas, superfluous incidents, or subjective analyses the narrator may develop the story in a manner suitable for telling.

Considering the essential, characterization, in story structure, the storyteller has to give a very keen analysis. Studies have shown that the listeners, losing themselves in the narrative, become identified either with the hero or with a minor character. This identification can be a healthy one if the portrayal of fictional people is convincing and true to life.

[26]From *Just So Stories*, by Rudyard Kipling, p. 63. Copyright 1902, 1907 by Rudyard Kipling; reprinted by permission of Mrs. George Bambridge and Doubleday & Company, Inc.

Good characterization is also dependent upon a clear understanding of behavior patterns which should be assumed by the fictional counterparts of the listeners. This indirect approach of presenting children with such information gives added value to proper story structure. Therefore, in story selection, the storied people should possess weaknesses as well as positive attributes. They should attain some degree of success in their pursuits. If they are characters of different racial and religious backgrounds, they should be presented fairly, accurately, and realistically. The fictional children included in the stories taken from the book *Told Under the Stars and Stripes*[27] are worthy examples of this essential.

Stories with animal characters should present these creatures in a manner which will make them appear natural and convincing to the listener. The Babar stories of Jean de Brunhoff[28] or those included by *Boy's Life Dog Stories*,[29] edited by Irving Crump, illustrate positively the worth of this factor.

Characteristics which make stories suitable or unsuitable for telling. Analyzing this essential, the storyteller has the experience of past tellers to guide him in his selection. With such welcomed standards he may evaluate story choice for the story hour. Simply stated in the chart below, these desirable or undesirable characteristics are self-explanatory. Illustrative examples are given for those which are suitable for use.

PREPARATION OF A STORYTELLER

Storytelling demands rigid requirements from its followers in order for them to achieve success in the art. These are (a) certain spiritual attributes and (b) an understanding of the technique to apply in learning a story.

Possession of spiritual attributes. A belief in storytelling and in his audience is a prime essential for the storyteller. Developing this art form through faith and labor, the tellers of the past have handed it down to succeeding generations. They have entrusted its perpetuation and further growth to today's inheritors. Unless a storyteller is able to perceive the intrinsic values inherent in the folk art, it will be impossible for him to establish any rapport between himself and this gift or between himself and a story. It is his responsibility, therefore, to approach his art as a storyteller with a sense of understanding and humility.

[27]Association for Childhood Education, *Told Under the Stars and Stripes* (New York: The Macmillan Company), 1945.

[28]Jean de Brunhoff, *Story of Babar* (New York: Random House, Inc., 1933).

[29]Irving Crump, ed., *Boy's Life Dog Stories* (New York: Thomas Nelson & Sons, 1949).

A SUGGESTED GUIDE TO STORY SELECTION

Characteristics of Stories Suitable for Use

APPEAL TO THE IMAGINATION
Brown, Marcia, *Stone Soup*
Geisel, T. S., *If I Ran the Zoo*

EMBODY UNIVERSAL TRUTHS
Pyle, Howard, *Apple of Contentment*
Tolstoy, Leo, *Where Love Is, God Is*

ENCOURAGE KINSHIP WITH ANIMALS
Potter, Beatrix, *The Tale of Benjamin Bunny*
Andersen, Hans C., *The Ugly Duckling*

ILLUSTRATE COMMON SENSE AND RESOURCEFULNESS
Brown, Marcia, *Dick Whittington and His Cat*
"The Leak in the Dike" in Baldwin, *Fifty Famous Stories to Tell*

INCLUDE DRAMA
King Arthur and His Sword
Icarus and Daedalus

INSPIRE LOVE OF BEAUTY
Alden, Raymond, "The Hunt for the Beautiful" in *Why the Chimes Rang*
Olfers, Sybil, *When the Root Children Wake Up*

MAKE FOR WONDER AND LAUGHTER
Bishop, Claire, *Five Chinese Brothers*
Wadsworth, Wallace, *Paul Bunyan and His Great Blue Ox*

OFFER ACTION AND EXCITEMENT
Davis, Norman, *Picken's Great Adventure*
Cruse, Amy, *William Tell*

PROMOTE DEMOCRATIC IDEALS
Paine, Alice, "The Magic Flag" in Schauffler, Robert, *The Days We Celebrate*, Vol. 3
Estes, Eleanor, *The Hundred Dresses*

REFLECT CHILD'S OWN EXPERIENCE
Felt, Sue, *Rosa-Too-Little*
D'Aulaire, *Ola*

Characteristics of Stories Unsuitable for Use

Appeal to fear (i.e., ghost stories)
Exaggerated and coarse fun
Extreme emotionalism
Lack of respect for other races, creeds, cultures
Matters beyond the realm of child's interest or understanding
Obvious moral to story (sermonizing)
Overabundance of humor
Profanity
Sadism, gruesomeness
Sarcasm and ridicule
Sensationalism
Sentimentality
Subjective analysis of motive or feeling

Still sharing this priceless heritage with children, the teller receives, in return, their offerings—frankness, spontaneity, sincerity. The young listeners give themselves wholeheartedly, emotionally and spiritually. If you are blind to these offerings of children, you may shatter beyond repair the delicate pattern which a child seeks to establish spiritually with the storyteller. Robbed of any opportunity for a close relationship, the children's valued treasures become valueless; an invaluable emotional and spiritual experience becomes mundane and meaningless.

A wider development of a creative imagination is also essential. The words "wider development" are used because the storyteller has possessed this gift of imagination since childhood. Growing older, however, one often fails to nurture it; thoughts and mental wanderings become directed more and more into prescribed channels. Consequently, freedom in exercising the imaginative powers is inhibited and the adult gradually finds himself imprisoned by a spirit of provincialism unknown to the world of children.

It is true that children may have a limited knowledge of the wider horizons surrounding them. Their everyday experiences and activities may be controlled considerably by family, community, and society. Expose these same children, through storytelling, to worlds beyond their immediate spheres of influence and knowledge. Now, watch how quickly they enter into the realm of creative imagination. Not stopping to reason, not wishing to question, they become absorbed in the storied elements described. For the adult, this same transition from reality to unreality is difficult to make. Psychological and social blocks prevent a similar acceptance of unreality. Examine your own creative imaginative powers and see if you as storyteller and adult, can enjoy with the same relish as a child the predicament of the Emperor walking in the Grand Procession with no clothes on.[30]

In this realm of fairy tales and fantasy children display the greatest difference from the adult in the intensity of imaginative powers. Unaware of the psychological implications of some of the stories, they take them for enjoyment, appreciating both the humor and the cruelty. Unlike their elders, they release the effects of these verbal pictures from their minds once the story reaches its happy end. The antics of Jack in "Jack and the Beanstalk,"[31] the death of the witch in "Hansel and Gretel,"[32] the daring rescue of "Rapunzel,"[33] are perfectly natural to the young audience. The symbolism and psychoanalyses read into these tales by adults mean nothing to the child. Such a lack of mental restraints enables the young listeners to live with the real and the unreal; order and chaos are understandable and accepted. This is the lesson which the storyteller must learn from his young friends.

A sense of responsiveness is another attribute which the teller has to

---

[30]Hans Christian Andersen, *Andersen's Fairy Tales* (several editions).

[31]Kathleen Adams, comp., *A Book of Giant Stories* (New York: Dodd, Mead & Co., 1926), pp. 78–91.

[32]Jacob and Wilhelm Grimm, *Grimm's Fairy Tales*.

[33]*Ibid.*

acquire. If the storyteller is able to react positively and surely to the story, he will have gained in his ability as a weaver of tales. Recreating the works of an author to a youthful audience, the storyteller forgets himself while he reveals in his speech and bodily expression the intensity of the hold of the story upon him. Mindful only of the story elements, he breathes life into the incidents and characters. This indicates sensitivity to the beauty of the language and to the tale. For the listener new vistas appear. Illumined by the inner glow of the teller, the graphic words of a printed tale carry him into strange regions far removed from the world about him.

Needing the ingredients of experience and wisdom in his interpretation of a story, the teller gains their possession only after a passage of time. They are not easily claimed but come only when the storyteller grows in responsiveness to his art. With such attributes, the narrator may develop an appreciation for the many kinds of stories. He may recognize those in which he finds the closest bonds. He will realize that there are personal limitations which prevent him from responding favorably to *all* stories. Thus, "The Old Woman and Her Pig"[34] or a Hodja tale[35] may be difficult to tell, but a story from Grimm[36] or an Indian legend may fire the teller with its appeal. If a story fails to kindle a spark of feeling within the teller, it should be left alone for the moment but not discarded. In time, return to the tale; try to relive it again as it is being read. What was once lifeless and meaningless may take on life and meaning. The story has not changed. It is, rather, the teller who has grown in his art. Responsiveness to the art and to the story has been attained.

These are just some of the many prerequisites for a storyteller. Not easily acquired, they form a major part of the preparation for telling stories. There remains, now, the learning of the tale.

Techniques to apply in learning a story. Techniques are relative. What may be a practical approach for one teller may become a stumbling block to another. However, there are certain fundamentals which any weaver of tales must follow.

Becoming acquainted with the story is the first essential. Reading it silently, the teller determines if it appeals, if it can become his. Once he has responded positively to the tale, he begins to seek its source of in-

---

[34]Feodor Rojankovsky, *The Tall Book of Nursery Tales.*
[35]Alice G. Kelsey, *Once the Hodja.*
[36]Jacob and Wilhelm Grimm, *Grimm's Fairy Tales.*

spiration. Visualizing the story as a whole, the storyteller gently unfolds the author's creation in his analysis. Noting the intricate, delicate threads of its pattern, he identifies himself more closely with the component parts of its structure.

He draws from the tale the central theme, for that is the substance out of which the rest of the story grows. Unmentioned by the teller, it will also serve as a guide for the audience in its journey with the narrator. Continuing his analysis, he carefully peruses the incidents and details used by the author to reinforce this theme. These also serve as a backdrop against which the characters will perform.

With the emergence of the characters, the storyteller identifies himself with each one as he visualizes their described acts and words. He becomes a part of their dreams and struggles. Step by step he goes through this process, first with one and then with another character. Scene after scene is presented until the whole tale moves in a rising crescendo to a dramatic climax. Along the way, the teller's attention is drawn at times to the incidents and details used by the author to give color to the story and depth to character development. Analyzing those which are highlighted and those which belong in the background, he determines their place in the total story pattern. Which of these can be eliminated without detracting from the fullness of the tale? Which ones need to be remembered and lived with again and again?

Still in his story analysis, the teller further unfolds the pattern to discover those peculiarities of the story which have made it appeal to him. Perhaps it was in the author's style of writing or in his manner of expression. How did he represent sounds, tastes, colors, or scents? What words evoked surprise or anger? What different uses of phrases or word structure lifted the story into an age different from the present? If the story is Biblical, the teller is moved by the sweep and grandeur of the language. These stories demand a slower pace in telling. The same is equally true of a Kipling, Andersen, or Pyle creation.

The analysis is nearly complete. There remains the task of taking these segmented parts and reassembling them into the author's original pattern. When this is done, the teller rereads the story, hoping to gain a deeper understanding. Small details which escaped him in his first reading are brought into focus and help give a clearer picture. Instead of losing a spiritual affinity with the story because of his close analysis, the storyteller will find a richer relationship. After reading the story aloud several times, the narrator approaches the final task of lifting it from the printed page and etching it upon his mind.

Learning the story embodies several essentials. At all times, remember one important principle: Memorize ideas; do not memorize words. Learn the story as a whole, keeping as close as possible to the author's wording and phrasing. If these impede the hearer's understanding, the teller may alter them without destroying the mood or style. Fully cognizant of the pattern, the storyteller memorizes the sequence of events and the ideas contained in each. He reproduces what he is learning as though he were actually seeing or experiencing it himself. Where there is dialogue, the storyteller should work over it until it becomes his as a story character, making it sound natural and spontaneous.

When the storyteller has completed these tasks, he should relate the tale aloud to himself. Stilted expressions, worried gropings for words, halting phrases, lose their power as constant practices brings improvement. Having fitted parts of the pattern into their respective places, the teller begins to strive for oral expression and proper body movements.

Oral expression for the storyteller is the principal means of conveying the ideas of the printed word to the audience. Supplemented at times by body and facial gestures, it depends upon a complete utilization of several effective voice qualities: speed, pitch, pause, and clarity. Speed has to be carefully controlled. Realize that your audience wishes to hear you. They want to enjoy with you the unexpected twists and turns of the story. They seek to grasp every point and shade of meaning which is injected into the telling. Give them an opportunity to do this by taking your time. The story may be a familiar one to you because of your previous contact with it, but to your listeners it is new. Hearing the tale, the group must first grasp the words mentally and then form the pictures which the teller is describing. In the next instant, the hearers must repeat the process in order to build a pattern similar to the storyteller's. This takes time; it cannot be hurried. Thus, the speed of delivery has to be carefully watched.

A varied rapidity of words accompanied by an altered change of pitch adds force to the telling. Employing no special "stage-effect" tones for the narration, the storyteller must avoid sounding artificial or pretentious. Sensed immediately by the least-discerning member of the audience, it will cause an immediate loss of rapport between the teller and his group. Altering the pitch of the voice, the teller is able to avoid monotony. Furthermore, it enables the listeners to discern the introduction of a new situation or a change in events. It is especially useful to denote different characters speaking.

Well-timed pauses allow the teller an opportunity to obtain effective pitch control. With a well-executed pause, a story can be made meaningful; its absence will cause confusion. As the teller skips hastily from one situation to another, from one character to another without a pause, he prevents the listeners from absorbing the full essence of the tale. Therefore, it is essential for the narrator to make use of this device in the most effective way possible. Pauses set the stage for contrast. They indicate a suspenseful moment. They provide the perfect setting for the introduction of a new storied character. Lastly, they give the teller time to assume the different tones of his story characters as they engage in conversation.

Clarity of expression is attained when the teller develops sensitivity to the choice of words in the story. The selection is based upon a keen perception of story style. Using specific or familiar words, the narrator secures clarity of meaning as he weaves them into a sentence structure which is easy to understand. Superfluous description, confused patterns of conversation become controlled and eliminated with an economy of words. This does not mean the employment of brevity to the detriment of the telling. Rather, it means a careful selection and arrangement of words which the teller includes in his telling.

Clarity also depends upon a clear articulation and enunciation. Careless endings given to words and improper pronunciations are pitfalls common to the inexperienced teller. The running together of syllables, phrases, or sentences will rob the listeners of much of the beauty contained in the author's expressions.

Proper body movements play a vital role as supplementary aids to the storyteller. While listening to the words of a story, the children keep a close watch upon the teller's face. It helps them to gauge the meaning of a word or share an emotional experience. By a flash of an eye, a ready smile, or a wrinkle of the brow you may convey more meaning to a particular idea or situation than a lengthy verbal description. Let your face be expressive but not overdone. Do not forget that any displeasure which you may have toward either a story or a reaction of a listening group finds a ready outlet in the facial expressions.

The storyteller should be deeply concerned with the movements of the body—head, shoulders, arms, fingers, legs, and feet. Limiting the body and its extremities to a minimum of movement, you achieve the maximum effect without an unnecessary distraction from the verbal pictures. Serving merely as the medium through which the author brings his work to an audience, the teller should never conceive of himself as an actor. Therefore, any activity which overshadows the story should be eliminated. This includes such overt mannerisms as clasping the hands nervously, moving them to the ear or other parts of the head. Continual striding about before the group, excessive waving of the arms, and frequent, hurried turnings of the head from one part of the audience to the other are to be barred by the teller.

The body expressions should be natural, appropriate, and spontaneous. Forced gestures and unfamiliar movements detract and give false impressions of the tale. As you stand before your group, strive for artistic restraint accompanied by a sense of ease and relaxation. Correlating the spoken word with the proper facial and body expressions, the storyteller comes closer to the source of the story's inspiration. Losing identity with all but the tale, you feel strangeness disappearing. In its place appears familiarity, warmth, and finally possession. You become as one with the author's creation. There only remains the task of presenting it to your listeners.

PRESENTATION OF THE STORY

The setting. Story hour! With these magical words you bring your young audience up to the closed doors. You turn the key. What will it be like? Where will you go? How will you succeed? It is difficult to recall the first moments of a first story hour in its entirety, but the memory of it will always be cherished. Unknowingly, the atmosphere for the story hour is created, partly, by the selection and arrangement of the story-hour site.

Serving as a frame to the teller and his art, the room may heighten or lessen a story-hour appeal. It should not be too small for the size of the group nor so large that its size dwarfs the spirit of those who enter. Furthermore, it should be located apart from any other activity and away from outside disturbances. The room, itself, should be clean, orderly in appearance, well lighted and well ventilated. Excessive sunshine should be avoided. If the story hours are to be conducted indoors, the arrangement of the furniture should be planned and executed before story hour begins. It is best to have the chairs in a semicircle with enough space between the rows to prevent cramping. If the story hour is held in a classroom, school, or church assembly hall, all desks and chairs should be cleared of pencils, papers, and books.

In those instances where a storyteller relates his story out-of-doors, careful selection of a site merits very close attention. The area should be shady, preferably. It should be free from such discomforting ele-

ments as stumps, sharp rocks, protruding tree roots, tall grass, or dampness. Similarly, it should be apart from other activity which may divert
the attention of the audience.

Regardless of the place of the story hour—indoors or out-of-doors—
the selected room or outside area should possess a focal point. Indoors,
this is usually a table facing the group and decorated with artistically
arranged books or some floral centerpiece. For a church story hour, a
table decorated with a Bible, cross, or flowers and flanked by lighted
candles is impressive in its very simplicity. In the camp or out-of-doors
site nothing creates an atmosphere any better than the fireplace with its
burning logs.

Assembling the group. In a library or community center the children should form into line and come quietly and orderly into the room.
For a school assembly or classroom group, proper procedure is often
governed by school practices. In all instances avoid public disciplinary
action for any misbehavior. This includes chastising children in a loud
voice, making them sit by themselves, or ordering them to leave the
auditorium, camp ring, or story-hour room. Such procedures create, immediately, an emotional block, dispelling for others some of the anticipated joy of the story hour. (Parenthetically, it should be stated that
story hour is *never* held forth as a reward for some accomplishment.
Nor is it withheld as a measure of punishment because of misbehavior.
In short, it is not a corrective device nor a meaningless bribe or prom-
ised activity granted in exchange for individual or group cooperation.
It is a voluntary, shared experience, free from such negative encumbrances.)

Preparing the group for the first story. When children come to a
community center, playground, or library for story hour, have them remove their wraps. Set aside all skates, umbrellas, books, and magazines. Small items such as candy, money, or keys are to be put into a
safe place. In a school auditorium or classroom have all desks and chairs
cleared during the story hour.

It may be expedient to remind the children that they should plan to
remain throughout the entire program. If anyone has to leave for the
purpose of looking at a favorite television program or listening to a radio
serial, it would be wise to excuse the child before the story hour begins.
This will prevent unexpected interruptions later in the program.

After all of the children are seated, wait for the first wave of excitement to pass away. You may attain that short period of silence which
comes before the first story by utilizing any one of the following tech-

niques. Play music softly either on a piano or on a phonograph. I have used the song "America" as recorded by the Boston Pops Orchestra or the engaging selection "In a Clock Store," a descriptive fantasy by Orth. The use of candles may bring the desired quietness. As a designated child lights the story-hour candle, it will serve as the moment to begin.

Presenting the program. Leading the children, mentally, up to the words of the first story, "Once upon a time . . ." is a puzzling task for some storytellers. Following a brief welcome to story hour, the teller may pause as he gropes for a beginning. If you are new to the group, you can establish a personal relationship very quickly by introducing yourself informally. Say just a few words to establish the mood for the story. This will also allow the children an opportunity to become accustomed to the sound of your voice.

As your eye travels over the group in the few seconds of silence, you gradually gain their attention. With their interest focused on you, you begin your story. Your practiced art becomes a reality. Progressing into your narrative, you lose your first moments of uneasiness as you slip into the familiar pattern and role of the storied characters. Of course, this occurs only if you have established a spiritual affinity with the tale. Watching carefully and unobtrusively the reactions of the group, you begin to gauge the effect of the story upon them. It is here that they give to you their emotional and spiritual gifts. It is here that you receive the added inspiration which brings you near to the pinnacle of your folk art.

But there will be moments when the audience shows no external response. This does not mean a lack of interest. Sometimes, it is a deliberate attempt to conceal the deepest feelings. These emotional experiences of the listeners are too precious to share, even with the one who has brought them into being. Gradually reaching the story climax, you draw your narrative to a close with a good ending. You return the audience, figuratively speaking, to the threshold of the castle. Finishing now, with a quietness, you wait while the youngsters slowly relinquish their mental hold upon this priceless treasure and return to the world about them.

Group activity during story hour. Before relating a second story, a brief period of relaxation is welcomed to ease the tension. In these few moments of digression from storytelling, it is still important to retain the atmosphere already created. The introduction of such activity permits group participation in story hours. It serves as another means for having shared experiences. Among the suggestive techniques which may be employed are the simple exercise games or volunteer reading of previously selected short poems. The latter can be done by the members of the audience. A few titles of poetry books are included in the bibliography at the end of this chapter. Group singing of a song learned in school is always effective and may be substituted for either one or the other suggested activities. This is particularly suitable for a school assembly which has large numbers of children. When the group has resettled itself once more in their seats or on the ground it is time to begin the next story.

Concluding the program. The effect of the story hour may be enhanced or destroyed by its conclusion. One excellent method of maintaining the mood created is to close with a story-hour thought for the day. This is simply a moment of reflection in which absolute quietness is kept; then the teller may quote a short, inspirational verse or thought as the group listens ("The Arrow and the Song" by Henry W. Longfellow, "My Creed" by Howard A. Walter, "Four Things" by Henry Van Dyke). Following the reading of the story-hour thought, the members of the group may make a personal story-hour wish, silently. If a candle has been used in the period, it may be extinguished at this time by one of the children. The value of such an ending is obvious. It allows the children to have a few moments in which to reflect upon the events which have gone before. It brings together in a compelling manner the dangling emotions of many listeners. It affords a group sharing of a common bond which exists between the storyteller and each member.

Dismissing the audience. Story hour is not over until the children have been dismissed from the story-telling room or out-of-doors area. For those attending story hours in nonschool agencies, an orderly recovery of articles is the first step. Donning of wraps and a quiet exit from the room follow. In school programs, the school procedure usually determines the manner of dismissal. It, too, should be systematic and in harmony with the other phases of the program. The dismissal is, in effect, part of the frame in which the story hour is bordered.

POSSIBLE OUTCOMES OF STORY HOUR

Story hour is over, the room deserted, and you sit alone amid the quiet of the hour. The room still seems to reecho to the sound of laughter, the quick intake of a breath, and the happy clapping of hands. Chairs slightly disarranged and an indescribable emotional warmth give mute testimony to a recently held activity. Reflecting upon the moments just past, the storyteller may ask: To where does it lead? Did the teller achieve his goals? What treasures became the possessions of those who listened?

These are queries difficult to answer, for they deal with intangibles and intangibles are never ascertainable or measurable. Yet, a storyteller has to make an evaluation of the story hour; it is indigenous to the teller's art. From such a review, the weaver of tales determines whether or not the completed program has produced the desired effects.

EVALUATION CHART FOR THE STORYTELLER

Storyteller_____ Date_____ Time_____ Place_____
Group_____ Attendance_____ Stories_____

Purposes of Storytelling: Develop well-delineated objectives which provide for teller and listener a *sense of direction, stability, and a means for growth*

    Entertain: provide enjoyment, satisfy the play spirit, and offer a mutually shared experience

    Motivate: provide a "bridge to" literature, introduce listeners to its inexhaustible sources

    Educate: provide a means for personal, social, and intellectual guidance; develop a feeling of social sensitivity to life and people of the past and present

    Inspire: provide concepts, without moralizing, which embody positive ethical, moral, and spiritual values

    Perpetuate Folk Art: add to a rich heritage; transmit its gifts to those who follow

Planning the Story Hour: Use some of the essentials related to good program planning

  A. *The Situation*: Answer these questions: *Who, what, where, when, how?*

      Type of Story Hour: Preschool story hours, picture book hour, regular story hour (learned stories), read aloud story hour, family story hour

      Agency: Home, library, school, camp, hospital, playground, recreation center, religious institution

      Schedule: Daily, weekly, monthly, seasonal, special observances

      Length: Determined by age, interest span, size, and composition of group

      Publicity: Posters, announcements, news releases, tickets

  B. *The Audience*: Develop a sensitive response to audience interests and potentials in story selections and presentations

      Age Groups: Preschool (3½–5 years), primary (6–8 years) intermediates (9–12 years), young adults, adults, senior citizens

Composition: Girls, boys, mixed groups; homogeneous or heterogenous age groups; cultural, national, religious backgrounds. Social, emotional, intellectual maturity and characteristics of various age groups
Number in Attendance: _____

C. *The Program Arrangement:* Develop programs with unity, balance, and coherence

Theme of story hour	Order of telling	Use of poetry
Number of stories	Balanced story selections	

Preparing the Story Hour:

A. *The Storyteller:* Recognize the depths of inner qualities needed to recreate a printed work into an oral masterpiece

Personal Attributes:

Artistry and dignity	Interpretative ability
Creative imagination	Rich literary background
Contagious enthusiasm	Positive response to story and audience

Essentials for Learning Stories:

Familiarity with material—read silently and aloud several times
Analysis of story—make a mental or written outline
Memorization of ideas
Retention of author's words and style
Repeated oral practice
Insertion of appropriate gestures, expressions, posture

Effective Storytelling Qualities:

Delivery: Speed, enunciation, clarity, pitch, full voice, pauses, breath control, good tonal qualities
Body Movements: Eye span, limited gestures, good posture, facial expressions

Negative Qualities to Avoid in Storytelling:

Over-dramatizing	Moralizing
Talking down	Interrupting or being interrupted
Going off on tangents	with questions
Stumbling, repeating	Frequent explanations
Indirect discourse	

Negative Qualities to Avoid in Reading Stories Aloud:

Eye span limited to page	Monotone
Improper position of book	Improper display of pictures
Leafing pages unconsciously	Stumbling
Rapid reading	

B. *The Story:* Types of stories are relative and the selections included under each apply to one or more of the categories

Type of Story:

Adventure	Myth	History
Animal	Parable	Holiday
Biography	Legend	Humor
Epic (hero)	Realistic stories	Picture book
Fable	Fantasy	Proverb
Modern fanciful	Fairy or traditional folk tale	Tall tale
		Cycle stories

Story Structure: Uncover the external structure of each story using a suggested written or mental outline to determine the component parts and their interrelationship:

Theme: Strong, understandable, well defined

Introduction: Indicates situation, setting, characters, problem to be solved or hope to be fulfilled

Plot: Logical development, economy of incidents, some elements of suspense, plausible

Climax: Answers the curiosity or anticipation aroused in introduction; resolves the problem or fulfills the hope

Conclusion: Follows climax quickly, finishes the story, avoids stated moral (except in a fable)

Style: Fluid, direct, recognize peculiarities of author's expressions, indicate story flavor

Characters: Appealing, believable, contrasting, natural, and appropriately suited for story role

Vocabulary: Simple, expressive; devoid of slang, stereotyped dialect, colloquialisms

C. *The Story-Hour Location*: Frame the storytelling with a proper setting and an atmosphere conducive to listening:

Selection of Site:

Absence of distractions	Good acoustics
Size suitable for number in audience	Clean, orderly

Appearance:

Indoors

Orderly furniture arrangement
Semicircular seating plan
Well lighted and ventilated
Table, book cases artistically
decorated

Outdoors

Shady location; grassy
Avoidance of natural obstacles—sunlight, damp ground, rocks, tall grass, tree roots
Free from glass, paper, etc.
Orderly arrangement of benches, chairs, stools

Presenting the Story Hour: Bring together all of the elements into an artistic pattern—a story, listeners, and a storyteller

A. Assembling children for story hour
B. Preparing group for first story
C. Presenting story
D. Conducting story-hour activity—poetry reading
E. Concluding story hour (story-hour wish)
F. Dismissing audience

Effects of story hour on listeners.   The evidence to be gathered should be considered in relation to the objectives determined earlier by the storyteller. It is evaluated, further, in terms of possible outcomes of various kinds: (a) deepening an appreciation for literature, (b) satisfying personal and social needs, (c) forming value concepts. Specific effects resulting from a given story hour cannot be determined by anyone except the teller who conducts the program. In his total appraisal, he analyzes purpose, situation, audience, and stories. Yet in all of these evaluative steps, the storyteller adheres very carefully to a principal tenet of his art: *Never probe children's minds in order to learn their reactions to a narrative.* The teller can only assume that children have taken away with them some shared experience with a storied character or situation. When children substantiate such assumptions with expressed thoughts such as those given below, then the storyteller is able to experience moments of happiness:

My reasons for immensely enjoying these stories are hard to express but as another student I will do my best to explain. Inside of a person there is a little light burning. That is the light of inspiration. Stories like those you told inspire people to do bigger, better things, and to set a goal to achieve. When that light warms my heart I know that I enjoyed and actually lived the story told. . . .[37]

SUGGESTED READINGS

INDIVIDUAL STORIES

"Africa 1725" in Elizabeth Yates, *Amos Fortune, Free Man.* New York: Aladdin Books, 1950.

"Ah Mee's Invention" in Arthur B. Chrisman, *Shen of the Sea.* New York: E. P. Dutton & Co., Inc., 1925.

"The Apple of Contentment" in Howard Pyle, *Pepper and Salt,* New York: Harper and Brothers, 1885.

"Beowulf's Encounter with Grendel" in Stratford Riggs, *The Story of Beowulf.* New York: Appleton-Century, 1933.

[37]Letter received from junior high school pupil, Brooklyn, New York, 1950.

"The Christmas Apple" in Sawyer, Ruth, *This Way to Christmas*. New York: Harper and Brothers, 1952.

"Crow's Nest" in Sawyer, Ruth, *Picture Tales from Spain*. New York: Stokes Company, 1936.

"Daniel" in Barnhart, Nancy, *The Lord Is My Shepherd*. New York: Charles Scribner's Sons, 1949.

"Doctor and Detective, Too" in Hatch, M. C., *13 Danish Tales*. New York: Harcourt, Brace & World, Inc., 1947.

"The Earrings" in Belpre, Pura, *The Tiger and the Rabbit, and Other Tales*. Boston: Houghton Mifflin Company, 1946.

"The Elephant Child" in Kipling, Rudyard, *Just So Stories*. New York: Doubleday & Company, Inc., 1912.

"The Good Samaritan" in *Bible (New Testament)*.

"Hansel and Gretel" in Grimm, Jacob and Wilhelm, *Grimm's Fairy Tales*. New York: Grosset & Dunlap, Inc., 1945.

"How the Camel Got His Hump" in Kipling, Rudyard, *Just So Stories*. New York: Doubleday & Company, Inc., 1912.

"Jack and the Beanstalk" in Adams, Kathleen, comp., *A Book of Giant Stories*. New York: Dodd, Mead & Co., 1926.

"The Juggler of Notre Dame" in Sawyer, Ruth, *The Way of the Story-Teller*. New York: The Viking Press, Inc., 1942.

"King Arthur and His Sword" from *The Boys' King Arthur* by Thomas Malory, ed. by Sidney Lanier, in Johnson, Edna, Carrie Scott, and Evelyn Sickels, *Anthology of Children's Literature*. Boston: Houghton Mifflin Company, 1948.

"Little Red Riding Hood" in Rojankovsky, Feodor, *The Tall Book of Nursery Tales*. New York: Harper and Brothers, 1944.

"My Song Yankee Doodle" by Carl Glick, in Association for Childhood Education, *Told Under the Stars and Stripes: An Umbrella Book*. New York: The Macmillan Company, 1945.

"The Old Woman and Her Pig" in Rojankovsky, Feodor, *The Tall Book of Nursery Tales*. New York: Harper and Brothers, 1944.

"The Paradise of Children" in Hawthorne, Nathaniel, *A Wonderbook and Tanglewood Tales*. New York: Dodd, Mead & Co., 1938.

"Paul Bunyan's Cornstalk" in Shepherd, Esther, *Paul Bunyan*. New York: Harcourt, Brace and World, Inc., 1924.

"Pecos Bill and His Bouncing Bride" in Malcolmson, Anne, *Yankee Doodle's Cousins*. Boston: Houghton Mifflin Company, 1941.

"Rapunzel" in Grimm, Jacob and Wilhelm, *Grimm's Fairy Tales*. New York: Grosset & Dunlap, Inc., 1945.

"Robin Hood and Little John" from *The Merry Adventures of Robin Hood* by Howard Pyle, in Johnson, Edna, Carrie Scott, and Evelyn Sickels, *Anthology of Children's Literature*. Boston: Houghton Mifflin Company, 1948.

"Rumpelstiltskin" in Grimm, Jacob and Wilhelm, *Grimm's Fairy Tales*. New York: Grosset & Dunlap, Inc., 1945.

"Ruth and Naomi" in Barnhart, Nancy, *The Lord Is My Shepherd*. New York: Charles Scribner's Sons, 1949.

"The Selfish Giant" by Oscar Wilde, in Harper, Wilhelmina, *Easter Chimes*. New York: E. P. Dutton & Co., Inc., 1942; and Wilde, Oscar, *The Selfish Giant*. New York: P. J. Kenedy & Sons, 1954.

"The Shepherd's Nosegay" by Parker Fillmore, in Fenner, Phyllis, *Princesses and Peasant Boys*. New York: Alfred A. Knopf, Inc., 1944.

"Three Fridays" in Kelsey, Alice, *Once the Hodja*. New York: Longmans, Green & Company, 1943.

"The Three Little Pigs" in Hutchinson, Veronica, comp., *Chimney Corner Stories*. New York: G. P. Putnam's Sons, 1925.

"Three Magic Oranges" in De Osma, Lupe, *The Witches' Ride and Other Tales from Costa Rica*. New York: William Morrow and Co., Inc., 1957.

"Three Questions" in Kelsey, Alice, *Once the Hodja*. New York: Longmans, Green & Company, 1948.

"The Tinker and the Ghost" in St. Boggs, Ralph and Mary Gould Davis, *Three Golden Oranges and Other Spanish Folk Tales*. New York: Longmans, Green & Company, 1936.

"To Your Good Health" by Andrew Lang, in Fenner, Phyllis, *Princesses and Peasant Boys*. New York: Alfred A. Knopf, Inc., 1944; Shedlock, Marie L., *The Art of the Story-Teller*. New York: Dover Publications, Inc., 1951.

"The Twelve Dancing Princesses" in Grimm, Jacob and Wilhelm, *Grimm's Fairy Tales*. New York: Grosset & Dunlap, Inc., 1945.

"Ulysses and the Cyclops" in Church, Alfred, *The Odyssey for Boys and Girls*. New York: The Macmillan Company, 1925.

"Waukewa's Eagle" by James Buckham, in Tyler, Anna Cogswell, comp., *Twenty-four Unusual Stories*. New York: Harcourt, Brace & World, Inc., 1921.

"Why the Sea Is Salt" in Dasent, George Webb, *East O' the Sun and West O' the Moon*. New York: G. P. Putnam's Sons, nd.

References to Children's Books

Andersen, Hans Christian. *Andersen's Fairy Tales*. New York: Grosset & Dunlap, Inc., 1945.

——. *The Emperor's New Clothes*. Boston: Houghton Mifflin Company, 1949.

Andrews, Mary R. S. *The Perfect Tribute*. New York: Charles Scribner's Sons, 1906.

Association for Childhood Education, *Told Under the Stars and Stripes: An Umbrella Book*. New York: The Macmillan Company, 1945.

Aulaire, Ingri and Edgar D. *Ola*. New York: Doubleday & Company, Inc., 1932.

Beim, Jerrold. *Thin Ice*. New York: William Morrow & Co., Inc., 1956.

Bemelmans, Ludwig. *Madeline*. New York: Simon & Schuster, Inc., 1939.

Bishop, Claire. *The Five Chinese Brothers*. New York: Coward-McCann, Inc., 1938.

Bowman, James. *Pecos Bill, the Greatest Cowboy of All Time*. Chicago: Albert Whitman & Co., 1937.

Brown, Marcia. *Dick Whittington and His Cat*. New York: Charles Scribner's Sons, 1950.

Brunhoff, Jean de. *Story of Babar*. New York: Random House, Inc., 1933.

Bulla, Clyde. *The Poppy Seeds*. New York: Thomas Y. Crowell Company, 1955.

Crump, Irving, ed. *Boy's Life Dog Stories*. New York: Thomas Nelson & Sons, 1949.

Estes, Eleanor. *The Hundred Dresses*. New York: Harcourt, Brace & World, Inc., 1944.

Flory, Jane. *The Cow in the Kitchen*. New York: Lothrop, Lee & Shepard Co., Inc., 1946.

Freeman, Don. *Fly High, Fly Low*. New York: The Viking Press, Inc., 1957.

Gag, Wanda. *Millions of Cats*. New York: Coward-McCann, Inc., 1928.

Garrett, Helen. *Angelo, the Naughty One*. New York: The Viking Press, Inc., 1944.

Geisel, Theodore (Dr. Seuss). *Horton Hatches the Egg*. New York: Random House, Inc., 1940.

——. *If I Ran the Zoo*. New York: Random House, Inc., 1950.

Grimm, Jacob and Wilhelm. *Grimm's Fairy Tales*. New York: Grosset & Dunlap, Inc., 1945.

Henry, Ralph, and Lucille Pennell. *My American Heritage*. New York: Rand McNally & Co., 1949.

Kelsey, Alice. *Once the Hodja*. New York: Longmans, Green & Company, 1943.

Kipling, Rudyard. *Just So Stories*. New York: Doubleday & Company, Inc., 1912.

McCloskey, Robert. *Blueberries for Sal*. New York: The Viking Press, Inc., 1948.

——. *Make Way for Ducklings*. New York: The Viking Press, Inc., 1941.

Politi, Leo. *Song of the Swallows*. New York: Charles Scribner's Sons, 1949.

Potter, Beatrix. *The Tale of Peter Rabbit*. New York: Frederick Warne & Co., Inc., 1904.

Rey, H. A. *Curious George Gets a Medal*. Boston: Houghton Mifflin Company, 1957.

Ruskin, John. *The King of the Golden River*. Yonkers, New York: World Book Company, 1946.

Ward, Lynd. *The Biggest Bear*. Boston: Houghton Mifflin Company, 1952.

REFERENCE AND BIBLIOGRAPHICAL AIDS FOR THE STORYTELLER

I. *Indexes*

Brewton, John E., comp. *Index to Children's Poetry*. New York: H. W. Wilson Co., 1942.

Eastman, Mary. *Index to Fairy Tales, Myths and Legends*, 2nd ed. Boston: F. W. Faxon Co., Inc., 1926.

Eastman, Mary. *Index to Fairy Tales, Myths and Legends*, supplement. Boston: F. W. Faxon Co., Inc., 1937.

Leach, Maria, ed. *The Standard Dictionary of Folklore, Mythology and Legends*, 2 vols. New York: Funk & Wagnalls, 1949.

II. *Books*

Arbuthnot, May H. *Children and Books*, rev. ed. Glenwood, Ill.: Scott, Foresman & Company, 1964.

Bulfinch, Thomas. *Bulfinch Mythology*. T. Y. Crowell, 1962.

Eaton, Anne. *Reading With Children*. New York: The Viking Press, Inc., 1940.

Hamilton, Edith. *Mythology*. Boston: The Little, Brown and Company, 1942.

Hazard, Paul. *Books, Children and Men*. Boston: Horn Book, Inc., 1932.

Hollowell, Lillian. *A Book of Children's Literature*. New York: Holt, Rinehart & Winston, Inc., 1966.

Sawyer, Ruth. *The Way of the Storyteller*. New York: The Viking Press, Inc., 1962.

Shedlock, Marie. *The Art of the Storyteller*. New York: Dover Publications, Inc., 1951.

Smith, Lillian. *The Unreluctant Years*. Chicago, Ill.: American Library Association, 1953.

Tooze, Ruth. *Storytelling*. Englewood Cliffs, N.J.: Prentice-Hall, Inc., 1959.

III. *Anthologies*

Arbuthnot, May H., comp. *The Arbuthnot Anthology of Children's Literature*. (Includes: *Time for Poetry; Time for Fairy Tales; Time for True Tales*), rev. ed. Glenwood, Ill.: Scott, Foresman & Company, 1961.

Gruenberg, Sidonie M., ed. *Favorite Stories Old and New*, rev. ed. Garden City, N.Y.: Doubleday & Company, 1955.

Hollowell, Lillian, ed. *A Book of Children's Literature*. New York: Holt, Rinehart & Winston, Inc. 1966.

Johnson, Edna, ed. *Anthology of Children's Literature* by E. Johnson, E. Sickels, and F. Eichenberg. 3rd ed. Boston: Houghton Mifflin Company, 1959.

Martignoni, Margaret E., ed. *The Illustrated Treasury of Children's Literature*. New York: Grosset & Dunlap, Inc., 1955.

IV. *Pamphlets*

American Folklore and Its Old World Backgrounds by Carl Carmer. Chicago, Ill.: F. E. Compton Co. (free)

Following Folk Tales Around the World. Reprint from *Compton's Pictured Encyclopedia.* Chicago, Ill.: F. E. Compton Co. (free)

For the Storyteller. Ed. by National Recreation and Park Association Committee, New York: National Recreation Association.

How To Tell A Story by Ruth Sawyer. Reprint from *Compton's Pictured Encyclopedia.* Chicago, Ill.: F. E. Compton Co. (free)

Let's Read Together: Books for Family Enjoyment. Children's Services Division. Chicago, Ill.: American Library Association.

Light the Candles! ed. by Marcia Dalphin. The Horn Book, rev. ed. Boston, Mass.: Horn Book, Inc.

Once Upon a Time. Rev. ed. by Picture Book Committee of the Children's & Young Adult Section of the New York Library Association. New York: The New York Public Library.

Stories: A List of Stories to Tell and Read Aloud, edited by Ellin Greene, new ed. New York: The New York Public Library.

Stories to Tell, edited by Jeanne Hardendorff, 5th ed. Baltimore, Maryland: Enoch Pratt Free Library (Publications).

Stories to Tell to Children, edited by Laura Cathon *et al.,* 7th ed. Pittsburgh: Carnegie Library of Pittsburgh.

Storytelling by Sara I. Fenwick. Lake Bluff, Ill.: The American Educ. Ency., Publishers House. (free)

Storytelling and Stories I Tell by Gudrun Thorne-Thomsen. New York: The Viking Press, Inc.

Storytelling and the Teacher by Ruth Viguers. Washington, D.C.: National Education Association. (single copy free)

Tell Me Another by Arlene Mosel. Reprint from Wilson Library Bulletin, October 1960. Bronx, N.Y.: H. W. Wilson Co.

Chapter 22

TOY AND CHILD PLAY

The craving for play opportunities is omnipresent. To the child, play is perhaps as essential as the air he breathes and as natural for his normal development. Whether we will it or not, children will play; for it is a normal manifestation of their growth and development. It is their manner of expression. It is their way of life. It is the laboratory in which the child experiments and learns of the world about him. The degree of learning is, to a great extent, dependent upon the success with which the playthings are chosen and put to use.

CHOOSING PLAYTHINGS

Hasty and unplanned toy purchases usually fall short of holding the child's interest. Playthings ought to be chosen to reflect the needs, interest, and development of the child. Is it any wonder that so many toys handed to children are discarded after but one or two attempts at their use?

The implements of childhood play are toys. Among the questions to ask oneself before purchasing a child's playthings are the following:

1. Is the toy creative?
2. Can the child learn something from its use?
3. Will it hold the child's interest?
4. Is it safe to use?
5. Will it further the child's physical, mental, emotional, and social development?
6. Does the toy suit the child's capabilities?

GUIDING THE CHILD

One should aim to select toys that stimulate the desire for activity within the child; adult guidance may be used at times with the element of choice of play materials left to the child. The ability of making a rational choice is a trait worth encouraging at the earliest possible moment of a child's training.

306

Playthings can be divided conveniently into two groups: (1) those that can be enjoyed alone, and (2) those that lend themselves toward use with other children. Also, there are varying degrees of active and sedentary types of toys. The purchaser should bear these classifications in mind when making selections of playthings.

VARIED PLAYTHINGS

The child should have a variety of playthings so that he may select the one which suits his needs at the moment. Since the child's interest span is a short one, he is more apt to enjoy a varied collection than one in which there may be as many toys but a poorer assortment. The needs of the child's level of maturity should govern an intelligent selection of toys. With such toys at his disposal, the child can then be said to truly have a choice.

Toys can be selected to meet the child's development needs for:

Creativeness and artistry. Blackboard, easel, modeling clay, pegboard, crayons, paints, water colors, basket-making set.

Construction. Blocks, tools, construction kits, workbenches, mold sets.

Rhythmical and musical development. Tambourines, child's phonograph, piano, tom-tom, xylophone, musical puzzles.

Imitative and dramatic play. Miniature household appliances, doctor's kit, cash register, play suits, magic sets.

Strength and skills. Ball, bicycle, hobbyhorse, roller skates, athletic supplies, jump rope, archer sets.

Manipulative skill. Peg sets, jigsaw puzzles, blocks, sound blocks, interlocking blocks.

Games. Checkers, dominoes, lotto, croquet, chess, anagrams, target games.

SCIENTIFIC BASIS FOR TOY SELECTION

For many, the haphazard selection of toys is becoming a thing of the past. The selection of a toy merely because of its color or the attraction it holds for the purchaser rather than its intended use is rapidly going out of style. Teachers and child psychologists have placed the purchasing of toys on a somewhat scientific basis. The toy is chosen to meet the needs and interests of a given age group. The selection of a toy that is too simple or elementary for a child may have a retarding effect upon his development.

Suggestions for age groups. The toys listed below are but suggestions of the types suitable for each age group. If the child is advanced in his toy "literacy" then the selection of toys from the subsequent period would be in order; conversely, toys from the previous age group would suffice for the less "literate" youngster.

Age Group	Dominant Characteristics	Suggested Toys
Infancy to one year	Needs chance to learn about objects by grasping, feeling, hearing, and seeing, thereby aiding muscular control	Stuffed animals, rattles, washable balls, bath toys, beads, bells, musical toys (rubber, squeaking)
One to two years	Creeping and walking call for better muscular control, displays great craving for activity, needs toys that stimulate varied interest	Building blocks, nests of blocks, pull toys, push toys, peg toys, stuffed animals, sandbox, wagons, dolls, large beads, kiddie car
Two to four years	Likes to pretend in his play and to explore with his new physical and sensory powers. Interested in playing with others	Wheelbarrow, dump truck, push wagons, hobbyhorse, kiddie car, tricycle, housekeeping sets, floating toys, jigsaw puzzles, finger paints, sandbox with appropriate toys
Four to six years	Play with a purpose becomes dominant. His old toys take on a new meaning with a practical tinge. Curiosity is rampant as to "what makes things tick"	Steam shovel, roller skates, construction sets (simple), pegboard table, coloring books, crayons, safety scissors, musical instruments (simple)
Six to eight years	There is a continuation of interests of the previous grouping. Opportunities for vigorous activity are needed to compensate for sedentary school life. Greater coordination evident. While there are play differences between boys and girls, they are not too marked	Simple construction sets, doll equipment, simple science sets, jump rope, craft work with tools, looms, paint, skates, musical toys, bicycle, elementary athletic gear
Eight to ten years	Marked interest in group play. Games based on school subjects of arithmetic, history, geography, science. Avid interest in sports and big muscle play. Hobbies involving collections and modeling (planes, boats, trains). A cooperative spirit is noticeable	Mold sets, puzzles, construction sets, printing press, athletic supplies, dominoes, checkers, mechanical games, crafts (hand loom, embroidery, bead loom, tool chest, workbench), magic sets, telegraph sets, records, jigsaw and musical puzzles

Age Group	Dominant Characteristics	Suggested Toys
Ten to twelve years	Changing interests indicate mental progress. Craving for adventure and vigorous physical activity. Games calling for skill lead in interest. Hero-worship is very evident. Activities that involve cooperation are sought. Outdoor sports often dominate	Chemistry, electrical, and mold sets, regulation-size tools and sports equipment, construction sets, boat and airplane kits, bird guide, entomology, typewriter, scouting equipment, chess, checkers, lotto, wagon, musical instruments

PLAY FOR WHAT?

While play is entered into for the sheer fun to be derived, it need not stop there. Rather, it is a means to a desired end. It is the avenue through which the child can express himself, whether it be through blocks, clay, or construction sets. Success in a play venture will invariably help the child find himself and help integrate his personality. It is therefore urged that parents encourage the successful completion of play projects.

Play situations offer vast opportunities for observing the child's personality traits. Since the child's whole personality is expressed during play, there are splendid opportunities for observation and teaching. Desirable personality traits can be encouraged and less acceptable ones forestalled. The selfish child may benefit most from games calling for cooperation in group play, whereas the bashful child needs toys which develop his ability to create a feeling of confidence. Make-believe and imitative play of adult activities can bring about improvement of imaginative powers and hasten the rate of maturity.

There are various theories which endeavor to explain play variously as a "blowing off" of excess energy, a "replay" of the stages of mankind, as a means of relaxation, self-expression, and re-creation. There is at least partial truth in all. They are exemplified by the various forms of play which, in addition, impart a knowledge of colors, shapes, numbers, letters, and skills.

The value of physical play is not to be overlooked in the development of the child. Development of the musculature proceeds from the larger muscle groups to the smaller ones. The larger muscles are called into action by the run-of-the-mill activities. Manipulative toys help advance the ease with which the smaller muscle coordinations can be enhanced.

In analyzing the need for physical activity, it is worthy of note that lower forms of life revealed first the development of a muscular system which led to the skeletal and then the nervous system. Moreover, physical activity produces a stronger physique and creates situations calling for mental adjustments. Not only does vigorous play improve the general muscle tone but it strengthens the supporting structures of the internal organs as well. As a result, the vitality and well-being of the child are increased. These benefits are predicated on the absence of strains and drains on the child's health.

Playthings that make it possible for the child to alter his environment are highly desirable. This "power of influence" provides the child with a challenge that will spark him toward continuing effort. It is well to bear in mind Bruno Bettelheime's caveat that "the child who cannot affect his environment gives up and loses the will to learn."

Play with other children is more apt to benefit the child's social development than solitary play. This is not meant to imply that playing alone is to be frowned upon. There is need and time for both forms of play, with special emphasis to be placed on group play. Granted, the resultant noise may be enough to try one's patience. At times, the scrapping and shouting may appear to outweigh the benefits that accrue. Yet, is it not better for the child to be exposed to social experience during his formative years than to face the more difficult task of having to make these adjustments after selfish behavior patterns have been instilled?

THE LEADER'S ROLE

The leader should not overlook the invaluable lift he can give to children by actively participating in portions of their play moments. Sharing their ball play, singing games, rhythms, construction projects, and toy play can add zest to play periods. Assisting children with their play problems can be of inestimable value to their progress and will further the development of rapport between the leader and child.

Whenever there are direct contacts with the home, the leader should suggest that the parents share at least a portion of the child's play at home daily. This experience stands to benefit the parent as well as the child. It can serve as a diversion that may prove highly beneficial as moments of relaxation. The joy to be derived from playing with one's child, observing his improved skill, marveling at his clever remarks, and revelling in his antics will more than compensate for the time spent.

Cooperation unlimited. It is not unreasonable to expect assistance from the children in putting away play equipment. In order to overcome any resistance that may develop, the leader can make a game or contest of this phase of the activity. The child can either be placed in full charge or be "permitted" to share the responsibility with the others. It is well to remember that the dividing line between work and play is an exceedingly thin one; the essential difference is self-motivation. If the child can feel that he is performing the task because he wants to rather than "You'd better do it or else" we can consider the round won.

Mark Twain illustrated this point poignantly when he revealed Tom Sawyer as a most depressed youngster upon being assigned the task of painting a fence, when he wanted to play. Since this was imposed from without with its accompanying displeasure, it became drudgery. When Tom adroitly directed his friends into a situation wherein they were trying the "privilege" of painting the fence, they were even willing to offer gratuities. Mind you, the task had not changed an iota. Rather, his friends were given an inner desire to paint, whereas, in Tom's case, painting was forced on him.

Work is felt to be time consuming, boring, and drudgery; play is challenging and fascinating. The recreation of the child to a request for assistance is dependent, to a great extent, on the approach used. No attempt is being made to oversimplify this problem, which often assumes serious proportions in many a household and play area.

SAFE TOY PLAY

Great care should be exercised in the choice of toys for children. The danger of swallowing small objects is a real one, especially in the case of tots. For the very young child, care should be exercised in choosing toys finished with nontoxic colors or paint. The danger of selecting metal toys with sharp edges or protruding parts should be stressed. Toys should be rounded, with the edges turned in. Wooden toys should be checked for slivers. Flimsily constructed playthings should be guarded against. Should a toy become broken, it should immediately be removed until such time as it is repaired. Misuse of toys often increases the likelihood of accidental injuries. The prevention of such injuries calls for constant vigilance on the part of the leader.

In addition, the flammability of the costume or cowboy suit may well be another reason for care. The same holds true for plastic toys which are often of a highly flammable nature. Electrical toys should be approved by the Underwriters Laboratories (UL) to help give assurance that they are safe; proper protection against defective construction that may account for the fire hazards and electrical shocks is thus certified.

As for the caring of toys, they should be stored in a specially designated spot. The use of peach baskets or bookcases in which to store toys has been proved very effective; the peach basket can be decorated with crepe paper so that it can be made to look more presentable.

INEXPENSIVE ITEMS ABOUT THE HOUSE

The price of the toy does not necessarily have a bearing on the amount of enjoyment it can hold for the child. As a matter of fact, there are many items about the house that can be easily constructed to help amuse as well as contribute toward the development of the child. Perhaps the most universally used household item is the tool chest. Tools provide an unaccountable amount of fascination for the average child; a chance to putter, to hammer, to construct, and to imitate the carpenter is intriguing. Quite often, both leader and child may team up in the construction of toy shelves, bookcases, kites, and the like. At other times, discarded toys can be rebuilt with a little ingenuity and effort.

The following items may be found about the house for toy construction: paper cartons, crates, cereal containers, bottles and jars, barrels, and butter tubs. For those who love to clown, discarded clothing, shoes, hats, jewelry, bed sheets, blankets, and rugs will prove helpful.

PLAY IN THE OUTDOORS

Whenever conditions warrant it, the play activities should be conducted out-of-doors. The values of fresh air and sunshine can be added to the many benefits to be derived from play.

An area where children can romp, dig, climb, jump, swing, and play table games in the open should be set aside and made conducive to play. Such fixed pieces as a table and bench, sandbox, swings, and slide can be set aside. A sheltered area should be available to protect the children against hot and sunny days as well as the occasional shower. Dramatic activities, arts and crafts, rhythm-band play, and table games can be conducted under this shelter. In addition, a paved all-purpose area should be available for low-organized games, singing games, rhythms, and the like.

SUMMARY

In summation, we can educate through play by:

1. Choosing playthings that meet the needs, interests, and aid the development of the child.
2. Selecting toys that are creative, instructive, safe to use, and able to sustain interest.

3. Apportioning plaything purchases among toys suitable for individual and group use as well as active and passive play.
4. Encouraging self-expression through play and integrating the personality through the successful completion of play projects.
5. Providing opportunities for physical activity so that normal growth and mental, emotional, and social betterment may result.
6. Furthering safe play through selection, vigilance, and guidance.
7. Keeping children busy through well-conceived play. Remember, an interested, occupied child is a happy one.

SUGGESTED READINGS

Gordon, Ira J. *Human Development: From Birth Through Adolescence.* New York: Harper & Row, Publishers, 1962.

Hawkes, Glenn R., and Damaris Pease. *Behavior and Development from 5 to 12.* New York: Harper & Row, Publishers, 1962.

Ilg, Frances L., and Louise Bates Ames. *Child Behavior.* New York: Harper & Row, Publishers, 1955.

Jenkins, Gladys, *et al. These Are Your Children.* Chicago, Illinois: Scott, Foresman and Company, 1966.

Reed, Carl, and Joseph Orze. *Art from Scrap.* Philadelphia: F. A. Davis Company, 1960.

Reeves, Robert. *Make It Yourself Games Book.* New York: Emerson Books, Inc., 1964.

Sapora, Allen V., and Elmer D. Mitchell. *The Theory of Play and Recreation.* New York: The Ronald Press Company, 1961.

Part V

PROGRAM ESSENTIALS:
C. OUTDOOR RECREATION

Chapter 23

CAMPING AND
OUTDOOR EDUCATION

Camping and outdoor recreation in general and family camping in particular have been achieving greater emphasis in the field of recreation and its parent, education. This recognition of their worth is justly earned. Moreover, it signifies growing appreciation of the worth activities suited and based on a sylvan setting can contribute toward a more complete educational experience.

Dr. Charles W. Eliot of Harvard once described camping as America's greatest contribution to education. His words comprise a challenge to us. While camping is not a new activity, it is undergoing a reemphasis as an educational medium. The popularity of school camps, community camps, and day camps is virtually taking the country by storm. This is justly so since camping offers a more interesting and natural setting for the learning process. Moreover, crowded city living, with its emphasis on brick, cement, and steel, has made little provision for nature. Even for the lad who comes from a country setting, the camp offers a most desirable setting for learning to get along with others, practicing the give and take of communal living, and developing self-reliance in the out-of-doors. While not a complete justification for camping, this explanation can at least partially account for its rapid rise in popularity.

In addition, camping can serve as a bromide to the highly strung and complex living of our time. It is an activity that can be practiced alone as well as with mixed groups, and by family groups regardless of financial standing. The individual, no matter what his age, can discover in camping an interest that will carry over into later life and one that will grow in appreciation along with each experience.

Camping as we know it today owes much of its success and acceptance to the private camp, for it served as the forerunner of our present-day camping program. It pioneered by experimenting and conducting varied activities. While there are many camps that simply transfer the physical education program of the school into a setting of trees and grass, this faulty emphasis is fortunately not attributable to all. Most camp leaders recognize that the locale of the camp is unique for acquiring the knowledge and skills of the outdoors with its nature lore, wood crafts, Indian lore, and the like.

The organization that has been instrumental in fostering advancement in camping more than perhaps any other is the American Camping Association. Its membership is countrywide with an individual membership of ten dollars and student membership of five dollars; a subscription to the publication *Camping Magazine* is included as part of the membership. It investigates and approves deserving camps for inclusion in its Camp Directory.

TYPES OF CAMPS AND CAMPING

There are assorted camps which derive their support from public and private sources. Nonpublic support can be broken down into nonprofit and commercial. Institutional camps are usually nonprofit and are exemplified by those conducted by the Boy and Girl Scouts, boys' clubs, 4-H clubs, settlement houses, "Y's," and church and school camps. They serve a unique purpose in that they make camp available for many who could not otherwise attend somewhat more costly private camps. In addition, there are health camps conducted by service clubs and charitable groups; sportsmen's club camps; public camps run by city, state, and federal agencies; conservation camps which are concerned with human and natural resource protection; and camps for the atypical, such as the crippled, blind, cerebral palsied, and cardiac, whose ailments make it difficult for them to fit into the regular camping activities. These are in addition to the hundreds of private camps usually attended for an eight-week period ranging in cost up to one hundred dollars or more a week.

School camping. Camping has become a recognized adjunct of the curricula of a growing number of school systems. The importance of this phase was highlighted by the undertaking of the Outdoor Education Project under the sponsorship of the American Association for Health, Physical Education and Recreation and the leadership of Julian W.

Smith. He has conducted outdoor education workshops throughout the country. The efforts of such states as Michigan, California, New York, Texas, and Pennsylvania have not only helped stimulate programs in their own borders but have exerted desirable influences on neighboring states and regions. A number of colleges have helped spearhead school camping by way of conducting demonstrations, workshops, seminars, and the issuance of descriptive literature. This is true of any number of other colleges throughout the United States.

A school can make effective use of facilities removed from its plant in the form of area campsites, parks, or farms. In addition, a recent conference report advises: "Private-, agency-, or state-owned summer camps offer opportunities for school use during the school year when they are ordinarily idle." It continues: "School systems may even own their own campsites singly or jointly and provide opportunity for school camping during the school year and recreational camping during the summer months" (*Conference on Education for Leisure*, American Association for Health, Physical Education and Recreation, 1957, p. 48).

Conservation camp. A concern for education in the protection and judicious use of the country's water, minerals, soil, forests, and wildlife is advocated in the conservation camp. Field trips and lectures are often used to impart an understanding of the importance of stream pollution, reforestation, farm fish ponds, forest game, land reclamation, and erosion to our natural resources.

Hobby activities involving the outdoors include fly and bait casting, firearm safety, target shooting, and fly tying. Other popular camp activities are hiking, map and compass orienteering, and the selection of edible wild plants for emergency feeding. Motion pictures dealing with wildlife and conservation round out the program.

Community camping. The drift toward community camping, which is unmistakable although still progressing at a slow pace, includes cities like Oakland, California, which recognized the need long ago, Dearborn, Michigan, and Columbus, Ohio, whose programs are of more recent date. An opportunity to camp at a minimal cost is needed greatly by countless communities.

Dearborn, a city of 90,000, administers its program through the city recreation department. A camp commission representing youth and civic organizations, clubs, fraternal organizations, and churches is appointed by the mayor to serve as an advisory body. On January 1, 1948, Dearborn purchased 240 acres of land for this purpose. While it was inaugurated as a day-camping experience, it became so popular that it was doubled in 1949. Although still predominantly a day-camping setup, overnight camping, family camping, and picnic camping are becoming increasingly popular.

There is a growing need for increased emphasis on family camping. In view of our growing leisure, longer paid vacations, renewed emphasis on togetherness, and the trend toward outdoor living, family camping warrants a more vital position in recreation programming. Although more communities are adopting this program feature, it is still short of the acceptance this worthwhile activity deserves. That camping is very much appreciated by the aged is attested to by the success achieved by Cleveland, Ohio, with its Camp Cleveland.

Outpost camp. A laboratory situation for the application of skills taught at camp is available in the outpost camp. Skills learned in camp such as axemanship, cooking, nature lore, camp making, outfitting, mapping, and first aid are afforded practice opportunities in a real situation. Projects dealing with the skills just mentioned or other activities may be assigned the group thereby providing added motivation and meaning to the experience.

A recommended number for an outpost hike is eight; one or two more or less is permissible. A minimum of two leaders should be assigned to each group so that full benefit from the venture will accrue. The length of time of an outpost hike may extend from half-day or one-day trial trips to three-day undertakings.

Outpost kit. That the camper should carry a minimum of gear on any trip is a maxim that cannot be overemphasized. The following items are suggested for an outpost hike to cover a group of ten:

> 1 axe
> 5 small tents
> 1 water bucket
> 1 folding shovel
> 1 camp cook kit
> 10 sleeping bags
> 10 ponchos
> 1 first aid kit

Other suggested items that may be added are a lantern, inflatable mattresses, water bag, kerosene stove, mess kits, wash basin, all-purpose jackknife, and a tent (nine feet by twelve feet) for headquarters. The number of items to be included are to be based on the duration of the trip and the needs of the group.

PROGRAM PLANNING

Program responsibility. The director is in complete charge of the activities to be featured in the program. He will invariably fall back upon his assistants for suggestions and advice. The suitability of the activities should be related to the needs of those who frequent the camp. The advice of the specialist and camp counselors is to be sought to help achieve this end. Obviously, the director should bear in mind that the program will be ineffective unless there are suitable leaders to execute it. A less elaborate program would be preferable to one that includes all the activities visualized by the director but with ineffectual leadership to conduct them. Facilities and equipment needs are also to be borne in mind in the selection of activities.

It is advisable to prepare a daily, weekly, and seasonal program. This will serve as a guide to the staff and will help them chart the course to be followed. Effective guidance and supervision are to be provided for, with conferences and meetings included, so that they may become positive forces for the betterment of the camp program.

Program: The camping program should be varied, flexible, and comprehensive. Activities that lend themselves to the camp's natural setting should be emphasized. This is not meant to preclude the use of sports, games, and physical education activities. By virtue of its setting, the unique atmosphere of the camp warrants the stressing of nature lore, campfire activities, cookouts, hiking, trail blazing, and ceremonials benefitting the camp situation.

To the camper, the primary concern is to have a good time by doing the things he likes to do. It is therefore the camp leader's responsibility to gear his program to the camper's needs. Furthermore, he must bear in mind that a well-balanced program is desirable not only because it is more apt to benefit the individual but also because it is likely to meet the varied tastes of the group. An overemphasis on games will be the case if such worthwhile activities as handicrafts, dramatics, music, storytelling, and varied hobby groups are slighted. A balanced program similar to the one indicated is more apt to leave the participant with a feeling of worthwhile accomplishment. Not only will there be fun in the doing but also gratification from having completed meaningful tasks. Moreover, there is tremendous value to be extracted out of camper participation in program planning. This feature is to be incorporated at every opportunity.

The schedule should be definite while still flexible in nature. Changes in weather and unexpected conditions are to be countered with a change in program. Rainy-weather programs should be worked out in advance so that worthwhile and meaningful activities can be substituted with ease. Any letup in the program may accentuate the problem of nostalgia or homesickness. A regimented program is not what is sought but rather one that sustains a camper's interests for the greater part of the day; a certain portion or set periods of the day are to be discretionary so that the camper may exercise a choice as he sees fit. The alert leader will see to it that even these periods of letup are interesting moments of fellowship.

Special events.   Special events can be used to stimulate interest and provide meaningful lifelike experiences wherein that which is taught can be practiced. These activities can also offer incentive for further effort and activity, since they may be referred to as the "dessert" part of the campers' "meal." Needless to say, the camp situation is resplendent with opportunities for this phase of the program. A partial list follows with the realization that the imagination of a leader can bring forth others that are perhaps more meaningful to his situation and more in keeping with the interests of his group.

Special Events

Splash parties	Trail laying
Socials and parties	Axemanship
Campfire programs	Knot tying
Storytelling	Fly tying
Camp sings	Bait-casting exhibitions
Quiz shows	Marksmanship
Forums	Nature expeditions
Barbecues—wiener roasts	Water pageants
Tournaments	Treasure and scavenger hunts
Hikes (short or overnight)	Visitations (farms, canneries,
Explorations	water works, etc.)
Fishing trips	Canoe trips

CAMP ADMINISTRATION

When operating a camp, it is highly desirable that it be done democratically. In order to effect this, many camps operate with the assistance of a committee of campers under the sponsorship of an adult leader. The committee is chosen by a duly conducted election. This committee or camp council, as it is often referred to, can serve as an advisory group which may be of inestimable assistance to the camp director. The pros and cons of the camp program and future plans and problems that may arise from time to time may well come before this group. Flagrant infractions of the camp's rules can also be handled by this council. This opportunity for democracy in action plus the leadership opportunities afforded warrant a try at this measure.

The staff. In the selection of personnel, the director will certainly look for essential leadership traits. These are discussed fully in the chapter on leadership principles and procedures. Here again, special skills may be desired, such as the ability to teach dramatics, dancing, camp craft, wood craft, and nature lore. Counselors are often drawn from the ranks of teachers, specialists in music, dramatics, the arts, and the clergy. In view of the unique setting of the camp and its own set of objectives and program of activities, it is essential that these leaders be well briefed prior to the start of the camping session. Experience in the varied phases of camping should indeed be one of the essential criteria to be used.

The camp director. The camp director is an educator who holds a position analogous to the principal of a school. He is the responsible head of the camp program and the leaders who conduct the activities. It is his duty to interview and to recommend the members of his staff, to consult with them in the organization of the camp program, to channel and direct the effort of the counselors, to conduct round table meetings, and to impart needed information to his staff while they in turn keep him posted as to what is going on throughout the camp. The business side of camp direction may include the purchasing of equipment, food and menu planning, kitchen management, the overseeing of the refreshment stand, trading post, and postal and deposit service for the campers.

In the training of camp directors a recent conference[1] recommended graduate training in the following areas of study: (1) Natural history and the interrelatedness of natural phenomena in the out-of-doors; (2) sociological, philosophical, and historical foundations of camping and outdoor education; (3) organization and administration of camping and outdoor education programs; (4) field techniques in the subject matter areas of the school curriculum as they relate to outdoor learning situations as well as to outdoor recreation experiences; (5) development and management of outdoor education areas and facilities.

In addition, the camp director should inform the candidates for po-

[1]*Professional Preparation in Health Education, Physical Education and Recreation Education* (Washington, D.C.: American Assn. for Health, Physical Education & Recreation, 1962).

sitions of the terms of employment, stressing salary, job duties, and hours of employment with the time off to be included in the contract or in a duly signed letter upon the agreement of both parties; a copy of the contract or letter is to be retained by the director, while the original is submitted to the employee. Principal staff members are often called upon to assist in recruiting new staff members, especially if they are to serve over them. A committee can be chosen to guide the camp director in the hiring of new personnel.

Staff assignments. If the camp is of sufficient size, an assistant director may be in order. The duties of an assistant director can include many that would normally belong to the director. In addition, he may be given some special leadership assignment or added supervisory duties.

Next in order comes the specialist or supervisor of music, arts and crafts, and the like. The specialist or supervisor may be called on to instruct designated groups in addition to supervising the counselors; the counselor is usually a veteran or older camp member who assists in the direction of the activities. Many camps operate on the ratio of one counselor for every eight to ten campers. The water-front leader is singled out, although he might well be included among the specialists. His duties encompass overseeing the water-front area and giving swimming and lifeguarding instruction. All camps should be required to have in attendance a full-time physician or nurse who will handle injuries or illnesses as well as help to keep the campers well. Should this be financially impractical, the services of a skilled first aider should be secured. A kitchen and maintenance crew are also "musts" in the camping setup. The staff just mentioned are considered to be a minimum, with special leaders to handle those who need special attention, a camp mother, secretary, and business office head often included.

Promotional methods. Wherever possible, it is desirable for a representative of the camp to have direct contact with the parents of each camper. The use of camp reunions, father and son, and mother and daughter parties, are often used to good advantage. In addition, pamphlets, letters, camp newspapers and magazines, demonstrations, exhibitions, movies, slides, and photographs will prove of assistance.

The importance of proper timing in promoting the camp program cannot be overemphasized. Get-togethers should be undertaken at a time when the desired results can best be achieved; the midwinter is often used, since it helps keep alive the camping spirit. Some camp directors desire to invite prospective campers for trial weekends. Another effective measure is to secure approval from the American Camping Association, since it indicates that the camp has met satisfactorily the standards set by this organization. This seal of approval may serve as an added criterion by which the camp may be judged.

Medical examination. In the selection of campers, it is most desirable that a thorough physical examination be conducted both by the family physician, reporting on a form issued by the camp director, and by the camp physician prior to the start of camp activities. In a similar vein, some camps resort to a recheck of each camper prior to departure from camp. Needless to say, the medical examination procedures should be thorough. An examination of the perfunctory type is of questionable value and has no place in an efficiently managed camp.

Order of events. At the outset, the camper should be made to feel at home as quickly as possible. Every effort should be made for him to feel that he is wanted. These measures will help to prevent a drooping of spirits which may cause homesickness. Our military leaders have found that an actively occupied recruit will be less apt to succumb to the dread disease, nostalgia.

The program should therefore start off right away with such highly popular recreational activities as swimming, games and sports, and entertaining films. This introduction to camp may help to ease the "breaking-in." Since the first day is perhaps the most crucial in the camper's stay, it should be highly entertaining and crammed with activity. An interesting evening program culminating in a campfire session of singing and storytelling should top it off. This regimen will result in a fairly tired camper whose desire for slumber will far outweigh any inclination to play a prank, become involved in tomfoolery, or brood.

The hour of rising is usually in the neighborhood of seven o'clock, with about three quarters of an hour between the first bugle call and breakfast. For the energetic, this interval will permit warm-up exercises. A ceremony of flag raising with a pledge to the flag may ensue. This is followed by a clean-up period with a half- or three-quarter hour allotment for the making of bunks, sweeping of tent or cabin, and the general tidying process. A morning assembly period may follow if there is a specially planned program. Otherwise, announcements can be read at any one of the three mealtime periods.

Mention is again made of the importance of balancing the program by including a variety of activities, alternating vigorous activities with those which make fewer demands on the camper's energy reserve. Among the vigorous activities are to be found games of low and high organization, softball, baseball, basketball, volleyball, tennis, paddle tennis, swimming, and diving, with hiking and mountain climbing included. On the less-active side, we note such activities as nature study, music, handicrafts, quiet games, discussion groups, and hobby groups.

Ceremonials and the campfire. The use of ceremonials to add color and stimulate the camping program is well recognized. They should be planned thoroughly so that every detail is anticipated and full benefit is derived. To state briefly the fundamentals of the ceremonials, they should be inspiring, stimulating to the majority, and clearly defined in purpose. The program should be suited to the occasion and staged in an appropriate setting.

Noteworthy examples are first-night campfire, candlelight ceremonials, campfire dramatization of a hero of the region, and closing and awards ceremonial. Ingenuity can be used by the leader to select meaningful ceremonials.

The campfire is ideally suited for talks dealing with desirable character traits to be gained under capable leadership, in addition to the wholesome physical outcome. Such concepts as being a modest winner and a good loser, not taking unfair advantage of one's opponent, and realizing the ideals of true sportsmanship ("how you've played the game" being of vastly greater importance than "whether you've won or lost") can be made a part of the stories told at the campfire gathering and can do much toward elevating the ideals of our youth.

Indian lore. Much of our present-day camping is based on Indian lore. Certainly, the Indian inhabited our land before the white man arrived; he is the native American. Hero worship is a powerful tendency in our youth, and the Indian's contribution to camping can be the core of interest.

The Indian is often maligned as a savage with boundless cruelty. We often overlook that he fought for his home and land, a cause which can arouse belligerence in anyone's breast. The tales, songs, and dances of the Indian are resplendent with heroism and valor.

Totem poles, placed in front of their homes, were carved with fish, birds, or animals, indicative of the family or clan to which they belonged. The totem would also be placed at the bow of the canoe as an animistic device to guard them against evil.

Indian symbols are useful for handicraft articles. Other activities adaptable to Indian lore are Indian dancing, trail blazing, songs, games, sign language, and smoke signaling.

FIRE BUILDING

Safety measures. People are apt to think of building a fire as one of those common skills which is as easy as falling off a log. This underestimation soon becomes apparent as one actually starts to build one.

In building a fire, it is advisable to select a spot that is clear of underbrush and overhanging branches and is removed from tree trunks. Leaf mold should be removed, since it can burn for days and the fire can travel quite far; the danger of starting a forest fire is to be considered at all times. The practice of surrounding the fire area with rocks, sand, and soil is a wise precautionary measure.

Preparatory hints. Cooking over a high flame is not advisable; it is apt to heat the food unevenly and char the cooking utensils as well. Soaping the pots prior to cooking will keep them from turning black. The use of aluminum foil as a food wrap to be placed on hot coals is highly recommended, with a double thickness to be used if the foil is of light weight.

The wood needed for the fire should be gathered in advance so that the camper will not have to leave the fire once it is lighted. Separate piles of tinder, kindling, and hardwood should be made to facilitate feeding the fire. The type of fire should suit the cooking to be done. In starting a fire, place a forked stick about six inches in length in the ground at about a forty-five degree angle. Keep the forked end out and place a handful of tinder on it so that it is kept off the ground to permit air to infiltrate. Broken, dry, plant stalks in a vertical position are suggested to start the fire. The type of fire that is desired can then be built above this.

Altar fire. An altar fire is particularly suited for a campfire meeting for it gives off a steady light with a minimal use of fuel. Logs about three inches in diameter and three feet long should be placed parallel on the ground two feet apart. Next, others should be crisscrossed above them in a square shape. Kindling wood can then be placed on top.

Reflector fire. This type of fire is desirable for reflecting warmth into a tent or for baking. The reflector is made by forcing two small logs about one and a half feet apart into the ground at a short angle away from the fire. Logs are then placed one on top of the other to comprise a wall which reflects the heat from a small tepee fire.

Tepee fire. This simple type of fire is a good one to start with. It provides a quick-burning fire since there is a good draft. Furthermore, it can be used as the foundation for other types of fires. Kindling wood plus some hardwood is stacked as a tepee. Whittling a few inches of the end of each twig so that the shavings remain attached will speed up getting it under way. By lighting the whittled portions, the fire will more readily spread to the remaining portions.

The cutting of green growing things is illegal in all national parks and in most state parks. In many places (Chicago Forest Preserve, for example) it is illegal even to pick up dead sticks.

MAP READING

The danger of getting lost while on a hike is a real one. To help offset this, a map of the area should be carried. A dominant spot like a mountain may help, providing the camper can orient himself as to north. The map should be turned so that the magnetic north is parallel to and lines up with the compass needle. One should bear in mind that true north and magnetic north differ in many sectors.

Should a compass not be available, it is possible to spot north with the aid of a watch and the sun. By holding the watch so that the direction of the hour hand points toward the sun, south will be found by cutting in half the space between the hour hand and twelve; this will hold true for the morning and afternoon. During the noon hour, south will be in line with the shadow cast by holding a matchstick at the hour hand. A more accurate reading may be secured by holding a matchstick at the hour hand for the morning and afternoon periods. An allowance should be made for the one-hour advance to daylight saving time.

CAMPING FACILITIES AND EQUIPMENT

Needless to say, wise administration of a camp calls for an advantageous use of the terrain upon which it is situated. The areas of high elevation are often used for such permanent structures as the cabins, administration buildings, and dining hall. Level areas are certainly desirable for the play areas and courts. Fixed equipment such as swings, slides, and baskets should be so situated that there will be no overlapping of areas and little likelihood of having the participants of one area overflow onto the other. Not only is efficient and pleasurable use desired but, what is of even greater importance, the safe use of these areas should be assured. The layout of the water front should be such as to permit the lifeguard(s) to have complete visibility and accessibility to the entire swim area.

Adequate camp facilities are essential for the fulfillment of most of the camp's objectives. Although experience will dictate the exact requirements, a point of departure to help guide the camp director can prove very helpful; the following standards may serve that purpose:[2]

Items	Number Required
Showers	1 to every 8 campers
Toilets	1 to every 10 campers; no farther than 150′ from any living unit
Infirmary beds	1 to every 16 campers
Water supply	50 gallons per day per person where flush toilets are used; 30 gallons per day per person where pit privies are used; plus a full day's supply in storage at all times
Swimming pools	27 sq. ft. of surface per swimmer
Kitchen storage, etc.	1/3 to 1/2 size of dining room
Size of camp site	1 acre per camper. (This area may vary considerably depending on location. Camps adjoining large public area, such as state or national forests, will not require as much acreage as those in agricultural areas or near cities. Possible growth of suburban communities and future expansion of camp should also be considered when determining size of camp site)

COMMON CAMP EMERGENCIES

Emergency situations are a possibility in any camping experience. Although these emergencies are on the whole unpredictable, it is wise to review the camping situation in an effort to ascertain beforehand the possible emergencies that may arise. Once this is achieved the recognition of hazards will be preliminary to concerted attempts at correcting them. Moreover, a clear-cut plan of action should be arrived at and made known to the camp staff; the equipment that is necessary in the light of likely emergency situations should be secured and centrally located.

Fire. The danger of a fire in a camping situation is omnipresent. The possibility of a fire in a camp involving its structures or the surrounding forest is to be recognized. The protective steps to be taken should include adequate fire-fighting equipment, both as to number and type, to protect the camp and its adjacent wooded area. Contact should be made with the fire department in the vicinity of the camp; the phone numbers of forest rangers should be posted at the telephone. A map indicating the

[2]Courtesy of *Camp Reference and Buying Guide* which is now incorporated in the March issue of *Camping Magazine.*

region in which the camp is situated and the area occupied by the camp, with its roads and paths, is essential. A fire patrol consisting of designated members of the camp staff and older campers who represent each structure and sleeping quarter should be organized and trained in the steps to be followed in the event of a fire. Periodic fire drills should be required to help familiarize the fire patrol and the campers with the procedures to be followed should a fire arise.

Missing camper. Should a camper get lost, go AWOL, or be unaccounted for for any reason, there is the possibility of grave concern and confusion. It may be helpful to have each counselor or leader be responsible for a designated number of campers. He should make a periodic check of all campers in his charge. Should any group of campers leave the camp for a hike or an overnight trip, the names of each camper making the trip should be filed at the camp office. Not only should periodic checks be made of the number on the trip but a responsible person should be placed at the head and the rear of the group. At the water front or pool, the safeguards should include the use of the "buddy" system and the presence of an approved lifeguard.

Communicable disease epidemics. The concern for an outbreak of a communicable epidemic of measles, scarlet fever, poliomyelitis, etc., is a real one. As a preventive measure, periodic inspection of the campers can prove helpful. Adequate space between bunks and alternate positions in the sleeping quarter, so that the head of one camper rests at the juxtaposition of the feet of the camper on either side of him, may do much toward reducing the likelihood of an outbreak of disease. An infirmary should be set up somewhat removed from the camp, where those who are ill can be confined. The names of the physicians in the neighboring community should be prominently posted in the event the camp physician is not available. Thorough dishwashing, careful handling of food, and periodic examination of the kitchen help are suggested. Adequate refrigeration and high sanitary standards for the grounds, sleeping quarters, kitchens, and dining hall will also prove invaluable.

Infirmary supplies. A well-stocked infirmary is indeed an essential among the provisions made by the camp director. The fact that the camp is usually removed from the beaten path makes this measure all the more necessary. Here again, the supplies required for the infirmary will be specifically determined by the needs of the individual camp. Until these needs are accurately ascertained, a suggestive list such as the one provided by the American Camping Association for twenty campers will certainly prove of inestimable value.[3]

[3]*Camp Reference and Buying Guide*, p. 25.

Item	Size or Type	Quantity
Adhesive compresses	1-inch	1 large package
Gauze pads	4 x 4 inches	1 package
Triangular muslin bandage	40-inch	8 or more
Absorbent gauze	½ yard	Several packets
Tourniquet		2
Adhesive tape	2-inch	1 roll
Antiseptic (or soap)		1 ounce
Boric acid	Powder or crystal	1 ounce
Aspirin		1 bottle
Aromatic spirits of ammonia		1 ounce
Burn ointment	1-ounce tubes	Several
Laxative		1 package or bottle
Rubbing alcohol		1 bottle
Baking soda		1 package
Absorbent cotton		½ pound
Applicators		1 box
Tongue depressors		5 dozen
Fracture splints	Arm, leg, thigh	2 sets of each
Stretcher poles		2 pairs

Tweezers, clinical thermometers, paper drinking cups, bar of soap, flashlight.

Emergencies requiring first aid. The camp nurse and/or the camp physician are to handle the usual camp emergencies. It is also advisable for the camp staff to be well versed in accepted first aid procedures. This will be particularly helpful during off-camp trips and for situations wherein immediate measures prior to the arrival of the nurse or physician may prove of great value. Knowledge of how to handle suspected fractures, submersion victims, serious bleeding, severe cases of sunburn, and other emergencies of equal severity may be of prime importance. A knowledge of how to administer first aid to a camper with a severe gastrointestinal upset when off on a camping trip can be of inestimable worth. How to handle these and similar emergencies are described in detail in the chapter on first aid and safety.

Short-term camping refers to day, overnight, and weekend camping. Even though this type of camping experience is of shorter duration than long-term camping, there are many situations that are comparable, so that undue repetition is not needed. A knowledge of how to make a fire, how to prepare and cook a meal, and how to cook without utensils through effective use of aluminum foil are among the skills that will prove valuable. Scouting has for years expounded these virtues and encouraged the practice of short-term camping. That the short-term

camp lacks some of the advantages inherent in those of longer duration is indeed true. Nevertheless, it does contribute many of the longer
camp's advantages while acting as an introduction to camping.

Day camping. The day-camp movement has been gaining in popularity at a very rapid pace. It is being adopted by many city recreation departments and by numerous settlement houses, boys' clubs, and "Y's."
Day camps are usually located within a large city park (as in the city of
Pittsburgh) or on rooftops (as in the case of many settlement houses and
boy's clubs in New York City and elsewhere).

The usual practice is for the camper to be picked up after breakfast,
to eat lunch at the camp, and to return in time for his evening meal.
Food is often provided by the camp itself. For many youngsters in city
areas, this experience offers an opportunity to exchange a tenement-
house setting for a countrified one with an opportunity to play in a
natural setting.

Suggested activities. An opportunity to exercise an adventuresome
spirit and to explore the countryside will prove captivating. A chance to
pioneer may stimulate the youngster to greater adventure in the out-of-
doors. During the course of hiking, an opportunity to blaze trails can
acquaint the neophyte with many of the skills associated with camping.
Learning how to use a compass and how to find one's direction by the
use of a watch and the sun can prove to be experiences that the camper
will never forget. Should the path followed on a hike be a rocky one,
stones can be placed so as to indicate the direction taken. In the building of fires, the knowledge of how to place the fire so that the direction of the wind will not disturb the campers can be surprisingly valuable in spite of its simplicity.

An opportunity to use a branch, twine, a bent pin, and some bread
crumbs for fishing invariably proves thrilling. As the campers' legs start
to give way, a chance to sit in a circle to hear stimulating stories and
pioneer tales can do much toward adding flavor to the occasion. These
experiences, although elementary, may well introduce the youth to the
values of a life in the out-of-doors and the joys to be derived from simple and natural living.

Preliminary steps. As a precautionary measure to assure maximum
benefits for the campers, a thorough medical examination should be
required of each camper, whether he is out for a long- or short-time
camping experience. This practice will help to prevent many emergency situations from arising in a difficult setting, such as while portaging
on a canoe trip or while mountaineering. In addition, general orientation
to the camp setting, introduction to the camp personnel, and establishing

familiarity with the camp's procedures and regulations are to be covered at the outset.

Camping out for a night calls for thorough planning so as to assure a reasonable degree of comfort and understanding of what it entails. For example, putting clothing and the like away in safe keeping for the night will protect against the night's dampness, a possible turn in the weather, and the chance that small animals may do damage to these essential articles.

The following admonitions are deserving of consideration by the camper:[4]

1. Take your axe to bed with you. Porcupines eat axe handles—they love the salt left by sweaty hands.
2. Take your canoe paddle to bed with you. Lay it flat on the ground-cloth beside you. If you lean it against a tree it may warp. Porkies love canoe handles too.
3. Roll your soap up in the towel and put it in the tent. Many small animals love soap.
4. Cache all food for the night. If you don't, you may go hungry the next morning.
5. Turn all pots and kettles upside down and leave them where the wind can't blow them away.
6. Check your campfire to make sure that it is out. A sudden wind may blow the coals and start a fire.
7. Put your shoes in the tent. Turn them upside down and lay them where the wind can't blow them away.
8. If you wear glasses put them in your shoes.
9. Take off your clothes and put on pajamas. You are sure to sleep cold in your clothes. It is dampness that keeps you cold and your daytime clothes have absorbed dampness. The colder the night, the more important it is that you take them off.
10. Put your underwear and other cotton clothing under your blankets. Cotton absorbs moisture and gets as wet as if it had been dropped in the lake. If you have an extra poncho, it's a good idea to wrap all your clothing in it.
11. Lay your handkerchief at the head of the bed for a blindfold. If the early morning sun keeps you awake, tie the handkerchief over your eyes. Some campers carry black blindfolds expressly for this purpose.
12. Put your flashlight where you can find it instantly.

Many find it more advisable to hold a training institute for day-camp

---

[4]Bernard S. Mason, *The Junior Book of Camping and Woodcraft* (Cranbury, N.J.: A. S. Barens & Co., Inc., 1943), pp. 44, 45.

leaders. Fundamentals of day camping can be imparted along with how to cook without utensils, fire making, nature lore, axemanship, compass reading, Indian Lore, and other recreational topics that are often slighted in recreational programs.

Facilities and equipment.   The importance of a shelter for the unpredictable summer shower is readily visualized. Other essential facilities are latrines, adequate first aid equipment, and such fire extinguisher equipment as sand, water, and the pyrene type of extinguisher. If tents are used, care should be taken that they are fire retarded. In the event that swimming facilities are at hand, a certified lifeguard should be in attendance with such paraphernalia as life buoys and catamarans or life boats so that "Throw, Row, Tow, and Go" can be practiced. A clearing wherein many of the activities can be conducted within a rustic setting; a supply of water for drinking, cooking, and washing purposes; toilet facilities; and a shelter to protect against the hot summer sun or shower are essential for a day camp. City departments will usually make the needed space available in one of its park areas. In smaller communities, public land or that belonging to a public-spirited citizen may be solicited. Wherever available, county, state, and federal land may be used.

Healty and safety practices.   Sanitary and healthful conditions at the camp are mandatory. Assurance that the water supply has been proved safe should be had prior to the opening of the camp season. Whenever there is cause to question the purity of water, as on a hike or trip, the use of Halazone tablets (two tablets per quart of water to be permitted to stand for thirty minutes before drinking) or boiling of water for at least twenty minutes is recommended. The flat taste of water so purified can be improved by pouring it back and forth from one receptacle to another. Cleanliness of utensils used for drinking and eating should be provided through thorough washing and drying measures. The waste disposal outlets (drains, septic tanks, and latrines) should be situated where they will not contaminate the water supply for drinking or bathing. Here again, the place to telephone for emergency situations should be easily reached. The telephone number of physicians (more than one is desirable) and a hospital should be prominently placed near the telephone.

Special events for the day camp.   In order to help give a lift to the activities in a camp, special events can be resorted to from time to time. The following are proved aids in this regard:

Hikes	Simulated search for lost campers
Explorations	Axemanship contests

Trail laying	Knot tying
Nature lore expeditions	Fly tying
Map making	Demonstrations
Cookouts	Bait-casting exhibitions
Compass hikes	

HIKES AND EXPLORATIONS

The craving for adventure can be nurtured by a hike or an exploration perhaps more than by any other activity. To benefit fully from this experience, it is essential that adequate preparation be made for this venture. The purpose of the hike should be made known to the campers so that they may share in it from the outset; they will want to know whether it is for overnight camping, delving into nature lore, trail laying, or whatever objective is being pursued.

Prior to the trip, the camper should be informed of the importance of carrying as light a load as possible without omitting essential items. The use of knapsacks will leave the hands free and the weight comfortably borne. Our military authorities wisely stress the importance of properly fitting shoes. Close-fitting and comfortable clothing are also important, with provisions to be made for the evening chill and the possible shower. A poncho can serve the dual purpose of providing protection against the camp ground for sleeping and serving as a raincoat. Added interest may be secured by making the hike purposeful. Examples of various hikes and the opportunities they afford are to be found in the chapter on hikes and excursions.

SPORTSMANLIKE CAMPING

As one of the outgrowths of camping, a respect and appreciation of the out-of-doors, should be sought. In this regard, the camper should be reminded that:

> Let it not be said
> And to your shame,
> That all was beauty here,
> Until you came.

Sportsmanlike behavior can be reemphasized as it applies to outdoor living. Cleaning up camp before leaving, caution in the use and disposal of matches (breaking the match in half is advisable), careful disposal of cigarette butts, and making certain that the fire is "dead and buried" (killing glowing coals with water and covering fire area with soil) are among the safety practices to be encouraged. Carry articles that will not burn to rubbish cans for deposit.

BENEFITS OF CAMPING

The attraction camp holds for the individual is fundamental, since it offers a primitive setting in which there is opportunity for new experiences. This challenges the imagination and provides countless opportunities for rugged adventure. It also places the camper in situations wherein self-reliance and independent thinking can be developed. Furthermore, camping serves to acquaint people with the vastness of the out-of-doors, with its streams, woodlands, and paths. This opportunity to commune with nature has a leveling effect on people, in that one becomes unmindful of social distinctions and mundane matters. It also inculcates an appreciation of the so-called simple and commonplace things in life; it emphasizes active participation rather than mere spectating, listening to the sounds of nature rather than to recordings or descriptions of them, and the living of adventuresome lives rather than just yearning for or reading about them.

SUGGESTED READINGS

Dimock, Hedley S. *Administration of the Modern Camp.* New York: Association Press, 1963.

Freeberg, William H., and Loren E. Taylor. *Programs in Outdoor Education.* Minneapolis: Burgess Publishing Co., 1963.

Goodrich, Lois. *Decentralized Camping.* New York: Association Press, 1959.

Hammett, Catherine T., and Virginia Musselman. *The Camp Program Book.* New York: Association Press, 1951.

Joy, Barbara Ellen. *Camping.* Minneapolis: Burgess Publishing Co., 1957.

Manley, Helen, and M. F. Drury. *Education Through School Camping.* St. Louis: The C. V. Mosby Co., 1952.

Miracle, Leonard. *Complete Book of Camping.* New York: Harper & Row, Publishers, 1963.

———.*Sportsman's Camping Guide.* New York: Harper & Row, Publishers, 1965.

Mitchell, A. Viola, and Ida B. Crawford. *Camp Counseling.* Philadelphia: W. B. Saunders Company, 1961.

Professional Preparation in Health Education, Physical Education and Recreation Education, Report of a National Conference. Washington, D.C.: American Assn. for Health, Physical Education & Recreation, 1962.

Smith, Julian, *et al. Outdoor Education.* Englewood Cliffs, N.J.: Prentice-Hall, Inc., 1963.

Standards Report of the Accreditation of Organized Camps. Martinsville, Indiana: American Camping Association, 1966.

Chapter 24

ACTIVE GAMES

What follows is a presentation of sample games which have proved to be popular in group situations under the author's leadership. Space limitations permit but a few examples of each type. Obviously, these games are not original in any sense since they were passed down from boyhood experiences at the neighborhood playground, school, and street play, from gymnasium experiences as a student and leader, and from student contributions in college classes in the author's charge. They have been retained on index cards for years prior to their transference to the present form. Credit to their original sources is therefore utterly impossible.

The aphorism that "there is nothing new under the sun" can find no better application than in game play. Much of value can be attained by trying to modify games to meet a local situation. The change of the name or the addition of a new regulation may add greatly to the game. The principles of game leadership, how to teach a game, and related information are presented in the chapter on leadership principles and procedures.

CHOOSING SIDES

Selection of players should be impartial. The play leader may select the "choosers" arbitrarily or, to avoid the possible accusation of playing favorites, suggest a preliminary event to decide the issue. Who shall pick sides first or start play first can be determined by the flip of a coin. It is also recommended that the games be varied so as to bring out different skills; otherwise the same players may find themselves left over time and again to be distributed only at the very end when it has become clear they are really no asset to the team. This same consideration applies to the selection of the "it" player: The contests should be varied so that the same one, whether the role happens to be a privilege or the opposite, is not repeatedly "it." As for penalties, they should be used sparingly, the leader to keep in mind that joyful play for all is the prime objective.

TAG, LINE, AND CIRCLE GAMES

The games included in the suggested readings can be modified to suit the facilities, the number of participants, and the equipment available. It is recommended that a portion of the games taught be those that require no equipment. This will ease their carry-over to the home play of children.

Some of the games are suitable for use by adults at PTA parties, socials, and the like. The fact that they are of a low-organized nature need not preclude their use. On the other hand, the astute leader will gauge the recreational literacy of his charges and will base his decision on the findings. A close observation and familiarity with the game interests and needs will prove helpful in handling all age groups. The time-proved admonition to start with the activities with which the group is familiar cannot be overstressed.

PRINCIPLES IN GAME LEADING

The leading of games is one of the most basic skills the leader will be called upon to handle. Games are the one activity that he may be called upon to lead more often than any other phase of the recreation program. It is not meant to intimate that games are the most important phase of the program but rather to reveal the popularity of this element of the recreation program.

To simplify the task of the game leader, the following suggestions are listed:

1. Plan the program thoroughly prior to the arrival of the class.
2. Arrange the equipment, marking the courts, goal lines, and so forth, beforehand.
3. From the start, teach the children to respect the sound of the whistle.
4. Select the games with the age group and "play literacy" of the participants in mind.
5. Start play as soon as possible so that there will be more time for play and less for mischief.
6. Stand in the semicircle while speaking to the group so that all can see you.
7. Describe the games in simple and concise language.
8. Explain the rules fully and see to it that they are followed; do not permit any exceptions.
9. Start your program with games familiar to the group, then branch off into the new ones.
10. Stop playing a game when the interest starts to wane: "Kill the game before it dies."

11. When selecting a player to be "it" or leader, use a competitive means, thereby avoiding any possibility of favoritism.
12. Use intermittently vigorous games and those that require less strenuous effort. For example, give the players an opportunity to recover from a vigorous game of Chicken-fight or Horse and Rider with a comparatively mild game of Snatch the Club or "Simon Says."
13. Encourage such attributes as joy of participation, play for "play's sake," play hard but clean, and be not only a modest winner but also a good loser, rather than merely the improvement of the player's ability.
14. Avoid the use of the elimination factor in games (dodge ball and hot potato) as much as possible. In its stead use the point system whereby the successful striking or pulling of an opponent results in the scoring of a point.

GAMES OF LOW ORGANIZATION

Games can be divided into "low-organized" and "high-organized" categories. While this division is often used as a matter of convenience and simplification, it is wise to emphasize that there is no clear-cut line that separates the two. Games of low organization refer to those in which the rules are simple, with a minimum of cooperation required of the players. The participant retains his individuality to such an extent that he often competes against everyone else. This type of play is suited to the self-centered makeup of the child and more apt to interest the "recreational illiterate." The equipment required is usually a ball, a bean bag, a club, or some such simple device.

GAMES OF HIGH ORGANIZATION

Unlike low-organized games, we note in the games of high organization more complex rules to observe, with a shifting of emphasis away from the individual and to the group side of play. It symbolizes the growth and progress achieved as a result of the participants' experience and development. It also marks a transition from elementary activities to those that are more advanced, while calling forth greater skill, agility, kinesthetic sense, and the ability to play with others—all this as part of a cooperative unit, the side or team.

TEACHING THE GAME

While there is no one best technique of teaching a game, it is certainly advisable that the leader bear in mind the fundamental steps to be covered when teaching a game. The following steps are presented to help guide the leader upon getting the group into the desired formation.

1. Name the game
2. Place the players in proper formation
3. Explain the game
4. Repeat the explanations with a demonstration
5. Ask questions
6. Start play

DODGE BALL VARIATIONS

Circle Dodge Ball. The players are divided into two teams, with team A in the circle and team B on the outside. Every time a player in the circle is struck by the ball, the team on the outside scores a point. At the end of five minutes of play, team B goes in the circle while team A shifts to the outside. Within the five-minute period, team A tries to outscore the total amassed by team B. The team scoring the greater number of "hits" is deemed the winner.

Note: Although the game of Circle Dodge Ball is usually played so that the player who is struck is eliminated from the game, the point system is recommended to forestall mischievous behavior on the part of those who are out of the game.

If the area is suitable, this game can be played by having the teams line up on opposite sides behind a restraining line. The rules of the "Circle" game will apply. Still another variation is Threeteam Dodge Ball wherein the court is divided into three sectors. Teams A, B, and C take turns at the center spot. The winning team is that one that was struck the fewest times while it was in the center spot.

Indian File Dodge Ball. A ring is formed by the players. Five players then step into the circle. They stand in single file, one behind the other. Each one places his hands on the hips of the one in front of him, making a trainlike appearance. The ball is then given to the circle. The object is to hit the last boy of the five with the ball. This will be difficult because the other four will stand in the way. The four must continually hold their hands on the hips of the one standing in front. Only by quickly passing the ball to another man in the circle who is in a better position to hit the end man will it be possible to hit the last man. When the last man is hit, he becomes a part of the circle. The object is then to hit the fourth man, then the third, etc. When the final man is hit, a new team of five is selected for the center.

Horse and Rider Dodge Ball. The horse is opposed to the rider on his back. While the rider is attempting to throw to another rider, the other horses try to keep the riders from catching the ball by wiggling and charging the riders out of position. As soon as the ball touches the floor the horses become the riders and the riders the horses. The catching of the ball gives the team one point; fifteen or twenty-one points win.

RELAYS

Relays have proved themselves an exceedingly popular form of play. For one, they invariably sustain interest until the very end. Furthermore, they can be used to incorporate skills and stunts. Capable coaches know the value of minimizing the boredom of teaching fundamentals by employing game situations. Added interest can be given to a relay by incorporating a stunt in it; sample stunts, such as resembling a duck by squatting as low as possible while grasping the heels by reaching between the legs, or a chicken by squatting low while clasping hands outside and around the legs in front of the ankles, can be used.

The simple and shuttle are the two common types of relays used in game play. In the Simple Relay, the players are placed in line and evenly divided in number. The first one in each line runs a designated distance to the wall, touches it, and returns to touch the hand of the second person who has moved up to the line; the first runner thereupon goes to the end of the line. This continues until all have competed. The side that completes the run first is called the winner. Under the Shuttle Relay plan, each line or team is divided in half with each half directly opposite the other, although a designated distance apart. The lines or teams are numbered A, B, and onward, while the halves have the odd numbers, 1, 3, 5, etc., on one side and the even ones, 2, 4, 6, etc., on the other. At a given signal, the first player of line A runs to 2A and tags him; 2A does likewise by running to tag 3A and so on; the numbers of line B do likewise. The line that finishes first is designated the winner. The shuttle principle can be extended so that the run is continued until each runner returns to his original position. Under the first described system, the players find themselves lined up opposite their original starting positions. Sports fundamentals such as dribbling and shooting in basketball can be taught interestingly in the shuttle or simple forms.

Wheelbarrow Relay. This relay can be played by having two or more columns competing against each other, or by having any number of pairs competing. The first one, A, in the column places his hands on the ground as the one behind him, B, grasps his knees while resting them on each hip, thereby simulating a human wheelbarrow. Upon traversing a given distance and returning, B becomes the wheelbarrow for C. C, returning, becomes the wheelbarrow for D, and so on until all have participated. The column that finishes first wins. When competing in pairs, the couple that finishes first is designated the winner.

Leap Frog Relay.   The players on each team line up one behind the other about four feet removed, with their hands on their knees. The rear man leaps over each player on his side and stoops over himself whereupon the new rear man does the same. This is continued until the first player has jumped over all his teammates and crossed a designated goal line.

Zigzag Relay.   Teams I and II form separate circles about ten feet apart. Designate the leader in each circle who is to start zigzagging to the right at the command "go." After he completes the circle, he returns to his original position and tags the player at his right. This is continued until all the players have run. The team that finishes first is the winner.

Pony Express Relay.   One man of each team is selected as the rider; the others are ponies and are stationed at intervals along the course, or in file if played in a gymnasium. The rider mounts the first pony who runs to the second one. The rider then must change ponies without touching the ground. If he accidentally touches the ground he must remount the last pony and attempt the transfer again.

Chinese Relay.   The first runner puts his hand between his legs and the second man clasps it. On the signal, they run to a goal. Number "two" then returns, and he in like manner leads the third man. The race is finished when the last man reaches the goal.

Matchbox Relay.   Use the rectangular safety-type matchbox (outer sleeve portion). This game is conducted on a shuttle relay basis. The partners line up about fifteen yards apart. Those at the starting line place matchboxes on their noses. After running to the opposite line, they are to transplant the boxes onto their partner's noses without the use of the hands. After this is done, those with the boxes on their nose are to run to the line formerly used as the starting line. The one to finish first is the winner. This game is suggested for social recreation as well as gymnasium and classroom use.

Overhead Relay.   Form two even parallel lines about two feet apart. The first person on each line passes a ball overhead until it reaches the last one. The last person runs forward, stands in front of the line and passes the ball the same as before. The line which makes the entire round first is the winner. Note: The same game may be played "underlegs," or combined as an "over and under" relay.

LEAD-UP GAMES

The use of lead-up games as situations wherein fundamentals can be practiced more interestingly is growing in popularity. As was mentioned before, relays offer numerous possibilities. That lead-up games of the nonrelay type are equally valuable may be gathered by examining the games that can be utilized for the sports of soccer, volleyball, baseball, and basketball.

SOCCER

Scrimmage. The rules are similar to those of Modified Soccer, except that the players are seated and not permitted to run. They can crawl. If the player stands up or rises above a crawl, he is eliminated from the game until a goal is scored whereupon he enters the game again.

Kick Ball. One team lines up at one end of the gym. The other team takes the field as follows: Two men stand on the farther end line, about twenty feet apart; the remaining players of the fielding team cover the playing area. The first man of the kicking team kicks the ball, which is resting on home plate. The ball must go past the foul line and into the playing area. The opponents, by the use of their feet only, pass-kick the ball to either of their two "linemen." The "lineman" receives the ball without using his hands and kicks it back to the opponents' end of the gym. The man who kicked the ball must run from home plate to the other end of the gym and must beat the ball back to his wall to score a point. No outs are kept. Each man kicks in order until everyone has had one turn. The teams then change positions. Play nine innings. The men should be numbered and always kick in consecutive order.

Modified Soccer. The group is divided into two teams. Each team is to designate one half as guards and the remainder as forwards. The guards are not permitted to pass the middle line of the court, whereas the forwards are. The hands are not to be used at all. After a goal is scored, the forwards of both teams become the guards and the guards become the forwards. The opposite wall or the area between the foul-shooting area (free-throw line) against the wall may be used as the goal. If a player touches the ball with his hands, he is eliminated from the game until a goal is scored, whereupon he enters the game again.

VOLLEYBALL

Volley Catch Ball. A ball is thrown by each team over the net from the back line of its court. The balls must be kept in the air at all times and must be caught each time, not batted with the hands. The ball so caught is passed either to a teammate or is thrown directly over the net into the other court. The balls are tossed back and forth from team to team. One point is scored against a team and given to its opponents each time a ball strikes the floor in its own court, but the ball that hits the floor should be continued in play. A net ball is in play. Use one ball at first and later advance to two or even three balls. Use a scorer or referee in each court. Twenty-one points is a game. Change courts after each game.

Keep It Up.   The leader starts the contest by giving a signal at which time one player in each group tosses the ball of that group in the air. The ball is then volleyed (batted preferably with two hands, not caught or thrown) from one player to another of the same team without any special order until it strikes the wall, ground, ceiling, or some obstacle upon which it is declared dead. Each time the ball is tapped by one of the players, his team calls aloud, "One two, three, etc.," counting this way the number of successful volleys made. After the ball has been declared dead, a new game is started; the counting starts again at one. Each group keeps a count of its best score, the highest determining the winning team at the end of the contest. There should be a judge for each team.

Variation: Each team is to have one continuous volley in each period. The team that volleys the most gets a point, twenty-one points win.

BASEBALL

Hit Pin Baseball.   A Club is placed at each of the four bases. The pitcher rolls the air-filled ball to home plate. When the batter kicks a fair ball, he runs around the bases and knocks down the club at each base. The fielders throw the ball first to the first baseman. If by hitting the Indian club with the ball the fielder knocks down the club before the batter can do so, the batter is out. No matter where a fair ball is fielded, it must be thrown to first base. If the first baseman cannot put the runner out, he throws the ball to the second baseman. Similarly, the second baseman, if he fails to knock down the club before the batter does, must throw to third, and the third baseman to home. If the runner reaches home first and kicks down the club, one point is scored for his team. The only way the batter can be put out is by a baseman knocking over an Indian club with the ball before the runner kicks it over.

Kick Baseball.   The rules used are similar to those of baseball except that the ball is kicked rather than batted. The ball can either be rolled in to the "batter" or kicked after placing the ball on home plate.

Roley Poley. By a competitive means the batter is selected. He either bats the ball by throwing it up himself, or has someone pitch it. If the batted ball is caught on a fly, the batter is out and the catcher gets up at bat. If it is a bounce ball, then the catcher tosses the ball at the bat and if he strikes the bat without the batter catching the ball, he gets up at bat. If the batter catches the ball, he remains at bat.

BASKETBALL

Bat Ball. The first man of the batting team tosses the inflated ball up, hits it with his fist into the playing area, and attempts to reach the far wall without being hit by the ball. The fielding team, observing basketball regulations, attempts to strike the batter with the ball to put him out; there must be no running with the ball. The hitter must run only to the far wall with his hit. He runs home on the next hit ball. After the runner has reached his wall or base, the ball is returned to the batting line. The second man now hits the ball and attempts to reach the far wall, while the first man, assuming he was safe, tries to reach the home wall without being hit. If he is successful, he scores a point. The fielders may play either or both of the men. The last batter of each team must try to make a home run every inning. All players are up in each inning. A thirty-foot short line is recommended.

Corner Ball. The court is divided in the middle, with a base marked in each corner. Team A takes half of the field and stations a player in each of the two bases in B territory. These players must stay on the base and the B players must stay off. The object of the game is for each team to make as many passes from their field players to men on bases as possible. The team winning the toss gets the ball first and keeps it until their opponents intercept a pass or until they fumble the ball and let it touch the floor.

Basket Baseball. One team is at bat at home plate. The batter tosses a basketball in the air, strikes it with his fist, and must run around the bases and make a home run before the opponents can shoot the ball through the farther basket. The batter must reach home plate before the basket is made to score a run. If the ball goes through the basket before the runner reaches home, he is out and no run is scored. A foul ball is out.

3–2–1. All players line up behind the foul-shot area and follow in rotation. During the first series, the players are allowed three tries in which to shoot the basket, then two tries, and finally one. If at any time a player fails to make the basket in the allotted number of tries, he is eliminated. If all fail, more attempts are permitted until one player is successful, whereupon all those preceding him in the series are eliminated and those who follow must also make the shot to continue. If not, the maker of the shot is the winner.

Clock Basketball.   Twelve-hour checks are marked about the basket area. All start at the foul-shooting line and shoot in rotation. When the foul shot is made, the player starts at "one o'clock" and advances "one hour" whenever the shot is completed. After "twelve o'clock" is completed a "long" shot is selected and the first one to make it is acknowledged the winner of the game.

SUGGESTED READINGS

Blake, O. William, and Anne M. Volp. *Lead-Up Games to Team Sports.* Englewood Cliffs, N.J.: Prentice-Hall, Inc., 1964.

Department of Health, Education and Welfare. *Recreational Games.* Washington, D.C.: U.S. Government Printing Office, 1961.

Donnelly, Richard, *et al. Active Games and Contests.* New York: The Ronald Press Company, 1956.

Edgren, Harry D. *1000 Games and Stunts.* Nashville, Tenn.: Abingdon Press, 1945.

Hindman, Darwin. *Complete Book of Games and Stunts.* Prentice-Hall, Inc., 1956.

Kraus, Richard. *Recreation Today.* New York: Appleton-Century-Crofts, 1966.

MacFarlan, Allan A. *New Games for 'Tween-Agers.* New York: Association Press, 1952.

Mulac, Margaret. *Games and Stunts for Schools, Camps and Playgrounds.* New York: Harper & Row, Publishers, 1964.

Van der Smissen, Betty, and Helen Knierim. *Recreational Sports and Games.* Minneapolis: Burgess Publishing Co., 1964.

Chapter 25

HIKES AND EXCURSIONS

The pleasures to be derived from taking a trip or hike are manifold. Benefits are to be derived not only from the excursion itself but also from the anticipatory joy, the preparatory steps, and the reminiscences that usually follow. The trip may be the result of a recreation project or a laboratory situation wherein the activities learned previously may be put into use in practical situations. It may also serve as the culminating event of an instructional period, class, or project. Moreover, new interests and activities may be spurred on by a visit, which may stimulate further activity and possibly open up new endeavors. In addition, it can be used as an incentive or rewarding event by the leader.

Hiking can be said to constitute both an "end in itself" and a "means to an end." It is an activity that leaves the body, mind, and spirit exhilarated and refreshed. To tramp through the woods, climb hills, elude branches, follow streams, blaze trails, or pursue beaten ones makes new acquaintanceships of nature's wonders and renews old ones.

As John Burroughs[1] so adroitly puts it:

The man who walks is always cheerful, alert, refreshed, with his heart in his hand and his hand free to all. He looks down upon nobody; he is on the common level. His pores are open, his circulation is active, his dige stion good. His heart is not cold nor his faculties asleep. He is the only real traveler. He tastes the real sentiment of the road. He is not isolated, but is at one with things, with the farms and the industries on either hand. He knows the ground is alive, he feels the pulse of the wind and reads the mute language of things. His sympathies are all aroused; his senses are continually reporting messages to his mind. Wind, frost, rain, heat and cold are something to him. He is not merely a spectator of the panorama of nature but a participator in it. He experiences the country he passes through—tastes it, feels it, absorbs it.

ORGANIZING AN EXCURSION

The selection of an excursion destination should be made after considering the age, interests, and project activities of the group to be

[1] John Burroughs, "Exhilarations of the Road" in *Selected Essays* (Cambridge, Mass.: Riverside Press, 1917), pp. 28–29.

345

taken. After this is ascertained, a signed parental permission form is to be received from each child; while it is of questionable value as a legal document, it can serve to acquaint the parents with the forthcoming event so that lively family discussions and parental advice for safe behavior may ensue. A notice to parents which can be attached to the permission form should contain information as to the day and time of departure, whether a bag lunch or other provisions for food are to be made, the amount of money for fare and incidentals, any special attire, if necessary, and the expected returning time.

Suggested excursions. As was stated previously, the type of excursion chosen should be suited to the group. The suggestions that follow are not to be taken as a prescription for any one group but rather are to be used as a general guide. A decision should be based on a careful appraisal of the group, its interests, and its program of activities. Points of interest will vary with each community. The suggestions that follow are based on a large city setup; adaptations can be made readily for those from smaller communities.

Aquarium. Opportunity to see an electric eel or any of hundreds of varieties of fish.

Airport. A trip to the control tower and hangars can often be arranged to the delight of the group.

Ball parks. Free admission or a nominal charge is often made for organized groups.

Boat and ferry rides. An exhilarating experience at any season and especially during the warmer months.

Botanical garden. A pleasant trip to take in the floral and plant beauties in a man-influenced setting.

Churches of prominence. The painstaking and devotional care plus the architectural splendor make a church visit memorable.

Civic center. The government can be observed in action, especially when the legislators are in session.

Dock and ship areas. In coastal areas, trips through naval vessels, passenger ships, and freighters may be arranged.

Factories. Steel mills, paper mills, automobile, clothing, shoe, airplane, electric light plants, and shipyards can prove to be fascinating and educational.

Food plants. Food establishments such as pasteurization, ice cream, soda bottling, slaughter and meat packing, baking, and canning plants prove interesting and informative.

Historical areas. The local historical society can help to designate the places of historical significance.

Museums. Art, children's, historical, natural science, and technical museums provide excellent media for visits; programs especially for children are often scheduled at museums. Planetariums have proved their popularity as an adjunct to the museum.

Newspaper plants. How news is transferred from the reporter's pad and ticker to the printed page. Determine in advance the time the presses operate so as not to miss them in action.

Parks. Outings, picnics, or field days find a pleasant setting in the park.

Radio and television studios. A tour of the station and a chance to see a live show broadcast and telecast will fascinate the group.

Zoos. A chance to visit the zoo and to feed the animals (be certain it is permitted) will be a memorable treat.

ORGANIZED HIKING

Hiking is becoming increasingly popular in recreation areas, public schools, and colleges throughout the nation. This interest may be indicative of a reaction to the complex and high-strung living of our day. It serves as a worthwhile influence in familiarizing people with the joys and benefits to be derived from the simple beauty and the revitalizing effects of a day out in the open. Certainly, we as a people have placed a disproportionate emphasis on spectating and vicarious experiences to the exclusion of self-participation.

In cities, a bus or car trip to the outskirts will often take the group away from the crowded conditions and hard pavements to destinations such as a lookout, cave, forest, and the like. A ride to within reasonable hiking distance of the spot to be visited will make more desirable areas accessible for hiking groups. Train systems such as the New York Central offer from time to time special weekend trips for hiking and climbing groups. In this instance a weekend trip from New York City to Lake Placid for a seven-dollar round trip was taken by the New York City High School Commerce Club. In a similar vein, college groups are placing great emphasis on hiking to college-owned camps and historical areas within the region. Combination hikes and motor or train expeditions are proving to be increasingly popular. Some college groups participate in European tours in conjunction with the youth hostels. The American Youth Hostels, Inc., annually plans organized tours at minimal rates to

European countries with the participants traveling on foot or by bicycle.

Destinations for hiking.   As a rule, there are myriad opportunities for interesting hiking trips within one's own region. Historical spots, lookouts, state parks, forests, lakes, and caves provide readily accessible destinations. In addition, there are often hiking trails to be found not too far removed. Two trails of national renown are listed.

1. In the eastern United States, there are more than 2000 miles of the Appalachian Trail; it starts at Mount Ratahdin in Maine, crosses the Hudson River at Bear Mountain, and ends at Mount Oglethorpe, Georgia.
2. The Pacific Coast Trailway extends 2245 miles for those who desire extensive hiking west of the Rockies.

During the depression years, the Civilian Conservation Corps constructed thousands of trails throughout the eastern United States. These constitute a permanent addition to the pathways for this magnificent outdoor activity.

Advantages of hiking.   It is perhaps a true indictment that we are a spectator nation with too little time, if any, devoted to actual participation. In our efforts at acquiring the material things in life, we often overlook the worthwhile benefits to be derived from getting out into the open and observing the wonders of nature. It is noteworthy that the human body operates rhythmically and finds such rhythmical activity as walking highly satisfying. Not only does walking permit one to reflect and to enjoy the out-of-doors, but it also makes it possible to ease nervous tension.

We are being plagued increasingly by obesity and the degenerative changes that often accompany excess weight. Among these are cardio-vascular-renal disorders which include high blood pressure, arteriosclerosis, heart disease, and kidney ailments. While it would be an outlandish claim to state that hiking can obviate these conditions, it is a fact that our tendency to lead a more and more sedentary type of existence contributes greatly toward this state of affairs. Along with hiking often go such related activities as camping, fire building, wood chopping, and pack carrying, which contribute toward the use of the muscles for more prolonged periods of time than they are usually brought into play.

Geist offers the following justifications for hiking:

1. It is an outdoor sport.
2. It requires no expensive clothing, equipment, stadia, etc.

3. It is enjoyed by both sexes, people of all ages, during all seasons.
4. There are no difficult techniques to be learned—only rhythm is required.
5. It may be enjoyed strenuously or moderately.
6. It may be enjoyed individually or in groups.
7. It is a safe pastime if enjoyed on trails away from congested highways.
8. Each hiking trip is an adventure in itself.
9. It has branches to suit all tastes: For the speedy there are heel and toe walking races; for the nature friend there is the long trail through the woods, and for the daring the thrills of a first ascent.[2]

Types of hikes. Interest in hiking can be increased by giving the hike a special designation and purpose. The hiker can be motivated by knowing that there is a special purpose behind the trip. The following are examples: (1) Collectors' hikes afford an opportunity to collect butterflies, insects, leaves, birds' eggs, and the like; (2) nature hikes can be used to investigate insects, animals, flowers, nests, and trees enroute; (3) exploring hikes are conducted to search for the "unknown"; (4) get-together hikes are undertaken by at least two groups who plan a common rendezvous after starting from different points; (5) visit hikes, taken on a reciprocal basis, afford the opportunity for an exchange of visits that proves beneficial to both camps; (6) trail-blazing hikes are made over a new trail with a camp site laid out at the other end; and (7) skiing hikes are coupled with trips to a predetermined destination.

Outfitting the hiker. A path road to ease the burden of the hiker and as little paraphernalia as possible are two of the essentials of a hike. Simplicity of gear as well as compactness are to be given primary consideration. Since the shoulders can support weight most efficiently, the use of a knapsack on the shoulders will prove highly effective.

The importance of properly fitting shoes is to be emphasized: a high-top shoe that provides ample room for the toes while giving a snug fit at the heel and the hollow part of the longitudinal arch of the foot. Woolen socks are preferred, since they absorb perspiration best and ease the amount of irritation. For those whose feet blister readily, the suggestion to wear cotton hose underneath woolen ones is proffered. The clothing to be worn should be suitable to the season of the year so that ample comfort results without overheating or chilling.

Wherever possible the use of dehydrated foods is recommended. Not only will they lighten the burden of the hiker, but they can help add variety to the meals. A first aid kit should contain the usual items

[2]R. C. Geist, "Hiking as a Sport," *Recreation* (May 1949).

plus talcum powder for irritations, a snake bite kit (if the region is noted for its poisonous snakes), a metal coat hanger which can be used for splinting, and a triangular bandage which serves a number of purposes in first aid work.

Hiking etiquette.   Good behavior need not take a holiday when one is out on a hike. If private property is used on a portion of the hike, permission should be secured from its owner. No attempt should be made to destroy branches or any of the fauna or flora. Certainly the rights of private property are to be respected. When starting a fire make certain that there is sufficient clearance of trees, brush, grass, and leaves. When you're leaving the fire area, make certain that the flame and coals are fully extinguished with water and earth.

It is usually preferable to hike cross-country rather than to use highways. If it should be necessary to use highways, the left side of the road should be used while walking in single file. Light-colored clothing should be worn if hiking into the dusk or dark part of the day; a flashlight is to be used to warn oncoming motorists. Whenever possible, the plan should be to reach the destination before dusk. Needless to say, hitchhiking is unethical for hikers.

Organizing a hiking group.   When there are enough prospects, added interest can be achieved by setting up an organized group. This practice has proved itself effectively in many communities. A notable one is that of Hohokus, New Jersey, where a Hiking Trips Bureau has been organized. The procedures that are recommended are as follows:

1. The prime concern in the selection of members is congeniality. The group must have that undefinable "something" which makes the group feel like singing on a rainy day.
2. A good hiking group has for its members people from varied occupations. One should experience for once the exhilaration that comes from getting away from the minute detail of his daily work by talking to other people about their hobbies, their hopes, and their aspirations.
3. A good hiking group uses many different leaders. No single hike leader can be expected to be expert in all areas. And no hiking group can be expected to be content with hiking, year after year, in the same small area.
4. A good hiking group strives constantly to develop new leaders and new trips.
5. A good hiking group offers a variety of trips. A group with a complete program might well offer its members weekend trips or joint trips with other hiking groups.
6. A good hiking group adheres strictly to its schedule.

7. A good hiking group knows no favoritism. There's something uplifting about being encouraged when you're the last one; but there's something uplifting about being discouraged in your attempts to speed up the group's stride too, when you come to think of it; for you realize that you are privileged to be hiking under the guidance of a leader who knows no favorites.
8. A good hiking group develops its own literature.
9. A good hiking group does not operate on education only. Merely is the plea made that education be a concomitant to the basic program of hiking.
10. A good hiking group is characterized by its informality. There is something about the spirit of a good hiking group that makes the swapping of food and the exchange of photographs the natural corollary of the midday campfire.[3]

Motivating the group. Once the group is organized, the problem of sustaining interest is next in order; "where" and "when" then become primary considerations. To start with, the spring and fall are usually the most suitable seasons for hiking, since the weather is neither too warm nor too cold; still, the summer and winter months must not be entirely discounted for hiking, for they are often periods when highly interesting trips may be taken.

The activities which can be conducted on hikes are unlimited in scope. An imaginative leader will encounter little difficulty in arriving at suitable ones. The wonders of nature offer ample subject matter, what with the trees, flowers, birds, and heavens to explore. Collectors find a haven in the outdoors. Stones, insects, leaves, flowers, fish, and frogs' and birds' eggs provide but a few examples. During the fall, there is an opportunity to observe and study seeds and fruits. The winter time offers vast opportunities for observing bark and twig tendencies. A chance to observe the flaming foliage during the fall is reason enough for a hike. A chance to photograph the scenic beauty with black and white or color film will serve as an added motivation.

There are many unexpected happenings during a hike that can add to its effectiveness. Blazing trails, inspecting a crow's nest, and examining an animal's tracks with the objective of determining its size and name provide unscheduled occurrences. Learning how to make a fire and prepare food out-of-doors as well as how to use an axe are representative of the great range of outdoor skills that offer unlimited possibilities for absorbing hike activities.

[3]*Woodland Trail Walks with the Hiking Trips Bureau* (Hohokus, N.J.: Hiking Trips Bureau), pp. 8, 9.

HOSTELING

Hosteling is a means of traveling, on the whole, by one's own "steam." It includes hiking, bicycling, canoeing, skiing, and horseback riding. The spirits of fun and fellowship prevail. It affords a splendid opportunity to know better the people in one's own land and in other parts of the globe. The gratifications are many, with bountiful indirect learnings such as the similarities, rather than differences, among people in our land and throughout the world. Hostels are open to all who possess a hostel pass and comply with simple customs. A Youth Pass for those under twenty-one is $2.00; an Adult Pass for those over twenty-one is $3.00; a Family Pass is $5.00.

The term "hosteling" derives its name from "hostel" which refers to an inn or lodge for overnight guests. The accommodations are modest and are supervised by houseparents. Separate sleeping quarters are available for men and women with blankets provided. Each hosteler provides his own sheet sleeping sack and mess kit, but uses pots provided by the hostel. The usual overnight fee is forty cents for hostelers under twenty-one and fifty cents for adults. Hostelers are expected to tidy the hostel before departing, at which time houseparents return the passes that were taken up as they registered. Hostels are usually situated in farm structures, barns, cabins, or lodges specially constructed for this purpose. In addition, garages, Grange Halls, Y.M.C.A.'s, and Y.W.C.A.'s, college dormitories, and community halls are used for this purpose. Hosteling is sponsored by public-spirited citizens representing schools, service clubs, churches, and civic and recreational organizations who recognize the great value of this wholesome youth activity.

THE HOSTEL ORGANIZATION

The American Youth Hostels, Inc., is the parent body, with its National Headquarters at 14 West 8th Street, New York, New York, 10016. There are A.Y.H. chartered councils in the states of California, Connecticut, Illinois, Indiana, Maryland, Massachusetts, Michigan, Minnesota, Missouri, New York, Ohio, Pennsylvania, Rhode Island, Wisconsin, and the District of Columbia. Most hostels in the United States are located in New England, the Middle Atlantic, Great Lakes, and West Coast regions.

It is a nonprofit organization that fosters, especially in young people, a deeper understanding and love of all peoples, both here and abroad, by virtue of its affiliation with the International Youth Hostel Federation of twenty-four countries. It provides Youth Hostels in this country and assists in the development of new ones. In addition, it assists its members in their travels abroad by planning sponsored trips and by encouraging individual hosteling. The cultural benefits of travel are made available at minimal costs, starting with $1.00 to $1.50 per day. Headquarter trips of from six to eight weeks in the United States and Canada start at $125.00, while overseas trips cost from $500.00 upwards, including transatlantic passage.

HOSTELING FOR GROUPS

While the privileges of hosteling are available to individuals, group activities are also encouraged; the A.Y.H. Sponsored Trips ease the task of the individual in planning a trip, while also extending this opportunity to any group that would care to take part. A special family membership is available for parents and all children under twenty-one for $5.00. Also, a youth organization pass for a group of ten is $5.00, whereas a similar pass for ten members of a bona fide adult agency or organization is $10.00.

It is noteworthy that A.Y.H. youth and adult passes are recognized by all other hostel associations belonging to the International Youth Hostel Federation. Family and organization passes are not valid outside the United States. The A.Y.H. issues *Hosteling*, a quarterly magazine, and the annual A.Y.H. *Handbook*, which are sent to all pass holders.

CUSTOMS

In order to assure lodging at a minimal cost and to maintain a standard of tidiness, adherence to hosteling customs is required of all. They are as follows:

1. Make reservations in advance and enclose a self-addressed stamped post card for a reply. This courtesy to houseparents is a necessity when a group is involved.
2. Arrive at the hostel early, preferably before dark. Should there be a delay, get in touch with the houseparents. Leave hostels at an early hour.
3. Hosteling equipment should include a pass, eating utensils (knife, fork, spoon, cup, and plate), dish towel, and a sheet sleeping sack.
4. Hand in your pass and register.
5. Hostelers purchase and prepare their own food.
6. Clean hostel and dispose of refuse. Pay fees, receive signed pass, and depart.
7. Hostelers agree not to drink or smoke in hostels.

8. Arrival by any method other than bicycle, foot, canoe, ski, or horse-back is not acceptable unless previous arrangements have been made.

BENEFITS

Hosteling is earning more and more recognition as a wholesome and reputable member of the recreational household. Like other recreational activities, it helps to develop an appreciation of the outdoors. Through such invigorating activities as hiking, canoeing, bicycling, skiing, and horseback riding, it encourages more extensive participation in activities that are beneficial to all age groups with definite carry-over value from one to the others. As an outgrowth, healthier, happier, more alert, and more understanding citizens may develop. Ample opportunities for self-expression, gaining confidence, and self-reliance are to be found in the multitude of experiences associated with hosteling. By reducing the costs of nationwide and worldwide travel, more people are able to take advantage of these opportunities. The educational and cultural benefits of travel both here and abroad make feasible friendships that are worthy of the "one world" concept. Franklin D. Roosevelt is quoted as having said, "I realize the need for hosteling. From the time I was nine till I was seventeen I spent most of my holidays bicycling on the Continent. This was the best education I ever had—far better than formal schools. The more one travels the better citizen he becomes, not only of his own country but of the world."[4]

RELATED PROJECTS

In addition to the benefits already discussed, there are numerous opportunities for incidental learning. The projects that follow are suggestive of the possibilities:

First aid instruction
Make first aid kit
Care of bicycle
   How to adjust seat and handlebars to height
   Oiling moving parts
   Repair of flat tire
   Adjustment of three-speed gears
   Adjustment of bearings
   Treating chain with oily rag and graphite
Handicrafts (activities in repairing hostel; making equipment)

[4]*Hosteling . . . Adventure at Home and Abroad* (New York: American Youth Hostel, Inc., p. 8).

Meal planning
  Nutrition
  Mathematics (planning quantities, prices, and so forth)
  Use of dehydrated foods
Camp cooking
  Fire making
  Use of axe
  Aluminum foil cooking
Trip planning
  Secure maps from Department of Conservation, National Park Service, or
    U.S. Geological Survey
  Topography
  Geography (map out bicycling and hiking trails)
  Mathematics (calculate distance to be covered, and so forth)
  Trail blazing
  Reading accounts of similar trips
  Correspondence with A.Y.H. Headquarters or Chartered Council
Nature lore
Science
  Astronomy—how to find way by stars; how to find north with a watch and
    the sun, and so forth
  Botany—flora en route
  Zoology—animal world en route
  Hygiene—how to care for overworked feet and legs; how to relax; solving
    personal-problem situations that may arise; importance of relaxation and
    rest
  Body mechanics—how to carry knapsack with a minimum of strain.
National and international relations
Language study
Recreational activities at hostels:
  Folk dancing
  Square dancing
  Social dancing
  Social recreation
  Group singing
  Arts and crafts
  Storytelling
  Group discussions
Photography (picture record of trip)

HOW TO ESTABLISH A HOSTEL

At the outset, a community committee and chairman should be chosen.
The committee should explore possible sites for the hostel, bearing in

mind the importance of a suitable location and facilities needed. Concurrent with this quest should go an avid search for youth-loving houseparents; the importance of interested and qualified houseparents cannot be overemphasized. They should rate highly in the community and be enthusiastic about hosteling.

The hostel site should have a pure water supply with desirable scenic and recreational features at hand. It is preferred that the distance between camps be about fifteen miles, with the hostel itself on a secondary road removed from traffic and somewhat out of town. While hostels can be modest and unpretentious, they should be safe structures and sanitary. Guidance and advice is available from the Chartered Councils or the A.Y.H. Headquarters; a representative will be sent who will advise how to proceed so that formal acceptance may take place.

SUPPLEMENTARY USE OF HOSTEL

Hosteling is primarily, although not exclusively, concerned with serving youth. It is, therefore, not averse to making its facilities available for use by the community. In fact, the community is encouraged to use its facilities for youth and church suppers and parties. It is eager to have the hostel be a very active portion of community life. Here again, smoking and drinking are not permitted at affairs held in the hostel. Smoking is forbidden partly because hostels are usually wooden structures such as barns or cabins, whereas the drinking of alcoholic beverages is harmful to the best interests of youth.

HOSTEL RECREATION

There are plentiful opportunities for recreational activities at the hostel. Since the hosteler usually arrives at the hostel rather early, he has some time for play. Dancing, both square and round, is usually very popular. Social recreation activities are also well-represented in hostel programs. Table games such as checkers, chess, bridge, and canasta, are also much in demand.

The chance to converse and exchange experiences is usually taken full advantage of by the hostelers. This opportunity can prove one of the most enlightening aspects of hosteling. Musical activities in the form of listening to records, group singing, barber shop harmony, harmonica playing, and vocal renditions are possibilities. Should the number warrant it, an Amateur Night can serve to knit together the assorted talents. Handicraft activities are also likely, with the service of and repair of gear the dominant motive.

EQUIPMENT NEEDED

Aside from one's personal needs, equipment should and can be kept to a minimum. In this connection, a hostel pass is an essential item with which to start. American Youth Hostel Youth and Adult Passes are valid for all hostel associations that belong to the International Youth Hostel Federation. However, Organization and Family Passes are not valid outside the United States.

Then there's the "means of transportation" to be considered; a bicycle, walking boots, or a canoe are to be provided. Arrangements for the rental of a bicycle or canoe will be eased by contacting the council nearest you. In addition, eating utensils (consisting of a knife, fork, spoon, cup, and plate) and a dish towel are essentials. Also, a sheet sleeping sack, or its equivalent, will help to insure the cleanliness of hostel blankets; one can be made readily from a sheet suitable for a twin-size or three-quarter-size mattress.

INTERNATIONAL ASPECTS

As in other areas of recreation, the hostel offers limitless opportunities for expression. This becomes even more apparent as hostelers from various countries undertake to share experiences, cultural outpourings, airing of photographic problems and knowhow, or any interchange of the myriad cultural attributes of each nation represented.

In an era marked by the availability of phenomenally destructive forces, our search must lead toward improved international and intercultural understanding. The availability of international youth hostels is a force that should be utilized more fully. As an added attribute, they provide inexpensive accommodations of a wholesome nature. The camaraderie and greater understanding that can result warrant their serious consideration as a force for peace as well as splendid recreation.

SUGGESTED READINGS

American Youth Hostels, *Personal Growth Leaflet Number 66*. Washington, D.C.: The National Education Association.

Ball, Edith. *Hosteling, The New Program in Community Recreation.* Washington, D.C.: The National Recreation and Parks Association.

Burton, Maurice. *Curiosities of Animal Life.* New York: Sterling Publishing Co., Inc., 1960.

Hosteling . . . Adventure at Home and Abroad, Tell Me About Youth Hosteling. New York: American Youth Hostels, Inc.

Hosteling (quarterly magazine). New York: American Youth Hostels, Inc.

Leechman, Douglas. *The Hiker's Handbook.* New York: W. W. Norton & Company, Inc., 1944.

MacFarlan, Allan A. *Living Like the Indians.* New York: Association Press, 1960.

Shuttleworth, Dorothy. *Exploring Nature with Your Child.* New York: Greystone Corporation, 1957.

Chapter 26

THE NATURALIST AND
HIS FIELD*

"This," says the naturalist, pointing with his stick at a large spreading tree, "is the maple. There are several kinds; this is the hard, or sugar maple. It makes excellent firewood, burns hot, and makes a deep bed of glowing coals.

"It is a very valuable tree. The lumber is used for floors and furniture mostly, but maple is also used for bowling pins, and for the heels of ladies' shoes. Maple sugar and syrup are made from the sap.

"See the bird in the top of the tree? It is red-eyed vireo, and it is eating worms and insects that live on the leaves. You see, the bird benefits the tree by destroying the organisms that prey on it, and the tree benefits the bird by furnishing food, as well as shelter. Any questions?"

Generally there are questions, plenty of them. And usually there are those in the group who are eager to add to the discussion with details from their own experiences; one has visited a sugar bush in the spring and has seen the syrup made, and another knows that the furniture in his home is made of maple. Someone finds leaves bearing the tiny larvae such as that upon which the vireo is seen to be feeding.

Through the forest they go, exploring, examining, discussing. The naturalist, poking about with his ever-present stick, points out such details he feels they should notice, the better to understand the world we live in.

THE NATURALIST'S REALM

Nature is so big, so vast, so omnipresent that it is often taken for granted or overlooked altogether. It is for this reason that every girl or boy should, sometime during the formative years, meet a naturalist who will point out to him or her some of nature's many phases.

The naturalist may be a teacher, a hobbyist in a club, counselor in a

*This chapter was prepared by Carleton A. Robertson. It is placed adjacent to "Hikes and Excursions" because nature lore is inextricably tied to hiking and trips in the out-of-doors.

359

camp, or a professional scientist. He may be one whose work has led him
to the very ends of the earth, or he may as easily be one who has spent
his life in a restricted locality. Be that as it may, he is an invaluable
man to know.

As nature itself is vast, so the study of nature is a tremendous field.
It is a vantage point from which are viewed the mountains, the rivers,
the sea, and the sky. It encompasses the small as well as the great; it can
consider the origin of a continent and turn to observe the fleeting life of
the luna moth.

Although nature lore contains the elements of many sciences, it is not
truly an exact science. Its boundaries are but loosely defined, and its
very breadth denies it depth and penetration.

The naturalist soon learns that to follow assiduously any single phase
of nature lore is to lose the greatest appeal that nature lore can possess;
to study birds exclusively may be interesting, but such a study is orni-
thology, not nature lore. It is the broad outlook on the entire field rather
than a detailed study of any of the many segments that becomes the
province of the naturalist; for the naturalist wants to know and enjoy
all nature, generally, not just a particular segment.

There are few opportunities in the professional world for the naturalist to find employment on a full-scale basis. The broad view of nature,
while important, seems difficult to market except in connection with
another occupation. There are many openings for specialists in the many
fields that nature embraces, and there are likewise many short-term
and part-time situations for those to whom this chapter is especially
slanted.

The naturalist referred to in these pages is of semiprofessional standing and views nature in its entirety, rather than one who limits his studies to a specific field. Nature lore is a good avocation, worthy of anyone's time and energy.

QUALIFICATIONS OF A NATURALIST

It is safe to say that almost anyone can become a naturalist. Good
health and possession of natural faculties are, of course, desirable though
not absolutely essential. Probably the most important characteristics of
the naturalist are: first, the mental attitude of the scientist which is
manifested by curiosity of all things about him, and second, the heart
of a pioneer which gives him the courage to seek out the answers to the
questions that his curiosity asks. These are the essential buds from
which the other characteristics sprout.

The study of nature is, in itself, a pleasurable experience. Nature study is a perfect example of a hobby that can be pursued through one's lifetime. For one reason, it is a healthful pursuit; it takes one into the open air and away from the irritations and distractions which, we are told, are responsible for many neuroses. It can be as strenuous as even the most athletic can desire, involving, if one wishes, climbing tall trees or toiling over rugged terrain; yet it can be enjoyed fully even by the physically handicapped.

The study of nature knows no season. It is a year-round proposition; weather means nothing to the naturalist. It requires a minimum of equipment, and for that reason, costs comparatively little. Because of its immensity, it never grows stale for there are always new avenues to explore.

TRAINING AND ROLE OF THE NATURALIST

To become a naturalist able to instruct nature lore, it is well to have a background of biology equivalent to that taught in the average high school. Coupled with this should be some field experience, such as prowling about the woods and fields, seeing what there is to see and developing one's observation. The beginning naturalist should permit his mind to ask all kinds of questions since, later on, his students will be doing that very thing. "What is this plant? What is this insect? Why is it found here? What is it doing?"

At first, of course, many questions will go unanswered. Possibly, too, there will be a tendency to jump to incorrect conclusions which will have to be corrected as one's knowledge and experience develops. Every good public library has reference books which the young naturalist can consult until he decides to collect his own library. Talking with other naturalists often clears up puzzling problems. The merit-badge programs of both Boy and Girl Scouts are invaluable in getting a start as a naturalist.

Gradually, a proficiency in recognizing some of the plants, trees, birds, and insects is developed; and the neophyte naturalist is ready to begin teaching. It is when he starts out with his first group of youngsters that his education becomes fortified, for it is no secret that the teacher stands to learn more than his students. Generally, it will seem to him that his knowledge is so pathetically meager that he is wasting his students' time, especially when they unearth specimens to identify and pose questions to answer that may never before have come to his attention. Instead of becoming dismayed, he should strive as soon as possible to learn the answers. With some good reference books and a little questioning in the proper places, he soon fortifies his knowledge and is confidently ready when someone thrusts a query at him.

The naturalist should never hesitate to say frankly "I don't know," when that is the case. To deliberately give a wrong answer, for the sake of a glib response, not only has its moral implications; it is one of the quickest ways to lose the confidence of the group. Teen-age people have a way of knowing when they are being deceived.

It is often quite possible, when leading the same group of students on successive hikes, to enlist a great deal of assistance in research from the students themselves. This procedure is especially useful since it has the added value of giving the students a responsible part in the program.

Choice of names. Many times, it will be found that a specimen has not one, but several names, all in good standing. The naturalist will say something like this: "Here is the purple boneset. It is also called queen of the meadow, but I like best the name Jo-Pye weed. Jo Pye was an old doctor who lived in New England years ago and who is said to have treated all diseases with a tea made from the leaves of this plant."

Quite often, the same name is applied to different items of nature, according to the region. A "gopher" is a rodent in the West and a tortoise in the South. A "partridge" may mean a quail in some sections and a grouse in others, while "pheasant" may designate either a grouse or a ring-neck, depending on the locality. The students should be made aware of these regional differences.

Common names should be used, except when the occasion demands precision. At such time, it may be necessary to fall back on the scientific name to establish an absolute identity, but it is not necessary for the students to memorize long Latin names when there are names in common usage that are more easily pronounced and remembered. When the common name is part of the scientific name (Cecropia, Promethia, and so forth) the students will take it in stride.

Approaches to nature lore. Because Americans are traditionally an outdoor people, a general knowledge of what the outdoors holds has become a part of the national culture. Hunting, fishing, hiking, skiing, and camping are sports that take one to the primitive environment of the wilderness, the enjoyment of which is greatly enhanced if one has learned how fully to appreciate it.

Much of our literature is filled with references to objects found in nature, to the true feeling and understanding which the printed page unfolds. "A spruce thicket," for example, may mean merely a grove of trees to some; but those who have fought their way through a tangled mass of resistant branches armed with sharp, fragrant needles, known exactly what an author attempts to convey. It can be said that nature lore has an important cultural approach.

There is a second approach, which we will call the aesthetic. Nature is filled with that which we call beauty. It is found in the sunrise, the sunset, the rainbow, in the bright colors of the flowers, the birds, and the insects. Closely akin to beauty is the majesty that is found in a noble old tree, a river, or a mountain. Nature has many moods, ranging from the cool tranquility of the moonlit night to the terrible anger of the storm.

It so happens that it is not fashionable, in this cynical age, to emphasize this phase of nature lore. Writers and poets of another era so completely stressed this aspect of nature appreciation that it has fallen into disrepute. Some of the writing was artificial and sentimental; modern-day students are too worldly to put high value on mere beauty. They are touched by it, nevertheless. Swashbuckling boys have suddenly become speechless at the sight of a scarlet tanager or a rose-breasted grosbeak; the brilliant vital hues contrasted against the verdance of the forest have overwhelmed them completely. The naturalist needs only, by gesture or word, to indicate what he wishes them to see; lengthy exposition is unnecessary to point out what is beautiful in nature. It is an aspect that must not be overdone, but neither should it be neglected.

The third approach of nature lore appeals to the practical. After the students have gone about with the naturalist on several hikes, and have observed and examined all of the more conspicuous features of the landscape, it will begin to occur to them that most of the things they have seen bear direct influence on man's very existence. "Why is this land so barren?" "Because improper agricultural methods have depleted the soil." "Why are there no fish or any other aquatic life in this stream?" "Because the waste products of industrial plants have poisoned it."

It is at this point that the phrase "The Conservation of Natural Resources" begins to take on significance. These trees, these many plants, these rocks that contain important minerals, this fertile soil, this pure water—all are resources, all are important.

Unquestionably, it is not for the naturalist to advocate specific programs of conservation. But he can and must point out the wasteful abuses of our great heritage and the desperate need for workable programs to preserve what is left of it.

A NATURE LORE PROGRAM

The nature hike.   Nature lore is essentially an outdoor activity, and most of the instruction can be effected in connection with organized hikes. These hikes should be conducted through "wildernesses," areas that are as primitive as possible. Such areas are usually to be found in the vicinity of summer camps, rural, and even suburban communities. In the larger towns, there may be parks, set aside long ago by wise and far-seeing city fathers, which still retain many of the characteristics of the virgin woods. In many urban settings, there are also tiny nooks and corners, often close to industrial areas, where neglect has allowed them to "go back to nature" and which are sometimes surprisingly interesting. The capable naturalist makes use of whatever resources he can find.

Hikes are planned and conducted, as far as possible, in the spirit of adventurous exploration. They are motivated by a purpose which is determined by the desires of the students and announced beforehand by the naturalist.

"Today," he says, "we will go to the east side of Sugar Loaf Mountain and look for ginseng. There are other choice plants to be found there as well." Or, "I know of a place out by the gas works along the bank of the river where migrating warblers stop to rest. Suppose we go there about daybreak tomorrow morning?"

By first stating clearly a definite objective and leading the students into an area where that objective is most easily reached, a feeling that a problem was solved and that something was accomplished results. Whatever may be the primary objective of any hike, it is very likely that something else may well be more vividly remembered. Possibly these unexpected developments are the most significant features of any hike.

"Remember that time," one student will say, "when we were out catching butterflies and we found those moccasin flowers? I'll never forget how surprised I was when you said they were native orchids, and wouldn't let us pick a single one."

It is, of course, a good idea to get permission to hike over certain areas, or at least make sure that permission is unnecessary. Care should be taken that no damage is done to property. Frequently, abandoned works of man will be encountered, such as a mill site, a mine, a sugar house, or old farm buildings. Unless trespass is specifically forbidden, and with all due regard for the safety of those in the naturalist's care, it is a high point of adventure to examine these places in detail. The naturalist should lead the way, cautiously, looking for unsafe floors, shafts, wells, and abandoned machinery.

Related outcomes. The objectives of the hikes vary with the seasons, but there is no time when nature is not interesting. Consecutive hikes are directed into different and contrasting areas. One day will be spent wandering in the shade of an upland forest, another day will witness a floundering journey through a swamp. Small brooks and shallow ponds are extremely productive of the interesting and unusual, and wading about in the cool water is especially enjoyable to youngsters.

The naturalist takes it for granted that the beginner sees the woods as a strange place; even, indeed, as a forbidding one. In the immature minds of many youngsters, there lurk tales of fierce animals, poisonous plants and reptiles, and vast, gloomy spaces from whence the lost never return. Therefore, the first lessons are aimed at developing a confidence in the woods. There are bound to be apprehensive questions which should be met honestly and courageously.

"Sure, there are rattlesnakes. There are also bears and wildcats. But we seldom see them, because they fear us more than we fear them, and they do all that they can to keep out of our way. So the least we can do is to stay out of theirs." "Poison ivy is found here and there, and some of us are allergic to it, but many of us can handle it without any fear at all. And when we do take it, there is usually found growing nearby the very thing that will cure it, the jewel weed, or touch-me-not."

The timorous students are led to the places where wild berries grow. They learn to collect the succulent pot herbs such as purslane or red-root pigweed, and cook them over an open fire in a tin pail. They learn how to make tea of the hemlock or sassafras. They learn to recognize the nut-bearing trees. It begins to appear that the forest is not a dreadful place after all, but one filled with a variety of good foods. It is easy to tell when confidence has been established, because there will be some spontaneous remark such as that voiced by an urchin who had just tasted wintergreen, birch, sarsaparilla, spearmint, and teaberries, "Just imagine all these *flavors* growing wild way out here in the woods!"

Much of the naturalist's time will be taken up with identification of anything that can be thrust at him, wherever he happens to be, with the demand, "What is this?"

But mere identification is far from enough really to be of use to the student unless he is able to relate it to something with which he is familiar. A strangely colored pebble may be just a piece of rock, but it has much greater significance if the naturalist can say something like this: "Here is a piece of sedimentary rock that has been rolled around on the bottom of the lake for a long time."

From this beginning the formation of rocks can be discussed, the action of the water on formations, and so forth. Perhaps the specimen has a mineral content: "This is iron, see this rusty streak? The very stuff that many of our tools are made of," and as nearly everyone is familiar with some phase of the vast steel industry, all the naturalist has to do is to fill in the gaps in the story. It is brought out that this iron, exposed under certain conditions to other materials found in nature, coal and limestone, becomes the well-known substance which has given its name to our age. It may be possible to find, in a sluggish stream, the ancient lowly iron plant (*Leptothrix*) which is the very foundation of the entire industry.

Conducting a hike. As a rule, boys and girls are so filled with excess energy that a hike, at its outset, may take the characteristics of a steeplechase. To prevent this, it is suggested that for the first ten or fifteen minutes, the group march briskly in a double line with the naturalist leading the way. No effort is made to do any studying of nature at this time, and not until the objective is reached or the place of departure is far behind is discipline relaxed. By this time, the desire to run has largely been dissipated, the group will stay together and the naturalist can then begin the teaching of nature lore.

For much of the time on the trail, only the voice of the naturalist is required to keep the group together. At every step are interesting things to talk about, and the naturalist speaks in tones low enough so that it is necessary to be close to him to hear what he is saying. Shouting and horseplay among the students is frowned upon; eyes and ears are kept open for possible wild creatures. Now and then, the naturalist orders the group to travel for a distance in complete silence.

A "headquarters" is established at a conspicuous object, such as a big tree or rock; and the group deploys in all directions while the naturalist remains at the headquarters. After about ten minutes, he blows his whistle, summoning them back, each student bringing with him some specimen he has found. The naturalist calls the roll, the specimens are examined and commented upon, and the journey is resumed. Little escapes the notice of a group of active, curious youngsters; and the naturalist should be prepared for almost anything.

It is well to make the periods of deployment short, because if too long a time elapses before the whistle calls the party together, somebody may have wandered out of earshot and may encounter difficulty in finding his way back. At last, laden with plunder in the way of specimens, the students will start the trek homeward. In returning, they march in the same brisk two-by-two formation observed when they left until they reach their starting point. At this time, the naturalist summarizes briefly what they have seen, mentions by name those who have achieved outstanding observation, and thanks the group for their participation.

Night hikes. At night, nature takes on a different aspect. Man is essentially a creature of the daytime; he cannot see in the dark and is at a disadvantage. The wood, familiar enough in the sight of day, becomes a gloomy, mysterious place upon nightfall. At most seasons of the year, it is filled with strange sounds and invisible beings. A hike in the darkness is an unforgettable experience. The usual reason for a night hike is for star study. A treeless hilltop is the best place to study the stars, a spot somewhat remote and apart, from which the entire heavens can be viewed. A good telescope is a useful adjunct to star study, but is not necessary unless the group expects to delve more deeply into the wonders of astronomy than the average naturalist is able to go. There is much of interest to be seen with the naked eye, and the naturalist points out the various constellations with the aid of a strong flashlight which sends a bright, narrow beam far into the sky.

There are legends that may be related at this time (for the mood is usually very receptive for the storyteller), legends that have come to us from two distinct sources: the deserts of Asia Minor and the plains and woodlands of America. Those of the desert nomads are the legends that have given the names to the constellations. Their stories are interesting indeed.

In addition to identifying some of the outstanding groups of stars, together with a discussion about how to tell directions at night, the students should learn something of the immense distances and sizes that exist in the regions beyond us. They should be made to see how the Earth, impressive though it may be, is only one tiny speck in a vast universe. Certain students who show more than the usual interest in star study may wish to undertake a special project. The ceiling of the clubroom or nature lodge is a suggested place upon which to reproduce the sky at night. The project is more effective if the stars can be powdered with luminous paint.

Bird walks. Bird walks are usually taken in the early morning, because the birds are most active at that time of day; there is no point in going forth before it is light enough to distinguish colors. An isolated tree or group of trees in an open field makes an ideal spot to see birds, and it is only necessary to sit motionless nearby while the birds come and go. Occasionally, one of the students can be sent to investigate a strange song ringing out of a nearby thicket.

"Go see what is making that noise," mutters the naturalist to one of the group. "I'm not sure what it is, but I suspect it is one of the rarer warblers. Get a good look at it, note the size and the coloration, and we'll look it up."

To each student chosen for special duty in this fashion, the quest becomes a personal adventure filled with responsibility, and with the opportunity to distinguish himself by bringing something outstanding to the group. Bird walks are apt to be short affairs, because it is necessary to get the group back in time for breakfast. In the average locality, twenty species seen in one morning is a good number, and it is not unusual to see fifty, sixty, or more, during the season.

Insect study. Insect study is included in some nature programs and offers a tremendous field of activity. The order *Lepodoptera*, being the most conspicuous, is usually the most sought after. Armed with nets and killing jars, the group sweeps across the fields and through thickets, around and across the swamps and swales. The forenoon and late afternoon are good times to study insects. As with other forms of nature lore, interest centers on great numbers of specimens of different kinds. The research necessary in insect study is probably greater and more precise than any other field. Each specimen should be carefully examined, for even the commonest butterflies occur in rare and various forms. A specialty such as insect study may lead some youth toward making it a lifelong hobby.

Mammals. It is virtually impossible to observe many wild animals on the average nature hike since the group is apt to make so much noise that the creatures go into hiding at their approach, and because many of them are nocturnal and are asleep at the time when hikes usually take place. There are more animals around than the casual passerby can even be aware of. Almost every brushy hillside supports a family of rabbits; woodchucks live in or near the grassy meadows; mink and muskrats inhabit the sluggish streams that are not polluted by waste; and the skunks make a living wherever they happen to be. Nut-bearing trees attract the squirrels, while deer are known to live within sight of metropolitan areas. Mice, several species of them, are fairly abundant everywhere; and tiny shrews are much more common than it is generally thought. The raccoon, the opossum, and the wily fox are not rare. But, in the course of a hike with the average group, few of these creatures are ever seen. Often, however, their tracks are abundant, their dens easily found, and their presence easily established. Occasionally, some young and foolish animal will be captured and can be displayed for a short time.

The naturalist, as he prowls about alone, as he often does to gain experience and knowledge beyond that of his pupils, will observe much more than is ever seen on his scheduled hikes. He will learn how to skulk through the woods like a predatory creature, he will develop the art of concealment, he will experience the satisfaction that comes from outwitting the wild folk in their own environment. But try as he will, he cannot teach a group to do as well. All he can do is to inspire certain individuals to learn to do likewise. Those who do will have developed within themselves the epitome of wilderness experience, a feeling of kinship with nature.

Trees. It will depend on the average age and experience of the group just how precise they will be when identifying trees. Those of the age group found in the primary grades may find it enough of a challenge to distinguish a maple from an oak. Older students will wish to know more; they will expect to learn the differences between varieties of the same species. It is easier to begin the study of trees while they are in leaf, because the shape and colors of the leaves are often the best means of identification; the lesson is only half taught, however, if there is no effort made to identify them in the winter.

Axes and hatchets have little place on hikes of this sort, largely because there is always the temptation to hack and wound the trees. Examples of the results of this practice are found in all woodlands frequented by irresponsible hikers; the scarred and decayed trunks can serve as object lessons. Carving one's initials in the corky bark of the beech does not impair the tree nor is it harmful to strip the dry bark from the paper birch, but cuts that are deep enough to damage the cambium layer will cause permanent imperfections in the wood. The trees will likely be the oldest living things that nature students will encounter. It is not impossible to find oaks, elms, and pines which have endured since the days of the founding of the country.

Plant life. Very likely, the greatest interest in plant life will be in those which have the brightest blossoms. Many such plants are abundant enough so that they can be collected without any danger of extinction, but some of them are rare enough to prohibit picking altogether. There are many parks and recreations where the collecting of plant life of all kinds is strictly forbidden. In the average rural area, there will be no enforced restrictions except those which the naturalist imposes. A rule-of-thumb basis for determining whether or not to take a rare specimen is as follows: If there are twelve, take one; if there are twenty-four, take two; and so on.

It has been suggested previously that many wild plants can be cooked as food. There are a few which are unwholesome as food while possessing value as sources of medicine. Certain mushrooms are excellent foods. Unless the naturalist is especially competent, it is wise to leave all of them alone, since some are highly poisonous.

Mosses, lichens, and liverworts appear to interest only the more advanced and serious of the students. They are too tiny and colorless to attract the notice of the younger ones. Likewise, the vast families of grasses and sedges deem to be overlooked in their very abundance. Both are huge fields and deserve at least a casual mention.

Nature handicraft.   Nature lore lends itself easily to various forms of handicraft. Animal and bird tracks found in the mud can be cast in plaster of Paris and incorporated into unusual book ends or paperweights. Interesting colorful plaques can be made of leafcasts. There are transparent plastic materials in which can be imbedded showy insects and blossoms to form the basis for attractive costume jewelry. Materials for basketry, such as grasses, reeds, and the like, are easily found in nature; and the naturalist knows best where they are. The ingenious incorporation of nature lore with arts and crafts can constitute a worthwhile and productive portion of an integrated recreation program.

Museums.   One of the outgrowths of the nature lore program is frequently a museum. Specimens of all sorts are bound to accumulate wherever a group of nature students gather and the development of the museum is largely a matter of mounting, classifying, and arranging the material at hand. In almost every group will be found certain ones who will need but little encouragement to do this, and thus relieve the naturalist of a pleasant, though time-consuming, occupation. Besides, the prime purpose of the activity is to further the knowledge of the youthful participants. However competent the student curators may prove to be, the naturalist should take an active interest in the proceedings, making certain that all labels are accurate and that the entire display reflects neatness and order.

The size, arrangement, and scope of the museum necessarily should follow the dictates of the available space. Often, a camp will dedicate an entire building as a nature lodge; a club may be able to set aside a small room for the purpose, while a school may have to be content with using a nature display to brighten an obscure corner. A very large space is not especially recommended because it will require so much material to make a good showing.

Specimens can be of many sorts. Pressed leaves and flowering plants mounted on sheets of cardboard; butterflies, moths and other insects; different kinds of woods, showing both the bark and a section of the heartwood; and samples of rocks. Charts for display can be drawn up tracing the stages from the raw materials to their finished products. Space can be devoted to Indian relics if any of the group are inclined in that direction, for archeology is a part of nature lore.

The walls of the museum are good places to display lists such as these: "Birds Seen This Year," "Trees and Shrubs," "Plants," "Insects Found."

These lists may be hand-printed, with good black ink, on long sheets of white cardboard; include the name of the species, when found, and by whom. In connection with the name of the finder, it is well to add some designation, like an address, or group number. Here are a couple of samples:

Cardinal: July 8. John Welton, Troop 27, Silver Lake.
Black Cohosh: August 12. Jane Phillips, Bumblebee Cabin.

These lists are started from scratch every season. They become actively growing entities and keep their appeal to the very end, as every student strives to discover new and strange items to record upon them. The specimens of the museum remain the properties of the donors. Because some of the materials which are displayed will eventually be taken home as souvenirs, there will be more or less constant replacement. Soiled and damaged objects ought to be replaced by better ones as often as necessary. Unless the specimen is of unusual rarity or interest, it should not be shown if it is not attractive. Mere trash should be eliminated.

The nature trail. Under certain situations, the development of a nature trail makes an excellent project. It is especially adaptable to summer camping, although it should be effective in any place where signs and labels can be posted. Briefly, a nature trail is simply a well-marked path winding its way through a woodland, alongside which are signs that identify and explain the many things that occur there. It might be described, in effect, as a sort of outdoor museum. The labels should be neatly prepared and small enough to be relatively inconspicuous so that they remain modestly in the background.

An ideal location for such a trail (somewhat difficult to find) would be a smooth well-drained path which meanders its way in an irregular circle over gently rolling terrain terminating at the place of beginning. In its course, it should skirt a grassy glade, a small section of marsh or swale, cross a small brook over a substantial bridge, and touch the shore of a crystal clear pond. It should be two or three hundred yards in length.

Signs should not be nailed to the trees, but displayed from posts set as close as possible to wherever the attention is directed. Small objects may be more precisely located by wires or strings stretched between them and the signs that relate to them. The labels can be typewritten or printed on small file cards. They are tacked to thin, soft wood, such as orange-crate material. There is nothing wrong in having a signboard large enough to contain three or four labels or even more if they can be hidden slightly by bushes. Great care should be taken that the labels do not mar the natural effect. The cards may be waterproofed after they are printed by dipping them in melted paraffin. If so treated, they should last for two seasons.

Zoos.   Zoos operated by amateurs with limited means are apt to be pretty sad affairs. This does not apply to balanced aquariums or terrariums since creatures of the lower orders seem able to withstand confinement to a certain extent. Snakes, likewise, are hardy; but it cannot be said that they adapt very easily to cages. It is poor practice to confine any creature when we know full well that it will be unhappy and eventually die. Such an attitude implies that life is cheap.

Urban students usually have access to municipal zoos where the animals are capably cared for by trained keepers; visits to such places are, by all means, recommended. Those students in rural areas and camps have access to the great outdoors and the opportunity to see indigenous creatures in their native haunts. They can be captured, if it is possible to do so without harming them, so that they may be observed in captivity for a brief period. They are to be then released near the spot where they were caught.

The naturalist's philosophy.   The thinking naturalist comes to realize that nothing in nature is useless, that everything has been created to fill a need. Entire books have been written to exemplify this fact. Nature, consisting as it does of interlocking relationships, becomes a wonderfully complex mechanism of which man is a part. These relationships are spoken of as "The Balance of Nature."

It is often something of a shock to the average person to learn that man, as highly civilized as he is, stands on the same level as the rest of the earth's creatures, though he will often resent and deny it. It seems to him to be bestial and degrading; he prefers to believe that man's position is above and apart from nature. He thinks that the world is his and all things are subservient to him. The students that the naturalist will contact will be sons and daughters of this "average man," with a similar subjective outlook. The naturalist must therefore meet them on their own familiar ground. He will teach them that the woodpeckers and nuthatchers are our friends because they rid the trees (which are useful to us) of larvae which prey upon them. By the same token, he will call the sharp-shinned hawk an enemy of ours because it preys on our friends, the nuthatchers, woodpeckers, and the rest of the songsters whose bright songs and colors delight us. This pleasant theory will fail to stand the acid test when someone who raises cherries will declare war on the robins and the waxwings, or when a state declares a bounty on foxes, despite the fact that few other creatures catch as many mice (enemies of man) as they do.

Only a few of the older and more alert pupils ever will question the naturalist on these glaring inconsistencies and to them the naturalist can explain man's true position in nature. Those to whom he imparts this knowledge are no longer mere students, but fellows in this fascinating hobby. When the naturalist has brought about this transformation, he has achieved the highest pinnacle of his calling.

Naturalists, as a group, are essentially highly religious. They may be of all beliefs and creeds, and they may differ radically in their methods of worship but none will deny the existence of a higher power. From his observations in the field, the naturalist will know for a certainty that summer will follow spring and autumn, summer. He knows there will be planting time and that it will be followed by a harvest. He beholds a woodland ruined by improper lumbering and is solaced by the knowledge that the trees will grow again. He knows that, in periods of hardship, the strongest and most adaptable will survive, that the weak and unfit will be weeded out, and that the resultant species will be the better for it. He knows that nature is stern and harsh but that it is just. Confident, optimistic, and cheerful, the naturalist observes the world and its wisdom. He sees everywhere the presence of a higher power and knows that it is good.

General benefits. One of the immediate effects of a nature lore program is that which comes out of any well-integrated recreational program. There are the physical values that are the result of moderate exertion in a wholesome, pure environment. There are the mental and intellectual values that stem from the desire to learn more and more as interest is aroused and curiosity whetted. Unquestionably, it can be said that there are spiritual values as well.

No naturalist should expect that his nature lore program, however excellent it may be, will appeal to all. There will be a few who will show little or no interest. By the same token, there will be a few who will, if allowed, neglect all other studies and activities and concentrate on nature lore exclusively. The great majority will fall somewhere between these extremes. It should be one of the naturalist's aims, therefore, to seek out and develop those minds in which latent powers are hidden. In general, however, as long as our complex industrial civilization holds sway, most of those whom the naturalist will teach will be destined to spend their lives at tasks that bear little relation to anything they may learn from him. Sojourns to the wilderness will be but brief vacations from the treadmill of existence.

In order that these short holidays be enjoyed to the fullest, there should be developed "an abiding kinship with nature." The wilderness should be remembered as a haven of peace, of beauty, as an eternal refuge for the harassed and weary. The naturalist should stress also the tremendous potential value of the many things found in the wilderness and the vital need for their protection and wise use. Lastly, the nature lore program should be a series of pleasant adventures that will remain in the memories of those who shared them.

SUGGESTED READINGS

Cassell, S. *Nature Games and Activities.* New York: Harper and Brothers, 1956.

Goodrich, Warren, and Carleen Hitchins. *Science Through Recreation.* New York: Holt, Rinehart & Winston, Inc., 1964.

Harty, William. *Science for Camp and Counselor.* New York: Association Press, 1964.

Ickis, Marguerite. *Nature in Recreation.* Cranbury, N.J.: A.S. Barnes & Co., Inc., 1965.

Melady, John H. *The Nature Dictionary.* Cleveland: The World Publishing Company, 1950.

Moldenke, Harold N. *American Wild Flowers.* Princeton, N.J.: D. Van Nostrand Co., Inc., 1949.

Morgan, Alfred P. *A Pet Book for Boys and Girls.* New York: Charles Scribner's Sons, 1949.

Peterson, Gunnar, and Harry Edgren. *The Book of Outdoor Winter Activities.* New York: Association Press, 1962.

Wyler, Rose, and Eva-Lee Baird. *Science Teasers.* New York: Harper & Row, Publishers, 1965.

Chapter 27

THE PICNIC

Eating is a popular activity in any setting. When it is transported to the outdoors, it becomes even more fascinating. Certainly, the picnic's origin is not a recent one. In fact, it was used as a socializing and energizing factor in the houseraisings of the frontiersmen. It was a popular front for the political rallies of over a century ago. Fraternal orders, clubs, and labor unions have used it for generations. Churches and industries have made extensive use of its ability to unify large groups from assorted walks of life. Families and friends have long found it to be a pleasurable way to make the lowly frankfurter and hamburger achieve the eminence normally attributed to the festive turkey and steak.

At the present, picnicking is virtually a year-round activity, with the greater portion taking place during the warm-weather months. Clam bakes, corn roasts, and camp cookouts need not be respecters of seasons. The rapid rise of tobogganing, skiing, and ice skating as winter sports makes the need for winter picnics an imminent one. With the growth in leisure, there is reasonable certainty that picnicking will assume even more popular proportions in the future.

The picnic is sufficiently attractive as an event by itself. That it can be adapted to most any occasion is readily apparent. It can be combined with field days, holiday celebrations, festivals, programs, pageants, and parties. Food can be supplied when larger groups are involved or each unit of this group can be responsible for its own supplies. While the usual family picnic may call for relatively simple assignments to the various members, there is need for specific responsibilities when large picnics are arranged.

PLANNING THE PICNIC

In organizing a picnic entailing large groups, it is essential that committees be appointed to handle the various functions to be performed. To begin with, the picnic is to be placed in the charge of a capable individual or committee which will administer the event. The various assignments that may be necessary to conduct the picnic are as follows:

1. Organization Committee to work with the person in charge or to be responsible for running the picnic with a chairman as the head of the group.
2. Facilities Committee to arrange for the use of the picnic area, permit to be secured, fee to be paid, areas to be roped off, courts and fields to be marked, provisions for bathing, indoor facilities in the event of inclement weather, public address system, and automobile parking.
3. Equipment Committee to prepare for the activities phase by rounding up sports equipment (horseshoes, softball supplies, etc.), prizes, and the assorted items needed for the games and contests to be held.
4. Publicity Committee to inform the public of the occasion sufficiently in advance. Publicity media most suitable for the group to be reached should be employed.
5. Transportation Committee for making the necessary provisions to get the food and equipment to the area. For those who do not own automobiles, the use of buses or the necessary arrangements to pool cars that are available should be made.
6. Food Committee to arrange for the preparation of food and refreshments. The number to be served, the menu, and how to serve those who are to attend should be decided. Steps are to be taken to serve the group with a minimum of delay. The cafeteria style has been found to be a very successful way of serving large numbers.
7. Program Committee to prepare and execute a program adapted to the interests and age groupings of the invited. Measures are to be taken to ascertain the interests and activities that are most likely to appeal to all. A simple questionnaire in written form or by word of mouth will prove of inestimable worth in arriving at a pleasurable program. The activities should be varied to meet the needs, both active and passive, for all age groups. By offering a varied choice of activities, the picnic will be more apt to please the vast majority. There should be ample planning to anticipate problems that may arise. Provisions are to be made for rainy weather by having a separate program arranged should the activities have to take place indoors.
8. Finance Committee to handle all transactions involving the exchange of goods or services for money. This would hold true especially if a fee is charged or a fund is available from which to meet the expenses.
9. Clean-up Committee to leave the area the way it was found.
10. First Aid Committee to handle injuries, cuts, bruises, and similar emergency situations.

Feeding the group. There are several ways of feeding a picnic group. One way is to serve all food and refreshments from a central source. Another is to have each family supply its own food and refreshments. A third way is to have each individual or family supply its own food while the refreshments are distributed from a central source.

The tureen technique is a very effective and simple way since it delegates the greater responsibility to the picnickers with the planning and management to be handled by a committee. Under this plan, each individual or family contributes an item, such as baked beans, meat loaf, or potato salad. A varied array of foods is possible through the tureen plan. While it is possible to assign refreshments also, it is more efficient to have the committee arrange for the brewing of coffee or the serving of soda with this cost to be borne by an available fund or by charging for this essential and the paper plates, spoons, napkins, and cups. The effort required of each individual or group is reduced greatly by the assignment of one item as against the usual problem of preparing a varied meal even for a small group. The joy to be derived from eating in a social setting in the outdoors makes picnicking one of the most pleasant of diversions. A menu that will meet the tastes of all will certainly be the aim of the committee in charge of food.

Program suggestions. The revelations of the questionnaire will help greatly in planning the program. Nevertheless, the leader will still resort to an appraisal and round out the program with activities that are bound to please the greatest number. The age groups to be served, the previous recreational experiences of the groups, and the activities that have proved popular in the past are to be given considerable thought.

For activities requiring little effort of a vigorous nature, the reader is referred to the games included in the chapter on social recreation. In addition, there are the popular lawn games, such as croquet, quoits, horseshoes, and badminton, which will prove popular throughout the day and serve the added purpose of taking care of the early arrivals' thirst for something to do. Group singing is also suggested at this point as well as after the eating phase is completed.

There are numerous novelty activities suitable for picnics. Among them are the following:

Potato and Spoon Race	Basketball Throw for Distance (Girls)
Sack Race	Wheelbarrow Race
Three-legged Race	Matchbox Relay
Peanut Scramble	Cracker Eating–Whistle Contest
Duck-walk Race	Rolling Pin Toss Contest
Paper Plate Distance Toss	Balloon-Wand Push Contest
Tug-of-War	Nail Driving Contest
Balloon Blowing Contest	Potato Race
Marshmallow Eating Contest	Shoe Scramble
"Beer" (milk bottle and nipple) Contest	Pie Eating Contest
Horse and Rider Contest	Watermelon Eating Contest

When the activities are forced indoors, the use of the quiet games and rhythmical play found in the chapter on social recreation are suggested. In addition, the progressive game theme is worthwhile for those who are interested in guessing contests. All who care to can take part during the course of the day with the winner to be decided later in the day; the one who scores the highest number of points is designated the winner. Members of both sexes can participate in this combined skill and guessing contest with their scores recorded on a mimeographed Progressive Games Score Card. The following are suggestive of the types of questions and skills to be sought:

1. Guessing the number of beans, coins, marbles, cherries, and so forth, in a jar. The one who is closest to the correct amount earns 10 points while 7, 5, 3 and 1 points to those next in line can be given.
2. Tossing ten playing cards into a hat from top part of a chair; 5, 3, 2, and 1 points may be given the four highest scores.
3. Guessing the exact time an alarm clock, the face of which is taped, will ring. Scoring similar to 1 or 2 above may be used.
4. Dropping ten clothespins into a milk bottle from the top portion of a chair. Score as in 2 above.
5. Tossing ten jar rubber rings at a board on which nails are numbered 1 to 10 in the order of difficulty. Score as in 2.
6. Tossing five darts at a numbered target board (1 to 10). Score as in 1.
7. Totaling the number of successful throws at an ash can or refuse basket 10 feet away from the target. Score as in 2.
8. Counting the number of coins (slugs) that can be tossed into a small glass at the bottom of a large glass receptacle of about two or three gallons filled with water. Score as in 2.
9. Totaling number scored by rolling a pair of dice three times. Score as in 1.
10. Taking ten tries to get a tennis ball into a wastebasket after a bounce. The table is to be waist-high with the basket removed six feet from the table's edge. Score as in 2.

FIRESTONE PICNIC

The Firestone Tire and Rubber Company, Akron, Ohio, has achieved notable success in the operation of its employee picnics. For that reason, the program of activities is presented in detail. The activities are directed at the mass appeal with the whole family included.

Morning

11:00 A.M. to 12:00 Midnight—Free Rides and Amusements.
11:00 A.M. to 8:00 P.M.—Registration at Special Booth near Exhibition Platform for:

Guessing Contest—Prizes $15.00, $10.00, and $5.00;

Firestone Employee Oldest in Age Attending Outing—Prize $20.00;

Firestone Employee with Largest Family at Outing—Prize $20.00.

11:00 A.M.—Band Concert—Bandstand.

11:15 A.M.—Clown Act—Exhibition Platform.

11:30 A.M.—Lucas Circus—Dog and Pony Show—Exhibition Platform.

11:45 A.M.—Band Concert—Bandstand.

12:00 Noon—The Valentinos—Flying Act—Near Exhibition Platform.

Afternoon

12:15 P.M.—Band Concert—Bandstand.

12:30 P.M.—Parallel Bar Act—Noble Trio—Exhibition Platform.

12:45 P.M.—Band Concert—Bandstand.

1:00 P.M.—Acrobatic Teeter Board Act—Bedell Troupe—Exhibition Platform.

1:15 P.M.—Band Concert—Bandstand.

1:30 P.M.—Trampoline Act—Bailey Trio—Exhibition Platform.

1:45 P.M.—Clown Act—Exhibition Platform.

2:00 P.M. to 5:30 P.M.—Dancing Summit Beach Ballroom—George Conway and His Orchestra—Dancing Contest—Prize Waltz—Prizes $25.00, $15.00, and $10.00 to Winning Couples.

2:15 P.M.—Parade of Youngsters—Three and Four Years Old, Dressed in Sun Suits—Outside Judges Will Select Winners in Each Contest—Prizes $20.00, $10.00, and $5.00.

Participation in Parade of Youngsters by Entry Blank Only—Each Contest limited to Sixty Youngsters, and Contestants Must All Be Three- and Four-Year Old Children of Firestone Employees—Each Youngster Participating in the Contest Will Receive $1.00—Obtain Entry Blanks from Your Foreman.

2:45 P.M.—Band Concert—Bandstand.

3:30 P.M.—Candy Eating Contest for Eight- and Nine-Year-Old Girls. Prizes $5.00, $3,00, and $2.00 for each contest.

3:45 P.M.—Band Concert—Bandstand.

4:00 P.M.—Apple Eating Contest for Eight- and Nine-Year-Old Boys. Prizes $5.00, $3.00, and $2.00 for each contest.

4:30 P.M.—Band Concert—Bandstand.

4:45 P.M.—Prize Waltz Dancing Contest—Summit Beach Ballroom. Prizes $25.00, $15.00, and $10.00 to Winning Couples. Outside Judges Will Select the Winning Couples.

5:15 P.M.—Clown Act—Exhibition Platform.

5:30 P.M.—Band Concert—Bandstand.

Evening

6:15 P.M.—Clown Act—Exhibition Platform.

6:30 P.M.—Lucas Circus—Dog and Pony Show—Exhibition Platform.

6:45 P.M.—Band Concert—Bandstand.

7:00 P.M.—Acrobatic Teeter Board Act—Bedell Troupe—Exhibition Platform.

7:15 P.M.—Band Concert—Bandstand.

7:30 P.M.—Parallel Bar Act—Noble Trio—Exhibition Platform.

7:45 P.M.—Band Concert—Bandstand.

8:00 P.M.—Trampoline Act—Bailey Trio—Exhibition Platform.

8:15 P.M.—Band Concert.

8:30 P.M.—Drawing for Prizes—Savings Bonds and Merchandise Orders—Stubs from Outing Tickets Deposited at the Entrance of Summit Beach Park Will Be Used for Drawing of Prizes. Please be sure to PRINT Name, Address, Department, and Clock Number of Salary on the Ticket Stub to Avoid Confusion and Errors in Delivery of Prizes to Winners. Drawing Will Be Held on Exhibition Platform.

9:00 P.M. to 1:00 A.M.—Dancing—Summit Beach Ballroom. "Ray" Robbins' National Radio and Dance Orchestra for Your Dancing and Listening Pleasure.

Dancing Contest—Prize Waltz.

9:15 P.M.—Band Concert—Bandstand.

9:30 P.M.—Announcing and Awarding Prizes to Winners of the Various Contests at the Exhibition Platform. Guessing Contest—Prizes $15.00, $10.00, and $5.00. Firestone Employee Oldest in Age Registering at the Outing—Prize $20.00. Firestone Employee with Largest Family Registering and Attending Outing—Prize $20.00. Registration for Guessing Contest—Firestone Employee Oldest in Age and Firestone Employee with Largest Family Must Register at Special Booth near Exhibition Platform.

10:00 P.M.—The Valentinos—Flying Act—Near Exhibition Platform.

10:30 P.M.—Prize Waltz Dancing Contest—Summit Beach Ballroom. Prizes $25.00, $15.00, and $10.00 to winning couples.

Outside Judges Will Select Winning Couples.

PICNIC KITS

As an added and much-needed service to the community, the recreation center can make available a picnic kit to be loaned to organizations and groups in the community. The activities most popular in a given community can help to govern the contents of the kit. For the average situation, the following items are suggested:

Softball equipment	Rope (for three-legged race)
Deck tennis	Sacks (for sack race)
Horseshoes	Croquet set
Volleyball	Mimeographed game sheet

It may be advisable to require a deposit before lending out a kit. A prearranged list of fees for objects lost or damaged should be shown to the borrower in advance to avoid misunderstanding. This list can be attached to the check list of items handed to the borrower. A mimeographed list and description of activities that require no equipment will prove invaluable as part of this picnic kit.

SUGGESTED READINGS

Eisenberg, L. and H. *Omnibus of Fun.* New York: Association Press, 1956.

Industrial Recreation Association, *Employee Picnics.* Chicago: Industrial Recreation Association Press, 1947.

Kraus, Richard. *Recreation Today.* New York: Appleton-Century-Crofts, 1956.

Leydet, F. *Time and the River Flowing.* San Francisco: The Sierra Club, 1965.

Picnic Booklet, Leader's Manual. Louisville, Kentucky: Department of Parks and Recreation.

Shallcross, John E. *The Complete Picnic Book.* Cranbury, N.J.: A. S. Barnes & Co., Inc., 1954.

U.S. Department of the Interior, *Quest for Quality*, Yearbook. Washington, D.C.: U.S. Government Printing Office, 1965.

U.S. Department of the Interior, *Outdoor Recreation Trends.* Washington, D.C.: U.S. Government Printing Office, April 1967.

U.S. Department of the Interior, *The Population Challenge . . . What It Means to America*, Yearbook. Washington, D.C.: U.S. Government Printing Office, 1965.

Chapter 28

ROWING, CANOEING, AND SAILING

There has been a tremendous upsurge in boating activities in recent years. There is obviously a limit to the amount of shoreline surrounding a body of water. However, boating extends the "shoreline" for the enthusiast aside from the tremendous satisfaction inherent in the sports of canoeing, sailing, water skiing, rowing, and the like.

The sport of boating offers one of the finest of recreational outlets. It is adaptable to people of all ages with a notable carry-over into the waning years. Whether it be rowing, canoeing, or sailing, the fact that one is in the out-of-doors with the variable colors of the water as a spectacle makes it relaxing and highly satisfying. The mind is diverted by this most relaxing of sports.

Motorboating, both inboard and outboard, has grown tremendously in recent years. The outboard has increased from less than 20,000 sold annually to roughly 393,000 in 1965. Accompanying the upsurge in power boating is a great interest in water skiing. Sales of boats for use with outboard motors has kept pace with this increase. Trailers for transporting boats increased from 4,000 in 1947 to over 130,000 in 1965.

RELATED ACTIVITIES

Boating also combines readily with other phases of recreation. The ability to swim is assuredly a highly essential skill. Safe behavior around the water calls for a reasonable amount of confidence in one's ability to cope with emergency situations. Outside of the emergency realm, swimming provides a refreshing activity in conjunction with sailboating, motorboating, canoeing, and rowing. When the boat is sufficiently sturdy, diving from it for a swim becomes one of the most memorable parts of the day.

Opportunities for handicrafts are indeed plentiful. The construction of the craft and its gear can keep the recreation center buzzing all winter. In fact, one of the outstanding sights this observer witnessed in his observations of recreational activities was the construction of a sailboat in a Chicago park center for use on Lake Michigan. Other related activities are weather detecting, sail making, knot tying and splicing, oar and paddle construction, repair of inboard and outboard motors, painting, and repairs along with improvements of the craft.

Skillful maneuvering may require extensive reading, observation, and practice. Competitive outlets are afforded by contests which include the various skills involved and racing, which is tremendously popular whether it entails sculling, rowboating, canoeing, speedboating, or sailing. Aquaplaning and water skiing often accompany motorboating. Participants in all forms of boating find in basking in the sunshine and picnicking pleasant supplements to a lifelong interest.

ROWING

As is true of many rather commonplace skills, and as is especially true of rowing, people are apt to feel that it is so simple an act as not to require any instruction. These underestimations become more apparent when members of this group are observed handling a rowboat; their floundering movements are often accompanied by stares of astonishment, indecision, frustrating motions, casting blame on the rowlocks, or some such spurious response.

While not a very difficult skill to acquire, it can be learned more readily if broken down into fundamentals and learned progressively. These instructions are but preliminary to their practical application on the water.

Fundamentals. Whenever feasible, one should enter a rowboat from the side with both hands on the gunwales. The first step should be somewhat equidistant between the gunwales to help keep the boat on an even keel. This holds true also when entering from the bow or stern.

In determining the length of the oar, measure the width of the oarsman's thwart from gunwale to gunwale plus the freeboard distance from the water line to the gunwale. Ash or spruce oars are most commonly used. The grip on the oar should be firm enough to keep it from turning.

Rowing calls for a rhythmical coordination of the entire body. The parts of the body that are used more prominently are the hands, wrists, arms, legs, feet, and back. The back is especially important since its pull can ease the strain on the other parts. The legs should be braced.

The fundamentals of rowing can be conveniently divided into four phases:

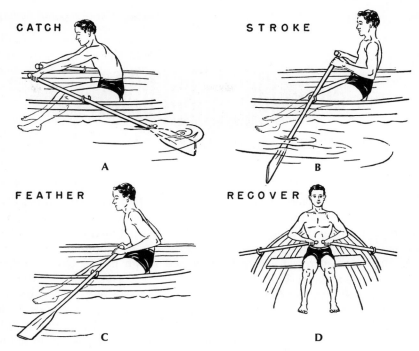

CATCH

STROKE

A

B

FEATHER

RECOVER

C

D

Figure 33. (a) **Catch**—when the blades strike the water at right angles with the arms fully extended and the legs bent (b) **Stroke**—the motion started under catch is continued with greater vigor as the blades are pulled through the water in a vertical position until they surface; the legs are extended as the back exerts a backward pull (c) **Feather**—upon clearing the water, the oars are feathered by flexing the wrists backward so that the blades are parallel to the water's surface; as a result, the wind or waves will exert minimal influence on the blades (d) **Recover**—the feathered oars are pulled to a position of momentary recovery with the grip portions of the oars almost touching each other

CANOEING

Canoe size and care. Canoes come in varied sizes ranging from eleven to thirty-five feet. As a utility canoe for juniors, the sixteen-foot craft is highly recommended while the fifteen-foot canoe is preferred for solo canoe mastery. The larger war canoe is useful for crew or group canoeing, competitive canoeing, or cruising.

The sixteen-foot canoe can be used to accommodate up to three paddlers so long as there is no equipment to be carted. Mass training opportunities are afforded by the war canoe with its thirty-five-foot length. The seventeen-foot or eighteen-foot canoe is often used for adult groups while the sixteen-foot size is usually best for youths.

On land, the canoe should be kept from contact with sand, mud,

385

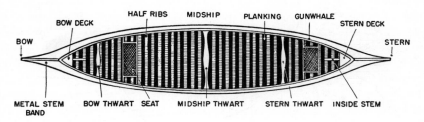

Figure 34. The canoe

gravel, or rocks. When afloat, canoeists must look out for submerged rocks and tree stumps. If damage occurs, canvas-covered canoes possess the advantage that they can be repaired and patched easily. Wooden canoes are somewhat more rugged. Canoes of aluminum or sheet metal can take even more of a beating and rough usage. On the other hand, they are noisy in rough water.

When refinishing the canoe, remove the old paint with sandpaper or paint and varnish remover. The addition of paint or varnish to previous coats will add weight to the craft. Finishes with linseed oil are not recommended for canvas canoes since oil tends to weaken the cotton fibers in the canvas.

Canoes should be stored on racks in the upside-down position. A shed or covering will shield the canoes while they are stored from the sun. If the canoe is used in salt water, hosing down with fresh water will help to protect the finish against the salt-water action.

Paddle selection. It is commonly recommended that the size of a single-blade paddle should be six inches shorter than the paddler himself. Another way to measure is to have the grip reach the eye level as the blade is turned downward. Paddles can be purchased in stock sizes from four to six feet in length at intervals of six inches.

Spruce paddles are light in weight, with the wood highly suitable for a camp paddle construction program. Ash makes a heavier paddle with its characteristic strength. Maple is similar to ash in strength but has a tendency toward warping unless given special care.

The double-blade paddle provides a readily learned and efficient means of handling a canoe. It is particularly suitable for the newcomer to canoeing since he can make more rapid progress with this type of paddle. The double-blade paddle length should be determined by the width of the canoe; the usual lengths vary from eight to nine and one half feet.

Canoeing strokes. The basic strokes are considered in the order of difficulty for the learner. They will be treated briefly here in view of the vast variety of subjects to be covered. More detailed information can be secured from any of the books listed as source material on this subject.

1. Bow stroke and back water stroke. The bow stroke is used by the paddler up front when there are two handling the canoe. For the right-handed person, the top of the paddle should be held shoulder high in the left hand as the right hand grasps the shaft and extends forward as far as possible. The stroke should be straight backward and close to the gunwale.

The back water stroke is the reverse of the bow stroke. With the blade as far back as possible, the right arm presses downward until the starting position of the bow stroke is reached. Both the bow stroke and back water stroke are completed as they reach the vertical position alongside the body.

2. Pull-to. In the pull-to, the starting position is the same as for the bow stroke except the blade is parallel to the gunwale. Reach out side-

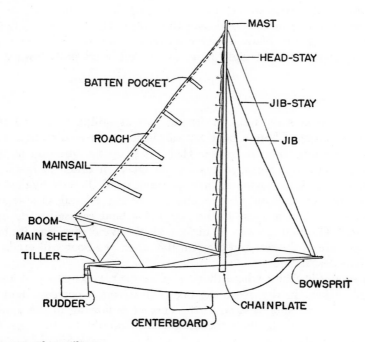

Figure 35. The sailboat

wards with the paddle and pull the canoe toward the paddle. Force should be exerted by both arms. Repeated stroking can be achieved best by turning the blade so that it is perpendicular to the gunwale as it is pushed and pulled until the paddle returns to the starting position. This stroke pulls the canoe closer to the side where the stroking is executed.

3. Pushover stroke. The pushover stroke is carried out in reverse fashion of the pull-to. It moves the canoe away from the paddle.

4. Sweep stroke and reverse. The sweep stroke is begun in similar fashion to the bow stroke with the sweep executed by reaching out close to the bow and making an arc. The size of the arc can be determined by the distance that the bow is to be turned away from the paddler's position without loss of momentum; the reverse is achieved by stroking the very opposite of the "sweep."

5. "J" stroke. The "J" stroke is a stern stroke employing the starting position of the bow stroke. Since the stroke up to this point causes the bow to turn away from the side of the paddler, the rounding out of the stroke to simulate a "J" causes the canoe to straighten its course. At the completion of the bow stroke, the right hand is near the side of the body with the left arm extended over the water. The "J" portion is executed by turning the blade counterclockwise with the left hand and by pushing away with the right hand as the left hand pulls toward the left.

SAILING

Tacking. Perhaps the most intriguing part of sailing to the landlubber is the problem of how a boat can sail in a southerly direction when the wind is coming from the south. This brings up the question of tacking which refers to a zigzag course to be taken in order to reach the southerly destination. Obviously, a boat cannot sail directly against the wind. On the other hand, by tacking or trying to sail close-hauled (with the sail pulled in close to the boat), the boat can sail fairly close to the wind. Through a series of tacks with the wind directing its force first on one side of the sail and then on the other, the boat will gradually approach its destination.

When sailing in water where there is no current, tacks of equal length are usually taken. In the event the boat encounters a current, then the length of the tacks should vary. If the current is flowing in the general direction one is sailing, then the longer tack would be the one that can take fuller advantage of this aid toward one's goal. Should the current flow against the boat's destination, then the short tack would be the one that meets the greater strength of the current; meeting the force of a current at an angle will set a craft back less than if head on. Maneuvering the boat so that its direction is changed when heading into the wind is referred to as "coming about." A jibe takes place when the sail shifts from one side to the other while the wind is blowing from the stern or rear of the boat. Jibing calls for skillful handling or else the force of the jibe may cause damage to the rigging.

Sail pull. Another question that is often raised, is "why is a boat able to move when its sails are in a close-hauled position?" The answer lies in a combination of forces. As the wind strikes the sail at an angle, it also creates a vacuum pull on the other side of the sail. The two combine to give the boat a forward pulling force. The fastest sailing point is attained when the wind strikes the sail at a right angle or 90° angle. Resistance to lateral sway is provided by the centerboard or keel which contributes thereby toward the boat's forward motion.

Adjusting sail to the wind. Some sailboat people recommend that the boom (pole at bottom of the sail) should be in line with the wind pennant at the top of the mast. While the more advanced sailboat enthusiast will want to develop his own feel of the boat and make his adjustments accordingly, this piece of advice will prove of some assistance. This hint is more accurate and useful when the boat is close-hauled while sailing close to the wind. It becomes less so as the wind approaches from the side (abeam) or slightly to the rear (abaft the beam).

There are varied rigs among sailboats. A boat with a cat rig has one sail with one line or sheet to control it; a sloop has two sails, a mainsail or larger sail and a jib or small triangular sail before the mast. If the mainsail is three-sided, it is a marconi rig. If it is foursided, it is gaff-rigged.

The following comments and drawings will serve to show how to adjust the sail in keeping with differing wind directions.

The helm. The helm is that portion of the sailboat where the tiller or steering device of the craft is situated. Varying the resistance of the rudder against the water causes the boat to turn. A turn of the tiller toward the left will cause the bow of the boat to head toward the right. Conversely, forcing the tiller toward the right will steer the boat toward the left. Facility at handling the tiller and familiarity with these maneuverings will come readily through practice.

Everything on board ship should be shipshape and properly stored. Moreover, the lines and gear throughout the craft and particularly at the

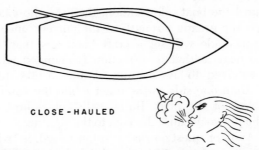

CLOSE-HAULED

Figure 36. Close-hauled—with the wind coming almost directly ahead, the boat is close-hauled with the main and jib sheets pulled in close to the boat. The boat can then be steered close to the wind

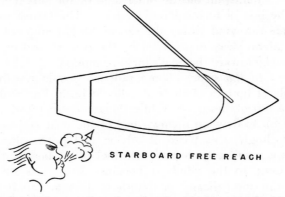

STARBOARD FREE REACH

Figure 37. Starboard free reach—when the direction is considerably away from the wind, we have a starboard free reach

RUNNING BEFORE THE WIND

Figure 38. Running—before the wind—should the wind's direction be from the rear or near it, we have running before the wind

helm should be free of encumbrances. A knock-down breeze may come along without any warning; inability to respond immediately by letting out the sail and heading over with the rudder may mean a swamped boat. Needless to say, the line attached to the mainsail should never be tied down.

SUGGESTIONS FOR SAFETY

1. Do not overload. Maintain adequate freeboard at all times; consider the sea conditions, the duration of the trip, the predicted weather, and the experience of the operator.
2. Be especially careful when operating in any area where swimmers might be. They are often difficult to see.
3. Watch your wake. It might capsize a small craft; it can damage boats or property along the shore. You are responsible. Pass through anchorages only at minimum speed.
4. Keep firefighting and lifesaving equipment in good condition and readily available at all times.
5. Obey the rules of the road. Neglect of this is the greatest single cause of collision.
6. Consider what action you would take under various emergency conditions —man overboard, fog, fire, a stove-in plank or other bad leak, motor breakdown, bad storm, collision.
7. Have an adequate anchor and sufficient line to assure good holding in a blow (at least six times depth of water).
8. Know the various distress signals. A recognized distress signal used on small boats is to raise and lower slowly and repeatedly the arms outstretched to each side.
9. Always have up-to-date chart (or charts) of your area on board.
10. Always instruct at least one other person on board in the rudiments of boat handling in case you are disabled—or fall overboard.
11. Water ski only when you are well clear of all other boats, bathers, and obstructions and there are two persons in the boat to maintain a proper lookout.
12. Before departing on a boat trip, you should advise a responsible friend or relative about where you intend to cruise. Be sure that the person has a good description of your boat. Keep him advised of any changes in your cruise plans. By doing these things, your friend or relative will be able to tell the Coast Guard where to search for you and what type of boat to look for if you fail to return. Be sure to advise the same person when you arrive so as to prevent any false alarms about your safety.[1]

[1]Excerpted from *Pleasure Craft*, U.S. Coast Guard, 1966.

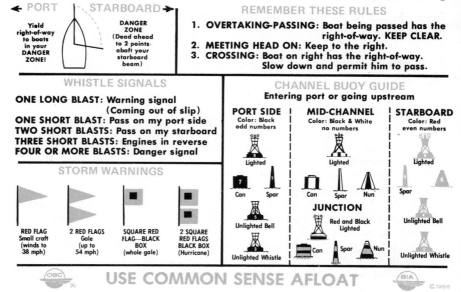

Figure 39. Sailing rules and signals

Source: Outboard Boating Club of America, 1966

Nautical Terms

Aft or abaft—toward the rear or stern.
Abeam—at right angles with the craft's keel.
Amidships—toward the middle of a craft.
Astern—in the rear or behind a craft.
Awash—on a level with the water.
Avast—stop or stay.
Beach—to drive onto a beach or strand a craft.
Beam—extreme breadth or width of a craft.
Belay—a pin or cleat around which a line is fastened.
Bow—forward part of a craft; also the prow or stem.
Calk—to drive oakum or cotton into the seams of a craft.
Capsize—to upset or overturn.
Chop—sudden wind shift; choppy or turbulent water.
Cleats—a wedge-shaped piece of metal or wood on which to fasten ropes.
Crest—the top of a wave.
Davy Jones' Locker—final resting place of those drowned or buried at sea.
Deck—floor portion of a craft.
Deck, aft—behind the midportion of a craft.
Dock—a slip between two piers or alongside a pier.

Draft—depth of water needed to float a craft.

Ebb—flowing back of the tide.

Eddy—a whirlpool.

Even keel—a balanced craft with both sides equidistant from the water.

Fair—clear weather.

Fast—firmly fixed.

Fathom—six feet in length.

Fore—portions of a craft between amidship and bow.

Fore and aft—in general line with the length of a vessel.

Frame—one of the craft's ribs.

Freeboard—distance between the water line and the gunwale.

Gunwale—upper edge of a boat's side.

Heel—the amount of tilting of a sailboat when the wind causes it to lean away from an even keel.

Helm—portion of the craft from which its direction is controlled.

Jib—the small sail.

Keel—built-up timber or metal extending along the middle of a craft's bottom.

Knot—a speed designation of a nautical mile (6,080.20 feet) per hour.

Landlubber—one who spends his life on land or anyone who is awkward on a craft.

Leeward—opposite to the wind's source; opposite of windward.

Midship—middle of a craft's length.

Port—left side of a craft.

Prow—front end of a vessel.

Rudder—steering device for maneuvering a craft.

Sheet—line attached to a sail.

Skeg—afterpart of a craft's keel.

Sloop—a sailboat with two sails: a jib and a mainsail.

Starboard—right side of a craft.

Stem—bow frame connected to lower end of keel.

Stern—aft end of a craft.

Thwart—wooden reinforcements extending across a rowboat; a seat.

Tiller—attachment to the rudder for steering.

Topside—side of the hull above the water line.

Trim—readiness of a craft for sailing.

Tumble home—receding of a craft's beam as it nears the rail.

Underway—craft that has started to move.

Veer—turning or changing of the wind.

Wake—churned water left by a craft under way.

SUGGESTED READINGS

Allen, Jim J. *Boating.* New York: The Ronald Press Company, 1958.

American National Red Cross, *Canoeing.* New York: Doubleday and Company, Inc., 1956.

Aymar, G. C., *Start 'em Sailing*. Cranbury, N.J.: A. S. Barnes & Co., Inc., 1941.

Basic Seamanship and Safe Boathandling. U.S. Coast Guard Auxiliary, National Board, 1961.

Gabrielsen, M. Alexander, *et al. Aquatics Handbook*. Englewood Cliffs, N.J.: Prentice-Hall, Inc., 1960.

Pleasure Craft. U.S. Coast Guard, Treasury Department, C.E.–290, November 1, 1966.

Sailboating. Greenwich, Conn.: Fawcett Publications, Inc., 1952.

Scharff, Robert. *The Complete Book of Water Skiing*. New York: G. P. Putnam's Sons, 1959.

Chapter 29

RECREATIONAL SWIMMING

Swimming is perhaps man's most pleasurable activity. By superimposing game and contest situations, a new dimension of satisfying experiences is uncovered.

In recreational swimming, emphasis is placed on the fun element. This is at variance with competitive swimming wherein speed and winning are of prime importance. Recreational swimming affords the participant an opportunity to add to the usual pleasures of moving about in the water. A chance to sense the exhilarating sensations of varying one's activities in the water increases the recreative and relaxing effects.

As a culminating project, the water pageant is perhaps unsurpassed. Its suitability as a means of displaying the achievements of those who take part in the program makes it a highly regarded special event. There are dangers in the offing if the emphasis and time devoted are excessive. Relegated to its rightful place, it can constitute a cooperative venture for so individualized an activity as swimming. Individual strengths and weaknesses can be so shuffled as to create a composite picture of pleasing pageantry. The participants should be afforded opportunities for creative effort and achievement. This one phase cannot be overemphasized in view of the overall objectives of recreation.

TRENDS

There are certain unmistakable trends evident in swimming in general and in recreational swimming in particular. Some of the more important of these are as follows:

1. Recognition of swimming as perhaps the most popular individual activity. It is usually at the top or near it as an activity in recreational interest polls.
2. Increased participation on the part of both sexes.
3. The vast increase in the construction of swimming pools.
4. Continued emphasis by the American Red Cross has increased the number of water safety instructors. Also, the quality of instruction has improved. Better analysis of swimming techniques plus their more effective applica-

tion in the light of individual needs have contributed generously toward this brightened picture.

5. With improved roads and faster means of getting to the shore, more spend their leisure moments swimming than ever before.

HOW TO ENCOURAGE ATTENDANCE

The periodic holding of special events can prove to be a most dependable way to increase attendance. Soundly conceived publicity can be brought into play prior to holding the event as well as photographs and releases for newspapers and magazines after the event is held. Newspapers are only too willing to give publicity to learn-to-swim campaigns, contests, or bathing beauty pageants. Announcements during station breaks can help greatly; newsworthy items may qualify usually for free radio coverage. The use of Father-and-Son and Mother-and-Daughter Nights, exhibitions, and similar special events are bound to promote attendance. Season tickets that are attractively priced are commonly used. Moreover, a polite and efficient staff devoted to a sanitarily operated pool with appealing activities will spell increased attendance.

Suggested special events. Conducting special events on a regular basis will stimulate interest in the swimming pool. Quite often, special events are held during days when attendance is apt to be poorest. Proper timing is an essential in any activity and no less in pool management. Some pool managers advocate holding these events on a good day, although not the best; *i.e.*, on a Friday rather than a Saturday or Sunday.

The following are suggested as special occasions and events suitable for a swimming area:

Carnival	Swimming Contest
Diving Contest or Exhibition	Telegraphic Meet
Gay 90's to Present Swimsuit Exhibition	Parents Night (Father-and-Son, Mother-and-Daughter)
Learn-to-Swim Program	Water Ballet
Bathing Beauty Contest	A Night in Venice
Baby Parade	Pet Parade
Lifesaving Exhibition	Stunt Night

Games and contests. Before the start of water games, it is advisable to think of the spectator as well as the participants. Certainly, the events should finish as close as possible to where the majority are seated. The swimming distances for each game should not strain the participant nor require so much time to complete that the spectator will become bored.

Some pools or camps find it a good policy to plan a special events program each week. While it may border on the obvious, the director should be certain that all participants can swim reasonably well.

The games that follow are suitable as part of a novelty night, special events program, or as part of an intermission program at a water carnival or pageant. Holding the games in the shallow area of the pool is advised to facilitate staging the games.

ACTIVITIES SUITED FOR A NOVELTY NIGHT

Swamp 'Em. Enlist as many partners as there are prams, rowboats, or canoes. One participant rows out or paddles while the other throws buckets full of pool water at the opponents' boats. The object is to swamp the opponents' boats while the rower manipulates his boat so as to keep his boat from taking too much water. This is continued until only one boat remains afloat thereby qualifying as the winning craft.

Boat Joust. The implement to be used is a bamboo pole of about five or six feet or a flagpole with a boxing glove or similar padding at the end. As in Swamp 'Em, one partner handles the craft while the other jousts with his opponents in the other boats in an attempt at either knocking them out of their boats or capsizing them. The one craft that avoids these predicaments is the winner.

Bronco Buck. A team of two takes part with one the horse and the other the rider. The two endeavor to unseat the rider or to cause the horse and rider to topple over by bucking or pulling. The team that remains upright wins.

Watermelon Polo. After dividing the sides evenly, the game is started by placing the watermelon in the center of the pool equidistant from both goals (any part of the end line of the pool). The side that forces the watermelon to its opponents' end line or goal scores a point. The first side to score 3 points is designated the winner.

Push Ball. The game of Push Ball is played similarly to Watermelon Polo, with a large, inflated ball. As for the scoring, that can be adjusted to the time available. The first side to score three or five points wins.

Greased-pole Walk. A heavily greased pole is suspended about nine feet over the water. The object is to walk the pole until the very end so as to qualify as the winner.

Three-legged Race. The participants compete in pairs shoulder-to-shoulder with the inner legs to comprise the third leg. By holding the event in the shallow-water area, the spectators can enjoy fully the proceedings.

Coin Fetch. Fifty or a hundred pennies are scattered in the deep end. At a given signal, those competing dive to recover as many coins as possible within the time allotted (two or three minutes). The winner is the one who comes up with the most pennies.

Tug O'War. Evenly divided sides line up opposite each other. They are to tug on a line with a buoy at the center. The buoy should be equidistant between markers on the deck. The side that pulls its opponents so that the buoy reaches an imaginary line in line with the deck marker is the winner.

Comedy dives and antics. The inclusion of clowning in the program can help to round out the Novelty Night. Slapstick rescue attempts, diving in pairs, and clowning on the pool's deck can add much to the evening.

GAMES FOR BEGINNERS[1]

Water Potato Race. The Water Potato Race is run much the same as the Land Potato Race. Five pucks for each team of five men are laid out in line with the direction in which the race is to be run. The first contestant stands about eight feet from the first puck. At the signal he goes out to the first puck, which he returns to the starting point, touching the hand of the next man in his line. This one now goes out to pick up the second puck. This is continued until the five pucks are brought in. The first team to finish is the winner.

Balloon Relay. Two teams are divided into two parts, one half going to stand at the deep end of the pool, the other standing in shallow water. The deep-end half has one balloon per man. At the signal, the first man in the deep-end section jumps into the water holding the balloon. After entering the water, he levels off, turns over, and does a kick glide with hands stretched out over his head holding the balloon in the water. When he reaches the shallow end of the pool, his teammate takes the balloon from him and does a kick glide on front to the deep end of the pool. He places the balloon on the edge of the pool and the next man in line jumps into the water to start the procedure over again. The first team to finish with the contestants at the deep end standing with the balloon tucked under their arms is the winner.

Artillery Skirmish. A group of twelve to eighteen contestants standing in waist-deep water form a circle at arms length from one another. Each contestant is given a number. The instructor throws a water polo

---

[1]This and the next two sections suggest games that can be adapted to use in the water. They are borrowed from a manual, *Recreational Swimming*, through the courtesy of the Brooklyn Chapter of the American Red Cross.

ball into the center of the ring, calling a number as he does so. The contestant whose number is called swims to the ball while all the others swim away. When he reaches the ball, he calls "Stop," and all the other contestants stand fast. He then tries to hit the nearest contestant with the ball. If a hit is made, that contestant is eliminated and the game continues in the same fashion. If the thrower misses, he is eliminated. The contest may be brought down to two winners.

The Wild Duck. Three separate pieces of one-fourth-inch rope long enough to form circles a foot in diameter when tied are placed in three feet of water, and a rock of a handy size is placed within each circle. The circles of rope should be placed about six feet from the edge of the pool, although the distance may be varied in the course of the game. The teams line up, either as individual contestants with three in one race, or as teams of two or three. Using a prone glide and holding their breadths, the "ducks" push off from the side of the pool, keeping their eyes open to look for the circle and the "food" within it. When found it is brought back to the starting point using a kick glide. A fellow "duck" takes the "food" and, gliding back to the circle, places the rock within it. When he returns to the starting point, the next contestant goes off in search of it. Any number of cycles may be made in the game. The first team to finish is declared the winner.

Floating Fiction. Any number of contestants are lined up at the starting point with their backs to the finish line. Each is given a sheet of newspaper. At the signal "Go," the contestants push off in a glide on the back, kick, and read aloud from the newspaper. The first to cross the finish line is the winner. Failure to keep the paper up, to read it aloud, or to remain in a floating position disqualifies a contestant.

Scramble. This game is much like water polo, but simplified so that there are almost no rules. It is usually played in shallow water by non-swimmers or beginners. Any method may be used to progress with the ball to the opponents' goal. (See *Water Polo.*)

Thru the Looking Glass. Successive beginners' skills may be learned by the imitation of things in the water such as fishes and boats.

1. Breath holding: The student takes a deep breath and lets it out with his head under water. The bubbling water sounds like a motorboat.
2. Rhythmic breathing: The instructor explains how a duck submerges to get food and returns to the surface to eat it. The child may then imitate by diving for a rock, returning to the surface, and again dropping the rock to retrieve it.
3. Prone float and back float: The child may be encouraged to float with his

arms and legs outstretched by explaining to him that this is how a turtle floats.

4. Prone glide: The figure presented by having the beginner stretch his arms out in front of him and glide through the water will resemble the long silhouette of a canoe.
5. Back glide: The shorter figure created by placing the arms beside the body will resemble a boat.
6. Kick glide: When done properly, the kick sounds like the firm hum of a steamboat. A good kick may be developed by suggesting to the children that they sound like a steamboat.
7. Arm stroke and leg stroke combined: The addition of paddling to the steamboat will complete the picture and encourage the children in the use of both arms and legs.

Wheelbarrow Race. The contestants are paired off. One lies in a prone float position with his legs apart. The other grasps the first contestant's ankles as in the wheelbarrow race on land. At the signal "Go," teams race to the other side, the floating child paddling with his hands. The first team to finish is declared the winner.

Snatch Game (a variation of Artillery Skirmish). Two teams line up facing each other and each team is numbered consecutively from one to the number of players. The instructor stands at the deep end of the pool with a water polo ball. He calls a number and throws the ball into the center of the swimming area between the two teams. The contestants whose number he calls run or swim out to retrieve the ball and return it to their teams. If tagged while carrying the ball, one point is scored for the tagging team. If home is reached safely, a point is scored for that team. The team with the highest number of points wins.

Baton Race. The contestants are split into two teams and a twenty-yard course is laid out in waist-deep water. The first contestant in each team is given a baton or any similar object that can be carried easily in the hand. At the signal, the contestant swims with the baton to the other end of the pool where the instructor is standing. He taps the instructor with the baton and returns on his back to his team where he passes the baton to the next man. If the baton is dropped, it must be recovered before progressing. The first team to finish is the winner.

GAMES FOR INTERMEDIATES

Arch Relay. Two teams line up in waist-deep water with their legs apart. The rear man in each column swims through the arches of the legs to the front of the column. The column moves back to make room for him and the new rear man comes forward through the arches. The first team to restore the original order is the winner.

Water Volleyball. Two equal teams are arranged on opposite sides of a rope stretched three feet above the head. The rules should be simple and the game played in shallow water. The object is to keep the ball going back and forth without falling into the water.

The first team to reach twenty-one points is the winner. The ball may be put into play from any position or the rules for ordinary volleyball may be applied.

Puck Snatch. Two teams, A and B, line up on opposite sides of the pool, and a puck or other easily visible object is placed in the center of the playing area. Numbers are given to each contestant and the number determines the stroke he will use in the game; (1) front crawl of arms and legs, (2) side stroke of arms and scissors kick, (3) breast stroke of arms and legs, (4) sculling with hands and flutter kick, and (5) elementary back stroke.

The instructor calls a number and a contestant from each team goes out to retrieve the puck. If the water is deep enough, a plain front dive may be executed; if not a running jump will serve. The object is to bring the puck to the surface and show it to the other contestants. Once a player touches the puck, it belongs to him unless he drops it, in which case it is again free. If touches are made simultaneously, the contestants bring it to the surface together and a point is scored for each side. The game should be played for a specified number of minutes and the team with the highest number of points at the end of that period is declared the winner.

Straw Hat Race. The contestants line up, each wearing a farmer's straw hat. They dive into deep water, recover the hat after completely submerging themselves and race to the other end of the pool or other finish line.

Water Punch Ball. The contestants are divided into two teams, of which one takes positions in the water to correspond to the field positions of Land Punch Ball, and the other sends its members to punch the ball until three outs are made. The positions are then reversed. The rules are the same as in Land Punch Ball with the following additions. When the player punches the ball, he makes a running jump into the water, and swims to first base under water. In going to second base, he must use a leg stroke. To third base, he uses an arm stroke, and may use free style to come home.

Balloon Relay. The teams line up in relay position, one balloon to a team. Swimming is done on the back using a leg stroke and the hands are used to keep the ball out of the water by light taps. If the balloon is dropped, it must be retrieved before progress can be resumed.

Water Spud. The contestants form a circle, face the center and count off consecutively. The leader stands in the center of the ring with the ball and calls a number. The person whose number is called swims to the center, while the others swim away. When he has the ball, the contestant calls "Stop," and the others stand fast. He will then try to hit one of the other contestants. Any person hit has one "spud" against him. The first to get three spuds goes through the mill.

Cracker Race. Teams are of six contestants each; three from each team stand on shore and three on the opposite shore or flat. At the signal, the first member of the team jumps into the water, picks up a cracker from the dock which he ferries to the opposite side without wetting it and gives it to his teammate who eats it, whistles, and jumps into the water to repeat the procedure. The first team to finish is declared the winner.

Kickboard Relay. Two equal teams line up, half at each end of the pool. The first swimmer on each team awaits the signal by holding the board in one hand and the starting marker in the other. At the signal, he kicks across the pool where he hands the board to his teammate, who returns it, and so on. The type of kick may be varied, such as flutter kick, breast stroke kick, scissors kick, and so forth. The first team to complete a cycle wins.

Apple Race. Members of two teams race to the center of the pool where fifty or so apples have been placed. Upon reaching the center, the contestants take one apple in each hand and return to the starting point doing the side stroke. They place the apples on the side and go back for more apples, continuing to do so until there are no more apples. The team retrieving the most apples wins.

GAMES FOR ADVANCED SWIMMERS

Water Punch Ball. A diamond is made by placing a rowboat at each base. The field team must tread water with the exception of the catcher who may lean against the dock or the edge of the pool. The batter must raise himself to punch the water polo ball and then swim to first base. Fielders try to tag him off base. The game is scored as in baseball.

Virginia Reel. The group is divided into two teams, numbered, and placed opposite each other:

1	2	3	4	5	6	7	8	9	10
10	9	8	7	6	5	4	3	2	1

The instructor calls a number and names an advanced skill. The contestants having that number exchange places by doing what the instructor has called for. The contestant reaching the opposing side first scores a point for his team. The skills are not called for in progression. Use crawl, breast stroke, backstroke, and so forth.

Survival of the Fleetest. The contestants are divided into two fleets, each consisting of one battleship, four destroyers, and two submarines. One fleet is stationed at the deep end; the other at the shallow end.

The object of the game is to sink the opposing fleet. Though the line of battle may be changed, it is suggested that a destroyer be a lead ship, followed by a destroyer on each quarter, and a submarine dead astern. The battleship follows the submarine with a destroyer on one side and a submarine on the other. Orders issued by the battleship may change the array. Touching a swimmer sinks that ship and he is eliminated from the game. Submarines attack under water and may be repelled by destroyers acting directly above.

The game is won when one team's battleship is sunk.

Red Rover. The teams face each other and one contestant calls to another by name (I call so-and-so over). The one called tries to swim past the one who called him without being tagged. If he is tagged by the "caller" they both "call" and endeavor to catch the next contestant. Contestants may surface dive and swim under water to avoid being caught.

Name It. The instructor names an article of the lifesaving equipment near at hand. The first person to find it scores a point for his team. However, if he is unable to demonstrate its use, the other team scores five points. The game gives practice in taking charge of elementary rescues using towels, paddles, shepherd's crook, ring buoy, surfboard, or canoe.

Passing the Puck. The group is divided into four teams and the lead man in each team is given a flat object such as a puck. Half of each team is stationed at the other end of the pool. At the signal, the lead contestant pushes off as for the backstroke and holding the object against his forehead with both hands proceeds to the opposite side using the breast stroke kick, inverted scissors, or flutter kick. Upon reaching the other side, he passes the object to his teammate who is already in position. This is continued until each man has swum the distance.

Disqualification may result from touching another man to force him to remove his hands, losing an object when in motion, or kicking an opponent. The instructor should act as referee.

Obstacle Relay Race.   Chairs, kickboards, bricks, and the like are arranged on the course. The first contestant jumps in with the ball and swims to the bricks. He leaves the ball there and carries the bricks to the receiving kickboard. He then carries the kickboard to the chair, where he climbs out, sits down, climbs back in, and continues the course. The next man swims to where the ball was left, carries it to the bricks, and so on.

Couple Tag.   The group is divided into pairs who swim while holding hands. One pair is "it." The object is to tag a pair without releasing the hands. Only one of the pair has to be tagged, and releasing the partner's hands to avoid being tagged makes that couple "it."

Modified Water Polo.   This game is a contact game and is considered to be valuable preparation for lifesaving since it prepares a swimmer against the frantic fear that often occurs when one is grabbed in the water. (Contact may be limited among girls and younger players in camp work.) Provision is made for scoring to be easier and the rules are made as simple as possible. Periods may be adjusted to suit the group being worked with; a suggestion is made that there be two halves, each composed of two quarters not to exceed five minutes in length. Any area not exceeding seventy-five feet in length may be used. Pool ends are preferred but ropes may be used instead. The entire end or rope length is the goal.

Play starts with the referee's throwing the ball (a regulation water polo ball, if possible) into the center of the pool and blowing a whistle. At the whistle, all players of both teams dive into the water. A race is made for the ball. The team securing it tries to progress with it by swimming or clever passing to striking distance for a goal. Plays and signals may be used. If a goal is made, both teams withdraw to their own ends, and the ball is given to the team scored upon. Play is resumed immediately upon indication of the referee. (Note: It is not necessary to get out of the water.) Play is continuous except for fouls or out-of-bounds balls. Cessation of play is indicated by the referee's blowing his whistle loudly. When a ball goes out of bounds, it is given to the opposite team at the point where it was thrown out of bounds. In this case, the defending team cannot approach closer than six feet to the contestant throwing it in. "Time out" is called for all foul throws, and the ball is again thrown in the center by the referee as in the start of the game.

A touch goal made by an attacking contestant's touching the ball to any part of the end counts five points; a thrown goal made by an attacking contestant's throwing the ball from at least fifteen feet away and striking the rope or end, before striking the water, counts three points; a foul throw made by a contestant's treading water at the fifteen-foot mark, throwing the ball, and striking the end or rope before the ball strikes the water, counts one point.

The number of contestants playing will depend somewhat upon the size of the area and local conditions. It is recommended, in order to keep the contestants distributed and to have some teamwork in passing, that the contestants be divided into: (1) forwards—those who are fast swimmers and swim down and attempt to score; (2) backs—those who play usually in an intermediate position and either pass the ball down to the forwards or receive it from the goal tenders and feed it to the forwards; and (3) goal tenders—those who are the poorest swimmers but who are seaworthy. Their duty is to defend the goal by intercepting thrown balls or fending off attacking players who have the ball.

Fouls are classified as follows: (1) Technical—called for unnecessary delay of the game, failure to play within thirty seconds after being instructed to do so by the referee, or holding to end or rope when in possession of the ball. One free throw is awarded. (2) Personal—roughness, slapping, kicking, tackling a player who does not have the ball, or holding a player under longer than three seconds. Two free throws are awarded.

Water Soccer or International Water Polo. This game is played in the Olympics and by teams in the Middle West and on the Pacific Coast. It is a game of skill and speed rather than contact. It may be highly technical, but for recreational use in camps is not played as such. It may be played with simple rules very much like Modified Water Polo.

A simple game of water polo may be set up according to the following rules: Goals are fixed at the ends in the center made by a cross bar ten feet wide and from three to eight feet high, depending upon the depth at the end. The regular number of contestants is seven, but any number may be used depending upon the area, so long as the sides are equally divided. A suggestion is made to divide the contestants into forwards, backs, and one goal tender. A score is made by throwing the ball into the net, and each score counts one point. Fouls are penalized by awarding a free throw to the opposite team at the point where the foul occurs. Foul shots are awarded for touching the ball with both hands at the same time, interfering with an opponent in any way unless he is holding the ball, holding the ball under water, unnecessary delay in playing the ball (ten-second limit), and roughing any player. Violators are penalized by giving the ball to the opposing team.

Note: For Modified Water Polo and Water Soccer, see the official rules for regular game played in colleges published by the American Sports Publishing Company, 45 Rose Street, New York City. These rules are published as a part of the official rules of the National Collegiate Athletic Association for swimming, diving, and water games.

SUGGESTED READINGS

Swimming for the Handicapped, Instructor's Manual. Washington, D.C.: American National Red Cross, 1955.

Affleck, G. B., and T. K. Cureton, Jr. *Swimming, Water Sports and Safety.* New York: Boy Scouts of America, 1958.

Armbruster, David A., *et al. Swimming and Diving.* St. Louis: The C. V. Mosby Co., 1963.

———. *Basic Skills in Sports for Men and Women.* St. Louis: The C. V. Mosby Co., 1967.

Gabrielsen, M. Alexander, *et al. Aquatics Handbook.* Englewood Cliffs, N.J.: Prentice-Hall, Inc., 1960.

McKenzie, M. M., and Betty Spears. *Beginning Swimming.* Belmont, California: Wadsworth Publishing Co., Inc., 1963.

Seaton, Don Cash, *et al. Physical Education Handbook.* Englewood Cliffs, N.J.: Prentice-Hall, Inc., 1965.

Smith, Hope. *Water Games.* New York: The Ronald Press Company, 1962.

INDEX